Calvin
in
Context

Understanding Cultures
through Their Key Words

OXFORD STUDIES IN ANTHROPOLOGICAL LINGUISTICS

William Bright, *General Editor*

Understanding Cultures through Their Key Words

English, Russian, Polish, German, and Japanese

ANNA WIERZBICKA

New York   Oxford
OXFORD UNIVERSITY PRESS
1997

Oxford University Press

Oxford   New York
Athens   Auckland   Bangkok   Bogota   Bombay   Buenos Aires
Calcutta   Cape Town   Dar es Salaam   Delhi   Florence   Hong Kong
Istanbul   Karachi   Kuala Lumpur   Madras   Madrid   Melbourne
Mexico City   Nairobi   Paris   Singapore   Taipei   Tokyo   Toronto   Warsaw

and associated companies in
Berlin   Ibadan

Copyright © 1997 by Anna Wierzbicka

Published by Oxford University Press, Inc.
198 Madison Avenue, New York, New York 10016

Oxford is a registered trademark of Oxford University Press

Portions of this book first appeared, in different form, as articles in journals or as chapters in collective volumes. I wish
to thank the following publishers for permission to include revised and expanded versions of the following publications
or parts thereof:

Lexicon as a key to history, culture, and society: "Homeland" and "Fatherland" in German, Polish and Russian. In René
Dirven and Johan Vanparys, eds., *Current approaches to the lexicon*, Frankfurt: Peter Lang Verlag, pp. 103–155.

Australian b-words (*bloody, bastard, bugger, bullshit*): An expression of Australian culture and national character. In
André Clas, ed., *Le mot, les mots, les bons mots / Word, words, witty words. Festschrift for Igor A. Mel'čuk* (Montreal:
Les Presses de l'Université de Montréal, 1992), pp. 21–38.

Speech acts and speech genres across languages and cultures. Anna Wierzbicka, *Cross-cultural pragmatics: the semantics of human interaction* (Berlin: Mouton de Gruyter, 1991), chap. 5.

Japanese key words and core cultural values, *Language in society* (1991), 20:333–385.

Library of Congress Cataloging-in-Publication Data
Wierzbicka, Anna.
Understanding cultures through their key words : English, Russian,
Polish, German, and Japanese / Anna Wierzbicka.
p.   cm. — (Oxford studies in anthropological linquistics ; v. 8)
Includes bibliographical references.
ISBN 0-19-508835-2 — ISBN 0-19-508836-0 (pbk.)
1. Language and culture.   2. Lexicology—Social aspects.
I. Title.   II. Series.
P35.W54   1997
306.4'4'089—dc20   96-8915

3 5 7 9 8 6 4 2

Printed in the United States of America
on acid-free paper

ACKNOWLEDGMENTS

Research for this book was supported by a grant from the Australian Research Council, which enabled me to obtain valuable research assistance throughout this project. I am extremely grateful to my very able research assistant, Helen O'Loghlin, whose help, both intellectual and organizational, was indispensable.

I would also like to express my gratitude to colleagues who read and commented on some of the chapters of this book, and in particular to Andrzej Bogusławski, Cliff Goddard, Igor Mel'čuk, and Alan Rumsey. Cliff Goddard read the whole manuscript and was, as always, more than generous with criticisms and suggestions for improvement. I would also like to acknowledge, with thanks, the contribution of my daughter Mary Besemeres, who has discussed with me many of the issues raised in this book and has contributed valuable ideas, observations, and references.

Finally, it is a pleasure to express my special thanks to Ellalene Seymour for her unfailingly efficient, thoughtful and good-humored typing and editing of the successive drafts of the book.

Canberra, Australia   A.W.
January 1996

CONTENTS

Understanding Cultures through Their Key Words

Language [is] a symbolic guide to culture.
Vocabulary is a very sensitive index of the culture of a people.
[L]inguistics is of strategic importance for the methodology of social science.

Edward Sapir

Introduction

1. Cultural analysis and linguistic semantics

In his introduction to *Vocabularies of Public Life* (1992) the well-known sociologist of culture Robert Wuthnow observes: "Perhaps more than at any other time in the present century, cultural analysis lies at the center of human sciences." A significant feature of the work in this area, according to Wuthnow, is its interdisciplinary character: "Anthropology, literary criticism, political philosophy, religious studies, cultural history, and cognitive psychology are all rich fields from which new insights can be derived." (2)

One discipline conspicuously absent from this list is linguistics. The omission is all the more striking in that Wuthnow links "the vitality and new thinking characteristic of the current sociological studies of culture [with] the depth of interest being given to questions of language" (2). This book seeks to demonstrate that cultural analysis can also gain important new insights from linguistics, in particular from linguistic semantics, and that the semantic perspective on culture is something that cultural analysis can ill afford to ignore. The relevance of semantics is not restricted to vocabulary, but perhaps in no other area is it so clearly obvious. It is therefore on vocabulary that this book concentrates.

More than sixty years on, Edward Sapir's profound insights, several of which serve as epigraphs to this book, have lost none of their validity or importance: first, that "language [is] a symbolic guide to culture" (Sapir 1949:162); second, that "vocabulary is a very sensitive index of the culture of a people" (27); and, third, that "linguistics is of strategic importance for the methodology of social science" (166).

2. Words and cultures

There is a very close link between the life of a society and the lexicon of the language spoken by it. This applies in equal measure to the outer and inner aspects of life. An obvious example from the material, visible domain is that of food. It is clearly not an accident that, for example, Polish has special words for cabbage stew (*bigos*), beetroot soup (*barszcz*), and plum jam (*powidła*), which English does not; or that English has, for example, a special word for orange (or orange-like) jam (*marmalade*), and Japanese a word for a strong alcoholic drink made from rice (*sake*). Obviously, such words can tell us something about the eating or drinking habits of the peoples in question.

The existence of language-specific names for special kinds of "things" (visible and tangible, such as food) is something that even ordinary, monolingual people are usually aware of. The existence of different customs and social institutions which have specific names in one language but not in others is also widely known. Consider, for example, the German noun *Bruderschaft*, literally 'brotherhood', which Harrap's *German and English dictionary* glosses laboriously as "(to drink) the pledge of 'brotherhood' with someone (subsequently addressing each other as 'du')." Clearly, the absence of a word for "Bruderschaft" in English has something to do with the fact that English no longer makes a distinction between an intimate/familiar "thou" and a more distant "you," and that English-speaking societies do not have a common ritual of pledging friendship through drinking.

Similarly, it is no accident that English doesn't have a word corresponding to the Russian verb *xristosovat'sja* (literally "to Christ one another"), glossed by the Oxford Russian-English dictionary as "to exchange a triple kiss (as Easter salutation)," or that it doesn't have a word corresponding to the Japanese word *miai,* referring to a formal occasion when the prospective bride and her family meet the prospective bridegroom and his family for the first time.

Most important, what applies to material culture and to social rituals and institutions applies also to people's values, ideals, and attitudes and to their ways of thinking about the world and our life in it.

A good example is provided by the untranslatable Russian word *pošlyj* (adjective) and its derivatives (nouns) *pošlost'*, *pošljak*, and *pošljačka*, to which the émigré Russian writer Vladimir Nabokov (1961) devoted many pages of detailed discussion. To quote some of Nabokov's comments:

> The Russian language is able to express by means of one pitiless word the idea of a certain widespread defect for which the other three European languages I happen to know possess no special term. (64)

> English words expressing several, although by no means all, aspects of *poshlust* [*sic*] are for instance: "cheap, sham, common, smutty, pink-and-blue, high falutin', in bad taste." (64)

According to Nabokov, however, these English words are inadequate, for first, they do not aim at unmasking, exposing, or denouncing "cheapness" of all kinds the way *pošlost'* and its cognates do; and, second, they do not have the same "absolute" implications that *pošlost'* does:

> All these however suggest merely certain false values for the detection of which no particular shrewdness is required. In fact, they tend, these words, to supply an obvious classification of values at a given period of human history; but what Russians call

poshlust is beautifully timeless and so cleverly painted all over with protective tints that its presence (in a book, in a soul, in an institution, in a thousand other places) often escapes detection. (64)

One could say, then, that the word *pošlost'* (and its cognates) both reflects and documents an acute awareness of the existence of false values and of the need to deride and deflate them; but to set out its implications systematically we would need to examine its meaning in a more analytical way than Nabokov chose to do.

The *Oxford Russian-English dictionary* assigns to *pošlyj* two glosses: "1. vulgar, common; 2. commonplace, trivial, trite, banal," but this is a far cry from glosses offered in Russian dictionaries, such as the following: "nizkij v duxovnom, nravstvennom otnošenii, melkij, ničtožnyj, zaurjadnyj," that is, "spiritually and morally base, petty, worthless, mediocre" (SRJ), or "zaurjadnyj, nizkoprobnyj v duxovnom, nravstvennom otnošenii, čuždyj vysšix interesov i zaprosov," that is, "commonplace (mediocre), base (inferior, low-grade) spiritually and morally, devoid of higher interests and needs."

The semantic range of *pošlyj* hinted at by the English glosses quoted earlier is remarkably wide (extending from "banal" to "morally worthless"), but what is even more remarkable is the speaker's disgust and condemnation included in the meaning of the word *pošlyj*, and given additional weight in the derived noun *pošljak*, which writes off a person with disgust, as a spiritual nonentity "without higher interests." (The gloss offered by the *Oxford Russian-English dictionary*, "vulgar person, common person," appears to imply social prejudice, whereas in fact the condemnation is made on moral, spiritual, and, so to speak, aesthetic grounds.)

From an "Anglo" person's point of view, the whole concept may seem as exotic as those encoded in the words *uxa* ('fish soup') or *boršč* ('Russian beetroot soup'), and yet from a Russian point of view, it is a salient, habitual mode of evaluation. To quote Nabokov again: "Ever since Russia began to think, and up to the time that her mind went blank under the influence of the extraordinary regime she has been enduring for these last twenty-five years, educated, sensitive and free-minded Russians were acutely aware of the furtive and clammy touch of *poshlust*'" (64).[1]

In fact, the peculiarly Russian concept of 'pošlost' ' may well serve as an introduction to a whole system of attitudes, a glimpse of which we can obtain by contemplating some other untranslatable Russian words like *istina* (roughly 'higher truth'), *duša* ('soul,' seen as a person's spiritual, moral, and emotional core and as an internal theatre where a person's moral and emotional life goes on); *podlec* ('base person who inspires contempt'), *merzavec* ('base person who inspires disgust'), *negodjaj* ('base person who inspires indignation'; for discussion, see Wierzbicka 1992b); or *osuždat'* (roughly 'condemn'), used conversationally in sentences such as:

Ja ego osuždaju.

'I condemn him'.

Ženščiny, kak pravilo, Marusju osuždali. Mužčiny, v osnovnom, sočuvstvovali ej.

'Women, as a rule, condemned Marusya. Men tended to be sorry for her.' (Dovlatov 1986:91)

The tendency to *osuždat* ('condemn') other people in conversation, to make absolute moral judgments, and to link moral judgments with emotions, is reflected in a wide variety of Russian words and expressions, as is also the cultural emphasis on "absolutes" and "higher values" in general (cf. Wierzbicka 1992b).

But although generalizations about "absolutes," "moral passions," "extreme value judgments," and the like are often valid, they are also vague and slippery. It is one of the major goals of this book to replace such vague and slippery generalizations with careful systematic analysis of words' meanings and to replace (or flesh out) impressions with evidence based on sound methodology.

The starting point, however, is obvious to the naked eye. It lies in the old insight that the meanings of words from different languages don't match (even if they are artificially matched, faute de mieux, by the dictionaries), that they reflect and pass on ways of living and ways of thinking characteristic of a given society (or speech community) and that they provide priceless clues to the understanding of culture. No one stated this old insight better than John Locke (1959[1690]):

> A moderate skill in different languages will easily satisfy one of the truth of this, it being so obvious to observe great store of words in one language which have not any that answer them in another. Which plainly shows that those of one country, by their customs and manner of life, have found occasion to make several complex ideas, and given names to them, which others never collected into specific ideas. This could not have happened if these species were the steady workmanship of nature, and not collections made and abstracted by the mind, in order to naming [*sic*], and for the convenience of communication. The terms of our law, which are not empty sounds, will hardly find words that answer them in the Spanish or Italian, no scanty languages; much less, I think, could any one translate them into the Caribbee or Westoe tongues; and the *versura* of the Romans, or *corban* of the Jews, have no words in other languages to answer them; the reason whereof is plain, from what has been said. Nay, if we look a little more nearly into this matter, and exactly compare different languages, we shall find out, though they have words which in translations and dictionaries are supposed to answer one another, yet there is scarce one of ten amongst the names of complex ideas . . . that stands for the same precise idea which the word does that in dictionaries it is rendered by. . . . These are too sensible proofs to be doubted; and we shall find this much more so in the names of more abstract and compounded ideas, such as are the greatest part of those which make up moral discourses; whose names, when men come curiously to compare with those they are translated into, in other languages, they will find very few of them exactly to correspond in the whole extent of their significations. (48–49)

And in this century, Edward Sapir (1949) makes a similar point.

> Languages differ widely in the nature of their vocabularies. Distinctions which seem inevitable to us may be utterly ignored in languages which reflect an entirely different type of culture, while these in turn insist on distinctions which are all but unintelligible to us.
>
> Such differences of vocabulary go far beyond the names of cultural objects such as arrow point, coat of armor, or gunboat. They apply just as well to the mental world. (27).

3. Different words, different ways of thinking?

In a sense, it may seem obvious that words with special, culture-specific meanings reflect and pass on not only ways of living characteristic of a given society but also ways of thinking. For example, in Japan, people not only talk about "miai" (using the word *miai*), and practice the social ritual of *miai,* but also think about *miai* (using either the word *miai* or the concept associated with this word). For example, in Kazuo Ishiguro's novel (1986), the hero, Masuji Ono, thinks a great deal—in advance and in retrospect—about the *miai* of his younger daughter Noriko; and clearly, he thinks about it from the point of view of the conceptual category linked with the word *miai* (so much so that he retains this word in his English prose).

Clearly, the word *miai* reflects not only the existence of a certain social ritual, but also a certain way of thinking about life's important events.

Mutatis mutandis, the same applies to *pošlost'*. Certainly, objects and phenomena meriting this label exist—the Anglo-Saxon world of popular authors contains a rich array of phenomena which merit the label *pošlost'*, for example the entire genre of bodice-rippers—but to call these volumes *pošlost'* would mean to view them through the prism of a conceptual category provided by the Russian language.

If a sophisticated witness like Nabokov tells us that Russians often think about such things in terms of the conceptual category *pošlost'*, we have no reason not to believe him—given that the Russian language itself provides objective evidence for this claim in the form of the whole family of words, *pošlyj, pošlost', pošljak, pošljačka,* and *pošljatina.*

It is often debated whether words encapsulating culture-specific conceptual categories such as *pošlost'* "reflect" or "shape" ways of thinking, but the debate seems misconceived: clearly, they do both. Just as the word *miai* both reflects and encourages a certain perspective on human actions and events, so does *pošlost'*. Culture-specific words are conceptual tools that reflect a society's past experience of doing and thinking about things in certain ways; and they help to perpetuate these ways. As a society changes, these tools, too, may be gradually modified and discarded. In that sense, the outlook of a society is never wholly "determined" by its stock of conceptual tools, but it is clearly influenced by them.

Similarly, the outlook of an individual is never fully "determined" by the conceptual tools provided by his or her native language, partly because there are always alternative ways of expressing oneself. But a person's conceptual perspective on life is clearly influenced by his or her native language. Obviously, it is not an accident that Nabokov views both life and art partly in terms of *pošlost'* whereas Ishiguro does not; or that Ishiguro thinks about life in terms of concepts such as 'on' (cf. chapter 6, section 4), whereas Nabokov does not.

To people with an intimate knowledge of two (or more) different languages and cultures, it is usually self-evident that language and patterns of thought are interlinked (cf. Hunt & Benaji 1988). To question the validity of the link on the basis of an alleged lack of evidence is to misunderstand the nature of evidence which is relevant in this context. The fact that neither brain science nor computer science has anything to say about links between ways of speaking and ways of thinking and about differences in ways of thinking associated with different languages and cultures hardly proves that such links and differences do not exist. Nonetheless, monolingual popular opinion, as well as the opinion of some cognitive scientists with little interest in languages and cultures, can be quite emphatic in their denial of the existence of such links and differences.

One particularly striking example of such a denial is provided by the recent linguistic best-seller by MIT psychologist Steven Pinker, whose book, *The language instinct* (1994), is hailed on the cover as "superb," "dazzling," and "brilliant," and praised (on the cover) by Noam Chomsky as "an extremely valuable book, very informative, and very well written." Pinker (1994:58) writes:

> As we shall see in this chapter, there is no scientific evidence that languages dramatically shape their speakers' ways of thinking. The idea that language shapes thinking seemed plausible when scientists were in the dark about how thinking works or even how to study it. Now that cognitive scientists know how to think about thinking, there is less of a temptation to equate it with language just because words are more palpable than thoughts. (58)

Pinker's book certainly offers no evidence of possible differences in thinking linked with different languages—but it is hard to see how it shows that "there is no such evidence." To begin with he never looks at any languages other than English. In general, the book is conspicuous for its complete lack of interest in other languages and other cultures, highlighted by the fact that of 517 works cited in Pinker's references, all are in English.

In his condemnation of the theory of "linguistic relativity," Pinker doesn't mince words. "It is wrong, all wrong," he declares (57). He ridicules the proposition that "the foundational categories of reality are not in the world but are imposed by one's culture (and hence can be challenged . . .)" (57), and doesn't even consider the possibility that while some categories may be innate, others may indeed be imposed by culture. He also dismisses in their entirety the views put forward by Whorf (1956) in the famous passage that deserves to be quoted once again:

> We dissect nature along lines laid down by our native languages. The categories and types that we isolate from the world of phenomena we do not find there because they stare every observer in the face; on the contrary, the world is presented in a kaleidoscopic flux of impressions which has to be organized by our minds—and this means largely by the linguistic systems in our minds. We cut nature up, organize it into concepts, and ascribe significances as we do, largely because we are parties to an agreement to organise it in this way—an agreement that holds throughout our speech community and is codified in the patterns of our language. The agreement is, of course, an implicit and unstated one, *but its terms are absolutely obligatory*; we cannot talk at all except by subscribing to the organization and classification of data which the agreement decrees. (213)

Undoubtedly, there is a good deal of exaggeration in this passage (as I will discuss later). Yet no one with genuine cross-cultural experience could deny that it also contains a great deal of truth.

Pinker says that "the more you examine Whorf's arguments, the less sense they make" (60). But what matters is not whether Whorf's specific examples and analytical comments are convincing. (On this point there is now general agreement that they are not; in particular, Malotki [1983] has shown that Whorf's ideas about the Hopi language were misguided.) But Whorf's main thesis that "we dissect nature along lines laid down by our native languages," and that "we cut nature up [in ways] codified in the patterns of our language," contains a profound insight which will be recognized by anybody whose experiential horizon extends significantly beyond the boundaries of his or her native language.

Pinker dismisses not only the "strong version" of Whorf's (and Sapir's) theory, which claims that "people's thoughts are determined by the categories made available by their language," but also the "weak version," which claims that "differences among languages cause differences in the thoughts of their speakers" (57).

When someone asserts that thought is independent of language, this usually means in practice that the words of his or her native language are absolutized and treated as adequate labels for supposed human "categories for thought" (cf. Lutz 1990). *The language instinct* is no exception in this respect. Pinker (1994) writes: "since mental life goes on independently of particular languages, concepts of freedom and equality will be thinkable even if they are nameless" (82). But as I will show in chapter 3, the concept of 'freedom' is not independent of particular languages (being different, for example, from the Roman concept of 'libertas' or the Russian concept of 'svoboda'). It is shaped by culture and history, and it is part of the shared heritage of the speakers of English. It is indeed an example of that "implicit agreement" of the members of one particular speech community that Whorf was talking about in the passage so emphatically dismissed by Pinker.

Whorf certainly went too far when he said that the world is presented to us "in a kaleidoscopic flux of impressions," because evidence (in particular, linguistic evidence) suggests that the distinction between "who" and "what" ("someone" and "something") is universal and does not depend on the way people in this or that culture "cut nature up" (see Goddard & Wierzbicka, 1994).

But the expression "kaleidoscopic flux of impressions" was perhaps a picturesque overstatement. In fact, Whorf (1956) did not claim that ALL the "foundational categories of reality" are "imposed by one's culture." On the contrary, in some of his writings at least, he recognized the existence of a "common stock of conceptions" underlying all different languages of the world:

> The very existence of such a common stock of conceptions, possibly possessing a yet unstudied arrangement of its own, does not yet seem to be greatly appreciated; yet to me it seems to be a necessary concomitant of the communicability of ideas by language; it holds the principle of this communicability, and is in a sense the universal language to which the various specific languages give an entrance. (36)

Whorf may also have exaggerated the differences between languages and cultures and the conceptual universes associated with them, and the degree to which the terms of the agreement that holds throughout a speech community "are absolutely obligatory." We can always find a way around the canonical "terms of agreement" by using paraphrases and circumlocutions of one kind or another. But this can only be done at a cost (by using longer, more complex, more cumbersome expressions than those which we can use relying on the habitual ways of speaking offered to us by our native language). Moreover, we can only try to avoid those conventions of which we are conscious. More often than not, the grip of people's native language on their thinking habits is so strong that they are no more aware of the conventions to which they are party than they are of the air they breathe; and when others try to draw their attention to these conventions they may even go on with a seemingly unshakable self-assurance to deny their existence. Once again the point is well illustrated by the experience of those who have had to adapt to life in a different culture and a different language, like the Polish-American writer Eva Hoffman (1989), whose "semiotic memoir" *Lost in translation: A life in a new language* should be required reading for all those professing an interest in this subject:

> "If you've never eaten a real tomato, you'll think that the plastic tomato is the real thing, and moreover, you'll be perfectly satisfied with it," I tell my friends. "It's only when you've tasted them both that you know there's a difference, even though it's almost impossible to describe." This turns out to be the most persuasive argument I have. My friends are moved by the parable of the plastic tomato. But when I try to apply it, by analogy, to the internal realm, they balk. Surely, inside our heads and souls things are more universal, the ocean of reality one and indivisible. No, I shout in every one of our arguments, no! There's a world out there; there are worlds. There are shapes of sensibility incommensurate with each other, topographies of experience one cannot guess from within one's own limited experience.
>
> I think my friends often suspect me of a perverse refusal to play along, an unaccountable desire to provoke and disturb their comfortable consensus. I suspect that the consensus is trying to colonize me and rob me of my distinctive shape and flavor. Still, I have to come to terms with it somehow. Now that I'm no longer a visitor, I can no longer ignore the terms of reality prevailing here, or sit on the margins observing the curious habits of the natives. I have to learn how to live with them, find a common ground. It is my fear that I have to yield too much of my own ground that fills me with such a passionate energy of rage. (204)

The personal insights of bilingual and bicultural insiders such as Hoffman echo analytical insights of scholars with a broad in-depth knowledge of different languages and cultures such as Sapir (1949), who wrote that in every large community "a mode of thinking, a distinctive type of reaction, gets itself established, in the course of a complex historical development, as typical, as normal" (311), and that since such distinctive habitual modes of thinking become entrenched in language, "the philosopher needs to understand language if only to protect himself against his own language habits" (165).

"People can be forgiven for overrating language," says Pinker (1994:67). They can also be forgiven for underrating it. But the conviction that one can understand human cognition, and human psychology in general, on the basis of English alone seems shortsighted, if not downright ethnocentric.

The field of emotions well illustrates the trap involved in the attempt to reach for human universals on the basis of one's native language alone. A typical scenario (where "P" stands for "psychologist" and "L" for "linguist") runs as follows:

P: Sadness and anger are universal human emotions.

L: *Sadness* and *anger* are English words, which don't have equivalents in all other languages. Why should these English words—rather than some words from language X, for which English has no equivalents—capture correctly some emotional universals?

P: It doesn't matter whether other languages have words for sadness and anger or not. Let's not deify words! I am talking about emotions, not about words.

L: Yes, but in talking about these emotions you are using culture-specific English words, and thus you are introducing an Anglo perspective on emotions into your discussion.

P: I don't think so. I am sure that people in those other cultures also experience sadness and anger, even if they don't have words for them.

L: Maybe they do experience sadness and anger, but their categorization of emotions is different from that reflected in the English lexicon. Why should the English taxonomy of emotions be a better guide to emotional universals than that embodied in some other language?

P: Let's not exaggerate the importance of language.

To show the reader that this dialogue is not fictitious, let me quote from a recent rejoinder by the distinguished psychologist Richard Lazarus (1995) directed, inter alia, at myself:

> Wierzbicka suggests that I underestimate the depth of cultural variation in emotion concepts as well as the problem of language. (255)
>   Words have power to influence, yet—as in the Whorfian hypotheses writ large—they cannot override the life conditions that make people sad or angry, which they can sense to some extent without words. . . .
>   I am suggesting, in effect, that all people experience anger, sadness, and so forth, regardless of what they call it. . . .Words are important, but we must not deify them. (259)

Unfortunately, by refusing to pay attention to words, and to semantic differences between words from different languages, scholars who take this position end up doing precisely what they wished to avoid, that is, "deifying" some words from their own native language and reifying the concepts encapsulated in them. Thus, unwittingly, they illustrate once again how powerful the grip of our native language on our thinking habits can be.

To assume that people in all cultures have the concept of 'sadness' even if they have no word for it is like assuming that people in all cultures have a concept of 'marmalade' and moreover, that this concept is somehow more relevant to them than the concept of 'plum jam', even if they happen to have a word for the latter but not the former.

In fact, the concept of 'anger' is no more universal than the Italian concept of 'rabbia' or the Russian concept of 'gnev'. (For detailed discussion of *rabbia,* see Wierzbicka 1995; for *gnev,* see Wierzbicka in press b.) To say this is not to argue against the existence of human universals but to call for a cross-linguistic perspective in trying to identify and map them.

4. Cultural elaboration and the lexicon

> Since before Boas first mentioned four Eskimo words for "snow," anthropologists
> have taken elaboration of vocabulary as an indication of the interests of particular
> cultures and of differences among them. (Hymes 1964:167)

Since Hymes wrote this, the familiar example of Eskimo words for *snow* has since
been called into question (Pullum 1991), but the validity of the general principle of
"cultural elaboration" would seem to be unassailable. Some illustrations of the
principle have not stood the test of time, but one doesn't have to be persuaded, for
example, by all of Herder's (1966[1772]) illustrations to be able to accept and admire
his basic insight:

> Each [language] in its own way is both lavish and lacking, but, to be sure, each in its
> own way. If the Arabs have so many words for stone, camel, sword, snake (things
> amongst which they live), the language of Ceylon, in accordance with the inclination
> of its people, is rich in flatteries, titles, and verbal décor. For the term "woman" it has,
> according to rank and class, twelve different names, while we discourteous Germans,
> for example, are forced in this to borrow from our neighbors. According to class, rank,
> and number, "you" is rendered in sixteen different ways, and this as well in the
> language of the journeyman as in that of the courtier. Profusion is the style of the
> language. In Siam there are eight different ways of saying "I" and "we," depending
> on whether the master speaks to the servant or the servant to the master. . . . Each one
> of these synonymies is linked to custom, character, and origin of the people; and
> everywhere the inventive human spirit reveals itself. (154–155)

Yet not only some of the illustrations but even the principle of cultural elaboration
itself has recently come under attack, although at times the attackers seem unable to
make up their minds as to whether it is false or, rather, a boring trusim.

For example, Pinker (1994) writes, with reference to Pullum (1991): "Speaking
of anthropological canards, no discussion of language and thought would be complete
without the Great Eskimo Vocabulary Hoax. Contrary to popular belief, the Eskimos
do not have more words for snow than do speakers of English" (64). Yet Pullum
himself ridicules the references to the reported multiplicity of Eskimo words for *snow*
in rather different terms: "Utterly boring, even if true. Only the link to those legendary,
promiscuous, blubber-gnawing hunters of the ice-packs could permit something this
trite to be presented to us for contemplation" (quoted in Pinker 1994:65).

What Pullum seems to overlook is that once the principle of cultural elaboration
has been established as valid on the basis of "boring" examples, it can then be applied
to areas whose patterning is less obvious to the naked eye. This is the reason (or at
least one of the reasons) why language can be, as Sapir put it, a guide to "social reality,"
or a guide to culture in the broad sense of the word (including ways of living, thinking,
and feeling).

If someone finds it boring that, for example, the Hanunóo language of the
Philippines has ninety different words for rice (Conklin 1957), that is their problem.
To those who do not find the comparison of cultures boring, the principle of cultural
elaboration is of fundamental importance. Since it is highly relevant to this book (in

particular, to the chapter on "friendship"), I will illustrate the principle here with some examples from Dixon's book, *The languages of Australia* (1980).

> As would be expected, Australian languages have a rich vocabulary for describing culturally important objects. . . . Australians typically have terms referring to different kinds of sand, but perhaps no unspecified lexeme corresponding to the English word *sand*. There are often many terms for referring to parts of emus and eels, among other animals; and there may be specific terms for each of the four or five stages of chrysalis that are recognised to intervene between grub and beetle. (103–104)

> There are verbs which distinguish culturally important actions—for instance, one verb will refer to 'spearing' in cases where the spear is aided into its trajectory by means of a woomera, another when it is held in the hand and the actor can see what he is aiming at, another when the spearer makes fairly random jabs in, say, thick grass in which he has seen a movement (none of these verb roots will be related in any way to the noun 'spear', unlike the situation in English). (106)

> One lexical area in which Australian languages excel concerns names for types of noise. For instance, I was able easily to record around three dozen lexemes in Yidiny referring to kinds of noise, including *dalmba* 'sound of cutting', *mida* 'the noise of a person clicking his tongue against the roof of his mouth, or the noise of an eel hitting the water', *maral* 'the noise of hands being clapped together', *nyurrugu* 'the noise of talking heard a long way off when the words cannot quite be made out', *yuyuruŋgul* 'the noise of a snake sliding through the grass', *gaŋga* 'the noise of some person approaching, e.g. the sound of his feet on leaves or through the grass, or even the sound of a walking stick being dragged along the ground'. (105)

Above all, Dixon emphasizes (with reference to Kenneth Hale's comments), the great elaboration of kinship terminology in Australian languages, and its cultural significance.

> Hale also notes that it is natural to find cultural elaboration reflected in lexical structures. Among the Warlpiri, for instance, where the algebra of kinship plays an intellectual role similar to that which mathematics plays in other parts of the world, one finds a flourishing, even vibrant, elaboration of kinship nomenclature which succeeds in enabling knowledgeable Warlpiris to articulate a truly impressive array of principles which inhere in the system as a whole—this elaboration, incidentally, goes far beyond the strictly practical needs of Warlpiri society, thereby revealing its true status as an intellectual field capable of providing considerable satisfaction to those individuals who, as they go through life, become increasingly expert in it. . . . Similar remarks apply to many other Australian tribes. (108).

It is hard to believe that anyone could indeed find these examples of cultural elaboration boringly obvious or uninteresting, but if someone does, there is really little point in arguing with them about it.

5. Word frequencies and cultures

Although elaboration of vocabulary is undoubtedly a key indicator of the specific features of cultures, it is of course not the only one. A related one that is often overlooked is frequency of use. For example, though a particular English word can be matched in meaning with a Russian word, if the English word is very common, and the Russian rarely used (or vice versa), this difference suggests a difference in cultural salience.

It is difficult to get an accurate idea of how commonly a word is used in a given society. In fact, the task of "measuring" word frequency fully objectively is inherently impossible. The results will always be affected by the size of the corpus and the choice of the texts entered in it.

Is it really worthwhile, then, trying to compare cultures through the frequencies of words recorded in the available frequency dictionaries? For example, if we find that in the Kučera and Francis (1967) and Carroll et al. (1971) corpus of American English (henceforth K & F and C et al.) the word *if* occurs 2,461 and 2,199, respectively, per 1 million words, whereas in Zasorina's corpus of Russian the corresponding word *esli* occurs 1,979 times, can we conclude anything from this about the role of the hypothetical mode of thinking in the two cultures?

My own answer is that (in the case of *if* vs. *esli*) we cannot and that it would be naive to try, for a difference of this order could be simply due to chance.

If, on the other hand, we discover that the frequency given for the English word *homeland* is 5 (in both K & F and C et al.) whereas that of the Russian word *rodina*, glossed in dictionaries as "homeland," is 172, the situation is clearly different. To dismiss a difference of this order (roughly 1:30) would be even more foolish than to attach great importance to a difference of 20% or 50%. (With small numbers, even much greater differences in proportions may of course be purely accidental.)

In the case of *homeland*, the two English frequency dictionaries quoted here happen to give the same figure, but in many other cases the figures given by them differ considerably. For example, the word *stupid* occurs in the C et al. corpus 9 times, and in the K & F corpus 25 times; *idiot* occurs 1 time in C et al. and 4 times in K & F; and the word *fool* occurs 21 times in C et al. and 42 times in K & F. All such differences can clearly be dismissed as accidental. When, however, we compare the English figures with the Russian ones, the pattern emerging can hardly be similarly dismissed:

English (K & F/C et al.)		Russian	
fool	43/21	durak	122
stupid	25/9	glupyj	99
stupidly	2/0.4	glupo	34
idiot	4/1	idiot	29

The generalization which emerges from these figures (concerning a whole family of words) is loud and clear, and it is entirely consistent with generalizations made independently, on the basis of nonquantitative data: that Russian culture encourages "direct," sharp, undiluted value judgments, whereas Anglo culture does not.[2] It is also consistent with other statistical data, such as, for example, those concerning the use of the hyperbolic adverbs *absoljutno* 'absolutely' and *soveršenno* 'utterly/perfectly' and their English counterparts:

English (K & F/C et al.)		Russian	
absolutely	0/12	absoljutno	166
utterly	27/4	soveršenno	365
perfectly	31/27		

One further example: the use of the words *terribly* and *awfully* in English and the words *strašno* and *užasno* in Russian:

English (K & F/C et al.)		Russian	
terribly	18/9	užasno	70
awfully	10/7	strašno	159
horribly	2/1		

If one adds to this the fact that Russian also has the hyperbolic noun *užas* 'terribly' (literally 'terror/horrors'), with a high frequency of 80, and with no counterpart in English at all, the difference between the two cultures in their attitudes to "overstatement" becomes even more striking.

Similarly, if we notice that one English dictionary (K & F) records 132 occurrences of *truth*, whereas another (C et al.) records only 37, we may at first be dismayed by the difference. When we discover, however, that the figure for the closest Russian counterpart of *truth*, namely, *pravda*, is 579, we will probably be less inclined to dismiss the differences as "accidental."

Anybody who is familiar with both Anglo culture (in any of its varieties) and Russian culture knows intuitively that *rodina* is (or at least has been until recently) a common Russian word and that the concept encoded in it is culturally salient—much more so than the English word *homeland* and the concept encoded in it. It is hardly surprising that frequency data, however untrustworthy they may be in general, confirm this. Similarly, the fact that Russians tend to talk about "pravda" more commonly than speakers of English talk about "truth" can hardly come as a surprise to people familiar with both cultures. The lexical fact that Russian also has another word for something like "truth", namely, *istina*, even though the frequency of *istina* (79), unlike that of *pravda*, is not spectacularly high, provides additional evidence for the salience of this general theme in Russian culture. Without wishing to undertake a proper semantic analysis of either *pravda* or *istina* here, I might say that *istina* refers not just to "truth" but rather to something like "the ultimate truth," "the hidden truth" (cf. Mondry & Taylor 1992, Šmelev 1996), and that it occurs, characteristically, in combination with the word *iskat'* 'seek', as in the first of the following two examples:

Zolota mne ne nužno, ja išču odnoj istiny. (Alexander Pushkin, *Sceny iz rycarskix vremen*).

'I don't need gold, I only seek the truth [*istina*].'

Ja po-prežnemu verju v dobro, v istinu. (Ivan Turgenev, *Dvorjanskoe gnezdo*).

'As before, I believe in the good, in truth [*istina*].'

Istina xoroša, da i *pravda* ne xuda. (Dal', 1882)

'*Istina is good, but pravda is not bad either.*'

But if the characteristically Russian concept of 'istina' ("absolute truth") plays a significant role in Russian culture, the concept of 'pravda' is even more central to it, as the numerous proverbs and sayings (many of them rhymed) illustrate (the first example is from SRJ and the others from Dal' (1955[1882])):

Pravda glaza kolet.
'Truth burns (pierces) the eyes.'

Bez pravdy žit' legče, da pomirat' tjaželo.
'Without truth, it is easier to live, but hard to die.'

Vse minetsja, odna pravda ostanetsja.
'Everything will pass, only truth remains.'

Varvara mne tetka, a pravda sestra.
'Barbara is my aunt, but truth is my sister.'

Bez pravdy ne žit'e, a vyt'e.
'Without truth, life is one long howl.'

Pravda so dna morja vynosit.
'Truth will uplift you from the bottom of the sea.'

Pravda iz vody, iz ognja spasaet.
'Truth will rescue you from flood and fire.'

Za pravdu ne sudis': skin' šapku da poklonis'.
'Don't take anyone to court for truth but take off your hat and bow.'

Zavali pravdu zolotom, zatopči ee v grjaz' - vse naružu vyjdet.
'You can bury truth in gold or trample it in the mud, but it will still out.'

Xleb-sol' kušaj, a pravdu slušaj!
'Eat bread-and-salt, but heed the truth!'

This is just a small selection. The Dal' (1955[1882]) dictionary of proverbs has dozens more concerning *pravda*—and dozens of others concerning its opposites, *vrat'* and *lgat'* (some of them excusing and justifying lying as a necessary concession to life, despite the supreme splendor of the truth).

Xoroša svjataja pravda—da v ljudi ne goditsja.
'The holy truth is good—but it is not for people.

Ne vsjaku pravdu žene skazyvaj.
'Don't tell every kind of truth to your wife'.

Similarly revealing are common collocations such as, above all, *pravda-matka* 'truth-mother' and *pravda-matuška* (*matuška* being a tender, peasant-style diminutive for 'mother'), which are often used in combination with the verbs *govorit'* 'speak' or *rezat'* 'cut' (i.e. 'speak' (see Dal' 1955[1882] and 1977[1862]); or in the phrase *rezat' pravdu v glaza* 'to throw the cutting truth into a person's face':

```
pravdu-matku           (matušku)           govorit'  (rezat')
truth-ACC-mother-ACC   (mother-DIM-ACC)    speak     (cut)
'to speak (to cut) the mother-truth'.
```

```
rezat'   pravdu       v      glaza
to cut   truth-ACC    into   eyes-ACC
'to speak the full (painful) truth to someone's face, without any attempt to soften or
hedge it'
```

The idea of vigorously throwing the whole "cutting truth into another person's face" ("to their eyes"), combined with the view that the "full truth" must be loved, cherished, and respected like a mother, is at variance with Anglo cultural norms, which value "tact," "white lies," "minding one's own business," and so on. But as the linguistic evidence mentioned here indicates, it is part and parcel of Russian culture. The sentence:

```
Ljublju  pravdu-matušku.
'I love   the-truth-the-(dear-little-)mother'
```

cited in SSRLJ is equally revealing of the traditional Russian preoccupation with and attitude toward truth.

I am not saying that a society's cultural preoccupations and values will always be reflected in common words, and in particular in abstract nouns such as *pravda* 'truth' and *sud'ba* 'fate'. Sometimes they will be reflected, rather, in particles, interjections, set phrases, or speech formulae (cf. e.g. Pawley & Syder 1983). Some words may be culturally revealing without being very common.

Frequency is not everything, but it is important and revealing. Frequency dictionaries are only broadly indicative of cultural salience, and they can only be used as one among many sources of information about a society's cultural preoccupations. But it would be foolish to ignore them altogether. They tell part of the story. For their message to be fully understood and correctly interpreted, however, figures have to be considered in the context of an in-depth analysis of meanings.

6. Key words and core cultural values

Next to "cultural elaboration" and "frequency," another important principle linking vocabulary and culture is the principle of "key words" (cf. Evans-Pritchard 1968[1940], Williams 1976, Parkin 1982, Moeran 1989). In fact, the three principles are interrelated.

"Key words" are words which are particularly important and revealing in a given culture. For example, in my *Semantics, culture and cognition* (Wierzbicka 1992b) I tried to show that the Russian words *sud'ba* (roughly 'fate'), *duša* (roughly 'soul'), and *toska* (roughly, 'melancholy-cum-yearning') play a particularly important role in Russian culture and offer invaluable insight into this culture.

There is no finite set of such words in a language, and there is no "objective discovery procedure" for identifying them. To show that a particular word is of special importance in a given culture, one has to make a case for it. Evidence is necessary for each such claim, of course, but evidence is one thing and a "discovery procedure" is another. For example, it would be ridiculous to criticize Ruth Benedict for the special attention she paid to the Japanese words *giri* and *on*, or Michelle Rosaldo, for her special attention to the Ilongot word *liget*, on the grounds that neither of them explained what led her to the conclusion that these words were worth focusing on, or justified her choice in terms of some general discovery procedures. What matters is whether or not Benedict's and Rosaldo's choices led them to significant insights recognized by others familiar with the cultures in question.

How can one justify the claim that a particular word is one of a culture's "key words"? To begin with, one may want to establish (with or without the help of a frequency dictionary) that the word in question is a common word, not a marginal word. One may also want to establish that the word in question (whatever its overall frequency) is very frequently used in one particular semantic domain, for example, in the domain of emotions, or in the domain of moral judgments. Furthermore, one may want to show that this word is at the center of a whole phraseological cluster, such as the following one in the case of the Russian word *duša* (cf. Wierzbicka 1992b): *na duše* ('on the soul'), *v duše* ('in the soul'), *po duše* ('after/to the soul'), *duša v dušu* ('soul to soul'), *izlit' dušu* ('to pour out one's soul'), *otvesti dušu* ('to relieve one's soul'), *otkryt' dušu* ('to open one's soul'), *duša naraspašku* ('a wide-open soul', that is, 'a communicative, sincere, frank person'), *razgovorivat' po dušam* ('to talk from soul to soul, that is, very intimately'), and so on. One may also be able to show that the proposed "key word" occurs frequently in proverbs, in sayings, in popular songs, in book titles, and so on.

But the question is not how to "prove" whether or not a particular word is one of the culture's key words, but rather to be able to say something significant and revealing about that culture by undertaking an in-depth study of some of them. If our choice of words to focus on is not "inspired" we will simply not be able to demonstrate anything of interest.

Using "key words" as an approach to the study of culture may be criticized as an "atomistic" pursuit, inferior to "holistic" approaches targeting more general cultural patterns rather than "a random selection of individual words." An objection of this kind could be valid with respect to some "studies in words" if these studies are indeed just a "random selection of individual words," viewed as isolated lexical items.

As this book hopes to show, however, a study of a culture's "key words" need not be undertaken in an old-fashioned atomistic spirit. On the contrary, some words can be studied as focal points around which entire cultural domains are organized. By exploring these focal points in depth we may be able to show the general organizing principles which lend structure and coherence to a cultural domain as a whole, and which often have an explanatory power extending across a number of domains.

A key word such as *duša* (roughly 'soul') or *sud'ba* (roughly 'fate') in Russian is like one loose end which we have managed to find in a tangled ball of wool: by pulling it, we may be able to unravel a whole tangled "ball" of attitudes, values, and expectations, embodied not only in words, but also in common collocations, in set phrases, in grammatical constructions, in proverbs, and so on. For example, *sud'ba* leads us to other "fate-related" words such as *suždeno, smirenie, učast', žrebij,* and *rok,* to collocations such as *udary sud'by* (roughly 'blows of fate') and to set phrases such as *ničego ne podelaeš'* ('you can't do anything'), to grammatical constructions such as the whole plethora of impersonal dative-cum-infinitive constructions, highly characteristic of Russian syntax, to numerous proverbs, and so on (for detailed discussion, see Wierzbicka 1992b).

Similarly, a key word such as *enryo* (roughly 'interpersonal restraint'), *on* (roughly 'debt of gratitude') and *omoiyari* (roughly 'benefactive empathy') in Japanese can lead us to the center of a whole complex of cultural values and attitudes, expressed, inter alia, in common conversational routines and revealing a whole network of-culture-specific "cultural scripts"[3] (cf. Wierzbicka in press a).

7. "Culture"—a perilous idea?

The idea that cultures can be interpreted in part through their key words may be attacked by questioning the notion of "key words" or the notion of "culture." To dwell for a moment on the second of these.

In the current debate on "culture," many voices have challenged the notion of "culture" itself, presenting it as a "perilous idea." One influential writer, Eric Wolf (1994), refers in this context to Franz Boas as someone who appreciated, ahead of his time, "the heterogeneity and the historically changing interconnectedness of cultures" and was therefore able to see cultures as "a problem and not a given":

> Just as Boas had disaggregated racial typologies and scrupulously severed considerations of race from considerations of culture, so he argued against the common presupposition that each culture constituted a distinctive and separate monad sui generis. Since all cultures could be shown to be interconnected and continuously exchanging materials, no culture was due to "the genius of a single people" (Boas, quoted in Stocking 1968:213). Since cultures were also forever breaking up and differentiating, it was not very useful to speak of culture in general; cultures needed to be studied in all their plurality and particular historicity, including their interconnectedness. (5)

Wolf charges that subsequently, anthropologists failed to fully appreciate the importance, and the full implications, of these points:

> Anthropologists have . . . taken seriously Boas's point about oppositions and contradictions in culture but have done little thinking about how these heterogeneous and contradictory perspectives and discourses can intersect, how divergent interests and orientations can be made to converge, how the organization of diversity is accom-

plished. Notions of a common cultural structure underlying all this differentiation sound a bit too much like a little cultural homunculus built into everyone through the process of socialization or a Maxwell's demon capable of sorting divergent messages to create negative entropy and order. (6)

Apparently forgetting that Boas himself was a major link in the historical tradition leading from Herder and Humboldt to Sapir and Whorf, Wolf contrasts the French "universalist" tradition with the German-style emphasis on *Volksgeist* and differences between cultures:

> It had become quite common, especially in Germany, where people opposed the universalist rationalism of the French Enlightenment, to assert the uniqueness of each people and of its *Volksgeist* or "folk spirit." That spirit was believed to be anchored in passion and emotion, not in reason, and manifest in art, folklore, and language. Educated Germans especially found it attractive to accept such unifying and holistic perspectives on other cultures. . . . A major tradition of intellectual thought and work—extending from Wilhelm von Humboldt . . . to Ruth Benedict—has employed the guiding notion of an ideational holism at the root of culture. To this kind of approach Boas was opposed. (6)

There can be no quarrel with the statement that cultures are not separate monads but, rather, heterogeneous, historically changing, interconnected, and "continually exchanging materials." However, the fact that the emphasis on *Volksgeist* in the German philosophical tradition may have contributed, in some ways, to the strength and shape of modern German nationalism (as Wolf, among many others, suggests) should not lead us automatically to condemn and repudiate the whole "major tradition of intellectual thought and work extending from Wilhelm von Humboldt. . . to Ruth Benedict" (with an honorary exception made for Franz Boas). To do this would be a spectacular example of throwing the baby out with the bath water.

There is a difference between, on the one hand, rejecting "static culturologies," as does Regna Darnell (1994) in her commentary on Wolf's paper, and, on the other, embracing the view that cultures have no "content" at all, being no more than cross-currents of myriads of influences, as Immanuel Wallerstein (1994) seems to do in his commentary on the same paper. According to Wallerstein, Wolf clearly shows that "races, cultures, and peoples are not essences. They have no fixed contours. They have no self-evident content. Thus, we are all members of multiple, indeed myriad, 'groups'—crosscutting, overlapping, and ever-evolving" (5).

I agree that cultures are not immutable "essences" and that they have no fixed contours. I also agree that their "content" is not "self-evident." But to deny the reality of that "content" altogether and reduce us all, as cultural beings, to members of myriad "groups"—cross-cutting, overlapping, and ever evolving, means to overlook the central reality. To repeat: no one is more acutely aware of this reality than a bilingual who lives his or her life in two languages and two cultures, and the testimony of bilingual and bicultural writers is loud and clear (cf. e.g. Huston & Sebbar 1986, Hoffman 1989, Nabokov 1961, Ishiguro 1986).

"What bilinguals, what two languages?" I hear the skeptics cry. Are languages "immutable essences with fixed contours"? Aren't they, too, cross-cutting, overlapping, and ever evolving?

Indeed they are. Yet to declare, for this reason, that the concept of "one language" (for example, French or Russian or Japanese) is a total fiction, misguided and probably reactionary, too, would be carrying theoretical extremism to the point of absurdity.

For those who do not acquire two languages by "immersion" but have to learn them by their own effort, the news that there is no such thing as "another language" might bring some relief (no need to study any further) but hardly much benefit. If people didn't believe in the existence of "other languages," then—apart from those bilingual by birth or circumstances—we would all be monolingual.

In fact, as Wallerstein (1994) himself pointed out, for different ethnic communities in a multicultural society (such as the United States), the news that the notion of "another language" is a total fiction would hardly be good news either (no more funding, perhaps, for Spanish language schools, there being no such thing as "the Spanish language"):

> Groupism is also the expression of democratic liberation, of the demand of the underdogs (those geoculturally defined as lesser breeds) for equal rights in the *polis*. This expresses itself, for example, in the call for "multiculturalism" in the United States and its equivalents elsewhere. The "universalist" response to multiculturalism—the call for "integration" of all "citizens" into a single "nation"—is of course a deeply conservative reaction, seeking to suppress the democratic demand in the name of liberalism. (5)

No language can be a better example of heterogeneity and lack of "fixed contours" than English. But does this mean that there is really no such thing as "English" and that there are only "the world's Englishes"?

There are undeniable differences between Australian English, American English, Indian English, and various other "Varieties of English Around the World" (to use the title of an important linguistic book series), but if these different "Englishes" were not perceived as different "varieties of English," then on what basis would they be grouped together as "Englishes"? Even if their presumed common core was not fully identifiable in terms of a finite list of features, "with fixed contours," would this mean that the notion of "English" has no content at all? To take a familiar example, the phenomenon of "baldness," too, has no fixed contours (for people with 30,000 hairs on their head are not bald, and neither are people with 29,999, or 29,998, and so on). This doesn't mean, however, that there are no bald people in the world, for "baldness" depends not on the number of hairs but on the overall impression that a person's scalp makes on other people.

Languages may be heterogeneous (to a varying degree) and may lack fixed contours, but this doesn't mean that they are total fictions; and it is in a clash with another language that the distinctness of a language (as a separate identity) reveals itself.

To quote another sophisticated bilingual, the semiotician Tzvetan Todorov (a Bulgarian living in Paris):

> Depuis que les sociétés humaines existent, elles entretiennent des relations mutuelles. Pas plus qu'on ne peut imaginer les hommes vivant d'abord isolément et ensuite

seulement formant une société, on ne peut concevoir une culture qui n'aurait aucune relation avec les autres: l'identité naît de la (prise de conscience de la) différence. (1986:20)

'Since human societies have existed, they have always maintained mutual relations. As one cannot imagine people living first in isolation and only later forming a society, so one cannot conceive of a culture which wouldn't have any relations with others: identity is born out of (the awareness of) the difference.'

Coming, linguistically, from the "Balkan Sprachbund," and living in one of the main centers of an increasingly unified Europe, Todorov is well aware of the foreign influences which both Bulgarian and French have undergone in the past and are undergoing in the present:

L'interaction constante des cultures aboutit à la formation de cultures hybrides, métissées, créolisées, et cela à tous les échelons: depuis les écrivains bilingues, en passant par les métropoles cosmopolites, et jusq'aux États plusri-culturels. (20).

'The constant interaction of cultures leads to the formation of cultures which are hybrid, "métisized," creolized, and this on all levels, from bilingual writers, to cosmopolitan metropolises, and even multicultural states.'

At the same time, however, being a bilingual writer himself, he is well aware of the "identity which is born out of the awareness of the difference."

For the same reason that bilingual witnesses are better placed than monolinguals to affirm the reality of different languages, bicultural witnesses are better placed than "monolingual monoculturals" to affirm the reality of different cultures, however heterogeneous and lacking in fixed contours these cultures may be.

One cannot discover the special "identity" of one's own culture (however heterogeneous it might be) until one becomes deeply and intimately acquainted with, and challenged by, another, to the point of developing a novel self. It is interesting to note, therefore, the quote from Maurice Merleau-Ponty with which Todorov closes his essay on "Le croisement des cultures":

L'ethnologie n'est pas une spécialité définie par un objet particulier, les sociétiés "primitives"; c'est une manière de penser, celle qui s'impose quand l'objet est "autre" et exige que nous nous transformions nous-mêmes.

'Ethnology is not a discipline defined by one particular object of study, "primitive societies"; it is a way of thinking, which imposes itself when the object is "the other" and which requires that we should transform ourselves.'

Of course, the term *culture* is used by different writers in different senses, and before anything is affirmed about "cultures" it is good to clarify in what sense one is using this term. For my part, I find particularly fruitful the definition proposed by Clifford Geertz (1979): "The culture concept to which I adhere denotes a historically transmitted pattern of meanings embodied in symbols, a system of inherited conceptions expressed in symbolic forms by means of which people communicate, perpetuate and develop their knowledge about and attitudes toward life" (89).

There is no need to invoke "a little cultural homunculus built into everyone through the process of socialization" (Wolf 1994) to recognize the validity of "a historically transmitted pattern of meanings embodied in symbols, a system of inherited conceptions expressed in symbolic forms . . . by means of which people communicate and develop . . . their attitudes toward life."

For example, the Russian word *sud'ba* expresses a historically transmitted conception of life by means of which Russian people communicate about people's lives and develop their attitudes toward life. The word *sud'ba* (with its high frequency in Russian speech) provides both evidence of this inherited conception and a key to its understanding.

Language—and in particular, vocabulary—is the best evidence of the reality of "culture," in the sense of a historically transmitted system of "conceptions" and "attitudes." Of course, culture is, in principle, heterogeneous and changeable, but so is language.

In the second chapter of this book I will study different conceptions of interpersonal relations historically transmitted in a few different cultures ("Anglo," Russian, Polish, and Australian) and reflected in key words. The inclusion of both "Anglo" and "Australian" cultures brings us face to face with the issue of unity and heterogeneity: Australian culture is associated with the English language, as is also "Anglo" culture in Britain, America, and elsewhere. Both the unity and diversity of "Anglo" culture are reflected in the lexicon: the unity in the pan-English word *friend*, and the diversity in the Australian-English word *mate* (with its own semantic profile and high cultural salience).

Furthermore, the changeability of culture is also reflected in the lexicon: although the word *friend* itself has remained stable in Anglo culture for several centuries, I show in chapter 2 that its meaning has changed (as reflected in its range of use, its collocations, and indeed its syntax)—in accord with independently established changes in the prevailing conceptions concerning interpersonal relations. (I am referring here not to the emergence of the new words *boyfriend* and *girlfriend*, revealing as they are of the changed patterns of living and of changed expectations and attitudes, but to the far less obvious changes in the meaning of the word *friend* as such.)

To say that "culture has no describable content" is to imply that culture cannot be taught. Languages CAN be taught, despite their lack of fixed contours, because they do have a describable core (in the form of basic vocabulary and basic rules of grammar). To say that cultures have no content and to imply thereby that they cannot be taught may seem a very liberal and enlightened position, but in fact the advocacy of this position hampers the possibility of cross-cultural understanding.[4]

Progress in cross-cultural communication will not be born out of slogans emphasizing only heterogeneity and changeability of cultures and denying the reality of different cultural norms and patterns (in the name of "deconstruction," misguided universalism, or whatever). Progress in cross-cultural understanding requires a basis in well-founded studies of different cultural norms and historically transmitted patterns of meaning.

The reality of both linguistic and cultural norms becomes evident when they are violated, as often happens in cross-cultural encounters. To deny the reality of such rules is to indulge in academic *schöngeist*-ery at the expense of persons and social groups (including, in particular, the ethnic underdogs) for whom successful cross-cultural communication is a matter of existential necessity (cf. e.g. Kataoka 1991; Darder 1995; Harkins 1994; cf. also Wierzbicka 1991a, chapter 2 and in press a).

The evidence for the reality of cultural norms and shared conceptions is provided by language and, in particular, by the meanings of words. Linguistic semantics provides a rigorous methodology for decoding such meanings and, consequently, for elucidating for cultural outsiders the tacit assumptions which are linked with them.

8. Linguistic and conceptual universals

To compare the meanings of words from different languages (such as, for example, *pravda* and *truth*, or *duša* and *soul*), we need a *tertium comparationis*, that is, a common measure. If the meanings of ALL words were-culture-specific, then cultural differences could not be explored at all. The "hypothesis of linguistic relativity" makes sense only if it is combined with a well thought out "hypothesis of linguistic universality": only well-established linguistic universals can provide a valid basis for comparing conceptual systems entrenched in different languages and for elucidating the meanings which are encoded in some languages (or language) but not in others.

The idea of conceptual universals as a possible "common measure" for comparing semantic systems is inherent, at least in embryonic form, in Leibniz's (1961[1903]) conception of "an alphabet of human thoughts":

> Although the number of ideas which can be conceived is infinite, it is possible that the number of those which can be conceived by themselves is very small; because an infinite number of anything can be expressed by combining very few elements. . . .
> The alphabet of human thoughts is the catalogue of those concepts which can be understood by themselves, and by whose combination all our other ideas are formed.
> (430)

Being a firm believer in the "psychic unity of humankind" (founded on the universal "alphabet of human thoughts"), Leibniz recommended comparative study of different languages of the world as a way to discover the "inner essence of man" and, in particular, the universal basis of human cognition (Leibniz 1981[1709]:326).

Just as Sapir and Whorf have often been chastized for emphasizing profound differences between languages and the conceptual systems associated with them, Leibniz has been chastized for emphasizing their underlying unity. For example, the distinguished British anthropologist Rodney Needham (1972) commented on Leibniz's proposal:

> This bold suggestion . . . was based on the tacit premise that the human mind was everywhere the same. . . . Methodologically, Leibniz was thus proposing a comparative analysis of the kind that Lévy-Bruhl was to put into effect almost exactly two centuries later, and even in terms that find ready agreement today; but it is not premises, not the type of research that he recommended, that have since been called into renewed question. Underlying his proposal was the conviction that human nature

was uniform and fixed, and it is precisely this idea that more recent conceptual analyses have made difficult to accept. (220)

Thus, scholars of Pinker's orientation dismiss the study of differences between languages as a possible source of insight into social cognition, for they identify such an endeavor with "the idea that thought is the same thing as language" (which they reject as an "absurdity" [Pinker 1994:57]). On the other hand, scholars of Needham's orientation dismiss the search for linguistic universals as a possible guide to conceptual universals because in their view there can't be any conceptual universals: to admit that such universals could exist would mean to accept the possibility that some aspects of "human nature" and human cognition may be constant.

What neither side seems prepared to consider is the possibility that languages, and the ways of thinking reflected in them, exhibit both profound differences and profound similarities; that the study of diversity can lead to the discovery of universals; that SOME hypotheses about universals are indispensable for the study of the diversity; and that hypotheses about conceptual universals have to be checked and revised in response to empirical findings emerging from systematic cross-linguistic investigations.

In fact, there is no conflict between an interest in linguistic and conceptual universals on the one hand and an interest in the diversity of language-and-culture systems on the other. On the contrary, to achieve their purpose, these two interests must go hand in hand.

Consider, for example, the following question: How do patterns of friendship differ across cultures? One standard approach to this question is to use broad sociological surveys based on questionnaires, in which respondents are asked, for example, How many friends do you have? How many of them are male and how many female? How often, on average, do you see your friends? And so on.

The procedure seems straightforward—except for one small point: if the question is asked in Russian, or in Japanese, what word will be used for *friend?* The assumption behind such questionnaires, or behind comparative studies based on them, is that, for example, Russian, Japanese, and English words for "friend" can be matched. This assumption is linguistically naive, and the results based on it are bound to present a distorted picture of reality (cf. Wagatsuma 1977). It is even more naive to assume that from a cognitive point of view such lack of correspondence doesn't matter, for "thought is [not] the same thing as language" (Pinker 1994:57). We can only reach thoughts through words (no one has yet invented another way). This is why in trying to say something about "human thoughts" we need to weigh our words carefully and try to anchor them in linguistic and conceptual universals.

9. "Natural semantic metalanguage": Exit from Babel

The idea that "there is no exit from language" (cf. e.g. Appignanesi and Garratt 1995:76) is not a twentieth-century invention, but it is certainly one which has been put forward with ever greater insistence in the last few decades (and also, with an ever greater range of interpretations). In a sense, this statement is true, in so far as everything we say we say in some language, so that even if we "translate" our thoughts from one language into another, we remain within the confines of a language.

In another sense, however, this idea is not true, for the existence of conceptual and linguistic universals does offer us an exit of sorts. This statement requires an explanation.

If we assume (at least as a working hypothesis) that, first, all languages have a common core (both in their lexicons and in their grammar), that, second, this common core is innate, being shaped by a prelinguistic "readiness for meaning" (cf. Bruner 1990:22), and that, third, this common core can be used as a kind of mini-language for saying whatever we want to say, then we can see that a door leading "outside language" has already opened. For although this common core can only be identified, and understood, via language, it is, in an important sense, language-independent: it is determined by an innate conceptual system, and it is independent of everything idiosyncractic in the structure of all individual languages.

To put it differently, by identifying a common core of all languages, we can carve within any language (for example, English or Japanese) a mini-language (a kind of "basic English" or "basic Japanese"), which we can then use as a metalanguage for talking about languages and cultures as if from outside them all. Since our "basic English" will be isomorphic with our "basic Japanese" (or basic anything else), from a theoretical (though of course not from a practical) point of view it will not matter which "basic language" we choose for our descriptive and explanatory formulae: each such "basic language" will be isomorphic to all the other ones, and each of them will be based directly on the prelinguistic conceptual system, presumed to be innate and universal.

If there is no "exit from language" in an absolute sense, there is, in some sense, an exit from the Babel of languages (via universal human concepts). Babel, that is, in the sense of the multiplicity of languages and the resulting confusion. But, as Derrida has discussed (1982:132–139; 1991), "confusion of tongues" is only the second meaning of the word *Babel*. In the original sense of the word, "Babel" was the tower of strength, the tower of a universal linguistic system. In this original sense of the word, natural semantic metalanguage (NSM) offers the possibility of a partial return to Babel (via universal human concepts). It presents a partial solution to what Derrida calls the "double bind" of the necessity of translation and the impossibility of translation and offers us some hope for achieving, or at least approaching (via universal human concepts), what Derrida calls "forbidden transparency, impossible univocity" (1991:253).[5]

This, then, is the fundamental assumption (or working hypothesis) on which the description and comparison of meanings in this book is based. In contrast to other approaches to meaning, the one adopted here relies neither on ad hoc formulations of meaning, given in ordinary language, nor on formulae of technical metalanguages requiring further explanation, but on paraphrases formulated in a self-explanatory "natural semantic metalanguage" carved out of natural languages and assumed to be independent of them all. Since this natural semantic metalanguage is based directly on natural language, the paraphrases formulated in it can be regarded as, essentially, self-explanatory (certainly more so than formulae of logical calculi); since, however, they do not utilize the full resources of natural languages but only their minimal shared core, they can be standardized, comparable across languages, and free of the inherent circularity which plagues semantic descriptions using the full-blown ordinary language as its own metalanguage.

For a full explanation of the methodology of semantic description in the NSM approach and for its theoretical underpinnings, the reader must be referred to some other works in the NSM literature (cf. in particular Goddard & Wierzbicka 1994, and Wierzbicka 1996). Here, I will only highlight a few basic points: semantic primitives, lexical universals, categories and "parts of speech," the universal syntax of meaning, polysemy, "allolexy," "valency options," and the trial-and-error approach.

9.1   Semantic primitives

As colleagues and I have tried to demonstrate for almost a third of a century, the key to a rigorous yet insightful talk about meaning lies in the notion of semantic primitives (or semantic primes). One cannot define ALL words because the very idea of "defining" implies that there is not only something to be defined (a definiendum) but also something to define it with (a definiens, or rather, a set of "definienses"). The elements which can be used to define the meaning of words (or any other meanings) cannot be defined themselves; rather, they must be accepted as "indefinibilia," that is, as semantic primes, in terms of which all complex meanings can be coherently represented.

This is, then, one of the main assumptions of the semantic theory, and semantic practice, presented in this book: meaning cannot be described without a set of semantic primitives; one can purport to describe meaning by translating unknowns into unknowns (as in Blaise Pascal's mock definition, "Light is the luminary movement of luminous bodies" [1667/1954:580]), but nothing is really achieved thereby. Semantics can have an explanatory value only if (and to the extent which) it manages to "define" or explicate complex and obscure meanings in terms of simple and self-explanatory ones. If we can understand any utterances at all (someone else's or our own), it is only because these utterances are built, so to speak, out of simple elements which can be understood by themselves.

This basic point, which modern linguistics has lost sight of, was made repeatedly in the writings on language by the great thinkers of the seventeenth century, such as Descartes, Pascal, Antoine Arnauld, and Leibniz. For example, Descartes (1931[1701]) wrote:

> Further I declare that there are certain things which we render more obscure by trying to define them, because, since they are very simple and clear, we cannot know and perceive them better than by themselves. Nay, we must place in the number of those chief errors that can be committed in the sciences, the mistakes committed by those who would try to define what ought only to be conceived, and who cannot distinguish the clear from the obscure, nor discriminate between what, in order to be known, requires and deserves to be defined, from what can be best known by itself. (324).

9.2   Lexical universals

In the theory on which this book is based, it has been hypothesized, from the start, that conceptual primitives can be found through in-depth analysis of any natural language, but also that the sets of primitives identified in this way would "match," and that in fact each such set is just one language-specific manifestation of a universal set of fundamental human concepts.

This expectation was based on the assumption that fundamental human concepts are innate, and that, if they are innate, then there is no reason to expect that they should differ from one human group to another.

Until recently, this assumption was based largely on theoretical considerations rather than on empirical studies of different languages of the world. This situation has changed, however, with the publication of *Semantic and lexical universals* (Goddard & Wierzbicka 1994, henceforth SLU), a collective volume in which conceptual primitives posited initially on the basis of a mere handful of languages were subjected to a systematic study across a wide range of languages from different families and different continents. The languages investigated in this volume included Ewe of the Niger-Congo family in West Africa (Felix Ameka), Mandarin Chinese (Hilary Chappell), Thai (Anthony Diller), Japanese (Masayuki Onishi), the Australian languages Yankunytjatjara (Cliff Goddard), Arrernte (Aranda) (Jean Harkins and David Wilkins), and Kayardild (Nicholas Evans), three Misumalpan languages of Nicaragua (Kenneth Hale), the Austronesian languages Acehnese of Indonesia (Mark Durie and colleagues), Longgu of Solomon Islands (Deborah Hill), Samoan (Ulrike Mosel), and Mangap-Mbula of Papua New Guinea (Robert Bugenhagen), the Papuan language Kalam (Andrew Pawley), and—the only European language besides English—French (Bert Peeters).

9.3   Categories and "parts of speech"

The work of the last thirty years undertaken by myself and colleagues has identified nearly sixty candidates for the status of universal semantic primitives, as outlined in the table below.

Substantives: I, YOU, SOMEONE/PERSON, SOMETHING/THING, PEOPLE, BODY

Determiners: THIS, THE SAME, OTHER

Quantifiers: ONE, TWO, SOME, ALL, MANY/MUCH

Attributes: GOOD, BAD, BIG, SMALL

Mental predicates: THINK, KNOW, WANT, FEEL, SEE, HEAR

Speech: SAY, WORD, TRUE

Actions, events, and movement: DO, HAPPEN, MOVE

Existence: (alienable) POSSESSION: THERE IS, HAVE

Life and death: LIVE/ALIVE, DIE

Logical concepts: NOT, MAYBE, CAN, BECAUSE, IF, IF . . . WOULD (counterfactual)

Time: WHEN/TIME, NOW, AFTER, BEFORE, A LONG TIME, A SHORT TIME, FOR SOME TIME

Space: WHERE/PLACE, HERE, UNDER, ABOVE, FAR, NEAR; SIDE, INSIDE

Intensifier, augmentor: VERY, MORE

Taxonomy, partonomy: KIND OF, PART OF

Similarity: LIKE

As the format of this outline suggests, the proposed set of primitives is not an unstructured set but, rather, a network of categories, which can be compared (somewhat metaphorically) with the parts of speech of traditional grammar. The main point is that the categories singled out (in a preliminary way) in the table above are, so to speak, both semantic and structural. They recognize certain natural semantic groupings such as, for example, time and space, and at the same time they pay attention to the combinatorial properties of the elements. Although the classification of semantic elements outlined above is by no means the only possible one, it is not arbitrary either.

What matters most from the point of view of this book is that the explications of meanings proposed here will be formulated largely (though not exclusively) in terms of the primitives listed in the above table.

Exceptions from this overall policy will be made sparingly, for the purposes of clarity and readability of the formulae. For example, in chapter 2 on "patterns of friendship," words such as *father*, *mother*, and *child* will be used as if they were semantic primitives, and the word *country* will be similarly used in chapters 3 and 4.

In addition to such consciously introduced exceptions, proposed semantic primitives will also be used in a number of different forms, or "allolexes," and with different "valency options." Both these points will be discussed briefly below, as will also the important issue of polysemy. First, however, I will discuss the grammar of the primitives, which is as important to the explanation of meaning as is the set of the primitives themselves.

9.4 The universal syntax of meaning

In what has been said so far, the emphasis was on the elements: the primitive concepts, the indefinable words. To say anything meaningful, however, we need more than words: we need sentences in which words are meaningfully put together. Similarly, to think something we need more than "concepts": we need meaningful combinations of concepts. Despite its obvious limitations, Leibniz's old metaphor of an "alphabet of human thoughts" is still quite useful here. Conceptual primitives are components which have to be combined in certain ways to be able to express meaning.

For example, the indefinable word *want* makes sense only if it is put in a certain syntactic frame, such as "I want to do this". In positing the elements I, WANT, DO, and THIS as innate and universal conceptual primitives, I am also positing certain innate and universal rules of syntax—not in the sense of some intuitively unverifiable formal syntax à la Chomsky but in the sense of intuitively verifiable patterns determining possible combinations of primitive concepts.

If one wants to explain the meaning of a sentence such as "I want to do this" to a nonnative speaker, the best one can do is to point to a semantically matching sentence in one's own language. For example, to a Russian one could offer the following equation:

I want to do this = ja xoču èto sdelat'

where *ja* matches with *I*, *xoču* (1st Sg) with *want*, *èto* with *this*, and *sdelat'* with *do*, and where the combination *ja xoču* matches with *I want*, the combination *èto sdelat'* matches with *to do this*, and the whole combination *ja xoču ėto sdelat'* matches with the whole combination *I want to do this*.

This is, then, what the universal syntax of meaning is all about: it consists in universal combinations of universal conceptual primitives. From a formal point of view, the grammar of the Russian sentence differs a great deal from that of the English one. But formal differences of this kind don't detract in the least from the overall semantic equivalence of the two sentences, which is based on the equivalence of the primitives themselves and of the rules for their combination.

Thus, the theory assumed in this book posits the existence not only of an innate and universal "lexicon of human thoughts" but also of an innate and universal "syntax of human thoughts." Taken together, these two hypotheses amount to positing something that can be called "a language of thought," or, as I called it in the title of my 1980 book, "Lingua Mentalis." It is this universal "lingua mentalis" which is being proposed, and tested, as a practical metalanguage ("NSM") for the description and comparison of meanings.

9.5 Polysemy

Polysemy is extremely widespread in natural language, and common everyday words—including indefinables—are particularly likely to be involved in it. A semantic primitive cannot be identified, therefore, simply by pointing to an indefinable word. Rather, it must be identified with reference to some illustrative sentences. For example, the English word *move* has at least two meanings, as illustrated below:

A. I couldn't move.
B. Her words moved me.

Of these two meanings, only (A) is proposed as a semantic primitive.

The NSM theory does not claim that for every semantic primitive there will be, in every language, a separate word—as long as the absence of a separate word for a given primitive can be convincingly explained (in a principled and coherent way) in terms of polysemy. The notion of different grammatical frames plays a particularly important role in this regard.

9.6 Allolexy

The term *allolexy* refers to the fact that the same element of meaning may be expressed in a language in two or more different ways. For just as one word (or morpheme) can be associated with two (or more) different meanings, one meaning can often have two or more different lexical exponents. By analogy with "allomorphs" and "allophones," such different exponents of the same primitive are called "allolexes" in NSM theory. For example, in English, *I* and *me* are allolexes of the same primitive concept (in Latin, EGO, in Russian, JA). Often, the allolexes of a primitive are in complementary distribution; for example, in Latin the three forms *hic, haec, hoc* are all exponents of the same primitive THIS, and the choice between them depends on the gender of the head noun. In particular, the combination with another primitive often forces the choice of one of a set of allolexes. For example, in English, a combination of the primitives SOMEONE and ALL is realized as *everyone* or *everybody*, and a combination of ALL with SOMETHING is realized as *everything*. In these particular contexts, *-one* and *-body* can be seen as allolexes of SOMEONE, on a par with *someone*; and *-thing* can be seen as an allolex of SOMETHING, on a par with *something*.

The notion of allolexy plays a particularly important role in the NSM approach to inflectional categories. For example, the forms *am doing*, *did*, and *will do* used without temporal adjuncts convey different meanings, but when combined with the temporal adjuncts *now*, *before now*, and *after now*, as in the sentences A, B, and C below, they are in complementary distribution and can be seen as allolexes of the same primitive DO:

A. I am doing it now.
B. I did it before now (earlier).
C. I will do it after now (later).

This is why NSM sentences can be said to match, semantically, across languages, even though inflectional categories can differ considerably from language to language.

9.7 "Valency options"

The notion of "valency options" refers to different combinability patterns available to the same primitive. For example, the primitive DO can occur in the following combinations:

A. X did something.
B. X did something to person Y.
C. X did something (together) with person Y.

Obviously, "doing something to someone" or "doing something with someone" implies "doing something." Nonetheless, sentences B or C cannot be analyzed in terms of A and something else. It has to be recognized, therefore, that in each case the difference in meaning is due to the sentence as a whole, not to the predicate as such, and that the three sentences share in fact the same predicate (DO), although they realize different valency options of this predicate.

9.8 The trial and error approach

The project of devising a "Natural Semantic Metalanguage" based on natural languages and yet, in a sense, independent of them all may seem utopian. It is important to point out, therefore, that the foundations of such a metalanguage have already been laid in the work of myself and colleagues, undertaken, with this goal in mind, over the last thirty years, and that a number of successive approximations to a workable, effective NSM have already been developed and put to the test in many languages, including languages as diverse as Chinese (cf. e.g. Chappell 1983, 1986a, 1986b), Ewe (cf. Ameka 1986, 1987, 1990, 1991), Japanese (cf. Travis 1992, Hasada 1994), Malay

(Goddard 1994b), the Austronesian language Mangap-Mbula (cf. Bugenhagen 1990), and the Australian languages Yankunytjatjara (cf. Goddard 1990, 1992a, 1992b) and Arrernte (cf. Wilkins 1986; Harkins 1992).

The building of the Natural Semantic Metalanguage was, and continues to be, a gradual process. In contrast to more speculative semantic theories, the NSM theory constantly seeks confirmation—or disconfirmation—in large-scale descriptive projects. For example, in my semantic dictionary *English speech act verbs* (Wierzbicka 1987), I attempted to analyze the meaning of more than two hundred English verbs; more recently, in a series of articles on another conceptual domain (cf. e.g. Wierzbicka 1990b, 1992a, 1994), I have similarly sought to analyze at least a hundred English emotion terms (see also Ameka 1987, 1990; Goddard 1990, 1991, 1992, in press; Harkins 1994; Hasada 1994; Kornacki 1995; and others).

It is through descriptive projects of this kind that the inadequacies (as well as the strengths) of the successive versions of NSM became apparent and that future directions of development could be seen more clearly. Perhaps the most important direction of change had to do with the growing simplification and standardization of the syntax of explications, linked directly with the search for universal syntactic patterns.

The present book can be seen as another such test, since it attempts to investigate several semantic domains, in several languages, in terms of the (latest version of) the Natural Semantic Metalanguage. This time, the focus is on the interpretation of cultures (via NSM) rather than on NSM as such. This means that NSM is being tested here as a descriptive tool rather than as an abstract system, but the two aspects of the verification process are, of course, closely linked.

10. Conclusion

Wuthnow et al. note that "for all the research that has been made possible by survey techniques and quantitative analysis, little has been learned about cultural patterns" (1984:6-7), and they ask "whether it is possible to construct cultural analysis as a basic tool capable of producing verifiable social scientific knowledge at all, or whether the study of culture necessarily remains a speculative venture" (257).

This book seeks to demonstrate that cultural patterns can be studied in a verifiable and nonspeculative way on the basis of linguistic semantics, rooted in empirically established linguistic and conceptual universals. It also seeks to vindicate the importance of words, which all too often are described these days as "isolated," "fuzzy," or "static" and, consequently, rejected in favor of "taskonomies," "everyday practices," "discourse," "schemas," "prototypes," and so on. For example, Wassmann (1995) writes:

> The opening of cognitive anthropology leads to new terminology appearing in publications: 'category' and 'semantic attribute' have been superseded by 'schema', 'prototype', and 'proposition'. . . . Thus, although language remains one of the focal points, it is treated differently: no longer as a lexicon, but in everyday use as 'discourse' from which inferences must be drawn as to the intended 'message'. (173–174)

But there is no conflict between studying the meanings of words and studying everyday discourse and everyday cognition. On the contrary, as this book seeks to show, the lexicon is the clearest possible guide to everyday cognition and to the patterning of everyday discourse.

For example, basic patterns of Japanese everyday discourse and the Japanese "cultural scripts" reflected in them (cf. e.g. Wierzbicka in press a) are closely linked with the semantics of Japanese key words such as *enryo* or *wa*, discussed in chapter 6; and the basic patterns of Anglo-Australian everyday discourse (cf. Wierzbicka 1991a and 1992b) are closely linked with the semantics of Australian English words such as *whinge, bullshit,* and *bloody*, discussed in chapter 5. In a sense, words of this kind provide a condensed introduction to patterns of discourse and present the essence of some everyday practices in a crystalline form.

While scholars such as Wassmann underestimate the importance of the lexicon, their attitude is at least not downright hostile, but there is no shortage of real enemies of "words." For example, Simon During (1995), a Professor of English at the University of Melbourne, attacks the concept behind the *Oxford English dictionary*: "[S]trange though it may seem, words do not have fixed and true meanings at all. They are not so much rigid designators of specific meanings as flexible counters used to build up phrases or sentences. It makes sense to say that a word has a different 'meaning' whenever it is used" (9).

In a sense, it is true that words have no "fixed" meanings because the meanings of words change. But if they were always fluid and without any "true" content, they could not change either. As this book seeks to demonstrate, words do have indentifiable, "true" meanings, the precise outlines of which can be established on an empirical basis by studying their range of use. Of course, these meanings change, but this change, too, can be studied and described only if it is understood that there is something there that can change. What is fuzzy, fluid, and lacking in clear content is not words but some recent theorizing about words, not supported, needless to say, by large-scale systematic study of the lexicon of any language.

It is an illusion to think that we will better understand cultures if we reject Sapir's fundamental insight that "vocabulary is a very sensitive index of the culture of a people." On the contrary. We will better understand cultures if we try to build on this insight and to learn to study vocabulary more deeply, more rigorously, and in a broader theoretical perspective.

Lexicon as a Key to Ethno-Sociology and Cultural Psychology

Patterns of "Friendship" Across Cultures

1. "Friendship"—a human universal?

There is a widespread assumption that friendship is a universal human need and that the concept of 'friend' is a human universal. For example, Davis and Todd (1985) ask, "Why do friendships have the importance that they do?" and they comment: "The general answer provided in many theories is that not to have friends is to miss something vital for full-fledged human development. The personal relationship of friendship is thus seen as providing the context within which a number of basic human needs can be met" (21). Having characterized what they call "a paradigm case of friendship" in terms of nine basic characteristics (such as equality, enjoyment of each other's company, mutual assistance, mutual respect, and intimacy), they affirm that these characteristics jointly "characterize a relationship taken to be central in normal personal development, and thus a relationship prototypical of people's capacity to enjoy a meaningful life" (p.22).

Assumptions of this kind are ethnocentric. The concept of 'friend', and the relationship linked with it, are important in Anglo culture, but it is an illusion to think that they must have their counterparts in all other cultures and that they are somehow part of human nature.

It is possible to look at other cultures through the prism of the English words *friend* and *friendship*, of course, but if it is not recognized at the outset that these words don't necessarily have exact equivalents in other languages, and that this fact is important and revealing, the inevitable result will be that the habitual Anglo perspective on human relations will be mistaken for the human norm. For example, Blieszner and Adams (1992) write:

From the days of the ancient Greek and Roman philosophers until now, throughout cultures, friends have been recognized as important sources of affection and enjoyment, understanding and support, companionship and counsel. . . . With the advent of empirical methods in psychology, sociology, and other disciplines comes a desire to understand the attributes of friends and friendship. (28)

But it is not true that "throughout cultures" "friends" have been recognized as an important social or psychological category. Taxonomies of human relations are just as culture-specific, and language-specific, as are taxonomies of emotions, or of speech acts, and the concept encoded in the present-day English word *friend* has no privileged status in them. It certainly does not represent a constant, a human universal. In fact (as we shall see), even within English the meaning of the word *friend* has changed in the course of the centuries, thus reflecting a profound change in the conceptualization of human relations and in the patterns of those relations themselves. To quote a sociological classic (Znaniecki 1965):

Perhaps the best-known voluntary, long-lasting relations between individual men, as intimate as fraternal relations, but independent of hereditary bonds, are those of *friendship*. They have emerged in various complex collectivities, but reached their full development only in ancient Greece and Rome—judging from the evidence contained in the works of Plato, Xenophon, Aristotle, the Epicureans, and Cicero. Friendship was seldom mentioned in medieval literature, where the basic cooperative relations between men were supposed to be religious; but it was revived during the Renaissance, and is now widely spread in the Western world. (138)

Although in the Western world, concepts encapsulated in words such as *amicus* in Latin, *friend* (in its older meaning) in English, *ami* in French, *amico* in Italian, *Freund* in German, and *przyjaciel* in Polish are indeed remarkably similar and do reflect a common cultural tradition, in this world, too, there are differences as well as similarities. The very fact that, as mentioned earlier, the meaning of the English word *friend* has changed shows that the Western cultural tradition in the patterns of human relations is less unified than it may seem at first sight.

Here as elsewhere, the crucial question is that of language. What is missing in most of the English language literature on the subject—psychological, sociological, and philosophical—is a clear realization that *friend* and *friendship* are English words, embodying concepts which are cultural artifacts of the society which created them. When this is not recognized, the meanings of the words *friend* and *friendship* tend to be either absolutized and treated as clues to human nature in general, or ignored, and treated as less important than personal judgments about human relations coming from individual informants. For example, Winstead and Derlega (1986) write: "In order to have an adequate theory of friendship, we must have a definition of friendship. Curiously, in reviewing the chapters in this volume, we find that the issue of definition was not addressed. . . . when authors refer to 'friendship,' they seem to rely on a consensual, but unspecified, idea of what friendship is" (2).

The very idea that there may be, and should be, "an adequate theory of friendship" is based on the assumption that "friendship" is something that exists independently of the English language and can be analyzed as a pre-existing, extralinguistic category.

The title of the section in which the authors put forward their proposal is: "A scientific approach to the study of friendship" (65).

This reliance on the word *friendship*, as if it were a label for a pre-existing fact, betrays an absolutization of this Anglo concept. At the same time, however, the authors fail to recognize the importance of this concept as a socio-cultural fact and want to base their "scientific approach to friendship" on some individuals' personal definitions of this concept:

> What is an appropriate starting place for a scientific study of friendship? Rather than continuing in the philosophical tradition that seeks the one definition of what constitutes the ideal friendship, we propose instead to focus on the individual: to examine individuals' personal definitions of friendship and the influence of their conceptions of friendship on the networks of their actual friendships and the social worlds within which they live. (65)

The desire to go beyond the philosophical tradition that seeks a definition of "ideal friendship" and to engage in an empirically based study of human relations is understandable, but a valid empirical investigation requires a previous conceptual clarification—and this cannot be achieved without some attention being paid to the language in which the "empirical" questions are framed.

Blieszner and Adams call, rightly, for an integration of "conceptual and empirical approaches to the analysis of friendship" and "of the friend relationship" (1992:123). It needs to be pointed out, however, that a fruitful conceptual approach must include an analysis of the words *friend* and *friendship* themselves, not as a focus for individual associations but as socio-cultural facts, and that a fruitful empirical approach must include an analysis of comparable socio-cultural facts embodied in languages other than English.

To give just one example of the kind of confusion which arises when language problems are ignored, consider the following statements from a psychology monograph (Duck 1977): "There is no Book of Common Sense, but magazines in dentists' waiting rooms seem to have a reasonable claim to embody the everyday view of life. . . . People set out consciously to make friends. . . . People like to feel that there exists some control over the selections which they make" (2, 3, 7).

Who are those "people" that Duck is talking about? The expression *to make friends* is indeed significant, and it does imply some expectation of "control," but it is a specifically English expression, without equivalents in many other European (let alone, non-European) languages; and moreover, it is an expression which emerged only in modern English, thus reflecting changes in the patterning of human relations and in their conceptualization in modern Anglo societies.

What this illustrates is that what people regard as "common sense" is bound up with a particular language, and that just as languages change and differ, so do "common-sensical" assumptions about human relations, as well as everything else. Reliance on one's native language as a source of universally valid "common-sensical" assumptions about human nature and human relations is bound to lead to ethnocentric fallacies. At the same time, ignoring the different "common-sensical" assumptions reflected in different languages is bound to lead to the obliteration of very valuable empirical evidence concerning both similarities and differences in the patterning and conceptualization of human relations in different cultures and societies.

To illustrate. In Japanese culture, two (main) "friend-like" types of relationship are lexically distinguished: *shinyu* and *tomodachi*. Loosely speaking, *shinyu* can be glossed as 'intimate friend', whereas *tomodachi* is closer to 'friend,' *tout court*. For example, children of kindergarten age can be said to have their *tomodachi*, but not their *shinyu*—presumably because small children are not seen as persons capable (yet) of genuine "intimacy" (Rie Hasada and Hiroko Quakenbush, personal communication).

But "intimacy" is not the only difference between the two categories. Normally, *shinyu* refers (at least for older speakers) to a person of the same gender (a man's *shinyu* are normally men, and a woman's *shinyu* women), whereas *tomodachi* is not similarly restricted. This link between "intimacy" and "being a person of the same gender" is highly revealing of Japanese patterns of interpersonal relations. Yet in two (otherwise highly informative) studies of "Japanese patterns of friendship" (Atsumi 1980, 1989) the distinction between *shinyu* and *tomodachi* is not mentioned at all, and although the word *shinyu* is mentioned, *tomodachi* is not. Instead, most of the discussion relies, confusingly, on the English word *friend* and thereby loses sight of vital linguistic evidence bearing on Japanese patterns of interpersonal relations.

This is only one example. Other Japanese words referring to interpersonal relations are also very revealing. For example, there is the word *doryo*, which refers to people whom one works with, but only people of the same rank. There is also the word *nakama* (from *naka* 'inside'), which refers to a group of "friends" (one's "crowd," so to speak), and its derivatives, such as *nominakama* (roughly 'one's drinking friends/companions'), *asobinakama* (roughly 'playmates') and *shigotona-kama* ('people whom one works with'). There is also the word *yujin*, described sometimes as a more formal equivalent of *tomodachi*. Each such word reflects assumptions and values characteristic of Japanese culture and absent from the less differentiated English concept of 'friend'.

In this chapter, I will explore the conceptualization and categorization of human relations in Russian, Polish, and Anglo-Australian culture, as reflected in the meaning of certain key words (such as *druz ja* and *tovarišči* in Russian, *koledzy* and *przyjaciele* in Polish, and *mates* in Australian English). I will also discuss the English word *friend*, showing how the meaning of this word has changed and how these changes reflect, and throw light on, changes in culture and society.

2. The changing meaning of the English word *friend*

2.1 How many friends does one have?

"Who was that?"
"Oh, just a friend. Someone I used to know"
(Brookner 1993:224)

The meaning of the English word *friend* has changed over the centuries in ways which are revealing of underlying changes in human relations. These changes could be crudely described in various ways as "devaluation," "broadening of scope," shift from "vertical" ("in-depth") to "horizontal," from "exclusive" to "inclusive," and so on.

The general trend of these changes is aptly illustrated by the emergence of the expression *close friend*, which though difficult to date, is definitely modern. Among more than two hundred classical quotations including the word *friend* in Stevenson's (1949) *Book of quotations*, not a single one includes the expression *close friend* (and there are no examples of it in Spevack's 1968 concordance to Shakespeare's works), whereas in contemporary sources this expression appears to be the most common collocation.[1]

Broadly, the meaning of the word *friend* has "weakened," so that to achieve anything like the same "force" it is now necessary to use the expression *close friend*. Something of the old value of the word *friend* has survived in the derived noun *friendship*: whereas in the older usage, *friends* were related to one another by *friendship*, in the current usage one can have many more *friends* than *friendships*, and only "close friends" can now be said to be linked by "friendship."

It is particularly striking that the number of "friends" that a person can be expected to have has increased over time in all major Anglo societies. A hundred years ago, Henry Adams wrote (in his *Education of Henry Adams*):

> One friend in a lifetime is much; two are many; three are hardly possible.

And an older quote, with a characteristic injunction:

> Choose thy friends like thy books, few but choice. (James Howell, 1659).

In the highly mobile present-day American society, people often count their "friends" by the dozen. To some extent, however, the same applies to other English-speaking countries, as the following sentence from an Australian book illustrates:

> One of our long-term survivors, Peter, had lost over forty friends to Aids. (King 1992:300)

Clearly, for this writer there is nothing odd about the phrase "forty friends." In fact, in modern English, even a person's "best friends" can be quite numerous. The fact that in modern English the expression *best friends* is often used in the plural is highly significant in this respect. For example, Rees' (1990) *Dictionary of popular phrases* includes the following expressions: "even your best friends," "my best friends," and "some of my best friends."

The same holds for the expression *close friends*, which (at least in American English) can now be applied to dozens of more or less casual associates. As Packard reports in his book on American mobility:

> A man who had moved sixteen times in twenty-two years of marriage contended he had at least acquired "a few close, lasting friends at every stop." (1974:174)

For this man at least, it would seem that the number of his "close, lasting friends" must have been at least fifty! This brings to mind the lines by the eighteenth-century English poet William Cowper:

> She, that asks
> Her dear five hundred friends, contemns them all
> And hates their coming . . .

For many other people interviewed by Packard, the numbers of "friends" were of a similar order. In most cases these "friends" were not seen as lasting but as transient and replaceable.

> A man can become a pal for two hours with a stranger he meets on the golf course with full knowledge that he probably will never see the person again. The trick is the knack for affability. The new gregarious can be fairly indiscriminate in their selection of new friends, who become as interchangeable as cars. (188)

In fact, it might be suggested that the idea of "friendship" as a lasting, permanent relationship has given way in Anglo-American culture to the new ideal of "meeting new people." To quote one more of Packard's respondents, "the remarkable wife of a plant manager in predominantly stable Glens Falls, New York, who had moved twenty times in fifteen years of marriage, . . . explained":

> I move to a new area with the feeling I will meet new people and will have many happy experiences—and I usually do. I join groups right away and get involved. (175)

Another woman, who had moved five times in eight years of marriage, made a similar comment:

> One cannot stagnate. You have to adapt, learn to change. There are always new, interesting people, fascinating places. (174)

"New people" whom one meets in new places are very readily called "friends". For example:

> The young wife of a new teacher in high-mobile Great Falls, Montana, said that though she still did not know anyone on her block, "We have developed a number of friends through the bowling alley where we play. I bowl one afternoon a week with a lot of real nice girls and we have met several couples at the alley. The alley develops leagues which any girls can join and you are periodically put on a different team with people you don't know" [2] (147).

Packard speaks in this connection of different methods of "instant plug-in" used by American people "when they move to a new community" (149).

Both the instant "plug-in" and the equally instant "plug-out" of contemporary "friends" are features quite incompatible with the classical conception of "friendship," including that reflected in the earlier English usage. This view of "friendship" as something that grows slowly and lasts "forever," is expressed in numerous traditional sayings and proverbs and in well-known works of literature. For example:

> Friendship's the wine of life; but friendship new
> Is neither strong nor pure.
> (Edward Young, *Night thoughts*)

Be courteous to all, but intimate with few, and let those few be well tried before you give them your confidence. True friendship is a plant of slow growth, and must undergo and withstand the shocks of adversity before it is entitled to the appellation. (George Washington, Letter, 1783)

It's an overcome sooth for age an' youth
    And it brooks wi' nae denial
That the dearest friends are the auldest friends,
    And the young are just on trial.
(R. L. Stevenson, "It's an overcome sooth")

Friendship is a slow grower, and never thrives unless ingrafted upon a stock of known and reciprocal merit. (Lord Chesterfield, Letter, 1747)

The traditional view of friendship as something permanent is reflected in common collocations such as *eternal friendship*, often combined, in addition, with *swearing* or *vowing*:

A sudden thought strikes me—let us swear an eternal friendship.

(J. H. Frere, "The rovers")

If I do vow a friendship, I'll perform it
To the last article.
(William Shakespeare, *Othello*).

Other common collocations involving *friendship* included the words *steady* and *constant*. For example:

A friendship that like love is warm;
A love like friendship, steady.
(Thomas Moore, "How shall I woo?")

To be capable of steady friendship and lasting love, are the two greatest proofs, not only of goodness of heart, but of strength of mind.
(William Hazlitt, "Characteristics")

Friendship is constant in all other things,
Save in the office and affairs of love.
(Shakespeare, *Much ado about nothing*)

But it is not only the word *friendship* but also the word *friend* whose common collocations reflect the old conception of friendship as something permanent. Thus, the most common collocations with the word *friend* included *faithful friend*, *steadfast friend*, and *old friend*. For example:

Above our life we love a steadfast friend.

(Chistopher Marlowe, *Hero and Leander*)

Ah, how good it feels

The hand of an old friend!

(Henry W. Longfellow, "John Endicott")

. . . There are certain signs to show

Faithful friend from faltering foe.

(Richard Barnfield, "Passionate pilgrim")

As old wood is best to burn, old horse to ride, old books to read, and old wine to drink, so are old friends always most trusty to use.

(Leonard Wright, "Display of dutie," 1588)

Clearly, the changes in the use of the word *friend* discussed here reflect historical processes and social transformations which are not unique to Anglo societies. America in particular has gone further along a road that many other modern societies are still traveling. There is, accordingly, nothing uniquely Anglo about the general direction of the semantic changes discussed here either (although the precise shape of the modern Anglo concept of 'friend' is no doubt due also to some specific features of Anglo culture). Given the key role that the English word *friend* plays in the modern literature on interpersonal relationships, it is particularly important to understand what this word really means. If we see clearly the changes which the meaning of this word has undergone, we will be less likely to absolutize the contemporary Anglo concept of 'friend' and to treat it as some kind of natural yardstick for assessing and comparing human relations in general.

2.2   A friend in need

The idea of permanence was linked in the traditional conception of "friendship" to the expectation of help in adversity. This, too, is reflected, in countless traditional sayings, as well as in a number of common collocations. For example:

A friend in need is a friend indeed.

(Richard Graves, 1772)

He that is thy friend indeed

He will help thee in thy need.

(Richard Barnfield, "Passionate pilgrim")

A friend is never known till a man hath need.

(John Keywood, "Proverbs," 1541)

A friend is not known but in need.

(George Meriton, 1683)

Among the collocations which attest (in reverse) to the same idea, particularly noteworthy are *fair weather friend*, *summer friend*, and *false friend*. For example:

Like summer friends,

Flies of estate and sunshine.

(George Herbert, "The answer")

O summer-friendship,

Whose flattering leaves, that shadow'd us .

In our prosperity, with the least gust drop off,

In the autumn of adversity!

(Philip Massinger, *The maid of honour*)

Evidence of this kind suggests that the older concept of 'friend' had a component of 'wanting to do something good for this person'. The examples adduced above may seem to suggest that this willingness to help (to do good things for) the other person was restricted to times of adversity. In fact, however, it appears that adversity was seen as a time when "friendship" was put to the test, rather than the only time when active benevolence was expected. The desire to do good things for another person is undoubtedly part of the concept of 'love' (as in "person X loves person Y") though not 'friendship'. But a "friend" in the older sense of the word was seen as a "beloved" person. Common collocations such as *sweet friends*, *loving friends*, *dearest friends*, now obsolete, certainly point in this direction, as do numerous references to "loving one's friends" (a point to which I will return later). Consequently, a desire to do good things for one's friends was (it seems) expected to be a permanent feature of the relationship and not something restricted to times of adversity. But this is not the case with the modern concept of 'friend'. For example, the numerous "friends" developed "through the bowling alley" are hardly expected to want to do good things for the speaker. Rather, friends are now expected to do things WITH us [or rather we are expected to do things with our friends]—and not so much "good things" as "fun things," things that make those involved "feel something good". These differences can be represented as follows:

A.
I want to do GOOD THINGS FOR this person
when I think about this person, I feel something very good
B.
I want to do THINGS WITH this person
when I am with this person, I feel something good

In nonformulaic English, one could say (roughly) that "friends" in the older sense of the word were expected to be loved, whereas "friends" in the modern sense are expected to be liked, and it is love, not liking, which may need to be put to the test (especially if the permanence of the relationship is not ensured by marriage or family bonds).

2.3 "Bosom friends" vs. "congenial fellowship friends"

Another important aspect of the older concept of 'friend' which has gone is that of special trust and a willingness to confide in the other person. This feature of the old *friend* is reflected in the old expression *bosom friend*, whose ironic echo resounds in the modern *bosom buddy*. Compare also the following nineteenth-century definitions of a "friend":

> A friend is a person with whom I may be sincere. (Ralph Waldo Emerson, "Friendship")

> What is a friend? I will tell you. It is a person with whom you dare to be yourself. (Frank Crane, "A definition of friendship")

Compare also the definition of a "true friend" offered by William Penn, a Quaker and founder of Pennsylvania:

> A true friend unbosoms freely, advises justly, assists readily, adventures boldly, takes all patiently, defends courageously, and continues a friend unchangeably. ("Fruites of solitude")

And George Herbert's injunction:

> Thy friend put in thy bosom: wear his eyes
>
> Still in thy heart, that he may see what's there. ("The church-porch")

The willingness to confide in a "friend" is of course related to the number of people whom one is willing to regard as "friends." As we have seen, one may now have even fifty "friends" (in the current sense of the word), but one can hardly "confide" in fifty people. A friend who is seen as someone with whom I may dare to be sincere and to whom I can truly open my heart implies a rather exclusive relationship. The willingness to confide and the exclusive relationship can be represented as follows:

> I think about this person like this:
>   I want this person to know what I think
>   I want this person to know what I feel
>   I don't want many other people to know these things
> I know this person thinks the same about me

2.4 A "circle of friends" vs. an exclusive relationship

The shift in perspective on human relations discussed throughout this chapter is reflected, in a particularly revealing way, in the syntactic construction "a friend of mine," in which, as it would seem, the word *friend* has started to appear more and more often in modern usage.

While some examples of this construction can be found in sixteenth-century English (e.g., in Shakespeare: "Dar'st thou resolve to kill a friend of mine"), it appears that the use of this construction increased considerably in modern times and that at the same time the use of *friend* with a definite possessive (e.g. "my friend") has decreased. Although I can't offer at this stage any serious statistical evidence for this contention, it is worth noting that according to Spevack's (1968) concordance of the complete works of Shakespeare, the construction "a friend of mine (his, N's etc.)" occurs 11 times for 452 occurrences of *friend*, whereas, for example, in Piper's (1970) concordance of F. Scott Fitzgerald's *Great Gatsby* it occurs 5 times for 17 occurrences of *friend*. In proportion to the corpus as a whole, this would be 2.5% for Shakespeare and 30% for Fitzgerald (or, roughly, one in forty for Shakespeare, and one in three for Fitzgerald). Although the two corpora are of course vastly different in size, a difference of this magnitude is nonetheless suggestive.

Furthermore, in the SEU (Survey of English Usage) Corpus of English (based on 1 million running words), all the occurrences of *friend* (excluding the parliamentary title "my honourable friend") amount to 80, of which 21, that is 24%, are instances of the "a friend of mine" construction. (If the 28 cases of "honourable friend" are included, the proportion of this construction is still very high: 18%.)

What is more, we can note some qualitative changes in the use of the "my friend" construction which support the hypothesis that the use of the alternative construction "a friend of mine" has extended over time. To illustrate these changes, I will quote a few sentences from Shakespeare's works where the use of "my friend" (or "mine friend") rather than "a friend of mine" sounds now archaic.

1 The knave is mine honest friend, sir.
(Second Part of *King Henry IV*, 5. 1.50)

2 For I shall never hold that man my friend whose tongue shall ask me for a penny
   cost.
(First Part of King Henry IV, 1.3.90)

3 There is not a man I met but doth salute me
As if I were their well-acquainted friend.
(*Comedy of errors*, 3.2)

4 Ye're welcome, my fair guests: that noble lady
Or gentleman that is not freely merry
Is not my friend: this, to confirm my welcome [Drinks].
And to you all, good health.
(*King Henry VIII*, 1.4,37)

In present-day English, one would normally say "he is a friend of mine" rather than "he is my friend" (unless under heavy emphasis, e.g. "I can't do it to him, he is MY FRIEND"); at the same time, sentences such as "he is my son" or "he is my brother" are perfectly natural. In fact, in current usage the phrase "my friend"—in contrast to "a friend of mine"—has started to be used as a euphemism for "boyfriend" or "girlfriend," as in the following example:

Dolly had a man friend. Quite possibly, although this seemed grotesque to me, Dolly was in love. All became clear when she said, in response to my mother's question as to how she had managed the journey to our flat—always a hazardous undertaking, as they both professed to believe—"My friend drove me over. Actually he owns the firm. You could say he was combining business with pleasure. Harry," she added, with deep satisfaction. "Harry Dean. A dear friend." (Brookner 1994:120)

If not used euphemistically, the phrase *my friend* tends to be, in current usage, accompanied at first by a specifier, as in the following example:

After tea my friend Marigold Chance might receive a visit. . . . She had been my friend since we had started school together at the age of four. . . . (Brookner 1994: 78)

But in older usage, phrases such as *my friend, thy friend,* or *your friend,* definite but without a specifier and non-anaphoric, were used commonly, as the phrases *my brother* or *my son* are still used in present-day English.

In current usage, it seems that a "friend" is usually introduced into conversation in one of four ways, all of which suggest a possible multiplicity of "friends": (1) with a possessive and a specifier ("my friend Marigold"); (2) in the partitive construction ("one of my friends"); (3) with an indefinite article ("a friend"); (4) in the highly characteristic "a friend of mine" construction, whose semantics deserves special attention.

To appreciate the full implication of this construction, consider the following phrases:

A. A friend (relative, servant) of mine was married in this church/is buried in this cemetery.
B. ?A brother of mine was married in this church/is buried in this cemetery.
C. ?A son of mine was married in this church/is buried in this cemetery.
D. ?A husband of mine was married in this church/is buried in this cemetery.

Phrases such as *a brother of mine, a son of mine,* and *a husband of mine* sound off-hand, ironic, and patronizing. The reason is, presumably, that the construction itself implies a whole class of persons, all equivalent to one another because all are related in the same way to a central figure. The phrase *a friend of mine* suggests that at the moment of speech the speaker is not interested in that particular friend's individuality, but views him exclusively as a member of a category, a category defined in terms of its relation to the speaker. It implies that I have, or could have, many friends (a "circle of friends"), and that I view myself as a figure at the center of that circle of friends, unilaterally related to them all.

The construction "an X of mine (yours, his etc.)" is particularly suited to collective categories, where all members can be viewed as equidistanced with respect to the person who provides the point of reference:

a colleague of mine
a student of mine
a fan of his

In the case of brothers or children, the construction "one of my Xs" is more appropriate because brothers or children differ importantly in their relative position with respect to the referent person and can hardly be regarded as "equidistant" to that person. As for inanimate objects, the following phrases sound perfectly natural (if somewhat dismissive):

> an old paper of mine
> an old photograph of mine

—more natural than, for example:

> ?an old toy of mine
> ?an old typewriter of mine
> ?an old camera of mine

The construction appears to require nouns which can be seen as inherently relational (e.g., papers written by me, or photographs showing me), and it sounds best if the assumption that there can be many items "like this" is self-explanatory. Roughly, then:

> an X of mine =
>   I can have many Xs
>   it doesn't matter how many I have
>   I think about all such Xs in the same way
>   this is one of such Xs

Jespersen (1965) says that "if I say *he is a friend of mine*, I need not at all imply that I have more than one friend. . . . To express the partitive sense we have the unambiguous expression *one of my friends*." What Jespersen says is correct, of course, but it doesn't explain why it sounds strange to say "he is a husband of mine," or even, "he is a son of mine."

It is true that one can say (in jest) "that husband of mine" or "that son of mine." but this only adds to the mystery. Jespersen argues (against Kruisinga) that in a phrase such as *that husband of yours*, "the disdainful tinge is caused by the application of the pronoun *that* to your husband, and not by the combination *of yours*," and he supports his argument with the example, "Where is that beautiful ring of yours?" But again, this doesn't explain why the sentences "he is a husband of mine" and even "he is a son of mine" sound odd.

In my view, to explain all these facts we need to hypothesize that in modern English the construction "an X of mine (his, etc.)" has a meaning of its own, not a "partitive" one but, so to speak, an "indefinite-indifferentive one," roughly along the lines of "it doesn't matter how many there are, it doesn't matter which one." In particular, this hypothesis accounts for the differences in acceptability between the sentences:

> He is a friend of mine.
> ? He is a son of mine.
> ? He is a husband of mine.

The related construction "this X of mine" (or "that X of mine") is different, in one respect, from "an X of mine," of course, but it, too, carries the semantic component which can be stated, very roughly, as 'it doesn't matter how many Xs I have'. This component explains why the phrase *this friend of mine* sounds neither odd nor playful, whereas the phrases *this husband of mine* and *this son of mine* do. (If one has several sons, the phrase *this son* doesn't sound at all playful [e.g. Was it this son who married an actress?] but *this son of mine* does.)

I am suggesting, then, that in the older usage *friend* tended to be seen as an individual related to us in a special way (rather like a brother, or a child), whereas in the current usage *friends* tend to be seen as a multiplicity of people related in an analogous way to a central figure (as reflected in the common expression *circle of friends*).[3]

This suggestion is further supported by the fact that the range of adjectives with which the word *friend*, and, in particular, *friends* (in the plural), can co-occur has apparently changed. Thus, among 445 quoted occurrences of *friends* in Shakespeare (cf. Spevack 1969), we find numerous examples of *sweet friends, good friends, gentle friends, loving friends, faithful friends, dearest friends, true-hearted friends, worthy friends, noble friends, precious friends, loyal friends*, and so on (as well as a few *false friends, hollow-hearted friends*, and even *monstrous friends*)—that is, evaluative terms, focusing on the personal qualities of the "friends" and the value of the relationship. What seems to be missing entirely are descriptive phrases specifying one particular category of people, such as, in contemporary literature, "my American friends" (Brookner 1994: 215), "my feminist friends" (Brookner 1994:217), or the following phrases listed in a concordance to the works of Bernard Shaw (Bevan 1971): "his English capitalist friends," "my clerical friends," "the American's American friends," "our Christian friends," and "English friends" (in the context "an Irishman may have . . ."). In these phrases, the adjective describes a kind of "people," not a kind of "person," and does not refer to the nature of the relationship.

What such phrases, apparently quite common in twentieth-century English, suggest is, first of all, a large number of possible "friends," who can even be classified into various collective categories on the basis of some (non-evaluative) characteristic. They also imply that the relation in question is not personal and exclusive but rather ranges over a whole class of people, defined by a single nonpersonal characteristic.

2.5 Making friends

The new "plural" orientation of *friends* is reflected, among other things, in the modern expression *to make friends*, with the object in the plural and without a further complement (e.g. "to make lots of friends," "to make new friends," "an opportunity to meet people and make friends.")

In modern usage, the set phrase *to make friends* (with the object in the plural, and with no further complements) seems to have largely supplanted the earlier expression *to find a friend* (not a set phrase). One obvious difference between the two phrases has to do with the voluntary character of the more recent, and the involuntary character of the older one. "Making friends" appears to be seen as an art and a skill which requires an active attitude to one's life and one's relationship with other people. (It is similar in this respect to the less idiomatic "winning friends," as in the title of a modern super-bestseller: *How to win friends and influence people* [Carnegie 1982(1936)]). But the expression *to make friends* implies also, significantly, a desire to have a multiplicity of friends, since while one can "make friends" one can hardly "make a friend." For example:

> I have made eight new friends (Bernard Shaw, *Good King Charles's golden days*)

> . . . in the teens it takes longer to make friends (?a friend) than in the grammar school years. (Packard 1974:237)

In the older usage (with the verb *to find*), both the singular (*a friend*) and the plural (*friends*) were perfectly natural. For example:

> Faithful friends are hard to find. (Richard Barnfield, "Passionate pilgrim")

> A friend may be often found and lost . . . (Samuel Johnson)

But in the characteristic modern usage (with the verb *to make*), the object is normally in the plural.

The combination of the verb *make* with the noun *friends* has been possible for a long time (for example, it occurs in Shakespeare) but apparently not in the construction discussed here ("to make friends," with no further complement). For example, in Shakespeare's works one can find examples with a double object or with a prepositional complement, such as the following ones:

> . . . for those you make friends
> And give your hearts to, when they once perceive
> The least rub in your fortunes, fall away . . .
> (*Henry VIII*)

> the poor advanc'd makes friends of enemies
> (*Hamlet*)

> Get posts and letters, and make friends with speed
> (*Henry IV*, Part Two)

However, among the 490 examples of the use of the word *friends* (in the plural) recorded in Spevack's (1969) concordance of Shakespeare's works, there is not one example of the construction "to make friends" (without a second complement) discussed here. This confirms the intuitive impression that this construction has probably appeared, and in any case spread, in modern times.

The common present-day expression *to make friends*, normally with a plural object (and without an explicit or implicit *with*-phrase), clearly reflects the modern outlook, which stresses an active forging of a whole multiplicity of associations with other people.

It should be added that in the older usage there was also another common collocation, next to *finding a friend*, namely, *choosing a friend* (or *choosing one's friends*). For example:

Be slow in choosing a friend, slower in changing. (Benjamin Franklin)

> True happiness
> Consists not in the multitude of friends.
> But in the worth and choice.
> (Ben Jonson, "Cynthia's revels")

Choose for your friend him who is wise and good, secret and just, ingenious and honest .... (Jeremy Taylor, *Discourse of friendship*)

The idea of deliberately "choosing a friend" may seem almost diametrically opposed to that of "finding a friend," and indeed closer to that of (voluntarily) "making friends." In fact, however, "finding" and "choosing" may represent two different aspects of the same process (one is lucky if one can "find" someone whom one can "choose" as a friend). On the other hand, "choosing" and "making" friends, while both voluntary processes, differ significantly in the attitudes implied. "Choosing friends" implies that one expects a small number and requires special qualities; "making friends" implies a desire for a large number (as in any "production process"), and a somewhat indiscriminate approach (the more the better), no special, individual qualities being necessarily required, and no exclusive relationship being envisaged. The expression *to make friends* is similar in this respect to the words *popular* and *popularity*, which point to a related cultural ideal of, roughly speaking, being liked by many people (cf. Stewart 1972:58).

2.6 "True friends" vs. "close friends"

One could object that since in the older usage "true friends" were sometimes distinguished from "friends," this distinction was in fact analogous to the modern distinction between "friends" and "close friends," so that the difference between the older and more recent approach to "friendship" is not as sharp as I have been suggesting. I would argue, however, that the similarity between the notions of 'true friends' and 'close friends' is more apparent than real.

First, a few quotes illustrating the use of the expressions *true friends* and *true friendship*:

To have the greatest blessing, a true friend.
(Philip Massinger, "Parliament of love")

They are rich who have true friends.
(Thomas Fuller, "Gnomologia")

A true friend is forever a friend.
(George Macdonald, "Marquis of Lossie")

The expressions *true friend* and *true friendship* implied an observed "corruption" and "misuse" of *friend* and *friendship* as such and were meant to defend them against that corruption, or, as Ralph Waldo Emerson put it, "prostitution":

> I hate the prostitution of the name of friendship to signify modish and worldly alliances. ("Friendship")

Indeed, there is plenty of evidence showing that in its earlier use the words *friend* and *friendship* without any modifiers were loaded with meaning going far beyond that associated with the modern Anglo *friends*. The expression *true friend* was clearly intended to defend that meaning rather than to draw a distinction between *friend* and some other category of human relations. The very high expectations linked with a *friend* as such can be illustrated with the following quotations:

> Life without a friend is death without a witness.
> (George Herbert, "Jacula Prudentum")

> The best elixir is a friend.
> (William Sommerville, "The hip")

> Love is only chatter,
> Friends are all that matter.
> (Gelett Burgess, "Willy and the lady")

> O friend, my bosom said,
> Through thee alone the sky is arched,
> Through thee the rose is red.
> (Ralph Waldo Emerson, "Friendship")

> A friend may well be reckoned the masterpiece of nature.
> (Emerson, "Friendship")

> A Father's a Treasure; a Brother a Comfort; a Friend is both.
> (Benjamin Franklin)

Similarly, *friendship* (without modifiers) was linked with expectations which could hardly have been greater with respect to *true friendship*. For example:

> Friendship is a union of spirit, a marriage of hearts, and the bond thereof virtue.
> (William Penn, "Fruites of solitude")

And on the value of "friendship":

> Friendship is the gift of the gods, and the most precious boon to man. (Benjamin Disraeli, speech, 1855)

Thus, a *true friend* was not seen as a special kind of *friend* (particularly close and valued), but simply as a *friend* in the most literal (rather than a "corrupted") sense of the word.

By contrast, the modern expression *close friend* is not meant to have the same range of referents as the word *friend*; it is indeed intended to stand for a different category of people, linked to the target person by a different kind of relationship. The notion that not all "friends" can be regarded as "close friends" does not represent (from the speaker's point of view) an attack on the current use of the word *friend*; rather, it establishes a new category including a special subset of the broader category. "Close friends" are "friends" with an additional feature of being "closely" related to the target person—the implication being that "friends" as such are not expected to be necessarily closely related to that person. Nonliteral, "corrupted" use is still seen as possible, but now it is the use of the expression *close friend* which may be scrutinized from this point of view rather than the use of *friend* itself (since one does not necessarily expect "friends" as such to amount to very much in the present usage).

For example, Packard (1974) repeatedly uses the phrase "really close friends," as if *close friends* was not sufficient to exclude weak and superficial relationships. For both Packard and his informants, the number of expected "close friends" clearly exceeds what used to be regarded as the "normal" number of "friends." For example, one of the questions in Packard's questionnaire was formulated as follows: "How many of the people that you regard as close friends (as distinguished from casual acquaintances and friends) live within five miles of your home?"

To this, the median answer in the high stability town Glens Falls was 6, whereas in the high mobility town of Azusa it was 3. (In both Glens Falls and Azusa the respondents wished that the numbers in question should be higher.) But if most people in Glen Falls have about six "close friends" living within five miles of their home, one wonders how many "close friends" they have altogether. It would seem that even if the man mentioned earlier who had moved sixteen times in twenty two years of marriage and had acquired "a few close, lasting friends at every stop" could be regarded as somewhat exceptional, neither Packard nor his respondents would regard a number of ten, fifteen, or twenty "close friends" as incongruous.

2.7 Friends and enemies

In the older usage of the word *friend*, this word was very frequently paired with the word *enemy* (or *foe*), and the two were clearly treated as opposites. For example:

Friends are as dangerous as enemies.
(Thomas De Quincey, "Essays")

You and I were long friends; you are now my enemy and I am
Yours, Benjamin Franklin. (Letter to William Strahan)

Do good to thy friend to keep him, to thy enemy to gain him.
(Benjamin Franklin, "Poor Richard's almanac")

He will never have true friends who is afraid of making enemies.
(William Hazlitt, "Characteristics")

When fails our dearest friend,
There may be refuge with our direct foe.
(J. S. Knowles, "The wife")

If I have not a friend, God send me an enemy that I may hear of my faults.
(Benjamin Whichcote, "Sermons")

In modern usage, however, *friends* and *enemies* are no longer treated as opposites. For one thing, if most people are expected to have "friends," it is not the case that most people are expected to have enemies. Moreover, even those people who can be expected to have "enemies," would not be expected to have a whole "circle of enemies," as they might have a "circle of friends." Most importantly, however, even for those people who do have a comparable number of "friends" and of "enemies," the two groups no longer seem to be related to the person in question in an analogous manner. This is not to say that there is no semantic relation between the two concepts anymore. There is—but presumably this relation is now restricted to a single contrast. Even this contrast is not based on full symmetry, as the following portrayal of the relevant components (not the whole meanings) shows:

This person is a friend. =>
   when I am with this person, I feel something good
   I think this person feels the same

This person is an enemy. =>
   when I think about this person, I feel something bad
   I think this person feels the same

As we have seen, however, in the older usage of *friend* (*friend*₁) this word referred also to a volition, a will directed toward the other person (good will). Since the word *enemy* also included a volitional component (ill will), the link between the two concepts was much stronger, and it is understandable why they should have been so readily perceived as opposites:

This person is my friend₁. =>
I want to do good things for this person
this person wants to do the same for me

This person is my enemy. =>
this person wants to do bad things to me
I want to do the same to this person

In the present-day usage, however, *friend* no longer includes a component of 'good will', whereas *enemy* still does include the component of "ill will." This explains why the two words have drifted apart. I do not think that *friend* and *enemy* have ever been perfectly symmetrical opposites, because *friend* included other components, such as the willingness to reveal thoughts and feelings to the other person, which were not matched by anything in the semantic structure of *enemy*. Nonetheless, the two concepts were sufficiently similar to be felt as quasi-opposites—much more so than they are now.

2.8 "Dear friends" vs. "enjoyable friends"

In the older usage, one of the most common collocations involving *friend* was *dear friend* or *dearest friend*. For example:

> Farewell, dear friend, that smile, that harmless wit
> No more shall gladden our domestic hearth.
> (H. F. Cary, "Epitaph on Charles Lamb")

> But Fate ordains the dearest friends must part.
> (Edward Young, "Love of fame")

In present-day English, however, the collocation *dear friend* or *dearest friend* is marginal or even archaic. It is true that it is still possible to address a group of people as "dear friends," but normally only older people would now describe a person as a "dear friend," let alone "dearest friend." Two other common collocations, *good friend* and *best friend*, have survived, but *dear friend* has largely gone out of use (as have also *sweet friend*, and many others, cited earlier from Shakespeare).

To account for this fact, I would posit a weakening (as well as reshaping) of the emotional component of the word *friend*, which can be represented as a shift from 'very good' to 'good':

*friend*₁
when I think about this person, I feel something VERY GOOD

*friend*₂
when I am with this person, I feel something GOOD

In the older usage, *friends* were mutually bound by something much closer to love than *friends* in the present-day sense of the word. To illustrate:

> So, if I live or die to serve my friend,
> 'Tis for my love—'tis for my friend alone,
> And not for any rate that friendship bears
> In heaven or on earth.
> (George Eliot, "Spanish gypsy").

> Having some friends whom he loves dearly,
> And no lack of foes, whom he laughs at sincerely.
> (Robert Southey, "Robert the rhymer's account of himself")

Thus, in the old usage of the word *friend*, people were usually expected to "love" their friends, but this is certainly not the case now. The distinction between 'feeling something very good' and 'feeling something good' is meant to account partly for this difference.

In addition to the difference of degree, however ('something very good' vs. 'something good') there is an additional qualitative difference, which, roughly speaking, can be linked with the contrast between "affection" and "enjoyment." As mentioned earlier, in the older English literature, people often "loved" their friends, or felt and thought of them as "dear" and "dearest." By contrast, in contemporary English (as mentioned earlier), people are more likely to talk about "friends" in terms of "enjoyment," "pleasure," and "fun."

This difference between "dear" friends and "enjoyable" friends can be represented as a shift from (habitual) affectionate thoughts to (occasional) pleasurable company:

*friend*₁
when I THINK ABOUT this person, I feel something very good

*friend*₂
when I AM WITH this person, I feel something good

For example, the sociologist Allan (1979), who bases his analysis of the category "friend" on accounts given by a large number of respondents, writes: "An assumption entailed in the idea that friendship is voluntary is that it is a relationship based on enjoyment. A friend is someone with whom one enjoys spending time and sharing activities" (41).

This is, of course, quite different from the classical (Roman) conception of *amicitia,* which (as presented by Cicero in "De Amicitia") was held to be based on mutual good will and affection, and which was seen as implying the duty of correcting a friend *(amicus)* when necessary. The older English concept of *friend*₁ was clearly closer to that Roman conception than the concept encoded in the modern English *friend*₂.

2.9   Summary and conclusion

The two meanings of the word *friend*, the earlier one (*friend*₁) and the present-day one (*friend*₂), can be portrayed as follows:

*friend*₁
(a) everyone knows: many people think about some other people like this:
(b)   I know this person very well
(c)   I think good things about this person
(d)   I want this person to know what I think
(e)   I want this person to know what I feel
(f)   I don't want many other people to know these things
(g)   I want to do good things for this person
(h)   I know this person thinks the same about me
(i)   when I think about this person, I feel something very good
(j) I think like this about this person

*friend*₂
(a) everyone knows: many people think about some other people like this:
(b)   I know this person well
(c)   I want to be with this person often
(d)   I want to do things with this person often
(e)   when I am with this person, I feel something good
(f)   I think this person thinks the same about me
(g) I think like this about this person

In the explication of *friend*₁, component (b) refers to personal knowledge which goes beyond a mere acquaintanceship or familiarity, component (c) refers to some valued personal qualities, components (d) and (e) define a dimension of something like "confidence" and "intimacy," (f) alludes to a "special" and rather "exclusive" relationship, (g) to "good will" and "willingness to help," (h) and (j) refer to "reciprocity," and (i) to something like "affection."

In the explication of *friend*₂, component (b) refers to a more superficial knowledge, components (c) and (d) substitute something like "gregariousness" for "confidence" and "intimacy" of *friend*₁, whereas (e) refers to the "fun-to-be-with" aspects of the modern "friends," replacing the earlier loving attitude (roughly speaking, a shift from "loving" to "liking").

Samuel Johnson in his *Dictionary of the English language* (1968[1755]) offered the following definition of the English word *friend* (as used at the time): "friend—one joined to another in mutual benevolence and intimacy." The striking differences between this definition and those offered by modern American dictionaries highlight the changes in the meaning of *friend* discussed in this chapter.

For example, *The American Heritage dictionary of the English language* distinguishes two meanings of *friend* (presumably, an earlier one and a more recent one) and offers the following two definitions: (1) a person whom one knows, likes, and trusts; (2) a person whom one knows; an acquaintance. The first of these two definitions is "thinner" in its implications than Johnson's (with no "benevolence" or "intimacy" being mentioned, and with an emphasis on mere "liking"), whereas the second one is so "thin" that hardly anything of the earlier meaning of *friend* is left in it at all.

Webster's third requires a bit more than just "knowing a person," but it offers the following characteristic comment, which explicitly denies "intimacy" and emphasizes "liking" and "pleasure": "*friend* applies to a person one has regarded with liking and a degree of respect and has known for a time in a pleasurable relationship neither notably intimate nor dependent wholly on business or professional ties."

The *New shorter Oxford English dictionary* (1993), too, reflects the change in the meaning of *friend* in the way it glosses phrases such as *be* or *keep friends (with)* ("be on good or intimate terms [with]"), and *make friends (with)* ("get on good or intimate terms with"). There is a big difference between being on "good" and on "intimate" terms with someone. Clearly, in older English more than "good terms" was required, but in present-day English being on "good terms" may be enough.

Certainly, the older sense of the word *friend* lingers on, to some extent, in the collective memory of native speakers of English, who are familiar with it through English literature and other cultural echoes from the past. If the modern expression *close friend* reflects the change in the meaning of *friend* (because in the past, all "friends" were "close friends," so no such distinction was necessary), the modern expression *real friend* expresses a sense of continuity in this word's meaning (because it seems to acknowledge, and even celebrate, the older sense of *friend* as a valid meaning of this word, and perhaps even as its "real" meaning, in contrast to the "loose" and "watered down" modern usage). For example, Allan (1979) writes:

To claim that some friends are allowed to discover the 'real self' more than others is to say that some are trusted more than others. This is the major difference between those people labelled 'real' or 'true' friends and the remainder. 'Real' friends appear to be trusted totally and can be relied on to protect their friend's interests. . . . Other friends not labelled real or true ones are likely to be treated more cautiously, . . . They are people who are found interesting and with whom one is sociable, but they are not people to whom one reveals innermost fears or worries.

As Suttles (1970) develops at length, an important way in which people become friends, and 'everyday' friends 'real' friends, is by breaking the normal 'rules of public propriety'. This serves to reveal the 'real self' and for the friends symbolises the strength of their friendship bond. (70)

Allan talks about the expressions *true friend* and *real friend* as if they were interchangeable, but in fact they are not. A *true friend* is an older expression, which, as we have seen, tried to protect the seriousness of the word *friend*. A *real friend* seems to be a predominantly modern expression (for example, there are no instances of it in Spevack's concordances of Shakespeare's works), which is closer in meaning to a *close friend* than to the older *true friend*, but which, nonetheless, recalls and acknowledges the older usage. In particular, Suttles' (1970) distinction between "everyday friends" and "real friends" highlights the fact that "real friends" tend now to be seen as a special category of "friends," distinct from the category of "everyday friends." This is not quite the same as "true friends" in the older usage.

Thus, semantic history of the word *friend* confirms the validity of Tocqueville's observation that "democracy does not create strong attachments between man and man, but it does put their ordinary relations on an easier footing" (quoted in Bellah et al. 1985:117). As Bellah et al. comment, with special reference to America, "in the mobile and egalitarian society of the United States, people could meet more easily and their intercourse was more open, but the ties between them were more likely to be casual and transient" (117). The change was visible by the 1830s, when Tocqueville wrote his classic work, and the trend has continued throughout the nineteenth and twentieth century. "'Friendliness' became almost compulsory as a means of arguing the difficulties of these interactions, while friendship in the classical sense became more and more difficult." (Bellah et al. 1985:118). In a similar vein, Stewart (1972) comments:

Personal relationships among Americans are numerous and are marked by friendliness and informality; however, Americans rarely form deep and lasting friendships. Friends and membership groups change easily as the American shifts status or locale; consequently, his social life lacks both permanence and depth. (49)

The generalized "friend" of Americans, standing for anyone from a passing acquaintance to a life-time intimate, is maintained according to activities. . . . But these patterns of friendship among Americans . . . do not imply a distrust of people. They signify more often the American reluctance to becoming deeply involved with other persons. In circumstances where a foreigner might turn to a friend for help, support or solace, the American will tend to search for the professional, preferring not to inconvenience his friends. (54)

What Bellah et al. mean by "friendship in the classical sense" involves not only a "deep involvement" with another person, and a "deep commitment" to him or her, but also the concept of a common good served by the relationship. I am not convinced that this latter idea was part of the older meaning of the word *friend* as such, although it was indeed part of the conception of "friendship" developed by the philosophers of antiquity and shared by many thinkers and writers in modern times. In more recent times, the ideal of a deep and lasting "friendship" involving strong attachments and an exclusive intimacy has given way to the ideal of "friendliness" and of "making friends" in the sense of extensive but limited and transient relationships is certainly corroborated by linguistic evidence. This applies not only to America but, to some extent, to the English-speaking world as a whole, although the fact that, for example, in Australia, another crucially important way of talking about human relations has developed, in addition to the idiom of "friends" (see below, section on "Mate"), shows that in this area, as in others, "Anglo culture" is far from monolithic.

As mentioned earlier, changes in the patterning and conceptualization of human relations, similar to those whose reflection in one fragment of the English language has been discussed here, have also occurred in other Western societies, during their gradual entry into "modern civilization." To what precise extent these changes have found their expression in other European languages is a matter for further investigation.

3. Patterns of "friendship" in Russian culture

Western, especially American, students of Russia are often struck by Russian patterns of "friendship" (I put the word "friendship" in quotation marks because this word itself embodies a certain categorization and interpretation of human relations, which, as we shall see, is different from that reflected in the Russian language).

For example, Hedrick Smith (1976), in his justly acclaimed *The Russians*, wrote:

> Their [the Russians'] social circles are usually narrower than those of Westerners, especially Americans, who put such great stock in popularity, but relations between Russians are usually more intense, more demanding, more enduring and often more rewarding.
>
> I knew of a couple sent off to Cuba for a two-year assignment, and another family put up their teenage son in an already crowded two-room apartment. When Bella Akhmadulina, the poet, married for the third time, she and her husband were broke, and their friends bought them an entire apartment full of furniture. Let a dissident intellectual get in trouble and real friends will loyally take the terrible political risk of going to his rescue....
>
> They commit themselves to only a few, but cherish those. Within the trusted circle, there is an intensity in Russian relationships that Westerners find both exhilarating and exhausting. When they finally open up, Russians are looking for a soul-brother, not a mere conversational partner. They want someone to whom they can pour out their hearts, share their miseries, tell about family problems or difficulties with a lover or mistress, to ease the pain of life or to indulge in endless philosophical windmill tilting. As a journalist I sometimes found it ticklish because Russians want a total commitment from a friend. (108–110)

Like many other foreign commentators, Smith linked Russians' need for intense and enduring friendships with the conditions of life under the Soviet regime.

Precisely because their public lives are so supervised and because they cannot afford to be open and candid with most people, Russians invest their friendships with enormous importance. Many of them, in cities at least, are only-children whose closest friends come to take the place of missing brothers and sisters. They will visit with each other almost daily, like members of the family. . . .

Friendships are not only compensation for the cold impersonality of public life but a vital source of personal identity.

"Friends are the one thing we have which are all our own," a mathematician confided. "They are the one part of our life where we can make our own choice completely for ourselves. We cannot do that in politics, religion, literature, work. Always, someone above influences our choice. But not with friends. We make that choice for ourselves."

The choice, among intellectuals at least, is made with special care, for one essential ingredient of Russian friendships is the political test of trust. This gives them special depth and commitment. Americans, spared the violence of Soviet political purges, repressions and constant pressures for ideological conformity, do not have to make the vital, acute judgment of sorting out true friend from devious informer. Soviets must make that judgment often, and always unerringly.

. . . For safety's sake, Russians hold each other at bay. "We don't want personal relations with that many other people," one man said bluntly.

But while the conditions of life in Soviet Russia have no doubt contributed to the exceptional importance of deep friendship, especially in milder times after Stalin's death, in other ways the dangers involved in trusting anybody at all outside the immediate family have had the opposite effect. In the chapter entitled "Russian character and the Soviet system" of their well-known study, *How the Soviet system works*, Bauer, Inkeles and Kluckhohn (1956) have commented on this reverse side of the coin:

Virtually all aspects of the Soviet regime's pattern of operation seem calculated to interfere with the satisfaction of the Russians' need for affiliation. The breakup of the old village community and its replacement by the more formal bureaucratic and impersonal collective farm is perhaps the most outstanding example, but it is only one of many. The disruption and subordination of the traditional family group, the church, the independent professional associations, and the trade unions are other cases in point. Additional effects of a marked kind are created by the strains which the regime has created on friendship relations between two or more individuals, by its persistent programs of political surveillance, its encouragement and elaboration of the process of denunciation, and its assumptions about mutual responsibility for the failings of particular individuals. (139)

The authors concluded, nonetheless, that Russians (and this applies to Soviet times as well) "value warm interpersonal relations to an unusually high degree":

The need for free, uninhibited social intercourse is both frustrated and accentuated under Soviet conditions. The desire to express pent-up feelings impels the individual to seek out confidants. The fear of talking makes him less likely to talk. The result is not a cessation of confidences, but rather the development of techniques of screening and assessing people in order to decide how much they can be trusted. (110)

The importance of deep friendship in the Russian hierarchy of values, reflected in the Russian literature and, as we will see, in the Russian language, is also confirmed by sociological surveys. For example, as noted by the Soviet sociologist Kon (1987:133–134), a survey conducted in America in the early 1970s showed that Americans ranked friendship tenth on a list of values, whereas in a comparable survey in Russia friendship was ranked sixth. Other studies conducted in the late 1970s and early 1980s found that in Russia young people responding to questions about their goals in life put friendship in the first place (cf. Shlapentokh 1989:174–176).

Intensive interpersonal bonds of the kind described by Smith and others no doubt continue patterns which were part and parcel of Russian culture in pre-Soviet times as well, and it has even been suggested that the political climate in tsarist Russia may have been a contributing factor, too; but generally speaking, all observers appear to agree that these patterns were intensified by the conditions of life under the Soviet regime. Shlapentokh (1984) comments on this as follows:

> The virtual cult of friendship in tsarist Russia strongly supports the notion that a lack of political freedom can greatly contribute to the development and preservation of close human relationships. The glorification of friendship in the poetry of Pushkin is linked directly to political opposition against tsarist despotism and the yearning for freedom. . . . The Soviet system, which has increased the political pressures on its citizens, has only enhanced the significance of friendship in Russia. (219)

But political pressures under the tsarist regime were incomparably less pervasive and oppressive than under the Soviet; it was in Soviet times that Russia became the true Gulag archipelago for everyone. It seems hardly surprising, therefore, that in the twentieth-century Russian conception of "friendship," mutual trust came to be seen as one of the most important features of this kind of relationship (Kon 1987:166, Sokolov 1981:207). Whether or not this has led to any changes in the meaning of words such as *druzja* (roughly 'close friends') is a point which requires further investigation.

3.1   Russian counterparts of the English *friend*— an overview

In Russian, the categorization of human relations is particularly richly developed, in comparison not only with Western European languages but also with other Slavic languages. If the wealth of Hanunóo words for 'rice' (Conklin 1957) reflects the special interest that the Hanunóo people (understandably) have in this area of reality, the wealth of Russian words for different categories of human relations (in addition to kin) provides evidence of Russian culture's special interest in the realm of human relations (a special interest also reflected in the extremely rich system of expressive derivation of Russian names, cf. Wierzbicka 1992b, chapter 7).

The main nominal categories are *drug, podruga, tovarišč* (in the sense *tovarišč₁*, to be discussed below), *prijatel'* (Fem. *prijatel'nica*), and *znakomyj* (Fem. *znakomaja*). Roughly speaking, the order in which these words are mentioned above could be said to correspond to the degree of "closeness" or "strength" of the relationship. *Drug* is someone extremely close to us (much more so than the English *friend*); *podruga* refers to a bond less powerful than *drug* but still stronger than *friend*; *prijatel'* (or *prijatel'nica*) is rather more distant; and *znakomyj* (or *znakomaja*) still more distant, although closer than the supposed English equivalent *acquaintance*, normally offered by Russian-English dictionaries. (*Tovarišč*, in the relevant sense, may seem either "stronger" or "weaker" than *prijatel'*, depending on context.)

In fact, as we will see shortly, the semantic differences among the words of this group are qualitative, not quantitative, with the impression of some differences in "degree" of strength or closeness following from the presence of distinct semantic components in their meaning.

None of the Russian words matches exactly any of the English ones. To give the reader some idea of the value of the Russian words, we could say that drug can be compared, roughly, to a close friend (male or female), *podruga*—to a (girl's or woman's) *girlfriend, prijatel'* (fem. *prijatel'nica*) to just *friend* (without a modifier), and *znakomyj* (fem. *znakomaja*) to a *close acquaintance*; whereas *tovarišč* (in the relevant sense) can only be compared to the bound morpheme *-mate* (as in *classmates* or *workmates*), or to the nominal modifier *fellow* (as in *fellow-prisoners*). But these are only very rough approximations.

Thus, in a situation where a speaker of English may describe someone as "a friend of mine" a Russian speaker is forced to analyze the relationship much more deeply and to decide whether the person in question should be described as *drug, podruga, prijatel'nica*, or *znakomaja* (in the case of a female), or as *drug, prijatel', tovarišč*, or *znakomyj* (in the case of a male). In English, one can differentiate between various kinds of "friends" if one wants to, but one doesn't have to do so: adjectival modifiers are only optional extras; but different nouns (as in Russian) provide a different grid and force speakers to make more specific choices. For example, explaining how the question of a person's nationality was decided in the Soviet Union, the Russian writer Sergej Dovlatov (1983) writes about his different "friends" as follows:

> Ja, dopustim, byl armjaninom—po materi. Moj drug, Arij Xajmovič Lerner—v russkie probilsja. . . . Moj prijatel' xudožnik Šer govoril:
> —Ja napolovinu russkij, napolovinu—ukrainec, napolovinu—poljak i napolovinu—evrej.
> . . . Zatem načalas' emigracija. I povalil narod obratno, v evrei. . . . Moj znakomyj Ponomarev special'no v Gomel' ezdil, tetku nanimat'. (11)

> 'I was, for example, an Armenian, after my mother. My friend [*drug*] Arij Xajmovič Lerner managed to get himself in among the Russians. My friend [*prijatel'*] Šer, an artist, used to say:
> "I'm half Russian, half-Ukrainian, half-Polish and half-Jewish."
> . . . Later the [Jewish] emigration [of the Brezhnev era] began. And everyone rushed back to being Jewish. Another friend [*znakomyj*] of mine, Ponomarev, made trips specially to Gomel' to hire himself an auntie.'

Dovlatov's careful distinctions between a *drug*, a *prijatel'*, and a *znakomyj* would normally be replaced in an English version with the all-inclusive term *friend*.

In what follows, I will discuss the Russian words one by one. (I have omitted from this survey *znakomyj*, which is similar in meaning to the Polish *znajomy*, to be discussed in section 4).[4]

3.2 Drug

Drug (Pl. *druz̆*ja) is one of the most important words in the Russian lexicon. Its very frequency in Russian speech is prodigious. In Zasorina's (1977) corpus of 1 million running words, the frequency of *drug* is 817, whereas that of *friend* in a comparable corpus of American English (Kučera & Francis 1967) is 298 (in Carroll et al. 1971, the corresponding figure is 346). Relatively speaking, *friend* is also a high frequency word in English; for example, it is much more frequent than *brother* (125 and 169). Nonetheless, *drug* is still much more common than *friend*; and the frequency of the abstract noun *druz̆ba* (155) is many times higher than that of *friendship* (27 and 8).[5]

The irregular plural of *drug* (*druz̆ja*, like *brat'ja* from *brat* 'brother') provides another interesting clue to this word's meaning: *druz̆ja*, like *brat'ja*, is an old collective form, and it suggests a group of people. Indeed, from an individual's point of view, one's *druz̆ja* form an important social category: they are the people on whom one can rely for help and support. Neither the word *podruga* nor *prijatel'* has that implication, but for drug it is very important.

Although no data on the relative frequencies of the singular *drug* and plural *druz̆ja* are available, I would judge that the plural is even more common and more salient in Russian speech than *drug*. The opposite is probably true for *prijatel'* (Sg.) and *prijateli* (Pl.): a person's *druz̆ja* form this person's vital support group, but *prijateli* don't form a collective category of any kind (one can more readily say *vse moi druz̆ja* 'all my druz̆ja' and even *vse moi znakomye* 'all my acquaintances' than *vse moi prijateli*). As a form of address, too, *druz̆ja* ('friends') is perfectly normal, but **prijateli* ('friends') is not acceptable.

Common phrases such as *rodnye i druz̆*ja 'family and *druz̆ja*' and *pomošč druzej* 'the help of *druz̆ja*' support the impression that the plural *druz̆ja* constitutes a salient conceptual category, as does the fact that the word *druz̆ja* is usually used without a possessive pronoun, whereas *prijateli* sounds better with a possessive pronoun:

Emu pomogla mat'/z̆ena.

to-him helped mother/wife

'He was helped by his mother/wife.'

Emu pomogli druz'ja/sosedi/ego prijateli/?prijateli.

to-him helped-Pl. *druz̆ja*/neighbors/his *prijateli*-Pl./?*prijateli*-Pl.

'He was helped by his *druz̆ja*/neighbors/*prijateli*.'

(This is not to say that the form *prijateli*, without a possessive pronoun, would be rejected by all native speakers, but *ego prijateli* is usually preferred. This is not the case with *druz̆ja*.) Similarly, in the following sentence from a novel by Sergej Dovlatov (1986:93) the word *druzej* (Pl. Acc.) occurs without a possessive modifier, as the word for 'mother' would, but if the word *prijatelej* (Pl. Acc.) were to be used instead, the sentence would sound much more natural with a possessive modifier:

Ty, Musen'ka, druzej ne zabyvaj.

'You, Musen'ka, don't forget [your] friends.'

Ty, Musen'ka, materi (mother) ne zabyvaj.

Ty, Musen'ka, svoix prijatelej ne zabyvaj.

?Ty, Musen'ka, prijatelej ne zabyvaj.

The importance of the concept of *druz'ja* in Russian life is nicely illustrated by the following six sentences, all drawn from one page of a memoir about two famous Russian dissidents, Anatolij Marčenko and Larissa Bogoraz (Litvinova 1994c:10–11):

Druz'ja pomogli Lare s Tolej tože kupit' v Taruse kusok doma.

'Friends [*druz'ja*] also helped Lara and Tolja to buy part of a house in Tarusa.'

V 73-m godu i pozže ja tuda [v Tarusu] priezžala navestit' druzej, guljat', kupat'sja i rabotat'.

'In 1973, and later, I used to travel there [to Tarusa] to visit friends [*druz'ja*], to go on walks, to swim, and to work.'

Gostili Sanja i Katja, priezžali i roditeli, navešcali druz'ja. . . .

'Frequently Sanja and Katja came to stay with them, their parents would also come, and so would friends [*druz'ja*]. . . .'

Letom poblizosti selilis' Lariny roditeli i druz'ja—Lavuty, Kulaevy.

'In summer, Lara's parents and friends [*druz'ja*], the Lavuts and Kulaevs, would come to live nearby.'

Priezžavšie na den'-dva druz'ja tože staralis' pomogat' [stroit' dom].

'Friends [*druz'ja*] who would come for a day or two also tried to help [to build the house for the Marčenkos].

Poka že oni, vtroem ili včetverom, i mnogočislennye rodnye i druz'ja, osvobodivšiesja iz zaključenija, i presleduemye, kotorye priezžali k nim—vse jutilis' v malen'koj izbuške, razdelennoj na tri časti doščatymi peregerodkami.

'In the meantime, the Marčenko family, together with their numerous relatives and visiting friends [*druz'ja*], who had been released from prison and were still being harassed, would all huddle together in a tiny hut divided into three by wooden partitions.'

These six sentences, two of which refer to giving substantial help and four to prolonged visiting, are highly typical, and they illustrate well what *druz'ja* are for: seeing one's *druz'ja*, talking to them, spending a lot of time with them, is one of the most important parts of a Russian's life; and so is helping one's *druz*ja when they need it. To quote Shlapentokh (1989) again:

> The notion of friend in the Soviet Union is different than in the United States. Americans use the term "friends" even for persons with whom they entertain only the most superficial relations (see, for instance, Pogrebin, 1986, who treats neighbors . . . as friends). But a friend, to Soviet people, is an individual with whom you have deep emotional, intimate relations. Friends in Soviet society characteristically maintain very intense contact. As Semen Lipkin, a Soviet author, became friends with Vasilii Grossman, the famous writer, they began to "meet each day" . . . and no Soviet reader would be amazed by this statement. (170).

On the importance of mutual help and support among friends, with special reference to the Soviet era:

> Soviet people provide each other with considerable assistance in "beating the system." Friends play an extremely vital role in procuring necessary goods, for they constantly buy each other food, clothing, shoes, or other items should the chance arise, i.e., should these items appear in stores. . . . (174)

> The mutual financial support between friends . . . is also one of the most significant aspects of Soviet private life. According to some data, up to three-quarters of Soviet people regularly borrow money from each other. (174)

Being a Russian, Shlapentokh assumes that the obligation to help a "friend," though particularly pronounced in Russian culture, is a human universal:

> In all societies, the role of friend tends to carry the expectation that, in a state of emergency—when one's life, freedom, or survival is in jeopardy—a friend will offer assistance and comfort in full measure. In Soviet society, the expectation of friends' active assistance, even when they may be put at risk, is particularly high. Again, the arbitrariness of political power in this society is largely responsible for the extraordinary demands placed upon friends. (230)

But it is highly questionable whether in all societies "friends" will be expected to "offer assistance and comfort in full measure." Certainly, no such expectation is built into the very meaning of the closest counterparts of the Russian *drug* in other languages, including the English word *friend*. It does appear, however, that such an expectation is indeed part of the very meaning of the Russian word *drug*.

Interestingly, both these key elements of the Russian concept of 'drug' (intense and intimate face-to-face communication and readiness to help) are included in Tolstoy's literary definition (given in Pierre's words to Nataša in *War and peace*):[6]

> . . . no ob odnom prošu vas—sčitajte menja svoim drugom, i ježeli vam nužna pomošč, sovet, prosto nužno budet izlit' svoju dušu komu-nibud'—ne teper', a kogda u vas jasno budet v duše,—vspomnite obo mne. (Tolstoy 1964:643)

> . . . one thing I beg of you: look on me as your friend [*drug*], and if you need help, advice, or simply need to open your heart to someone [literally to pour out your soul to someone]—not now, but when your mind [soul] is clearer—think of me. (Tolstoy 1930–1931:710)

The bond implied by the word *drug* is far stronger than that of *prijatel'*, not to mention *znakomyj*, as the following contrasts in acceptability show:

nastojaščij drug, istinnyj drug
*nastojaščij prijatel', *istinnyj prijatel'
*nastojaščij znakomyj, *istinnyj znakomyj

where *nastojaščij* (*-aja*) means 'real' or 'genuine' and *istinnyj* (*-aja*) means 'true'. Only *drug* can be described as "real" or "true" because, of the three, only *drug* implies a powerful hidden bond which could be put to the test.

The Academy of Sciences' *Dictionary of synonyms* (SSRJ) defines *drug* as "čelovek blizkij po duxu, po ubeždenijam, na kotorogo možno vo vsem položit'sja," 'a person close in spirit, in their convictions, on whom one can rely for everything'; and SSRLJ (the *Dictionary of the Russian literary language*), as "a person closely linked to someone by mutual trust, devotion, love." According to these definitions, too, the defining elements of *drug* appear to be, roughly speaking, readiness to disclose to the other person one's thoughts and feelings, complete trust, readiness to help, and intense "good feelings":

> S prijateljami v kino xodjat, futbol gonjajut, a s drugom vse napopolam idet—i radost' i gore. (Mixalkov, SSRLJ)

> 'With *prijatel's* (Pl.) one goes to the movies, or kicks a football around, but with a *drug* one shares everything, fifty-fifty, both joy and sorrow.'

> Čerez dva-tri dnja my stali uže druz'jami, xodili vsjudu vmeste, poverjali drug drugu svoi namerenija i želanija, delili porovnu vse, čto perepadalo odnomu iz nas. (Gor'kij, SSRLJ).

> 'Within a few days we had already become friends [*druz'ja*], went about everywhere together, confided to each other all our hopes and desires, and shared everything that came our way.'

A *drug* is someone on whom one can rely for help. The expression *bud' drugom*, used "dlja vyraženija usilennoj pros'by" (SSLRJ) (that is, "to intensify a request") provides evidence for this:

> Na svjatkax L'vov stal ugovarivat' Platona:—Ty—xrabryj, bud' drugom, pomogi mne. (Gor'kij, SSRLJ)

> 'At Christmas, L'vov tried to persuade Platon: "You are brave, be a *drug*, help me." '

The expression *ne v službu a v družbu* '[please do it] not out of duty but out of friendship [*družba*]' points in the same direction.

Interestingly, the Russian *drug* is frequently used as a form of address, especially in letters, which often begin with phrases such as "Nataša, moj drug" ('Natasha, my *drug*') and end with similar expressions of *družba* 'friendship', such as "tvoj drug Andrej" ('your *drug*, Andrej').

The use of the word *drug* as a form of address may seem to have a parallel in the English phrase *my friend* used sometimes in conversation, but this is an illusion: in

English, when the phrase *my friend* is used as a form of address, its use is ironic, sarcastic, or patronizing. One doesn't address a real friend in this way. On the other hand, in Russian, phrases such as *drug, moj drug* and *dorogoj drug* 'dear *drug*' can be used affectionately to real friends (and even family members).

The fact that *drug* can be used in this way (rather like *darling* or *sweetheart* in English) suggests that it has an emotive semantic component such as 'when I think of you I feel something very good'. Neither the English *friend* nor the Russian *podruga* or *prijatel'* (or *prijatel'nica*) would justify positing such a component.

The most common collocations with *drug* include adjectives referring to the "closeness" and "specialness" of the bond, for example, *blizkij drug* 'close friend', *zaduševnyj drug* 'soul friend', *lučšij drug* 'best friend', *edinstvennyj drug* 'only friend', and *nerazlučnye druz'ja* 'inseparable friends', and reliability, e.g. *vernyj drug* 'faithful friend', *nadežnyj drug* 'reliable friend', *predannyj drug* 'devoted friend', and *istinnyj drug* 'true friend' (cf. Mel'čuk & Žolkovskij 1984:293, USSSRJ 1978:147).

On the basis of all these considerations, I would propose the following explication of the concept *drug*:

(my) drug
(a) everyone knows: many people think about some other people like this:
(b)   I know this person very well
(c)   I think very good things about this person
(d)   I want to often be with this person
(e)   I want to often talk [say things] to this person
(f)   I know: I can say anything to this person
(g)   nothing bad will happen because of this
(h)   I want this person to know what I think
(i)   I want this person to know why I think this
(j)   I want this person to know what I feel
(k)   I want to do good things for this person
(l)   when something bad happens to this person,
       I can't not do something good for this person
(m)   I know: this person thinks the same about me
(n) when people think like this about other people, they feel something very good
(o) I think like this about this person

As in the several subsequent explications, the first component (a) shows that *drug* refers to a common pattern of human relations, and the last that this pattern is thought of as shaping this particular relationship. Components (b) and (c) reflect the assumption that the relationship is based on knowing the other person very well (not just well, but very well), and (c) the related assumption that one holds this person in high regard. The components (f) and (g) jointly spell out something like complete trust, components (d) and (e) represent the need for frequent face-to-face interaction, components (f)–(i) correspond to the desire to "pour out one's soul" to the other person, components (k) and (l) spell out the willingness and indeed obligation to help, (m) refers to the assumption that the relationship is symmetrical, and component (n) stands for the intensive emotion.

The *Explanatory combinatorial dictionary of modern Russian* (ECD, Mel'čuk & Žholkovskij 1984) offers the following carefully phrased and very detailed definition of *drug*:

X—drug Y-a—čelovek X takoj, čto ljudi X i Y, xorošo znaja drug druga, emocional'no raspoloženy drug k drugu, ponimajut drug druga, duxovno blizki, predany drug drugu i gotovy pomogat' drug drugu, i eto kauziruet to, čto X i Y xotjat imet' kontakty (obyčno očnye) v sfere ličnyx interesov, pričem vse eto—ne v silu kakix-libo inyx otnošenij [naprimer, rodstvennyx] meždu X- om i Y-om. (292)

'X is Y's *drug*—X is a person such that persons X and Y, who know each other well, are emotionally well disposed towards each other, understand each other, are spiritually close, are devoted to each other and are ready to help each other; and this causes the fact that X and Y want to be in contact (usually, face-to-face), in the domain of personal interests; and all this not by virtue of some other relationship (for example, kin) between X and Y.'

Clearly, this definition does not endeavor to use semantic primitives or simple syntactic patterns, but in content it is fairly close to the one proposed here. It contains, in a different form, all the components proposed in my explication and adds two more: the exclusion of kinship as a basis of the relationship in question, and the inclusion of spiritual closeness.

In principle, I agree with the spirit of these two additional components, but I don't think they have to be mentioned explicitly: a family member can well be described in Russian as a *drug*, and since the family ties are simply not relevant to this relationship they don't have to be mentioned in the definition at all.

The question of "spiritual closeness" is more problematic, largely because it is not quite clear what is meant by this phrase. I presume, however, that it is intended to refer to the domain of moral judgments and is probably meant to imply that in Russian culture *druzja* are expected to often agree, in important matters, on what is "good" and what is "bad." If we accepted that this expectation was indeed a necessary ingredient of the Russian concept of *drug* (*druzja*), we could spell it out in the explication along the following lines:

when I think that it is good if someone does something
often this person thinks the same
when I think that it is bad if someone does something
often this person thinks the same

Given other evidence for the importance of absolute moral judgments in Russian culture (cf. e.g. Bauer, Inkeles & Kluckhohn 1956:142; Walicki 1980:100–110; Wierzbicka 1992b:435–440) the idea that this kind of moral unity is seen as a necessary ingredient of Russian "družba" (close friendship) is appealing; whether or not it is a necessary semantic component of the word *drug*, however, is a question which I would like to leave open.

I would add that "spiritual closeness" as an ingredient of the relationship between "friends" (*druzja*) is also mentioned by Shlapentokh (1984:229), in whose view the relationship between *druz̃ja* (especially men) is often closer and more open than that between family members and even that between husbands and wives:

> ... lying to family members is only a part of a general pattern of lying in Soviet life. ... Thus, it is to friends that the Soviet people are more likely to turn to fulfill the expressive need in their lives. (225)

> ... quite often the spiritual closeness between friends is greater than that between husbands and wives, the role of friends in such interpersonal communication is probably greater. This is especially true among men. (229)

It seems to me, however, that the components 'I know: I can say anything to this person' and 'nothing bad will happen because of this' (in combination with the other components of the proposed explication) sufficiently account for all those aspects of the concept 'drug' which are implied by the word as such.

3.3 Podruga

Russian-English dictionaries (e.g. Smirnickij 1961, Wheeler 1972), gloss the word *podruga* (etymologically related to *drug*) as "(female) friend," and since *drug* is glossed as "friend," this seems to imply that *podruga* is simply a female counterpart of *drug*. But this impression is deceptive, first, because a woman or a girl, too, can be called a *drug*, second, because calling a woman a *drug* does not mean the same as calling her a *podruga*, and third, because a man's or a boy's female friends are normally not called his *podrugi* (Pl.).

Before discussing the different implications of these two words (*podruga* and *drug*) as applied to relations between women or girls, we must note that in addition to its main use, *podruga* also has three other uses, which offer helpful clues to the main meaning of this word: first, when applied to nonpermanent heterosexual relationships, *podruga* has a meaning similar (though not identical) to that of the English word *girlfriend* (as in "his girlfriend"); second, in the expression *podruga žizni*, 'life *podruga*', it refers to a man's wife, seen as someone who shares his life (Wheeler 1972 glosses this meaning as "helpmate"); and third, *podruga* is often used in a metaphorical sense, as "loving companion," especially in poetry—often with reference to a woman but in poetry also to a concrete object or an abstract idea (when the Russian word for it has the feminine gender). For example (from Pushkin):

Podruga dnej moix surovyx,
golubka drjaxlaja moja.

'*Podruga* of my sombre days,
My poor old darling.' [to his old nanny]

Goriš li ty, lampada naša,
Podruga bdenij i pirov.

'Are you burning, our lamp,
The *podruga* of wakefulness and all-night feasts.'

Zadumčivost', ee podruga
Ot samyx kolybel'nyx dnej,

Tečenie sel'skogo dosuga
Mečtami ukrašala ej.

'Pensiveness, her companion [*podruga*]
even from cradle days,
the course of rural leisure
with daydreams beautified for her.'
(Nabokov's translation, Pushkin 1975:138)

The phrase *podruga dnej moix surovyx* ('*podruga* of my sombre days'), implies that at the time the addressee, Pushkin's old nanny, was his constant (and only) companion and that her presence softened the loneliness and the bleakness of his days. Similarly, the phrase *zadumčivost', ee podruga* ('pensiveness, her *podruga*') implies that pensiveness "was always with" Tat'jana, and the verb *ukrašala* (beautified/colored) implies that Tat'jana felt something good because of that constant companion. Finally, the phrase *lampada naša, podruga bdenij i pirov* ('our lamp, a *podruga* of wakefulness and [long-night] feasts'), implies that the lamp "was always there" and that it made the atmosphere pleasant and enjoyable. The phrase *podruga žizni* 'one's life's *podruga*' (referring to a man's wife) has similar implications (the wife is always with her husband, and her presence is a source of "good feelings"). These additional uses of *podruga* highlight the elements of companionship and 'sharing of life' present in its meaning but absent from the meaning of *drug*. In fact, some dictionaries hint at this aspect of *podruga* without spelling it out in definitions.

For example, Rozanova (1978) glosses *podruga* in English as *friend*, but in French as *amie, compagne* ('friend, companion'); and Smirnickij (1961) glosses the expression *podruga detstva*, literally 'a childhood *podruga*', as *playmate* (thus highlighting the aspect of shared activities).

Similarly, the *Dictionary of the Russian language* (SRJ) defines *podruga* as follows: "devočka, devuška ili ženščaja sostojaščaja v družeskix, tovariščeskix otnošenijax s kem-nibud'" ('a girl or a woman who has a *družeskoe, tovariščeskoe* relationship with someone'), thus describing the relationship in question as not simply *družeskoe* (adjective derived from *drug*) but also *tovariščeskoe* (adjective derived from *tovarišč*). Since, as we will see later, *tovarišč* refers crucially to sharing (of life experiences), this definition, too, highlights an important difference between *podruga* and *drug*. In the case of *podruga*, this sharing has to be long-term, as reflected in the following definition: "devočka, devuška ili ženščaja, s detskix ili s davnix let blizko sdruživšajasja s kem-nibud'" ('a girl or a woman who has been for a long time, often from childhood on, someone's close friend') (TSRJ 1940).

All these definitions offer helpful hints, but they all fail to mention the specifically "inter-female" character of the relationship implied by the word *podruga* and, more generally, to sort out the distinct meaning of this word from others in the group. To see that the word is indeed polysemous, and that the implications of specifically "inter-female" kind of friendship are not due to context, it is sufficient to consider common expressions such as *podruga detstva* 'childhood friend (*podruga*)' and *škol'hye podrugi* (Pl.) 'school friends (*podrugi*)'. If *podruga* really meant something like 'female friend', there would be no reason why such expressions could not refer to boys' childhood friends, or school friends, but in fact they normally refer only to inter-female relationships,[7] and a sentence such as

? On pošel guljat' s podrugami.

'he went for a walk with his *podrugi*'

sounds very strange.

To see the main meaning of *podruga* more clearly, therefore, it is better to consider first the meaning of the plural form *podrugi*, which cannot apply to the other meaning of this word. Roughly speaking, this form refers to female friends who have for a long time shared life experiences and whose existential situation is similar—with the implication that these shared life experiences have something to do with the nature of women's lives and that women's existential situation is linked with their gender. In a more formulaic form, these "specifically female" implications of the form *podrugi* can be spelled out along the following lines (to be refined later):

many women think about other women like this:
   this person is someone like me
   often, when I do something, this person does similar things
   often, when something happens to me, similar things happen to this person
   often this person feels similar things to me

A *podruga* is someone who can provide a woman or a girl with much needed and highly valued company of "someone like herself." The following nineteenth-century example illustrates these implications very nicely:

Ona žalela o tom, čto ee vospitannica ne budet imet' podrug v derevne. (Černyševskij, SRJ)

'She was sorry that in the village her adopted daughter [ward] would not have any *podrugi* [Pl.].'

It is also interesting to note that Dal''s 1955[1882] dictionary of Russian includes the following comment about the use of *podrugi* and its diminutive *podružki* in folk speech: "O devicax odnoletkax, vyrosšix vmeste," 'about girls of the same age who have grown up together'. Dal' illustrates this use with the words of a folk song and with two proverbs:

Kak pošli naši podružki v les po jagody guljat'.

'When our *podružki* (Pl. Dim.) went for a walk in the forest to gather berries.'

Podružka—poduška (drugoj net).

'A *podružka* is [one's best] pillow (there is no other).'

U xorošej nevesty po semi podrug.

'A good prospective fiancée has seven *podrugi*.'

The fact that one can talk about *druz'ja po perepiske* '*druz'ja* by correspondence, pen-friends', but not **podrugi po perepiske*, '*podrugi* by correspondence', points in the same direction: *podrugi* have to be together and to share life experiences.

Mutual help (though very common) is not a necessary ingredient of this relationship: for this concept being together (with a like-minded person) in a shared mood is more important than doing things for one another. The contrast between *podruga* and *drug* used in close succession in the following passage provides a good illustration of this (Litvinova 1994d:12):

Èto kto u tebja, Larissa? Podruga? Xorošo, a to tjažko odnoj. Toska.
I čto on, bedolaga, sejčas peredumyvaet, kak ob vas duša u nego bolit. . . .
   Priexala k Lare okolo 7 večera—na prjamom poezde. Zdes' Nina Petrovna—dobryj, tixij, dejatel'nyj drug. V dome porjadok—vse postirano, N.P. gladit.

'Who is with you, Larissa? A girlfriend [*podruga*]? That's good, it's hard to be alone. It is painful. And what is he, poor soul, thinking about now, how his heart must ache for you. . . .
   I came to Lara's about 7 in the evening—by express train. Nina Petrovna is here—a good, quiet, helpful friend [*drug*]. Everything is in good order in the house—everything has been washed, N.P. is doing the ironing.'

The woman referred to in this passage, Larissa, is tormented by anxiety about her husband, Anatolij Marčenko, who has been arrested by the KGB. A sympathic woman-neighbor, worried about Larissa, is pleased to see that she has the company of a *podruga*. Two sentences further, another woman-friend of Larissa's is mentioned, who comes in and simply starts doing Larissa's household chores for her (washing, ironing). In the first case, (focusing on company), the word *podruga* naturally comes to mind, in the second (focusing on help), *drug* (and the phrase *dejatel'nyj drug* 'an actively helping *drug*').

Consider also the following example (again from Pushkin's *Eugene Onegin*, with Nabokov's translation):

Kogda že njanja sobirala
Dlja Ol'gi na širokij lug
Vsex malen'kix ee podrug,
Ona [Tat'jana] v gorelki ne igrala,
Ej skučen byl i zvonkij smex
I šum ix vetrenyx utex.

'Whenever nurse assembled
for Olga, on the spacious lawn,
all her small girl companions,
she did not play at barleybreaks,
dull were to her both ringing laughter
and noise of their giddy diversions.' (138)

Ol'ga's little *podrugi*, gathered for her by her nanny, are other little girls with whom Ol'ga likes to share her activities and her fun. These other little girls would probably not qualify as *druz'ja*, but they are like-minded companions, of a similar position in life, with whom little Ol'ga likes to be together, feeling that each of them is someone like herself (partly because they are all girls).

Yet, despite all this existential closeness, *podruga* does not have the emotional warmth of *drug*. This absence of "warmth" is reflected in the fact that, except in metaphorical usage, *podruga* cannot be used as a form of address; for example, one cannot start a letter with the phrase *Anna, moja* ('my') *podruga*, or *Anna, dorogaja* ('dear') *podruga*. In metaphorical usage, on the other hand, *podruga* is often so used (as in one of the examples from Pushkin quoted earlier).

Given the specifically "inter-female" character of friendship implied by *podruga*, one might expect that this word will also imply a willingness to confide in one another, to open one's heart to one another (at least as much as *drug* does). But this is not exactly the case. In Russia, both women and men are expected to "open their hearts" (or, as Tolstoy says, to "pour out their soul") to their close friends, regardless of gender, and this cultural expectation is reflected in the semantics of the word *druzja*. *Podruga* focuses on something else: a bond based on perceiving the other person as being someone like me, both with respect to our existential position (doing and happening) and with respect to feelings ("someone who feels the same things as I do").

The fact that the bond between *podrugi* (Pl.) is seen as largely existential may explain, to some extent, why *podruga* does not imply a "high opinion" of, or high regard for, the other person in the way *drug* does. Some good opinion is implied, but not necessarily "very good" opinion, as in the case of *drug*.

To sum up all these considerations, I would propose the following explication of *podruga* (in the sense under discussion):

(my) podruga
(a) everyone knows: many women think about some other women like this:
(b)   I know this person very well
(c)   I have known this person for a long time
(d)   I think something good about this person
(e)   this person is someone like me
(f)   I have often been with this person
(g)   often, when I did some things,
        this person did similar things
(h)   often, when some things happened to me,
        similar things happened to this person
(i)   often, when I felt some things,
        this person felt similar things
(j)   when I am with this person, I feel something good
(k)   I know: this person thinks the same about me
(l)   I think like this about this person

3.4   *Prijatel'*

Alexander Pushkin's masterpiece *Eugene Onegin* introduces the hero with the following lines:

Onegin, dobryj moj prijatel'
Rodilsja na bregax Nevy.

'Onegin, a good pal [*prijatel'*] of mine
Was born upon the Neva's banks' (Pushkin 1975:96)

These lines define the narrator's attitude to the hero—friendly, but rather distant. The set of modifiers that the word prijatel'takes underscores this distance: while both a *prijatel'*and a *drug* can be described as *dobryj* or *xorošij*, only *drug* would be normally described as *lučšij* 'best', *edinstvennyj* 'only', *bol'šoj* 'great', *zaduševnyj* 'soul-friend', or *zakadyčnyj* 'bosom-friend' (cf. e.g. **bol'šoj prijatel'*), and only *druz'ja*, not *prijateli* (Pl.), would be normally described as *nerazlučnye* 'inseparable'.

Similar contrasts can be observed in the collocations *rodnye i druz'ja* 'family and druz'ja' vs. **rodnye i prijateli* 'family and prijateli', the second of which could be compared to the bizarre combination *family and distant friends*, in contrast to *family and close friends*.

The Academy of Sciences' *Dictionary of synonyms* (SSRJ) describes the meaning of *prijatel'* as follows:

prijatel'—čelovek, s kotorym složilis' xorošie, prostye, no ne očen' blizkie otnošenija

'prijatel'—a person with whom one has good, simple, but not very close relations'

Many examples of the use of the word *prijatel'* gathered in dictionaries support the gist of this definition and highlight the difference between *drug* (very close) and *prijatel'*(not very close). For instance:

S prijateljami v kino xodjat, futbol gonjajut, a s drugom vse napopolam idet—i radost' i gore. Prijatel'—čto! Ix mnogo byvaet. A drug—odin. (Mixalkov, SSRJ)

'With one's *prijateli* [Pl.] one goes to the movies, or chases a football, but with a *drug* one shares everything, fifty-fifty, both joy and sorrow.'

Prijatelej u Gavrika bylo mnogo, a nastojaščix druzej vsego odin: Petja. (Kataev, SSRLJ).

'Gavrik had many *prijateli*, but only one real *drug*: Petja.'

V ego družbe ko mne bylo čto-to neudobnoe, tjagostnoe, i ja oxotno predpočel by ej obyknovennye prijatel'skie otnošenija. (Čexov, SSRJ).

'In his friendship (*družba*) for me there was something uncomfortable, awkward, and I would have preferred to have an ordinary *prijatel'*-like relationship with him.'

As these examples (the first of which we have already seen) suggest, *prijatel'*, in contrast to drug, does not imply a willingness to confide in the other person, to open one's heart to them, and to "share with them one's joys and sorrows." Nor does it imply that one can always count on the other person's help and support. Instead, it implies that one knows the other person well (but not necessarily very well) and that one enjoys their company. There is no implication that one thinks very good things about this person. More precisely, the meaning of *prijatel'* can be represented as follows:

(*my*) *prijatel'*
(a) everyone knows: many people think about some other people like this :
(b) I know this person well
(c) when I am with this person, I feel something good
(d) when I do something with this person, I feel something good
(e) I think this person thinks the same about me
(f) I think like this about this person

The examples from Russian quoted earlier, which explicitly contrast the two words *prijatel'* and *drug*, highlight the importance of this distinction in Russian and, more generally, the importance that Russian culture attaches to the classification of human relations. Furthermore, judging by the frequencies of the two words (as reported in frequency dictionaries), the category of *drug* (very close "friend") is far more important in Russian culture than that of *prijatel'*(a more casual kind of "friend").

The explication of *prijatel'* sketched here is in fact quite similar to that assigned to the English *friend* (*friend₂*). The main difference is that *friend* expresses a more active attitude: one seeks, as well as enjoys, the company of "friends" and shared activities with them. In this respect, *friend* resembles *drug* rather than *prijatel'*; but otherwise, *friend* is more like *prijatel'* than *drug*.

3.5   *Tovarišč*

The word *tovarišč* was of central importance in the Soviet era in its political meaning, usually rendered in English as "comrade". Although the use of the word *tovarišč* in this sense was politically driven and imposed from above, its status in the Russian language of the Soviet era cannot simply be compared to that of the English *comrade*. Being addressed as *tovarišč* was a sign of belonging; losing this title and losing the right to apply it to others was a sign of exclusion and could have easily been a prelude to arrest, incarceration, and death.[8]

If only one word were to be nominated as the key word of the Soviet Russian, it would probably have to be this one. Although after the collapse of communism in Russia this politically driven use of the word *tovarišč* quickly started to recede, it will always keep its place in Russian history as a symbol of a long and terrible era, and as such it certainly deserves analytical attention. It should be noted that throughout the Soviet era *tovarišč* also retained its earlier, nonpolitical meaning, and that that nonpolitical meaning has never lost ground. To avoid confusion, I will distinguish the two meanings as *tovarišč₂* (political) and *tovarišč₁* (nonpolitical).

Although we do not have any statistical data on the relative frequencies of these two meanings in Russian speech, we do have some data on the frequency of the word *tovarišč* as such, and these data suggest that in the Soviet era *tovarišč* was one of the most frequently used nouns in the Russian language (in Zasorina's frequency dictionary it is the sixth most frequent noun, following only such basic nouns as *god* 'year', *delo* 'matter', *čelovek* 'man', *žizn'* 'life', and *den'* 'day', and its frequency in a corpus of 1 million running words is a phenomenally high 1,162; in a comparable corpus of American English [Kučera & Francis 1967], *comrade* doesn't appear at all, and *brother* has a frequency of 124; in Carroll et al. 1971 *comrade* occurs 7 times, and *brother* 169 times).

In fact, the *Dictionary of the Russian language* (SSRLJ) distinguishes as many as six distinct meanings of the word *tovarišč*, but this is clearly a case of "multiplying beings beyond necessity": all that is justified is the distinction between the relational (nonpolitical) sense, as in *moj* ('my') *tovarišč*, and an "absolute" (political) sense (as in *tovarišč* tout court). Accordingly, in the discussion which follows, I will distinguish only two meanings: the relational *tovarišč₁* and the absolute *tovarišč₂*.

SRLJ assigns to the relational meaning of *tovarišč* (my *tovarišč₁*) three different definitions:

1. A man participating with someone in the same case, affair, enterprise etc.
2. A man linked with others by a common profession, place of work; a colleague.
3. A man linked with someone by ties of friendship [*družba*]; a close friend [*prijatel'*, *drug*].

Undoubtedly, a *tovarišč detstva* ('childhood friend'), a *škol'nyj tovarišč* ('school friend'), or *tovarišč po škol'noj skam'e* (literally 'someone sharing the same school bench') is not the same thing as a *tovarišč po rabote* ('fellow-worker'), *tovarišč po universitetu* ('fellow-student'), *tovarišč po nesčast'ju* ('fellow-sufferer'), or *tovarišč po kamere* ('fellow-prisoner, sharing the same cell'), but the differences are here due to context, not to the word *tovarišč* itself. What all these different uses of *tovarišč₁* have in common is the idea of a bond based on shared life experiences, linked with a shared position in life, and a shared "lot."

The *Dictionary of synonyms* (SSRJ), which wisely attributes a unitary meaning to *tovarišč₁*, defines this meaning as follows: *tovarišč* —a man close [to someone] by virtue of his kind of activity, occupation, conditions of life, etc., and tied [to this person] by common views, and friendly relations.

Although not fully accurate, this is not a bad definition, and its reference to shared conditions of life is insightful. Like the English word *fellow* (as in *fellow-prisoners*), *tovarišč₁* refers to a bond based not on a purely voluntary association but on one imposed on us by, so to speak, life itself: not on what we choose to do but on what happens to us. The main formal difference between the Russian *tovarišč₁* and the English *fellow* (as in *fellow-students* and *fellow-prisoners*) is that the former is, syntactically, a noun, whereas the latter (in the relevant sense) is not a full blown noun but a kind of prefix, almost on a par with the prefix *co-*. This formal difference is associated with a semantic difference: *tovarišč₁* is one of the basic categories for categorizing human relations (like *friend* in English, or *drug* in Russian), whereas *fellow-* is not; like its fellow-prefix *co-*, *fellow-* is both syntactically and semantically a modifier, not an independent category of thought.

The concomitant cultural difference seems quite clear: it is only in Russian that the idea of "sharing the same lot" is so salient that it has become a basis for one of the fundamental categories in the interpretation of human relations. It is, in a way, an echo of *sud'ba* (cf. Wierzbicka 1992b, chap. 2).

It is important to point out, therefore, that the dictionary's reference to a shared "kind of activity" (as well as shared "conditions of life") is not part of the word's semantic invariant. For example, the common phrase *tovarišči po nesčast'ju* 'fellow-sufferers' does not refer to any activity at all; and the frequent use of the word *tovarišči* in the prison and camp literature (as illustrated below) also highlights the central relevance of "conditions of life" over and above any shared activities.

Of course, some common "conditions of life" imply also some kinds of activities, and, for example, the existence of schoolboys, or soldiers, can be viewed either from the point of view of what they do or from the point of view of what happens to them. But as the phrase *tovarišči po nesčast'ju* 'fellow-sufferers' shows, the word *tovarišči*₁ as such highlights an undergoer's, not an agent's, perspective.

Some examples:

Soldaty bezmolvno smotreli na èto strašnoe zrelišče [kazn']. Nikto iz nix ne rinulsja na zaščitu svoix tovariščej. (Novikov-Priboj, SRLJ).

'The soldiers were silently watching the terrible sight [execution]. None of them made a move to try to defend his *tovarišči* [Pl.].'

A čto, vy drug emu?—drug ne drug, a tovarišč. (Semenov, SSRJ.)

'What, are you his *drug*?—Perhaps not a *drug*, but a *tovarišč*.'

U nego zavjazalas' družba s tovariščami po rabote. (Gorbatov, SSRJ).

'He developed a friendship [*družba*] with his workmates [work *tovarišči*].'

And some more recent examples:

Tri goda ja ležala tixo-tixo noči naprolet i myslenno rasskazyvala. Obo vsem. Ne tol'ko o sebe. O tovariščax po nesčast'ju, s kotorymi menja svela sud'ba, ob ix gorestnyx stradanijax, tragičeskix slučajax ix žizni. (Adamova-Sliozberg 1993:8).

'For three years, I lay awake at night telling the story of it all in my thoughts. About everything. Not just about myself. About my companions in misfortune with whom fate [*sud'ba*] had brought me in contact, about their grievous sufferings, the tragic circumstances of their lives.'

A est' takie zavlekatel'nye tjurmy, gde dajut obryvki knižnoj pečati—i čto èto za čtenie! ugadat' *otkuda* . . . —pomenjat'sja s tovariščami. (Solzhenitsyn 1973:211)

'And there are prisons which have the engaging practice of providing fragments ripped out of books—what a great read that is—to try and guess where it comes from . . . , swap bits with your comrades [*tovarišči*].' (On prison latrines)

Edut [na poxorony Marčenko] krome Pavlika i Sani [Danielja], Katja s Mišej, Kolja Mjuge, Genja Lubeneckij—tovarišč Sani. (Litvinova, 1994a:10)

'Those traveling [to Marčenko's funeral] include Pavlik and Sanja [Daniel], Katja and Miša, Kolja Mjuge, and Genja Lubeneckij—a *tovarišč* of Sanja's.'

If one considers the time, the effort, and the political risk involved in traveling to the funeral of a leading dissident in a remote island of the Gulag archipelago, the participation of someone described as "a *tovarišč* of Sanja's" (a son of Larissa's,

Marčenko's wife, by an earlier marriage) illustrates well the human weight of the concept encapsulated in the word *tovarišč₁*. Clearly, the relationship between the two men is not considered to be close enough for the word *drug* to be used here, and yet few "friends" would be expected to do as much.

The assumption of similarity in one's existential position links *tovarišč₁*, in one respect, with *podruga* (in the plural, *podrugi*), but there are also important differences between these two concepts. My *podruga* is someone whose existential position, so to speak, is similar to mine (as, for example, in the phrase *škol'naja podruga* 'a school-Adj. *podruga*'); but it cannot be someone who is simply "in the same boat" because the same misfortune has befallen us both. Hence the unacceptability of a phrase such as **podruga po nesčast'ju* ('*podruga* in misfortune') or **podruga po kamere* ('*podruga* by prison cell'). Unlike in *tovarišč₁*, in *podruga* there is also an element of personal attraction and personal choice.

This asymmetry between *podruga* and *tovarišč₁* throws an interesting light on the different expectations with regard to males' and females' lives in Russia. Let us compare, for example, the position of schoolgirls and schoolboys in an Anglo society (say, in America), in Poland, and in Russia. In an Anglo society, both a girl and a boy would usually refer to some of their classmates as "friends." In Poland, the basic word used for classmates is *koledzy* (referring to boys) and *koleżanki* (referring to girls). The Polish dictionary equivalents of *friend*, namely *przyjaciel* (male) and *przyjaciółka* (female) are normally not used for the classmates that one associates with. Usually, they are reserved only for one person, roughly the equivalent of the English *best friend*. This means that while the basic social grid applied in Anglo schools and Polish schools is different, nonetheless in both systems girls and boys are treated essentially in the same way.

This is not the case in a Russian school. Here, there are no colloquial words applying to all classmates (as in the case of the Polish words *koledzy* and *koleżanki*), and there is no colloquial word for those boys and girls who one usually associates with (as in the case of the English *friend*). Instead, girls are expected to have *podrugi* (a specifically female form of friendship), whereas boys' classmates can be seen as their *tovarišči₁* (unless they are especially close friends, that is, *druz'ja*). A girl's close friends (male, or a mixed group) can also be seen as *druz'ja*, but for girls, there is no colloquial equivalent of *tovarišči₁* and for boys, there is no equivalent of *podrugi*.

This is not to say that the word *tovarišči₁*—unlike *druz'ja*—can never be used with reference to women. It can, especially in contexts where the focus is on solidarity (often, the solidarity of prison or camp inmates, as in the example from Sliozberg quoted earlier or in the example from Solzhenitsyn which follows); but prototypically, it refers to men (or at least did in pre-Soviet times).

Anna Skripnikova ... požalovalas' sledovatel'ju, čto ee odnokamernic načal'nik Lubjanki taskaet za volosy. Sledovatel' rassmejalsja i sprosil: "A vas tože taskaet?"— "Net, no moix tovariščej!" (Solzhenitsyn 1974:301)

'Anna Skripnikova complained to her interrogator that the head of the Lubyanka prison had been pulling her cellmates around by their hair. Her interrogator laughed and asked, "And does he pull you by the hair as well?" "No, but he does my comrades [*tovarišči*]!'"

Nonetheless, women companions with whom one is on friendly terms are more likely to be referred to as *podrugi*, and if they are very close, as *druzʹja*, as in the following example:

Proev neskolʹko rublej, sobrannyx lagernymi druzʹjami, Stoljarova vernulasʹ k zone, sovrala oxrane . . . , i—v svoj barak! . . . Podrugi okružili, prinesli s kuxni balandy. (Solzhenitsyn 1975:467)

'Having eaten her way through the few rubles her camp friends [*druzʹja*] had collected for her, Stolyarova returned to the zone, tricked the guards into letting her back in—and went straight to her hut. . . . Her friends [*podrugi*] clustered round her and brought her some gruel from the kitchen.' (A prisoner released from a camp decides the only way she can survive is by getting back into the camp.)

Another way of describing the situation in Russian is to say that Russian singles out, lexically, a special category of human relations (namely *tovarišči*$_1$), which refers to prototypically male solidarity based on shared experiences of groups of males thrown together by "fate"—as in the case of soldiers or prisoners. There is no element of personal choice in that solidarity, but there is an expectation of mutual good feelings and good will based on the fact of having been thrown together into the same circumstances, as equals (like brothers in misfortune). The following examples illustrate this bond particularly clearly.

Za denʹ ili za dva dnja pered ètim oni xorošo pogovorili s Alekseem i oba kak-to vnutrenne daže poradovalisʹ, čto oni tovarišči po nesčastʹju i u nix oboix odinakovo složnoe sostojanie ličnyx del. (Polevoj, SSRLJ)

'One or two days before that, he had had a good talk with Aleksej, and they both felt very pleased that they were fellows in misfortune [*tovarišči* in disaster] and that they were both in a similarly difficult personal situation.'

Vot Vasʹka, on u nas molodčina! . . . Ni nad čem dlja tovarišča ne zadumaetsja. (Veresaev, SSRJ).

'That Vasʹka, he is a great chap! He would do anything for a *tovarišč*.'

. . . a takoe čuvstvo, budto serdce otorvala ot samogo dorogogo i ljubimogo, ot tovariščej po nesčastʹju. (Solzhenitsyn 1975:476)

'And a feeling as if one's heart had been torn away from that which is dearest to it—one's comrades [*tovarišči*] in suffering.' (a camp prisoner's feelings just after her release)

In particular, one normally doesn't want "bad things" to happen to one's *tovarišči*, as one doesn't want "bad things" to happen to oneself, as the following example illustrates:

Ja smotrela na svoix tovariščej po nesčast'ju i žalela ix ščemjaščej žalost'ju potomu, čto znala, čto éti ljudi osuždeny na tot strašnyj krestnyj put', kotoryj ja uže prošla. (Adamova-Sliozberg 1993:177)

'I looked at my companions in misfortune and felt the keenest pity for them, for I knew that these people were condemned to undergo that same terrible ordeal that I myself had already undergone.' (Sliozberg was imprisoned for a second time.)

Thus, although not chosen voluntarily, the bond with one's *tovarišči* can be expected to be strong—often as strong as with a *drug*, as evidenced by the collocation *drug-tovarišč* or, rarely, *tovarišč-drug*:

Ja s otkrovennoj dušoj prišel k tebe . . . kak k drugu-tovariščů. (Gladkij, SSRLJ)

'I have come to you with an open heart—as to a friend [*drug-tovarišč*].'

. . . kak s tovariščem-drugom, govorit on s toboj. (Tvardovskij, SSRLJ).

'He talks with you as with a friend [*tovarišč-drug*].'

On the basis of all these considerations, I would propose the following explication:

(my) tovarišč$_1$
(a) everyone knows: many people think about some other people like this some-
    times:
(b)   these people are people like me
(c)   these people are in the same place as I
(d)   the same things happen to these people as to me
(e)   I don't want bad things to happen to these people as I don't want bad thing
      to happen to me
(f) when people think like this about other people, they feel something good
(g) many men think like this about some other men
(h) I think like this about this person

Component (a) reflects the "collectivist" perspective of the concept *tovarišči*$_1$ and allows for the inclusion of women, while component (g) shows that prototypically the word refers to groups of men. Component (b) shows the equality of the members of the group, (c) their togetherness, and (d) their shared condition and their perceived status of undergoers rather than agents. Component (e) reflects the solidarity and group identification implied by this word, (f) the warmth, (g) a prototypical male group focus, while (h) reflects the fact that despite its group orientation, it can also refer to one person.

Unlike in the case of *druz'ja* (Pl.) or *podrugi* (Pl.), there is no implication that one knows one's *tovariščej* (Acc. Pl.) well or very well, or that one thinks of them good, or very good, things; and there is no question here of any desire to be together, to talk, or to open one's hearts to one another. Nonetheless, a fellow-feeling is certainly there—frequently leading to the emotion of *žalet'* (roughly 'warm, intense compassion'). The frequent co-occurrence of the words *tovarišči* and *žalet'* in Russian literature is certainly striking, as the last example from Adamova-Sliozberg and the following one illustrate:

> Ja tol'ko gorjačo žalela svoix tovariščej' po nesčast'ju i nenavidela našix palačej. (Adamova-Sliozberg 1993:220)
>
> 'I just pitied with all my heart my companions in misfortune and loathed our murderous tormentors.'

One may wonder whether the components (f) and (g) are compatible with examples such as the one quoted earlier about the soldiers, none of whom tried to defend their tovariščej (Acc. Pl.) from execution, but I think it is. The whole point of the quoted sentence was the contradiction between the soldiers' observed behavior and their presumed or expected feelings. The same applies to the following sentence about a student forced by her interrogator in prison to make false accusations against other students:

> On fabrikoval i zastavljal ee podpisyvat' čudoviščnye protokoly, obvinjat' desjatki ee tovariščej. (Adamova-Sliozberg 1993:189)
>
> 'He fabricated, then forced her to sign grotesque protocols implicating dozens of her fellow-students (tovarišči).

3.6 Tovarišč$_2$ ('comrade')

Tovarišč$_2$ has no doubt developed out of the earlier meaning tovarišč$_1$. One can almost see this transition in examples such as the following one, where the word tovarišč is still accompanied by a possessive pronoun but where it clearly refers to political and ideological "comrades":

> V rasprostranenii že učenij nazvannyx pisatelej [Marksa i Engelsa] imenno i zaključaetsja cel' moix tovariščej. (Plexanov; SSRLJ).
>
> 'The goal of my tovarišči is precisely to spread the teachings of these writers [Marx and Engels].'

Subsequently, however, the possessive pronoun was dropped and an absolute use of tovarišč developed in which the very absence of a possessive pronoun signaled that both the speaker and the audience were presumed to belong to the same speech and thought community and to be permanently united in a common ideology, a common struggle, and a common pursuit. As Majakovskij put it:

> Nado obvjazat' i žizn' mužčin i ženščin
> Slovom nas ob"edinjajuščim: "Tovarišč"
> (SSRLJ)
>
> 'We should bind together the lives of men and women with this word which unites us: "Comrade."'

Who would be seen as tovarišč in that new sense of the word was spelled out in Lenin's words, designed to ignite the October revolution:

Tovarišči rabočie, soldaty, krest'jane i vse trudjaščiesja! Berite vsju vlast' v ruki svoix sovetov! (SSRLJ)

'Comrade workers, soldiers, peasants, and all working people! Take the power into the hands of your councils (soviets)!'

As a force unifying the Soviet people (and implicitly excluding others) the word *tovarišč₂* came to be valued and cherished almost above all other Russian words:

Naše slovo gordoe "tovarišč"
Nam dorože vsex krasivyx slov.
(Lebedev-Kumač, SSRLJ)

'Our proud word "comrade"
is dearer to us than the most beautiful words.'

Used in this new sense, the word *tovarišč₂* implied a kind of collective identification: if X called Y a *tovarišč₂*, X assumed that Y was someone like him (X); and at the same time, X was referring to many other people with whom they both (Y and X) could identify ('there are many people like this; Y is one of them, I am one of them').

This collective identification presupposed common ideals and common goals ('these people want the same things to happen', 'these people want to do many things because of this'). Presumably, the common ideals and goals hinted at in the concept of *tovarišč₂* were, in an embryonic form, the basic ideals and goals of the communist ideology: the future good of the masses of the "working people," class struggle, struggle against all the forces of "counter-revolution." This can be represented as follows: 'these people (i.e. all the "comrades") want good things to happen to very many people', 'these people want bad things to happen to some other people (because of this)'. The common struggle of all the *tovarišči₂* (Pl.) implied shared experiences and similar risks ('the same things can happen to these people because of this'). Finally, the word *tovarišč₂* implied appreciation and high regard for those on whom it was bestowed. I will represent this as follows: 'I think something very good about these people'.

Before proposing my own explication of *tovarišč₂*, I will first adduce Nikita Khrushchev's definition, which in fact tallies quite well with all the points mentioned above:

Slovo "tovarišč" vyražaet edinomyslie, i ravenstvo, i bratstvo, i uvaženie, i sotrudničestvo. (SSRLJ)

'The word "comrade" expresses unanimity, and equality, and brotherhood, and respect, and cooperation.'

I propose, then, the following explication:

tovarišč₂
(a) everyone knows: many people think about some other people like this:
(b) these people are people like me
(c) there are many people like this
(d) these people want the same things to happen

(e)   these people want good things to happen to very many people
(f)   these people want bad things to happen to some other people because of this
(g)   these people want to do many things because of this
(h)   I think something very good about all these people
(i)   when I think about these people, I feel something good
(j)   I think about this person like this

As this explication suggests, in *tovarišč₂* the emphasis has shifted from things that happen to people to things that people want to happen and to things that people want to do. One might say that the "solidarity of undergoers" (not to say "victims") has been replaced by the "solidarity of agents"; and while the positive affective attitude remained ('when I think about these people I feel something good'), the attitude of "solidarity of undergoers" ('I don't want bad things to happen to these people, as I don't want bad things to happen to me'), natural in people who see themselves as potential victims of life, disappeared, being replaced by an attitude of mutual regard ('I think something very good about these people'), natural in self-confident agents, aware of their numbers and their power.

The component 'these people are people like me' remained, but it was expanded and broadened (and diluted) by the reference to many people ('there are many people like this'), united not by the vicissitudes of fate but by a common ideology and purpose (b)–(g). Interestingly, the group identification implied by *tovarišč₂* was no longer focused on men: there is no reference to men, only to people, in the explication of *tovarišč₂.*

It is hardly necessary to point out that, from the first to the last component, the whole explication sounds phony, as the word *tovarišč* itself (in its political sense) has always done.

3.7   *Rodnye* ('one's own people, close relatives')

The concept of *rodnye* is another important Russian category of thought. Russian-English dictionaries usually translate this word with the English word *relatives*, but the two words are far from equivalent. In fact, Russian does have a lexical equivalent of *relatives*, namely, *rodstvenniki*, but this is not the same as *rodnye*.

First of all, the word *rodnye* refers normally to close relatives, not to distant ones; and the phrase *dal'nie rodnye*, unlike *dal'nie rodstvenniki* 'distant relatives', sounds ludicrous.

But the phrase *blizkie rodnye*, unlike *blizkie rodstvenniki* 'close relatives', is also very odd, at least as odd as the phrase *close immediate family* would sound in English: *rodnye*, like *immediate family*, are, by definition, very close to us, and this closeness cannot be qualified in any way because it is seen as an absolute, an existential given.

In principle, *rodstvenniki*—like *relatives* in English—refers to people who are not members of the immediate family, whereas *rodnye* refers primarily to the immediate family. In certain special contexts, the words *rodstvenniki* and *relatives* can be used more broadly, in a way which would include family, and *rodnye* can be extended to people outside the family; but prototypically, *rodstvenniki* (like *relatives*) focuses on those outside the family, whereas the opposite is true for *rodnye*. Furthermore, *rodnye* implies closeness, emotional attachment, belonging, whereas *rodstvenniki* has no such implications.

Although it is cognate with the verb *rodit'* 'give birth', and although it is roughly coextensive with *sem'ja* 'family' (in its broader sense, including not only parents and children but also brothers, sisters, and grandparents, as well as various in-laws), the concept of *rodnye* is defined, primarily, in existential and emotional terms rather than in biological or legal ones. From this point of view, being a member of the same household may be more important than being related by blood. For example, for Nataša Rostova (in Tolstoy's *War and peace*), her cousin Sonja, who is being raised by Nataša's parents together with their own children, belongs undoubtedly to her *rodnye*—probably more so than her own married older sister Vera, who is no longer a member of the same household.

It is perceptive, therefore, of Taube's (1978) Russian-English dictionary to offer the Russian word *domašnie* (from *dom* 'house', 'members of the same household') as a synonym of *rodnye*. The two words (*rodnye* and *domašnie*) do not mean exactly the same, but in a sense they are closer than *rodnye* and *rodstvenniki* ('relatives'). It is also perceptive of another Russian-English dictionary (Wheeler 1972) to illustrate the meaning of *rodnye* with the phrase *v krugu rodnyx*, literally 'in the circle of *rodnye*', glossed as 'in the family circle, with one's people': the phrase *v krugu* 'in the circle' suggests a group of people who are often together, who sit around the same table, and who share their life, as well as their meals. For this image, being a member of the same household (though not necessary either) may be more important than being a close blood relative.

> Bolezn' Nataši byla tak ser'ezna, čto, k sčast'ju ee i k sčast'ju ee rodnyx, mysl' o vsem tom, čto bylo pričinoj ee bolezni, ee postupok i razryv s ženixom, perešli na vtoroj plan. . . . Čto že by delali Sonja, graf, i grafinja, kak by oni smotreli na slabuju, tošćuju Natašu, ničego ne predprinimaja, esli by ne bylo ětix piljul' po časam, pit'ja teplen'kogo, kurinoj kotletki i vsex podrobnostej žizni predpisannyx doktorom, sobljudat' kotorye sostavljalo zanjatie i utešenie dlja okružajuščix? (Tolstoy 1964:60–62)
>
> 'Natasha's illness was so serious that, fortunately for her and for her parents [*rodnye*] all thought of what had caused it, of her conduct and the breaking off of the engagement, receded into the background. . . . What would have become of Sonya and the count and countess if they had had nothing to do but look at Natasha, weak and fading away—if there had not been those pills to give by the clock, the warm drinks to prepare, the chicken cutlets, and all the other details ordered by the doctors, which supplied occupation and consolation to all of them. The stricter and more complicated the doctor's orders, the more comfort did those around her find in carrying them out.' (Tolstoy 1930–1931:776–778)

Another image which may be helpful here is that of a nest: one's *rodnye* are like people who form one's existential "nest". This nest provides one with existential and emotional support, warmth, and a frame of orientation and belonging—not just in childhood but throughout one's life.

Given the double, existential and emotional, bond implied by the word *rodnye*, the English expression *nearest and dearest* gives a better idea of what this concept really involves than the cold descriptive term *relatives*, although the strength of the bond implied by the Russian word is much greater. In English, people often make disparaging comments about their relatives, as reflected, for instance, in the celebrated linguistic example of a sentence with two possible syntactic interpretations:

Visiting relatives can be a nuisance.

In Russian, a sentence of this kind could only be translated with the word *rodstvenniki*, not with the word *rodnye*. From a Russian perspective, *rodnye* are, by definition, beloved and indispensable, not a nuisance, and they are beloved not because of any personal attraction or preference but simply because they are an inalienable part of one's own life. I am not saying that from a Russian perspective relatives are necessarily "beloved," but only that *rodnye* are. One CAN speak about relatives in Russian in a cold or hostile manner, but the word which would be used for this would be *rodstvenniki*, not *rodnye*.

Ja terpet' ne mogu moix rodstvennikov/? rodnyx.

'I can't stand my relatives.'

Even the ironic definition of the concept *rodnye*, offered by the cynical narrator of Pushkin's *Eugene Onegin,* confirms this:

Pozvol'te: možet byt', ugodno
Teper' uznat' vam ot menja
Čto značit imenno *rodnye.*
Rodnye ljudi vot kakie:
My ix objazany laskat',
Ljubit', duševno uvažat'
I, po obyčaju naroda,
O roždestve ix navešcat'
Ili po počte pozdravljat',   `
Čtob ostal'noe vremja goda
Ne dumali o nas oni . . .
Itak, daj bog im dolgi dni!

'Perhaps you would like
to learn from me now
what "kinsfolk" [*rodnye*] means exactly?
Well, here's what kinsfolk are:
we are required to cosset them,
love them, esteem them cordially,
and, following popular custom,
at Christmas time, visit them,
or send them postal greetings,
so that for the rest of the year
they will not think about us.
So grant them, God, long life!
(Pushkin 1975:184)

The warm, emotive character of the word *rodnye* is also reflected in the fact that—unlike *relatives* or *rodstvenniki*—it can be used as an endearment, that is, as a form of address, as in the loving graffitti scratched out on prison walls in the following example:

> Vernuvšis' v kameru, ja stal čitat' nadpisi, nacarapannye na narax, na stenax i na podokonnike. Po bol'šej časti éto byli obraščenia k materi, žene ili detjam; obyčno oni končalis' slovami: proščajte, rodnye, na tri goda ili na pjat' let, itp. (Amal'rik 1970:51).

> 'When I came back to the cell, I started to read the graffitti scratched on the bunks, on the walls, and on the window sill. For the most part, these were addressed to mothers, wives, or children; and usually they ended with the words: goodbye, *rodnye*, I won't see you for three years, or for five years, etc.'

Although it is impossible to be quite sure whether *rodnye* is meant here as a noun or as an adjective, its use as an endearment standing on its own is none the less quite telling.

The word *rodstvenniki* (in contrast to *rodnye*) is also used in contexts where for some reason the speaker wishes to speak about relatives in a fully detached, objective manner.

Consider, for example, the following dialogue (Litvinova 1994b:11), in which the words *rodnye* and *rodstvenniki* are used in close succession (the speakers are a KGB officer and the dissident Larissa Bogoraz, whose husband, a human rights campaigner, Anatolij Marčenko, is on the verge of death in a Soviet prison):

ON: My predlagaem vam drugoj vyxod—nemedlenno podat' zajavlenie ob émigracii v Izrail' vašej sem'i—muža, syna, i vas.

L: . . . ja dolžna obsudit' vaše predloženie s rodnymi i druz'jami.

ON: S synom Pašej?

L: I s nim, i so staršim synom.

ON: No ved' on tože možet vyexat' v Izrail'. U ego ženy tam rodstvenniki.

L: Rodstvennikov net. . . .

'HE: We would suggest a different solution: that you apply immediately for emigration to Israel for your family—your husband, your son, and yourself.

L: I would need to discuss your suggestion with my *rodnye* and *druz'ja* (family and friends).

HE: With your son Paša?

L: With him too, and with my older son.

HE: But you know, he, too, can go to Israel. His wife has relatives [*rodstvenniki*] there.

L: No, she doesn't.

Thus, Larissa's sons are for her *rodnye* with whom she wants to consult before taking any important decision concerning herself and her family; clearly, they are not in the same category as some presumed relatives of her daughter-in-law.

The phrase *rodnye i druz'ja* used in this passage is also very characteristic and very common in Russian: given the strength and the warmth of the word *druz'ja,* and the marked coolness and detachment of the word *rodstvenniki*, a phrase conjoining the two (?*rodstvenniki i druzja*) would sound odd. Interestingly, even the phrase *semja i druzja* 'family and friends' sounds less felicitous than *rodnye i druzja*, presumably because *semja* doesn't have the connotations of an emotional bond that both *rodnye* and *druzja* share. But the fact that Russian—unlike English or even Polish—has a separate word for one's close relatives seen in that "nearest-and-dearest," "inseparable-and-inalienable" perspective, is culturally revealing. One is reminded in this context of the Russian proverb cited in Dal''s 1955[1882] dictionary of Russian, "Russkij čelovek bez rodni ne živet," roughly "Russians can't live without their kinfolk," and also of various social commentaries emphasizing the importance of family ties in Russia.[9]

But while the word *rodnye* reflects and documents the perceived value of close family ties in Russian culture, it also shows that the boundary between kin and non-kin can be blurred: what is really essential is the existence of enduring and unconditional emotional ties, which are perceived as an important aspect of one's identity, rather than "blood relations" as such. This is why the gloss "one's people," offered for *rodnye* by some Russian-English dictionaries in preference to the less imaginative "relatives" captures the meaning of this word better. In addition, this gloss provides also some insight into the semantic link between the noun *rodnye* and the adjective *rodnoj* (in the plural *rodnye*), although the phrase "one's own people" would be even better, as a parallel to the phrase "one's own" often used by dictionaries to describe one of the meanings of the adjective *rodnoj*.

Usually, dictionaries ascribe three different meanings to the adjective *rodnoj* (fem. *rodnaja*); for example, Wheeler (1972) offers the following glosses:

1. own (by blood relationship in direct line), *rodnoj brat* 'one's brother' (as opposed to cousin, etc.)

2. native, e.g. *rodnaja strana* 'native land', *rodnoj jazyk* 'mother tongue'

3. (as a form of address) (my) dear.

Descriptions of this kind, though useful as a first approximation, do not really explain what is conveyed by this adjective in any one of the following sentences (Dal' 1955[1882]):

Ja prišel k mysli, čto ne po krovi ljudi ljubjat drug druga, ne po rodstvu oni *rodnye* i blizkie, a po duše, po serdečnoj svjazi. (Gladkov).

'I have come to think that people don't love one another because of blood ties, that they are not *rodnye* and close because of kinship, but because of the heart [soul], because of ties of affection.'

Esli svoju dal'nejšuju žizn' Doronin ne predstavljal bez služby v armii, to i svoju voennuju službu on ne predstavljal vne rjadov *rodnoj* divizii. (Čakovskij).

'If Doronin couldn't imagine his future life outside the army, nor could he imagine his military service outside his *rodnaja* division.'

Ax njanja, sdelaj odolžen'e.—Izvol', rodnaja, prikaži.
(Pushkin).

"'Oh, nurse, do me a favor."
"Of course, darling [*rodnaja*], just tell me.'"

A *rodnaja* division (in the army) is not one to which one is "related by blood in direct line," or one where one was born, or a form of address. Rather, it is a division of which one feels a part, which, furthermore, one perceives as an inalienable part of one's life, and to which one feels bound "by one's heart" ("po duše, po serdečnoj svjazi").

The same assumptions are also part of the adjective *rodnoj* (fem. *rodnaja*) when it is used as a term of address, which is why when Pushkin's heroine Tatjana addresses her old nanny as *rodnaja*, this form of address means infinitely more than "dear." When this adjective is used as a form of address outside the family, and outside the domestic circle, its great emotional strength is also linked with the implications of belonging, a total lack of distance, and the existence of ties felt to be absolute and unseverable.

The land where one was born (*rodnaja strana*), the language spoken in that land (*rodnoj jazyk*), the family one was born into (*rodnoj otec, rodnaja mat', rodnye bratʹja, rodnye sestry*), all these things define (from a Russian cultural perspective) who one is and where one's heart is going to be. These cultural assumptions are reflected in the semantics of both the adjective *rodnoj* and the noun *rodnye*. One's *rodnye* are people who are related to one by ties that cannot be severed and whom one values and cherishes as an inalienable part of one's life and one's identity, people to whom one is "attached" both existentially and emotionally in some absolute sense.

As a first approximation, then, I would propose the following (partial) explication of this key concept:

(my) rodnye
(a) I think about these people like this:
(b) these people are like a part of me
(c) I am like a part of these people
(d) it cannot be otherwise
(e) when I think about these people, I feel something very good

It has often been suggested that the importance of friendship in a society grows as the family ties weaken. But in Russia, both friendship and family ties appear to be valued very highly (at least from an Anglo perspective). Words such as *rodnye* and *druzʹja* support the view that "Russians . . . value warm interpersonal relations to an unusually high degree" (Bauer, Inkeles & Kluckhohn 1956:110), and that this applies to family and friends alike. The survival of these words as key Russian words supports the view that in Russia, as in many other countries, certain basic personality patterns and patterns of interpersonal relations have a tendency to be enduring despite sweeping changes in politics, economy, and social structures.[10]

4. Patterns of "friendship" in Polish culture

The area of human relations which is covered in English by the term *friend* is divided
in Polish into three different categories, corresponding to three nouns (all of them very
common in everyday speech). These nouns are *przyjaciel* (glossed by Polish-English
dictionaries as "friend"), *kolega* (cognate to, and in some uses corresponding to, the
English word *colleague*), and *znajomy* (derived from *znać* 'to know', and glossed by
Polish-English dictionaries as "acquaintance"). It could be objected that—leaving
aside more or less "slangy" words such as *pal*, *chum*, and *buddy* (which will be
discussed later)—English has two nouns, not one, for classifying the semantic area
under discussion: *friend* and *acquaintance*. But in fact, *acquaintance* is only a
marginal word in colloquial English. Its frequency is very low and the range of
syntactic frames in which it can appear is also quite limited. For example, while one
can say

She is an old acquaintance of mine.

one can hardly use this word referentially:

? I talked about it with an acquaintance of mine.
? I had lunch with two acquaintances.

There are no similar limitations on the use of the Polish word *znajomy*.

Since each of the three Polish nouns listed above has its counterpart of the
feminine gender—*przyjaciółka*, *koleżanka*, and *znajoma*—it could be argued that
Polish provides a basic grid with six rather than three categories in the area of *friend*.
Unlike the Russian pair *drug* and *podruga*, however, Polish pairs such as *przyjaciel*
and *przyjaciółka* do not exhibit any semantic differences in addition to gender and can
be regarded as purely grammatical variants of the same lexical unit.

In examining these three Polish "folk categories," the social anthropologist Janine
Wedel (1986) writes: "Apart from family, in general Poles maintain contact with
przyjaciele (close friends), *koledzy* (colleagues from school, work or other common
experiences) and *znajomi* (acquaintances)" (103). And, "Family, very close friends,
colleagues and 'good acquaintances' are the four types of individuals Poles invite into
their homes for dinner or 'parties'" (112).

Assuming, then, that in Polish the basic lexical grid for interpersonal relations
(apart from family) has three categories, not six (*przyjaciel*, *kolega*, and *znajomy*), I
will note that this is still three times as many as English (with its cover-all category
of *friend*), though not quite as many as Russian (with its five basic lexical categories
of *drug*, *podruga*, *prijatel'*, *tovarišč*, and *znakomyj*). This suggests that Polish culture
places a greater emphasis on different types of interpersonal relations than Anglo
culture but doesn't go quite as far in this direction as Russian culture. This is consistent
with the implications of the different systems of expressive derivation of names, with
both Polish and Russian systems being much more highly developed than the English
one, but with Russian having an even more elaborate system than Polish.

To give the reader some idea of how common the three Polish words under
discussion are, I will adduce some data from frequency dictionaries. In Carroll et al.'s

(1971) dictionary of English, the frequency of *friend* is 226 to 1 million running words, whereas that of *colleague* is 6, and of *acquaintance* 5, and the corresponding figures in Kučera and Francis (1967) are 298, 32, and 9. In the Kurcz et al. (1990) dictionary of Polish, the frequency of *przyjaciel* (and *przyjaciółka)* is 132, that of *kolega* (and *koleżanka*) 242, and that of *znajomy* (and *znajoma*) 46.

Of course (as mentioned earlier), frequency data of this kind are only broadly indicative and can only be taken as an approximation. Nonetheless, they strongly support native speakers' intuitive impression that in English, *friend* is a very common word, whereas *colleague* and *acquaintance* are not; and also, that in Polish all three words (*kolega, przyjaciel,* and *znajomy*) are common, though not to the same degree, with *kolega* being the most common one in the group.

4.1   *Koledzy* (Masc. Pl.) and *koleżanki* (Fem. Pl.)

The *Kościuszko Foundation dictionary* (1959–1961) glosses the word *kolega* as "fellow companion; comrade, (in an institution etc.) colleague; (among workers) mate; *colloquial* buddy." It also offers glosses for two common collocations: *serdeczny* (Adj. from *serce* 'heart') *kolega*—"chum," and *kolega szkolny* (adj. from *szkoła* 'school')—"classmate."

As this rather heterogeneous collection of glosses suggests, *kolega* is really quite a different concept from the English *colleague*. Not only is it—unlike *colleague*—a very common everyday word, but its sphere of application is very wide, ranging from "chums" and "buddies" through ordinary classmates (among schoolchildren) and "mates" (among workers) to professional colleagues.

Like the English concept of 'friend', the Polish concept of 'kolega' can cover a wide range of degrees of closeness and intimacy, from very close to very distant. The difference is that Polish, unlike English, does have a separate word for a relation involving a high degree of closeness and intimacy, namely, *przyjaciel.* The wide range of use of the word *kolega*, therefore, does not suggest that closeness and intimacy are not perceived as sufficiently important in Polish culture to merit lexicalization but rather that there are some other values in this culture which are also perceived as extremely important.

Since the most common use of the words *koledzy* (Masc. Pl.) and *koleżanki* (Fem. Pl.) is no doubt with reference to schoolchildren and university students, it is natural to look for a clue to the core values reflected in these words in this use; and the clue offered by this most common use is clear: *koledzy* are equals who are doing the same things and doing them together. For example, classmates are students of equal rank who are "doing the same things" (studying) in the same place (at school).

In the case of *koledzy*, however, the "equality of rank" is not interpreted as specifically as in the case of *classmates*. Normally, it is assumed that one's *koledzy* are from the same grade, but a *starszy kolega* (literally 'an older *kolega*', i.e. a boy from a higher grade) is also possible; and at the university, *koledzy* can be at different stages of their university career. What really matters, then, is not equal age but equal status; and this equal status has to be based on shared activities within some sort of institutional framework.

The idea of shared activities is one of the dimensions which distinguish the Polish concept of 'koledzy' from the Russian concept of 'tovarišči'. Although at school, a Polish boy has a set of *koledzy* (classmates), and a Russian boy, a set of *tovarišči*, and although both these words refer to equal status and to shared life experiences, for the Russian concept, the most important thing is that the same things HAPPEN to the whole group, whereas for the Polish concept, the most important thing is that the whole group DOES the same things.

This is why in Russian one can also speak of *tovarišči po nesčast'ju* ('fellow-sufferers' or 'comrades in misfortune') or *tovarišči po kamere* 'fellow prisoners', whereas the Polish word *koledzy* cannot be used in such contexts. For example, to refer to one's "fellow sufferers" one would have to say in Polish *towarzysze w nieszczęściu*, not **koledzy w nieszczęściu*. The Polish word *towarzysz*, cognate with the Russian *tovarišč*, can be used in such contexts, but it is a much more marginal word in modern Polish and is not used for describing "normal" human relations such as those prevailing in schools, universities, army, or the workplace. In Polish, one speaks of *koledzy z pracy* 'koledzy from work', *koledzy z wojska* 'koledzy from the army', *koledzy szkolni* 'koledzy from school', and so on, not *towarzysze z pracy, z wojska,* or *ze szkoły* (from work, the army, or school).

The shared institutional framework mentioned earlier is also important, which is why English words such as *buddy* or *chum* mentioned by the Kościuszko dictionary can be misleading as glosses for *kolega* (although there is also in Polish an expressive word *koleś*, derived from *kolega*, which jocularly extends the use of *kolega* outside institutional frameworks, and which can indeed be loosely compared with *buddy*).

Of course, the main difference between *chum* or *buddy* on the one hand and *kolega* on the other is sociolinguistic rather than semantic: the former two are (more or less) slang words, whereas the latter has no links with slang whatsoever. In addition, however, there are also important semantic differences, which illuminate certain aspects of the meaning of *kolega*.

First, *buddy* implies an exclusive relationship based on personal preferences and restricted to a very small number of participants (typically, two), whereas *kolega* applies to an entire set of equals within a certain institutional framework, regardless of any personal preferences. *Chum* doesn't necessarily imply an exclusive relationship, but it, too, implies a degree of personal attraction and personal preference. Consequently, one's relations with one's *buddies* or one's *chums* are, by definition, good: if they spoil, the *buddies* cease to be *buddies*, and the *chums* cease to be *chums*. By contrast, one's relations with one's *koledzy*, while expected to be good, can also be bad, because this relationship is defined by the institutional framework, not by personal choice.

Importantly, in institutional frameworks there are many people in the same position. In this sense, being a *kolega* is not a private, interpersonal relationship but a social relationship, defined with reference to a whole social group. Even when a waiter in a cafe (in "People's Poland") tried to fob off an exasperated customer, after a long wait, with the customary phrase *kolega załatwi* 'a *kolega* will take your order', there was an implicit reference to the establishment as a whole, with a set of employees with equal status and the same duties.[11]

This is not to say, however, that *kolega* has no affective component. Although one's *koledzy* are not personally chosen but are given to one within a certain institutional framework, the word carries an implication of solidarity and mutual good feelings: even if my relations with my *koledzy* happen to be poor, or temporarily soured, nonetheless the word still carries an implication that when I think of them 'I feel something good' (although these "good feelings" may be mixed with temporary "bad feelings").

The solidarity with one's *koledzy* is based on the perception that within a certain framework we are all equals, that we do the same things, and that I know these people well (though not necessarily very well), and with a kind of concomitant group identification: 'these people are people like me'.

All these considerations lead us to the following explication:

(my) koledzy
(a) everyone knows: many people think about some other people like this:
(b) these people are people like me
(c) I know these people well
(d) I do many things in one place
(e) these people are often in the same place
(f) these people do the same things as I
(g) I think these people think the same about me
(h) when people think like this about other people, they feel something good
(i) I think like this about these people

In this explication I have not used a format starting with the component 'I think about this person/these people like this' in order to account for the fact that *koledzy* can be either people with whom "I DO the same things, in the same place" or people with whom "I DID (have done) the same things, in the same place." Since the relationship is conceptualized as unitary, whether it has its basis in the present or in the past, I don't want to use a disjunction in the explication ("I do or I did"). The phrasing suggested here overcomes this difficulty: the prototypical *koledzy* relationship refers to the present situation (components [d], [e], [f]); at the same time component (i) indicates that I see my own relationship with some people (my *koledzy*) in the same light, without actually implying that I do now the same things as those people do.

The explication proposed here, therefore, is consistent with the fact that phrases such as *koledzy z wojska* 'koledzy from the army' or *koledzy ze studiów* 'koledzy from the university' may refer to relationships rooted in the past.

This analysis of the concept of *koledzy*, corresponds, on the whole, quite closely to that proposed, from a different perspective, by Wedel (1986):

> *Koledzy* are colleagues brought together by formal organizations or common experience. *Koledzy* can be close friends—often those with whom one forms lasting bonds. But *koledzy* and *koleżanki* (the female form of *koledzy*) are also everyone with whom one works, even if one started work one week ago. *Koledzy* are relationships formed through an institutional base or common experience. Hence, schoolgirls have *koledzy* or *koleżanki* from school; university students have *koledzy* or *koleżanki* from the university; most adults have *koledzy* or *koleżanki* from work; many people over 50

have *koledzy* or *koleżanki* from the war or the resistance; and almost all males 18 years of age and older have *koledzy* from the army. (105)

The only aspect of Wedel's analysis that I would disagree with is that concerning the permanence of the *koledzy* relationship:

People are *koledzy* and *koleżanki* for life, years after the formal organization or common experience that first made them so no longer brings them together.

Poles who lived through the war together, comrades in the underground or the Warsaw uprising developed special *koledzy* relationships. *Koledzy* and *koleżanki* from school or work from days past often operate as "old boy networks," relying on each other to solve problems. Though *koledzy* and *przyjaciele* are people through whom one can *załatwić sprawy* [get things arranged], these relationships are often of a moral quality, as in family relationships. *Koledzy* may now be engaged in vastly different pursuits, yet they continue to meet getting together for drinking parties, reunions and nameday celebrations. In some cases their ties may be even stronger than kin ties.

A 50-year-old professor of mathematics still meets frequently with her *koleżanki* from secondary school for coffee klatsch and nameday celebrations. She has a higher position than her *koleżanki*, but they all belong to one *środowisko*. Likewise, a 62-year-old working class man meets often with his *koledzy* from a World War II underground resistance organization. (105–106)

It is quite true that people are often *koledzy* and *koleżanki* for life. But the concept as such implies, roughly speaking, equality within an institutional framework, without necessarily implying permanence: whether or not the bond will be regarded as permanent depends on the importance of a given institutional framework in people's lives. In this respect, therefore, the bond of *koleżeństwo* (abstract noun derived from *kolega*) is not like the family bond.

Nonetheless the salient role of this kind of relationship in Polish culture, reflected in the prominent place of the words *koledzy* and *koleżanki* in the Polish lexicon (alongside *rodzina*, *przyjaciele*, and *znajomi*), calls for an explanation. I believe that such an explanation can be found in Poland's history and, in particular, in the concept of the "noble ethos," expounded particularly well by the British historian Norman Davies (1984):

Of all the products of Polish life before the Partitions, the Polish nobility—the *Szlachta* and all their works—might seem to have been the most discredited. . . . In fact, though the legal status of *szlachta* was annulled in 1795 by the partitioning powers, its ideals lived on. The *kultura szlachecka* (the noble ethos) has become one of the central features of the modern Polish outlook.

As it happened, the annulment of *szlachta*'s legal status rendered a signal service to their reputation . . . The mass of the *déclassé* nobility shared the misfortunes of the common people, and, as the main educated element, could act as their tribunes. What is more, in mourning the fate of their own defunct estate, they could interpret the attacks on their own battered ideals as an assault on the beliefs of the entire population. In this way, the ex-*szlachta* became the pioneers of the new intelligentsia; the former 'noble nation' was transformed and expanded to include all social classes of the new, universal Polish nation; and the *kultura szlachecka*—with its ideas of exclusivity, equality, unanimity, resistance, and individualism—continued to provide the guidelines for Polish social and political thought. In the old days, only the *Szlachta* could address each other as *pan* (Lord) or *pani* (Lady). Nowadays, it is the normal form of address for everyone. Two hundred years after the formal abolition of the *Szlachta* most people in Poland are content to think of themselves as honorary nobles. (331–333)

Most important in the present context is the *Szlachta's* old ideal of equality (within their own class). Having described the *Szlachta's* deplorable attitudes labeled sometimes as "Noble Racism" and "Vanity of Birth," Davies goes on:

> More attractively perhaps, the *Szlachta* were devoted to the principle of treating each other as equals. All noblemen called each other 'Brother'. Except for the princes of Lithuania, whose titles had to be confirmed to gain their acceptance to the Union of Lublin, all titulation in the old Republic was legally banned. All noble citizens, irrespective of wealth or office, enjoyed the same civil liberties, and full equality before the Law. Phrases implying that some nobles were more equal than others— such as 'magnate' or 'lesser nobility'—were struck from the record of the Diet. No one could seriously contend that all members of the *Szlachta* were equal in all respects, since the gamut of wealth and power was enormous. But the final fiction of equality was an important social lubricant, which added greatly to the sense of solidarity within the broad mass of the nobility as a whole. After the partitions, the ex-nobles shared the 'democracy' of the oppressed and the deprived—where the old ideal could be preserved in new forms. (333)

I would suggest that the old ideal of the "solidarity of equals" (within the confines of one social group) has found its expression in the key Polish concept of *koledzy* (and *koleżanki.*)

Speaking of the ideal of the "solidarity of equals," it is impossible not to think of the name of the Polish Solidarity union and the Solidarity movement of 1980–1981, which is widely believed to have initiated the process of the collapse of communism in Eastern Europe. It would be difficult to doubt that the rush of nationwide popular support for Solidarity had something to do with the fact that the ideal referred to in this name struck a vital chord in the Polish national psyche. As Norman Davies (1981) wrote, perceptively and sympathetically, at the time: "The Polish working class can be seen to be reviving the political traditions of the Noble Democracy—traditions which appear to have survived almost two hundred years of suppression" (724). The fact that in Polish the concept of *koledzy*, with its emphasis on equality and solidarity of existentially linked free individuals, has become a key concept in the national folk-philosophy is also a reflection of the strength of those traditions.

The word *kolega* is, of course, a loan word in Polish, as *colleague* is in English. But the fact that on Polish soil this loan word has greatly expanded its range of use (and its meaning) and has turned into one of the language's key words for categorizing human relations suggests that there was something in its meaning which tallied well with the Polish ethos.

In English, the word *colleague* (which, as we have seen, has a very low frequency anyway) is restricted to professional elites, and it doesn't have the implications of "shared existence" characteristic of the Polish *kolega*. Its meaning can be explicated as follows:

(my) colleagues
(a) I think about these people like this:
(b)   these people are people like me
(c)   these people do things of the same kind as I do
(d)   not many other people do things of this kind
(e)   I think something good about these people
(f)   I think these people know a lot about some things
(g)   because of this, these people can do things of this kind
(h) I think these people think the same about me

The first two components of this explication, as well as the last one, are essentially the same as in the explication of the Polish word *koledzy*, but the other ones are different. In particular, component (d) points to the somewhat elitist connotations of the word *colleague*, (e) to the respect implied by it, and (f) and (g) to its professional implications. On the other hand, this explication does not include the components of familiarity ('I know these people well'), of affection ('when I think about these people, I feel something good'), or of an existential bond, based on doing things together in the same place that is characteristic of the Polish concept of 'koledzy' (cf. components [d]–[f] in the explication of this word). Furthermore, the word *colleagues* does not embrace the past in the way *koledzy* does: whereas in Polish, people with a shared past may well be referred to as *koledzy*, in English, people from one's past are usually referred to as "former colleagues" rather than simply "colleagues." This is why the explication of *colleagues* can start with the component 'I think about these people like this', whereas that of *koledzy* needs to be done via a prototype.

Since the original meaning of the French word *collègue* (and the Latin *collega*) was similarly restricted to privileged elites and didn't have the existential implications of *kolega*, one could say that within Polish this word has both increased in "existential weight" and undergone far-reaching democratization.

Nonetheless, the salience of the concept 'kolega', with its emphasis on equality, in Polish language and Polish culture should not be taken to mean that the Polish ethos is superegalitarian (in the way, for example, the Australian ethos is). As Wedel (1986) rightly emphasizes, the concept of 'koledzy' celebrates the equality of people who share the same status, and so, in a way, it emphasizes, rather than de-emphasizes, differences between different social statuses:

For example, a professor at the university is on very friendly terms with her secretary. While on vacation in Romania and Bulgaria, they have met several times, the professor taking the secretary out to dinner. The secretary did not elect to take sick leave from work (to the amazement of her physician) even when she was quite ill. She felt obligated to finish a typing job, even working overtime without extra pay, to meet her boss's deadline. Despite their affection and respect for one another . . . they will not become *koleżanki* (colleagues) or refer to each other as *ty*. The two women appreciate the difference in their status, which will remain clearly defined. Though it is often in the best interest of both parties to establish a personal relationship, this by no means blurs the distinct social hierarchical structure. (111)

Observations of this kind tally well with the wide use of professional titles in Polish, especially as forms of address (e.g. *Panie Profesorze* 'Mr. Professor', *Panie Doktorze* 'Mr. Doctor', *Panie Inżynierze* 'Mr. Engineer', *Panie Mecenasie* 'Mr. Lawyer', *Panie Naczelniku* 'Mr. Head', and so on; cf. e.g. Bogusławski 1990), which Poles themselves often ridicule as the Polish *tytułomania* 'mania for titles'.

In the passage adduced earlier, Norman Davies mentions that in the past, all Polish nobles called each other "Brother." Speaking more precisely, they commonly called each other *Panie Bracie,* that is, so to speak, "Lord Brother," thus emphasizing both their equality and their status. The modern Polish word *kolega*, which can also be used as a title, has a similar double point: while it seems to emphasize equality more than status, it still celebrates both: equality AND status, or equality within a certain status.

4.2 *Przyjaciel* ('close friend')

Przyjaciel (the feminine counterpart *przyjaciółka*) is normally glossed by Polish-English dictionaries as "friend," but in fact it means much more. Eva Hoffman (1989), writing from the perspective of a Polish teenager transplanted with her family to North America, comments on these differences:

> I trust Penny to explain some of these things to me. She is a happy, bouncy young person, curly haired and ruddy cheeked, and she is the smart girl in class, the one who always gets the best grades. Penny is a native Vancouverite, and Vancouver, as far as she is concerned, is the best place on earth, though I, of course, know that it is Cracow. We like each other quite well, though I'm not sure that what is between us is "friendship"—a word which in Polish has connotations of strong loyalty and attachment bordering on love. At first, I try to preserve the distinction between "friends" and "acquaintances" scrupulously, because it feels like a small lie to say "friend" when you don't really mean it, but after a while, I give it up. "Friend," in English, is such a good-natured, easygoing sort of term, covering all kinds of territory, and "acquaintance" is something an uptight, snobbish kind of person might say. . . .
> As the word is used here, Penny is certainly a friend, and we spend many hours together, gossiping about our classmates and teachers and futures. And, of course, about dates. (148)

Clearly, the Polish words that Hoffman has in mind are *przyjaciel* (Masc.), *przyjaciółka* (Fem.), and *przyjaźń* (abstract noun); and trying to show how these "more weighty" words differ from the "good-natured," "easygoing" English word *friend*, she mentions "strong loyalty and attachment bordering on love." Other commentators concur in the view that *przyjaciel* "means more" than *friend*, but try to explain the difference in other terms. For example, the Polish sociologist Stefan Nowak (quoted in Wedel 1986) emphasizes the readiness and, indeed, obligation to help as one important function of "friends" in Polish culture:

> When Americans say about someone "he is my best friend," at the most we can say that the Polish equivalent of that is "good acquaintance." That which would correspond with friendship in our understanding is simply lacking in many cultures. To our friends we can go for help in many difficult situations and, in relation to them, we are obligated to offer help. A lot of Poles would go very far both in their

expectations of real help and in terms of offering such help to their friends. Having a circle of *przyjaciele* increases the feeling of safety, both in psychological as well as in very "practical" aspects of life. (104)

But while both Hoffman's and Nowak's remarks are apt and valid as sociological comments, the meaning of *przyjaciel* (and *przyjaciółka*) is, I think, even more clearly illuminated by the following examples of use from Polish literature quoted in the *Dictionary of the Polish language* (SJP):

> Miałem serdecznego przyjaciela, który, jak sądzę, otwierał przede mną swoją duszę na oścież. (Świętochowski)

> 'I had a close *przyjaciel*, who, I believe, used to fully open his heart (soul) to me.'

> Przyjaźń prawdziwa tylko tam istnieć może, gdzie pomiędzy przyjaciołmi [przyjaciłmi] istnieje ustawiczne i nieprzerwane porozumienie. (Kaczkowski).

> 'True *przyjaźń* (friendship) can exist only where there is constant communication and understanding between the *przyjaciele*.'

> Nie lubiła zwierzeń i nie miała przyjaciółki pomiędzy koleżankami, z którymi żyła na stopie pewnej wyniosłści. (Reymont)

> 'She didn't like confidences and she had no *przyjaciółka* among her *koleżanki*, from whom she maintained a somewhat haughty distance.'

> Zrób ze mnie swoją powiernicę, przyjaciółkę: miej do mnie zaufanie, jak do własnej matki. (Sewer)

> 'Make me your confidante, your *przyjaciółka*: trust me, like your own mother.'

What these examples highlight is the assumption of a "special relationship" based on "intimate communication." Compare also the comment made by the poet Czesław Miłosz (1972:147) about another Polish writer, Ksawery Pruszyński:

> Stosunki nasze były kordialne, ale nie zasługiwały na miano przyjaźni. Prowadziliśmy czasem zupełnie szczere rozmowy, ograniczone jednak do polityki; inny wymiar, który mnie interesował, był Ksaweremu obcy.

> 'Our relations were cordial, but they did not deserve the name of friendship [*przyjaźń*]. We sometimes had long talks which were completely open, but they were restricted to politics; another dimension, which interested me, was alien to Ksawery.'

This assumption of a "special relationship based on an intimate communication" can be represented along the following lines (as in the explication of the earlier meaning of *friend*):

> *(my) przyjaciel/przyjaciółka*
> (a) everyone knows: many people think about some other people like this:
> (b)   I know this person very well
> (c)   I think good things about this person
> (d)   often when I think something, I can't say it to other people
> (e)   I can say it to this person

    (f)   I want this person to know what I think
    (g)   I want this person to know what I feel
    (h)   I think this person thinks the same about me
    (i) I think like this about this person
    (j) I don't think like this about many other people
    (k) when I think about this person, I feel something very good

As for the "strong loyalty" mentioned by Hoffman and the "obligation to offer help" mentioned by Nowak, I believe that they simply follow, or can be seen as following, from the defining components of this relationship spelled out above. In particular, I would argue that *przyjaciel*—unlike the Russian *drug*—does not embody assumptions about mutual help as a necessary part of the concept. The members of one's *rodzina* ('family'), too, are expected to provide help, but this expectation has not found its way into the very meaning of the word *rodzina*; and I think the same is true of *przyjaciel*.

It is difficult to prove the absence of a component, of course, and the onus should be on the person who would wish to argue that such a component is necessarily included. Nonetheless, I can point to some differences in the collocations of *drug* and *przyjaciel* which suggest that the meanings of these two words differ in this respect.

To begin with, we should note that the most common collocations of the Polish word are *bliski* ('close') *przyjaciel*, *najbliższy* ('the closest') *przyjaciel*, and *serdeczny* (Adjective from *serce* 'heart') *przyjaciel*. What these collocations imply is something like intimacy and affection.

Similar collocations are also characteristic of *drug*; in addition, however, *drug* has a different set of collocations, referring to something like "reliability in need" (such as *nadežnyj drug* 'reliable *drug*' and *ispytannyj drug* 'tested *drug*'). In fact, phrases such as *nastojaščij drug* or *istinnyj drug* 'true *drug*' would normally be interpreted in Russian as referring to reliability in need. By contrast, the Polish phrase *prawdziwy przyjaciel* 'true *przyjaciel*' would normally be interpreted as referring to "true closeness" (linked with a true baring of hearts and sharing of hidden thoughts), rather than to "true reliability."

Even the parallel collocations *wierny przyjaciel* and *vernyj drug* 'faithful friend' would tend to have somewhat different interpretations. The Polish phrase would be likely to be taken to refer to someone who is constant in maintaining the relationship and doesn't discontinue it in changed circumstances, whereas the Russian phrase would be more likely to be taken to refer to someone who is constant in his or her support and help in need.[12]

In addition to the differences in collocations and in the interpretation of comparable collocations, it is also noteworthy that Polish has no phrase corresponding to *bud'drugom* ('be a *drug*'), which in Russian introduces a request for help. This is not to say, of course, that in Poland people don't expect to receive help from their *przyjaciele*, or to offer it in case of need, but only that this is not how the conceptual category in question is defined. Readiness to help is a (likely) consequence of the relationship, not its basis.

4.3   *Znajomi* ('close acquaintances')

Ukłoniłsię znajomym z daleka, bez zbytniej uprzejmości. (1953, SJP)

'He bowed to his *znajomi* from afar, without excessive politeness.'

.   Wyszli razem, bo mial ją odprowadzić do parku, gdzie czekały na nią znajome. (1949, SJP)

'They left together, because he was to see her off to the park, where her *znajome* were waiting for her.'

Po paru godzinach spędzonych w tym miłym saloniku, gwarzyli już z sobą jak starzy znajomi. (1901, SJP)

'After a few hours spent in this pleasant drawing-room, they were chatting with one another like old *znajomi*.'

Wszystkich przyjacioł i znajomych swoich, bez względu na wiek i płeć, zaprosił do siebie na bankiet, chcąc się z nimi pożegnać. (1779, SJP).

'He invited all his friends [*przyjaciele*] and *znajomi*, regardless of their age and sex, to his house for a banquet, because he wanted to say good-bye to them.'

Znajomi (glossed by Polish-English dictionaries as "acquaintances" and derived from *znać* 'to know') are, literally, "known ones," that is, people whom one knows. But in fact, 'being known' is only one component of the meaning of this important word. As many "participant observers" of both cultures (Polish and Anglo) have noted, the relationship between "znajomi" would often be described in English by means of the word *friends*, and only a small proportion of Polish *znajomi* could be described in English as *acquaintances*. If the English word *friend* means, so to speak, less than the Polish *przyjaciel*, *acquaintance* means less than *znajomy*. To put it differently, the English *friend* covers most of the territory shared in Polish between *przyjaciel* and *znajomy*, and—from a Polish point of view—it seems to obscure an important conceptual distinction. Consequently, for many Polish immigrants to English-speaking countries, accustomed and attached to their own universe of social relations, the need to preserve the distinction between *przyjaciele* and *znajomi* leads to identifying *przyjaciele* with *friends* and *znajomi* with *acquaintances*. For example, Hoffman notes that while she herself, after a while, gave up trying to preserve the distinction between "friends" and "acquaintances" scrupulously, her parents "never divested themselves of the habit, and with an admirable resistance to linguistic looseness, continue to call most people they know my acquaintance—or, as they put it early on, mine acquaintance." But in fact, what Hoffman's parents show is not really "admirable resistance to linguistic looseness" but rather unconscious transfer of Polish conceptual categories into English: they say "acquaintances" when they mean *znajomi*.

One wonders in this connection whether Joseph Conrad's insistence on distinguishing a "friend" from a mere "acquaintance" (as in the quote below) is not similarly due to the influence of Polish: "You understand that I am not their friend. I am only a holiday acquaintance" (quoted in *Webster's third*).

Janine Wedel (1986), too, tends to identify *znajomi* with "acquaintances" when she writes:

The most distant relationships are those of *znajomi* (acquaintances). *Znajomi* has a broad meaning; it can refer to people that one sees frequently, or to those one has just met. Neighbours often become close acquaintances, aided by their proximity and the long time period, often years, in which they have to build relationships and engage in exchange. Hence there are "close" and "distant" acquaintances, as well as long-term and short-term acquaintances. (107).

But this is not quite accurate. *Rodzina* can indeed be described as *bliska* or *najbliższa* ('close' or 'closest') and *daleka* or *dalsza* ('distant' or 'more distant'), but *znajomi* cannot be described as *dalecy* or *dalsi* (plural). They can, on the other hand, be described as *bliscy* or *dobrzy* ('close' or 'good'). The same applies to *przyjaciele*, who can be either *przyjaciele* tout court, or *bliscy przyjaciele* 'close *przyjaciele*', but not *dalecy przyjaciele* ('distant *przyjaciele*').[13] What these collocations suggest is that *znajomi*, unlike *acquaintances*, are seen as people whom one knows fairly well and with whom one has a bond which is far from negligible: not only *bliscy znajomi* and *dobrzy znajomi*, but any kind of *znajomi*. From this point of view, *znajomi* are more like English *friends* than like English *acquaintances*.

The very fact that one often speaks in Polish of *dobrzy znajomi* 'good *znajomi*', and *bliscy znajomi* 'close *znajomi*', highlights the difference between *znajomi* and *acquaintances* and the similarity between *znajomyi* and *friends*: in English, one can speak of "good friends" and "close friends" but not of "good acquaintances" or "close acquaintances."

Eva Hoffman's friend who doesn't quite qualify as a *przyjaciółka* could not be described as Eva's *znajoma* either. In Polish, Penny would be described as a *koleżanka*, and although one of one's *koleżanki* can become one's *przyjaciółka*, a *koleżanka* can never be described as a *znajoma*. Loosely speaking, the reason seems to be that the category of *znajomi* implies a certain reserve and voluntary distance, which are incompatible with the solidarity of *koleżanki*. It is also interesting to note that children can't have *znajomi* at all, although the categories of *przyjaciele/przyjaciółki* and *koledzy/koleżanki* are perfectly applicable to them. The word *znajomi* is parallel in this respect to the polite titles *Pan* and *Pani*, which also cannot be used for children. Normally, *przyjaciele* and *koledzy* would address each other with the "familiar" form *ty*, whereas *znajomi* would use the "unfamiliar" forms *Pan* and *Pani*. The correspondence between the forms of address and the lexical categorization of human relations is certainly striking. One could say that both forms of address and lexical categories of human relations suggest that Polish culture values gradation in and barriers to intimacy and closeness, as well as intimacy and closeness as such.

Consider, for example, the possibilities available for addressing a Professor Tadeusz Kowalski. When I address this person, my basic options include: *Tadziu, Tadek, Tadeusz, Panie Tadziu, Panie Tadku, Panie Tadeuszu, Panie Profesorze*. Each of these options implies a different kind of relationship and, roughly speaking, a different degree of "closeness," "intimacy," and "familiarity." For example, the combination of the diminutive form *Tadziu* with the polite title *Panie* in *Panie Tadziu* implies that I wish to convey something like affection for the addressee while also setting a certain barrier between us.

Given the value placed in Polish culture on "degrees" of familiarity, closeness, and intimacy, one can well understand why the Polish emigré poet and professor of Slavic literatures at Harvard University, Stanisław Barańczak, includes the following item on his "list of things American which E.E. [East European] will never be able to come to terms with": "being addressed on a first-name basis by strangers" (1990:11).

What I am suggesting, then, is that by defining many of their personal relationships in terms of *znajomi*, Poles are also setting and acknowledging certain barriers in these relationships. Relationships without social barriers (those with *przyjaciele* and *rodzina*) are also valued, of course, but so are those with deliberately set barriers (i.e. those with *znajomi*). This can be represented as follows:

(my) znajomi
(a) everyone knows: many people think about some other people like this:
(b) I know these people well
(c) I don't want to say: very well
(d) I can say things of some kinds to these people
(e) I don't want to say things of some other kinds to these people
(f) when I say things to these people, I often feel something good
(g) I think these people think the same about me
(h) I think like this about these people

In this formula, the "barriers" are represented in the components (c) and (e), whereas the closeness of the relationship is represented in (b) and (f). Component (b) reflects the fact that *znajomi* are people of one's own social circle, people with whom one maintains social relations, whereas (f) reflects the voluntary and the pleasurable character of these contacts.

It could be argued that the English concept of 'acquaintance', too, sets barriers in social relations. But first, as mentioned earlier, this concept is quite marginal in English, whereas in Polish the concept of *znajomi* has considerable significance in people's lives; and second, the concept of 'acquaintance' does not apply to fairly close relationships at all, whereas that of *znajomi* does. *Znajomi*, in contrast to *acquaintances*, are seen as people whom one knows well and contact with whom is perceived as pleasurable or satisfying.

Unlike *przyjaciel*, the concept of *znajomy* does not imply any willingness to confide, to share one's thoughts and feelings with the other person; it does, however, imply a willingness to talk—though not without some barriers on what one is willing to say. Unlike *przyjaciel*, *znajomy* doesn't necessarily imply affection ('when I think about this person, I feel something good'); it does imply, however, "good feelings" related to social (mainly conversational) contact ('when I say things to these people, I often feel something good'). The fact that one could never use the word *znajomi* as a form of address, and hardly as a form of introduction, supports the absence of a 'when I think of these people I feel something good' component in its meaning:

*Znajomy! *Znajomi!
*Przyjaciele i znajomi!

'Friends and acquaintances!'

?*To jest mój znajomy X.

'This is my *znajomy* X.'

The explication of *znajomi*—like that of *koledzy*, and unlike that of *przyjaciel*—has deliberately been phrased in the plural. Although *znajomi* does not refer to any set of people within an institutional framework, as *koledzy* does, it does refer to a circle of people whom one knows and maintains contacts with, and only secondarily to individual members of this circle.

This primacy of the plural is confirmed, to some extent, by statistical data. In the case of *przyjaciel* (and *przyjaciółka*), the frequencies of the singular and the plural (as recorded by Kurcz et al. 1990) are similar (78 vs. 72), in the case of *znajomi* the plural is much more common (14 vs. 32). (As mentioned earlier, such statistical data are not conclusive, but they are nonetheless suggestive.)

Wedel's observation that, for example, "Family, very close friends, colleagues and 'good acquaintances' are the four types of individuals Poles invite into their homes for dinner or parties" (1986:112) acknowledges the importance of *znajomi* as people with whom Poles deliberately maintain contact.

Wedel repeatedly stresses the value of *znajomi* in "People's Poland" as people who could call on each other in times of need, and the derived word *znajomości* referring to networks of mutual help (often stretching the law for private purposes) supports this. At the same time, it is important to recognize that mutual help (whether within the law or not) is not part of the meaning of the word *znajomi* (as it is not part of the meaning of *przyjaciele* or *koledzy*). People like to do something, from time to time, with their *znajomi*—to meet in a coffeehouse, to talk, to visit, to swap political jokes (under communism), to go to the theater or cinema together, and so on—because such contacts and conversations satisfy their social needs and make them "feel something good," and not merely because they expect to get something out of it. The proposed explication reflects that, and it deliberately omits any reference to mutual help.

4.4 Rodzina ('family')

The word *rodzina* is outside the scope of this chapter, strictly speaking, but since it is, as Wedel (1986:103) says, one of the four basic categories used in Polish for categorizing human relations, it does merit a few brief comments.

Looking at the concept of 'rodzina' from an Anglo point of view, one is struck, first of all, by how much territory it covers, in comparison with the English *family*:

> In Poland "the family" may include extended family members such as aunts, uncles and cousins, or the term may refer to immediate family members—children, parents, sometimes grandparents, often people who share a household. People speak of "the closest family," which is defined as either of the above. They speak of "more distant family," those wider kin relations with whom they may or may not have frequent contact. Wedel (1986:99)

Wedel's point referring to the common collocations *najbliższa rodzina* 'the closest family' and *dalsza rodzina* 'more distant family' is very important because it highlights the difference between the concepts 'rodzina' and 'family'. Without a modifier, *rodzina* covers a territory extending far beyond the so-called nuclear family. A distinction between "the closest *rodzina*" and "the more distant *rodzina*" can be made, but "the more distant *rodzina*" is not seen as an "extension" of the same basic core; rather, the whole "extended family" is seen as simply *rodzina*. The expression *najbliższa rodzina* ('the closest *rodzina*') cuts off, so to speak, some real members of the *rodzina*, not some "extensions" to the *rodzina*. This could be compared with the English distinction between *close friends* and *friends*: *close friends* constitute only a subset of *friends*, and similarly, *najbliższa rodzina* constitutes only a subset of *rodzina*. In English, on the other hand, *immediate family* is not seen as a subset of *family*; rather, this phrase seems to emphasize that what is meant is "family" in the strict sense and not "extended family."

I would add that in English, the phrases *extended family* and *nuclear family* belong to the technical language of sociology, not to everyday speech, and that even the phrase *immediate family* sounds like a sociological comment rather than like a "normal" everyday way of speaking (for example, it does not belong to the same register as *close friends*). Normally, one says simply *family*, and while this may include brothers and sisters, or grandparents, it would normally not include aunts, uncles, or cousins.

In Polish, too, one normally says *rodzina*, without modifiers, but this would normally include aunts, uncles, and cousins. The expression *najbliższa rodzina* does not sound like a sociological comment but has a stylistic status comparable to that of *close friends* in English; and the adjective *najbliższa*, like *close* in English, serves here to narrow down the basic category to a subset of this category. To illustrate the meaning of *rodzina* (which she glosses as "family") in Polish, Wedel (1986) cites the following dialogue between herself and one of her Polish friends, Barbara:

> Barbara explained how she plans to go about obtaining a refrigerator when she eventually moves into her brother's apartment.
> "But on whom can you most depend to help you get the refrigerator?" I inquired.
> "Well, on my family. Always."
> "Family, meaning your parents and brother?"
> "No, no," she adamantly replied. "Family means the closest family. Brothers and sisters of my mother, their husbands, their families, the family on my father's side. We can really count on each other." (99)

Wedel comments: "Barbara depends not only on her parents and brother and his in-laws but also on her entire extended family unit." What is worth adding is that Barbara calls this "entire extended family unit" *rodzina* and, when queried, *najbliższa rodzina*.

Thus, what would count for Barbara as *dalsza rodzina* 'more distant *rodzina*' would in English correspond not to *extended family* but to *relatives*. This shows that in Polish, *rodzina* not only covers "immediate family" and "extended family" but extends even further than that, into the territory covered in English by *relatives* (although the word *relatives* as such has a counterpart in the Polish word *krewni*).

But what matters is not only a term's range of use but also its focus (cf. Berlin & Kay 1969), and for *rodzina* and *family* these are different, too. *Family* without a modifier is normally taken to refer to the nuclear family, although it can be extended further than that, whereas *rodzina* without a modifier is normally taken to refer to a group extending far beyond that.

The point is nicely illustrated by Wanda Chotomska's (1967) children's story about a lonely hedgehog who wants to have a *rodzina* and who dreams therefore of finding not only a *żona* (wife) but also a *stryjek* (uncle), a few *ciotki* (aunts), and a *dziadek* (grandfather). The story ends happily with the hero finding some cousins, getting married, and leading a happy life with his *rodzina*, playing Monopoly with his father-in-law and his uncle.

An additional difference between *rodzina* and *family* is that the former emphasizes one's roots (parents, grandparents, past generations), whereas the latter places a special emphasis on one's offspring. Thus, *family* can be used to refer specifically to a couple's children (e.g. "we want to have a family"), but *rodzina* can never be used like that. On the other hand, *rodzina* is often used in combination with the preposition *z* 'from' to describe a person's background. The phrase *z dobrej rodziny* 'from a good *rodzina*' is particularly common:

> One mother asked a series of questions as she tried to assess whether the boyfriend of her engineer daughter would make a suitable husband: "Is he educated? Is he from a good family? . . ." The mother's questions were illustrative of the categories often used to gauge social position.
>   . . . Part of a person's moral status is coming from a good family. In every social milieu or stable community in which families have known each other for many generations, certain families are considered good and certain ones bad. It was said about a prominent Polish journalist, "How can it be that he came from such a 'good family' and became an alcoholic?"
>   A good family may have a history of high moral standards, abilities and discipline for generations. As part of a cultural elite with a particular ethos, members of the traditional intelligentsia have a heritage of education, cultural competence and social service. (Wedel 1986:152–153)

The concept of 'rodzina' can be compared in this respect with that of 'ojczyzna' ('homeland'): they both link a person's personal identity with "where he or she comes from."

Schematically (and without trying to use only primitives), the difference between a comprehensive and "backward-looking" concept of *rodzina* and the much trimmer and "forward-looking" concept of *family* can be represented as follows:

(X's) rodzina
many people
these people are like one thing
because every one of these people is a mother, father, wife, husband, or child of
another one of them
X is part of this thing
X's mother and father are part of this thing
other people are part of this thing

X's family
some people, not many people
these people are like one thing

because every one of these people is a mother, father, wife, husband, or child of
another one of them
X is part of this thing
X's children are part of this thing

4.5 Summary and conclusion

Apart from *rodzina* ('family' and 'extended family'), the Polish taxonomy of human
relations includes three basic categories (*przyjaciel, kolega,* and *znajomy*). None of
these categories has an equivalent in English, although *przyjaciel* is relatively close
to the older English concept 'friend₁' (different from the present-day concept
'friend₂'). *Znajomy*, which can be compared with the Russian *znakomyj* (and the
German *Bekannte*), implies a certain distance and a lack of intimacy, and it extends
over a whole range of relationships covered in English by the words *friends* and
acquaintances, excluding, however, "close friends." *Kolega*, which has a very broad
range of use (applying to schoolchildren and soldiers as well as to professional elites)
is a uniquely Polish concept which emphasizes both equality and status and which
appears to embody the traditional values of the so-called Polish "noble ethos."[14]

5. *Mate*—a key to Australian culture

If one word had to be nominated as a key word in traditional Australian culture, few
would hesitate to nominate the word *mate*. From the first half of the nineteenth century
to the present time, it has been widely felt that the word *mate* provides a key to the
Australian spirit, Australian national character, Australian ethos; and even those who
do not wish to subscribe to this view have to recognize that the word *mate* holds an
exceptionally important place in the Australian national mystique. If it is not a key to
the Australian culture, then it is a key to the Australian self-image. But there is a great
deal of evidence that it is in fact a key to both (cf. e.g. Bell 1973, Kapferer 1988, Ernst
1990).

To start with some recent examples (from a volume of interviews with two young
Australian rugby league players, Daley & Clyde 1995):

> And I liked hanging out with my mates. We were the cool cats at school and at
> lunch-time we'd be left alone by the other kids to meet on the back oval to do our
> own thing, which was to play sport.

> I wasn't a big television viewer. I'd prefer to be outdoors with my mates doing
> whatever came naturally, such as swimming at the creek, playing footy and listening
> to my music at night, than imitate a couch potato.

> It has certainly been a huge roller-coaster ride, but I reckon I've been fortunate to
> come through it all with a bloke who is a true mate, solid and strong. . . . Apart from
> being considered one of the game's top players, Laurie Daley is also one of the most
> popular blokes to have laced on a pair of boots. The fans love him simply because,
> despite his success, he has never once put himself above them . . . he's the people's
> person and gives a lot of himself.
>   Lozza, you're a champion and I take my hat off to you.[15]

No bones about it, a strong team spirit can help win games because a side whose players play for one another is a pretty tough unit to crack. And not only that, I find the will to win for your mates is also a pretty reliable pick-me-up when tiredness sets in late in a match and your thoughts stray.

About the best tribute I can offer Brad Clyde is to say I think of him as a good mate . . . he is someone I like to have a mag and beer with, and I'm pretty sure that's how it will always be.

Several of the main themes of "mateship" (to be discussed in this chapter) are here: the ideas of spending a lot of time together, doing things together, drinking together—of equality, solidarity, mutual commitment and mutual support, of companionship and fellowship in good fortune and in bad fortune.

As has often been pointed out, the Australian ethos is a direct descendant of the "bush ethos" which developed in the outback in the lives of the early (white) Australian bushmen, many of them convicts and exconvicts. As Russel Ward (1966[1958]) put it, in Australia—as in America—"the frontier was a forcing ground for the growth of distinctive national habits and sentiments." Most importantly (from the present point of view), these distinctive "habits and sentiments" were clearly reflected in language and, for the most part, have remained entrenched in it to this day:

> In Australia, the frontier has not had so much lasting effect on the external forms of life, political, legal, institutional and so on, as it has had upon men's attitude to life and so, at one remove as it were, upon the way in which these institutions are made to work in practice. Most Australians no longer bake dampers or wear cabbage-tree hats, but their ethos, like the speech which clothes it, differs from that of their British congeners more than it did a hundred years ago. (223).

According to many historians and social commentators, in the second half of the nineteenth century the "bush ethos" if anything gained in significance in the life of the country as a whole—and with it did the concept of 'mateship':

> Unionism came to the Australian bushman as a religion. . . . It had in it that feeling of *mateship*, which he understood already, and which always characterized the action of one "white man" to another. Unionism extended the idea, so a man's character was gauged by whether he stood true to Union rules or "scabbed" it on his fellows. (Spence 1909, quoted in TAND; emphasis added)

In the second half of the twentieth century, the significance of the traditions of the Australian "bush ethos" in the life of the nation has no doubt declined, and with it has declined the importance of "mateship." Nonetheless, these traditions have not completely died out yet, and the continued use of the word *mate* provides evidence for their vitality. The fact that in current Australian speech the use of *mate* has in some ways expanded and that this traditionally male word can be increasingly heard in the speech of women, also gives witness to their tenacity. One example:

—Sarah, do you know Susan Parker?
—Susan? She's my best mate!
(heard in Canberra, January 1995)

In fact, as Kapferer rightly points out, "many women in Australia are now stressing a kind of mateship among themselves" (1988:158).

The continued appeal to this concept by politicians points in the same direction. For example: "In his summit launching speech, he [Mr. Hawke, then Australia's prime minister], said: 'Our problems call for the application of those qualities of innovation, initiative, independence, tolerance—and, need I say, mateship—the qualities which we like to think are distinctly Australian (1983, quoted in Wilkes 1985[1978]:268). Similarly, in a 1988 speech, John Howard, leader of the Federal Opposition (and now prime minister), referred to "certain timeless traditional qualities about Australian life that . . . ought to be preserved and complemented in a contemporary fashion," citing "mateship and the equal treatment of people" as "the best of these qualities" (cf. Ernst 1990:110).

In any case, by "Australian culture" I do not mean the trends prevailing in the last decade of the twentieth century but those which have emerged and prevailed—to a varying degree—over the last two centuries. Seen in this perspective, the importance of the concept of 'mate', and of the ideal of "mateship" based on it, can hardly be doubted, and it takes a good deal of determination and ideological parti pris to try nevertheless to deny it, as Donald Horne (1989:183) does in his ironic comments on the subject (to which I will return in section 5.5).

The idea that "mateship" may be a unique cultural form in the whole history of human sociability seems to strike Horne as laughable, but careful semantic analysis shows that this is precisely what it is. The characterization of "mateship" as "bonded (male) comradeship" is vague and superficial; and on this level of superficiality many parallels can indeed be pointed to (beginning with 'comrade', or with the Russian concept of 'tovarišč').

At a deeper level of analysis, however, it can be shown that the concept of 'mate' is different not only from 'comrade' or 'tovarišč', but also from the French concept of 'camarade', or the Russian concept of 'drug', or the Polish concept of 'kolega', and probably from any other concept embodied in a noun in any other language. What Horne fails to appreciate is that concepts of this kind are very complex and that each of them reflects one particular perspective on human relations due to special historical and cultural sets of circumstances.

"Mateship" is not just a "bonded male camaraderie" (whatever that might mean), but a unique cultural ideal, based on a uniquely Australian perspective on human relations. Even though *mateship* itself is not a common everyday word in Australia, *mate* IS such a word; and the meaning encoded in it reveals a unique combination of assumptions, expectations, attitudes, and values.[16]

Before trying to analyze the meaning of *mate* which underlies the concept of 'mateship', let me first adduce some quotes from *The Australian national dictionary*, illustrating the importance of this concept in Australian culture.

River banks were grassy—grassy in the bends,
Running through the land where mateship never ends.
(1913, H. Lawson)

But nevermore shall I forget, not though I live for ever,
The days when we in mateship met along the Moonie River.
(1915, T. Skeyhill, *Soldier-Songs from Anzac*)

So mateship became the lonely poet's watchword, and he made it the watchword of Australia.
(1931, Lawson & Brereton, H. Lawson.)

The one compensating aspect of life as then lived was the element of mateship.
(1935. J. P. McKinney).

And some more recent quotes:

Historians have come to accept fairly calmly the notion that the Australian national philosophy of 'mateship' emerged from what was perhaps the world's only homosexual social ordering of things. (1973, Max Harris; quoted in Wilkes 1978).

Mateship is an important aspect both of the conceptions Australian males have of themselves, and of conceptions Australians generally have of their 'culture' [and] of an 'Australian way of life'. It is part of the legendary history of the nation, common parlance in the press and most other popular media and, not infrequently, an object of sociological inquiry. (Ernst 1990:110).

If anything, it's the lack of mateship in the House that will get to him. (About a footballer, Paul Osborne, turned MP, *The Canberra Times* March 11, 1995).

5.1   Different senses of mate

The Australian national dictionary (TAND) distinguishes four different though interrelated senses of the (Australian) word *mate*. Of these four, the crucial one is sense number three, but to understand it fully, it is necessary also to consider the others.
    TAND defines sense 1 as follows: "an equal partner in an enterprise. Also working mate." This sense of *mate* was associated with a special grammatical frame: "to go mates" (that is, as TAND puts it, "to work as an equal partner"). For example, TAND quotes an advertisement in the Sydney *Morning Herald*: "Wanted mate to go rabbiting." Other crucial quotes illustrating and commenting on this sense of *mate* include the following:

These men when they contract to do heavy work, as clearing, fencing, etc., almost always do it in parties of two, or more, being prompted to this in the first place by the hardness of the work, which a man cannot face alone, requiring always the assistance of 'neighbours', or 'mates', or 'partners', as they are severally called, even in the minute details. (1838)

Two generally travel together, who are called mates; they are partners, and divide all their earnings. (1845)

Two working mates occupy the same tent if working together. (1859)

A 'mate' was a 'mate'—share and share alike, no matter how bad might be the times. (1887)

I have alluded several times to 'partners', or 'mates', which was the more popular term. These partnerships were quite common amongst carriers and diggers in bygone days. It was simply chums, owning and sharing everything in common, and without any agreement, written or otherwise. (1921)

As these quotes suggest, the essence of the original *mate* relationship (i.e. *mate*1) can be represented as follows:

*(my) mate*1
(a) everyone knows: many men think about some other men like this:
(b)   this person is someone like me
(c)   I have to do some things
(d)   I couldn't do them if another person didn't do them with me
(e)   I want to do them with this person
(f)   this person is often in the same place as I
(g)   this person does the same things as I
(h)   this person does these things with me
(i)   the same things happen to this person as to me
(j)   I think like this about this person
(k) I know: this person thinks the same about me

Component (b) refers to the equality of the "mates1," (f) to their spending a great deal of time together, (g) and (h) to their shared activities, and (i) to their shared experiences; (c) shows that the shared activities constituted work (and not, for example, a game); (d) refers to the heaviness of the work, which a man "couldn't face alone;" (e) indicates that the relationship was entered into freely, as a free partnership; (k) shows the symmetrical and reciprocal nature of this relationship; and (a) shows that this type of relationship was seen as common among men.

It should be added that although at the outset "*mate*-partner" referred typically to one person, at the times of gold rush it spread to teams of half a dozen or more. In keeping with the earlier traditions, the miners working in such cooperative groups were reluctant to work for wages and preferred to share their earnings, with one digger acting as a cook and tentkeeper, as was earlier done at out-stations (cf. Ward 1966[1958]:109). This use of the word *mate* in the context of group endeavors has no doubt facilitated the transition from the "*mate*-partner" sense of the word to the sense of *mate* focusing on a group and embracing companions in contexts other than those of partnership.

5.2   *Mate*2: a transitional stage between *mate*1 and *mate*3?

According to TAND, the second sense of *mate* was that of "an acquaintance; a person engaged in the same activity." This definition suggests that my *mate*2 is simply someone whom I know and who does the same thing or things as I do. But the examples adduced by TAND show that in fact much more was involved in that. Significantly, all these examples are in the plural. The relationship between "mates" in this second sense of the word is in some ways analogous to that in the first sense, but in the second sense there is no question of a partnership entered into freely; rather, the reference is to activities that groups of men have to do (for example, as soldiers, or as miners).

We told him our mates were gone, and that we had heard two shots fired. (1841)

Boasting, among his mates in the bush. (1849)

Kipper Tommy was . . . acknowledged by his mates to be the crack driver of the district. (1879)

Covered with large green ants . . . how they stang! and how my dusky mates laughed! (1911)

The boy had joined his mates in one of the little cemeteries on the Western front. (1919)

Seventeen of our mates were killed in the mining industry last year. (1934)

The old soldiers watch him, look around at their mates and don't listen. (1971)

The "mates" mentioned in the above sentences are not only people doing the same things (as suggested by TAND), but also people doing these things together (with one another, in the same place). Furthermore, there is clearly an assumption of equality or similar status ("these people are people like me"); and clearly, here, too, there is an expectation that the same things are likely to happen to all the "mates."

It is by no means clear that the second sense posited by TAND is indeed a separate meaning of the word *mate* and that one can distinguish it in a principled way from sense 3, from which the abstract word *mateship* is derived. For the time being, however, I will go along with the classification of meanings proposed by TAND and will discuss *mate₃* as if it were indeed a meaning separate from *mate₂*. Given the central position of this meaning (*mate₃*) in Australian English, I will call it simply *mate*, without a subscript (in contrast to the early nineteenth century *mate₁*, i.e. "*mate*-partner"), and I will return later to the question of whether this crucial meaning (TAND's *mate₃*) can be distinguished from that described by TAND as *mate₂*.

The intention behind TAND's hypothetical meaning *mate₂* is clear. What this category was intended to capture was sentences referring to one's "co-workers" without attitudinal components characteristic of references to people's "special mates," "good mates," "mates-friends." The intended category can be seen as intermediate between *mate₁* in the sense explicated in the preceding section (roughly, voluntarily chosen partners), and *mate₃* (to be discussed in the next section (roughly, companions seen as special "friends").

5.3   Mates and mateship

Moving now to the crucial sense of *mate* widely used in Australia for defining human relations and constituting the basis of "mateship" (TAND's *mate₃*), I will note that TAND defines this sense as "one with whom the bonds of close friendship are acknowledged, a 'sworn friend.'" This definition implies that a *mate* (in the relevant sense) is simply something like "close friend." In fact, the whole point about "mateship" is that it is not the same as "friendship," or even "close friendship," and that these two categories ("friendship" and "mateship") differ in culturally significant ways. As Kapferer says, "To reduce the idea of mateship to friendship or comradeship is not to comprehend its meaning fully" (1988:158–159).

To begin with some examples:

Where his mate was his sworn friend through good and evil report, in sickness and health, in poverty and plenty, where his horse was his comrade, and his dog his companion, the bushman lived the life he loved. (1891)

No matter what you do, your Australian mate will defend you—'A mate can do no wrong.' (1965)

'He's me mate. I gotta help 'im' he stated simply and incontrovertibly. . . . There was no answer to that, Gunner knew: the outcome of this incident had been predetermined by the peculiar chemistry of compatibility, by social mores and by the almost tribal ties of marriage, all pledged with countless beers. It was personal, traditional, and deeply masculine. (1977)

My "mate" in the crucial Australian sense of the word is someone whom I perceive to be "someone like me" (as in *mate*₁) but whom I also see, more specifically, through the prism of the collectivist concept 'people like me'. It is also—as in the original sense—someone who is often with me, who does the same things as I do, and who does these things with me.

But in the "*mate*-partner" sense of the word, being together was simply a consequence of doing something together—something that one needed to do (work) and that one couldn't do alone (heavy work). By contrast, in the "*mate*-friend" sense of the word, being together could be, and can be, mainly "hanging around together"—precisely because one wants to be together with that person.

Given the traditional (male) Australian ethos—anti-intellectual, anti-verbal, anti-overtly emotional—being together, for men, could not mean a great deal of "talking together," exchanging ideas, swapping confidences, articulating and revealing one's feelings. In this culture, being together for pleasure had to mean, primarily, "doing things together" and enjoying shared activities and shared experiences (that is, doing the same things together and feeling the same because of this).

There was mateship, sharing a billy of bitter-black tea, a smoke and a yarn. (1985, Dorothy Hewett; quoted in Wilkes 1985).

Even the verbal activity of "having a yarn" (in the Australian sense of the word *yarn*, see chapter 5) was more an instance of "doing something together" (and "feeling something because of this") than of verbal self-disclosure.

The emphasis on spending time together and doing things together rather than on talking, and in particular the abhorrence of any verbal intimacies is also well illustrated by the following statement from Hawkes's book: "We don't say it in so many words. When I see those Hollywood movies where they bleed their hearts, it actually makes me sick. It's just knowing that each other's around"[17] (1990:60)

It is interesting to note in this respect that one can talk of *good mates, best mates,* and *old mates,* but not of *close mates* (as one can talk of "close friends"). This shows again that what really matters in "mateship" is not something like "closeness" or "intimacy" (in the sense of intimate knowledge of the other person's inner life) but how much time one has spent with another person (sharing the same activities and the same conditions), and to what extent one can rely on them (a point to which I will return shortly). To quote an example from an Australian play:

ALF: Wack and me are old mates. At the war together. (. . .)
MUM: 'E's never got married. 'E's never 'ad no one.
WACKA: I've had youse.
ALF: You said it, Wack, what d'y'mean 'e never had no one? We bin mates
        for years. I've looked after him, haven't I, Wack? I seen 'im through. .
        . . What I c'n work out, my old man seen 'im through the first show [i.e.
        WWI], I looked after him all through the last lot. (Seymour 1962:32-33)

In the case of *mate₁*, the shared activities had to be work, and heavy work at that;
in the case of *mate* ("*mate₃*"), the shared activities may be simply fun activities
(drinking, smoking, occasionally "yarning"). Schematically (formula B is only a
partial explication and will be expanded later):

A. (*mate₁*)
(a) I have to do some things
(b) I couldn't do them if another person didn't do them with me
(c) I want to do these things with this person
(d) because of this, this person is often in the same place as I
(e) this person does the same things as I
(f) this person does these things with me

B. (*mate₃*)
(a) this person is often in the same place as I
(b) this person does the same things as I
(c) this person does these things with me

Given the common practice of pleasurable "hanging around" with one's "mates"
(for example, in a pub), one may be tempted to add two further (identical) components
to formula B, namely (a') 'because I want this' and (c') 'because I want this'. Such
additional components would stipulate that (apart from "mates-partners"), being
together with one's mates and sharing activities with them is voluntary.

I don't think that this would be justified, however. In the "modern" (i.e. not
"*mate*-partner") sense of the word, *mates* are often together, and do things together,
either because they want to or not for this reason (but, for example, because they work
together). The essential thing is that they are often together, and do things together,
not that this being together, and doing things together, is voluntary.

In fact, it is one of the main differences between "mateship" and "friendship" that
"friendship" does involve "voluntary association," whereas "mateship" may link
people who are simply thrown together by circumstances. What matters for "mateship" is the attitude of those involved, not their voluntary choice of their associates.
(For example, army cadets, who have not come together voluntarily but have been
"thrown together by fate," may still be "mates," if their attitude to one another satisfies
the expectations of "mateship," to be discussed below).

The sharing of "being somewhere" and "doing things," which applied to both
mate₁ and the later *mate*, has continued to be linked with an exposure to the same
experiences ('the same things can happen to this person as to me') and with a male
perspective (two points to which I will return shortly).

As a first approximation, therefore, I would propose the following explication for the crucial Australian sense of *mate* (*mate₃*):

> *X is my mate₃*
> everyone knows: many men think about some other men like this:
>> these people are people like me
>> these people are often in the same place as I
>> these people do the same things as I
>> these people do these things with me
>> the same things happen to these people as to me
>> I know: these people think the same about me
> I think like this about this person (X)

(This is not a complete explication; further components will be suggested shortly.)

Thus, the main shift in the semantics of *mate* (from the original *mate₁* to the main *mate*) involved a transition from an emphasis on sharing work, out of necessity (usually, with one person), resulting in sharing company and sharing experiences, to an emphasis on sharing company, sharing activities, and sharing experiences—not necessarily because of sharing work and usually with a group of men.

The emphasis on equality ('someone/people like me') and on a specifically inter-male character of the relationship remained unchanged. Although in the past, the word *mate* (in the quasi-friend sense) was occasionally applied to women (TAND has included two such examples dated 1928 and 1930), there can be no doubt that throughout its history the idea of a 'mate' included a reference to a specifically inter-male style of relationship (continuing the cultural tradition of mates-partners going rabbitting or timber-sawing together).

Emphatic statements such as the following one may overstate this obligatory maleness of a "mate," but they capture correctly the necessarily "inter-male" proto-type, and style, of "mateship":

> "My mate" is always a man. A female may be my sheila, my bird, my charley, my good sort, my hot-drop, my judy or my wife, but she is never "my mate." (1960, Donald McLean, quoted in Wilkes 1985).

When one recalls that, as Baker pointed out, "For more than half a century Australia was almost entirely a masculine country" and that "as late as 1840 the proportion of males to females was two to one" (1970:121), it becomes clear that the masculine bias of the traditional Australian ethos, reflected in the concepts of 'mate' and 'mateship', had its roots in historical conditions and was related to the absence of women and to the fact that many men were dependent on other men for companionship and human contact. In fact, common references to Australian men "needing" mates suggest another dimension of continuity in the use of the word *mate*: just as it was once assumed that a man needed a "mate" (partner) to go rabbitting or timber-sawing, it was also assumed that a man needed a "mate" or "mates" to spend time with:

> A mate in Australia is simply that which a bloke must have around him. Mates do not necessarily want to know you. (1972, K. Dunstan, Knockers 52, quoted in TAND)

The male who hasn't a male mate is a lonely man indeed, or a strange man, though he have a wife and family. (1913, H. Lawson, quoted in TAND)

And a recent quote:

It is necessary to have good mates. (Hawkes 1990:52)

The supreme value of a man's *mate* was clearly linked with this notion, rooted in Australia's history, that men were dependent on men.

Stevie is more to me than a man is to a girl—yes, I know you'll grin at that, but you don't rightly know what men are to each other out here. He's my mate—we're mates, and good mates. (1917, B. Cable)

You've been a good mate and a man can't say more than that. (1948, F. Clune).

What exactly being a "good mate" means is a point which will be addressed in the next section.

5.4   The attitudinal components of mate

As mentioned earlier, throughout its history (after *mate*₁, i.e. "mate-partner"), the word *mate* has implied the same interpersonal attitudes—attitudes which in the literature on "mateship" are usually referred to with words and phrases such as "loyalty," "solidarity," and "mutual support." These attitudes, often contrasted with the American ideal of "self-reliance," are generally linked with the harshness of the conditions confronting the first European settlers in Australia and the economic conditions, which made individual success unlikely. To quote first an American observer, George Renwick: "Emerging from their particular heritage are the Australians' fundamental beliefs that one has a responsibility for his or her neighbor and that loyalty to one's friends is not only appropriate, it is essential" (1980:16).

Contrasting these Australian cultural attitudes with the American ones, Renwick writes:

Consistent with their interest in limiting the depths of friendships while increasing the number of friends, Americans are careful to minimize their commitments to others.
. . .
Australians have traditionally expressed the priority they give to personal relationship in terms of "mateship." Through the loneliness, vast distances, and the difficulties of existence experienced by the first Australians, men and women learned to help and trust each other. Australians still respect and share a genuine spirit of mateship, a sense that "we're in this thing together." . . .
Australians therefore believe strongly that "a man's got to stick to his mate and see him through." An American is more conscious of sticking to his job and seeing his work through to completion. (17–18)

What Renwick doesn't address is the difference in the original conditions for Australian and American settlers, which must have contributed to these differing cultural attitudes. These differences between the conditions in America and in Australia were discussed, with particular clarity, by Ward (1966[1958]):

The plain fact is that the typical Australian frontiersman in the last century was a wage-worker who did not, usually, expect to become anything else. The loneliness and hardships of outback life, as on the American frontier, taught him the virtues of co-operation, but his economic interests, unlike those of the American frontiersman, reinforced this tendency towards a social, collectivist outlook. By loyal combination with his fellows he might win better conditions from his employer, but the possibility of becoming his own master by individual enterprise was usually but a remote dream. So far from being 'precipitated by the wilderness into a primitive organization based on the family', he was precipitated into an equally primitive organization of 'nomad tribesmen', if one may conceive of a tribe without women and children. Thus it came about that differing frontiers in the United States and Australia produced two different kinds of frontiersmen, with mental attitudes which were very similar in some respects but very different in others. (226–227)

Ward's comments are echoed by Bell (1973), among many others, who wrote (with reference to Turner 1968): "The Australian dream, according to Ian Turner, had no element of the American dream of rising from the log cabin to the White House. In Australia the individual could rise only with the collective" (5).

As Ward (among many others) pointed out, in Australian "mateship" the idea of solidarity with one's equals had not only an egalitarian but also an anti-authoritarian ring and combined "the strongly social sense of solidarity with the nomad tribe, and the equally strong, antisocial hostility to any control, or even patronage, from above" (Ward 1966[1958]:227). This somewhat "aggressive" dimension of "mateship" is well illustrated by Henry Lawson's often quoted quatrain from his poem "The Shearers":

> They tramp in mateship side by side —
> The Protestant and Roman —
> They call no biped lord or sir,
> And touch their hat to no man!

The "collectivist" ring of the word *mate* can be accounted for if we formulate the first component of its meaning in the plural:

> these people are people like me

Of course the word *mate* can also be used in the singular, but—like the Polish *kolega* or the Russian *tovarišč*—it refers to a prototype that is plural and collective, as well as clearly defined in gender: to a group of men. The very common use of phrases such as "Barry and his mates" or "me and a few old mates of mine" in Australian English points in the same direction. In the formula proposed earlier I have represented this as follows:

> everyone knows: many men think about some other men like this:
>   "these people are people like me"

This formulation suggests that *mate* is exclusive as well as inclusive. By emphasizing the notion that "these people are people like me," the speaker is implicitly referring to some other people who are not like me. It has often been pointed out that this group identification excluded "Abos" and "sheilas" (i.e. Aborigines and women, cf. e.g. Horne 1989:184) as well as various immigrant groups (cf. e.g. Medding 1973), but the original emphasis was no doubt above all on people who might consider themselves as being "above" people like me and superior to people like me (in particular, the authorities, the police, the British). The following early example quoted in OEDS is characteristic in this regard:

> When the diggers address a policeman in uniform they always call him 'Sir', but they always address a fellow in a blue shirt with a carbine as 'Mate'. 'Mate' is the ordinary popular form of allocution in these colonies. (1852)

Of course, as mentioned earlier, "mate" as a form of address is not the same thing as "mate" used in reference or predication, and non-mates are more likely to be addressed in this way than mates. The vocative "mate" indicates that the speaker wants to show that he wants to treat the addressee "like a mate," or pretends to do so, and there is no need to do so with someone who knows that he is a real "mate." Nonetheless, the very existence of the two alternative forms of address ("mate" and "sir") reflects the assumption that there are two different categories of people: those who can be (really or ostensibly) treated "like a mate" and those who cannot. There can be little doubt that this assumption had real consequences in social interaction. For example, Garvin notes this about the Australian miners of the period: "You wouldn't dare be caught removing a mate's shovel, yet you were regarded as a bit of a hero if you outwitted the 'Joes'—the local police (1988:38).

The solidarity with "the people like me," which is justly emphasized in the literature as an essential aspect of "mateship," was clearly based on the shared existential conditions, including (1) doing the same things together (as in the case of Polish *koledzy*), (2) having the same things happen to you (as in the case of the Russian *tovarišči*), (3) helping each other at all times, (4) relying on mutual support in trouble, and (5) identifying with one another in the case of misfortune. These last three components can be represented as follows:

> I want to do good things for these people when I can
> when something bad happens to one of these people,
>   it would be bad if I didn't do something good for this person
> I don't want bad things to happen to these people,
>   as I don't want bad things to happen to me

As pointed out by Ian Green (personal communication), "mates" like and actively seek to do things for each other all the time, and in particular to help each other with specific projects that they have got going (such as building a fence or overhauling an engine). But they also have a commitment to looking after each other and standing by each other in times of trouble. The components 'I want to do good things for these people' and 'if something bad happens to one of these people, it would be bad if I didn't do something good for this person' reflect those two aspects of mates' mutual support. To quote Garvin again: "When fire, flood, or any difficulty arose you needed a man to stand beside you—and you had to be prepared to stand with your mate when hardships hit him" (1988:38).

Although in modern times the emphasis on helping one's "mates" in adversity may seem less pronounced than in the olden times, it is definitely still there (to the extent to which the concept of 'mate' is still there).

But while the attitudinal components proposed so far account for one crucial aspect of *mate* and *mateship*, they do not seem to fully capture the "loyalty" dimension, which is also widely felt to be as essential to the concept of 'mate'. After all, people could believe in the necessity of helping one another in general, and when misfortune strikes in particular, without feeling the need to "stick to one another" when one of them does something wrong, or when one of them thinks that the others are doing something wrong. Yet, as Frank Hardy put it, "a mate can do no wrong" (quoted in TAND), and the idea of "dobbing a mate in" (cf. chapter 5) or of "betraying" one's fellow workers by acting as a "scab" (i.e. strike breaker) is completely unreconcilable with the notion of 'mateship'.

The assumption of equality, existential bonding, and mutual dependence in the face of hardship and danger lead to attitudes which are loosely referred to by means of words and expressions such as *solidarity, mutual support, loyalty,* and *sticking to one another through thick and thin;* but without more fine-grained analysis it is impossible to see what exactly these labels are meant to stand for and how the attitudes in question differ from those encoded in other ethno-sociological categories, such as *koledzy, tovarišči,* and *druz'ja.*

Linking the basic features of the Australian outback ethos with Australia's convict past, Ward noted also: "Take, for example, the strongly egalitarian sentiment of group solidarity and loyalty, which was perhaps the most marked of all convict traits. This was recognized as the prime distinguishing mark of outback workers fifty years before Lawson and others wrote so much about mateship" (1958:77).

Consider also the following conclusion reached by Ward on the basis of his analysis of Australian folk ballads: "The greatest good is to stand by one's mates in all circumstances, and the greatest evil is to desert them" (188). Clearly, this is not quite the same as the belief that one must help one's companions in misfortune—or rather, it is more than that. Yet the idea of "standing by" and "sticking with" is generally felt to be essential to the traditional Australian folk philosophy of "mateship." To account for this "loyalty" dimension of "mateship," I would propose for it the following additional components:

> I don't want to say bad things about one of these people to other people
> I don't want other people to say bad things about one of these people
> I don't want other people to do anything bad to one of these people

Needless to say, these components are not meant to define the whole meaning of the word *loyalty*, or to fully explicate the assumptions behind condemnatory terms such as *scab* or *dob in*, but only that aspect of the concept 'mate' which was related to them.

According to the mateship ethos, a man is supposed to "stick up" for his mates. While it is an accepted part of mateship to "rubbish" one's mates (i.e. to say bad things about them) to their faces, for fun, it would be felt to be disloyal to say bad things about them to outsiders (in particular, to "dob them in") or to listen willingly to outsiders saying bad things about them.

The assumption that one doesn't say bad things about one's mates to outsiders is closely related to the assumption that one doesn't want "other people" to do something bad to one's mates. In a way, both these assumptions are reflected in the traditional

Australian abhorrence of "dobbing a mate in," that is, saying something bad about one's mate to someone in authority (a boss, a policeman, even the mate's wife) and thus possibly causing trouble for the mate.

Stressing how deeply the concept of 'mateship' is embedded in the "Australian psyche," Hornadge (1980) quotes, with approval, the following definition offered by Thomas Dodd and quoted in the *Australian Worker* (1926):

> What is a mate nowadays? Somebody you can rely on—through thick, thin and middling; past hell and high-water. Like the mariner's compass he always points north to you. In any trouble, you know what he will do, without argument; because, since he is your mate, it is exactly what you would do yourself. Your mate is indeed yourself in another fellow's skin. (129)

This psychological identification and solidarity with one's "mates," implied by the very word *mate*, is reminiscent of those implied by the Russian word *tovarišči*. In the case of *tovarišči*, I have represented this psychological identification and solidarity in the form of the component 'I don't want bad things to happen to these people, as I don't want bad things to happen to me', and in a sense, this could be said to apply to *mates*, too. But in the case of *mates*, this "solidarity" has the added "loyalty" and "anti-authority" dimension, and this requires a different phrasing of the explication. I think that the additional components proposed here account adequately for this aspect of "mateship."

The attitudinal components of *mate* discussed here are reflected with particular clarity in the meaning of the expression *good mate*, used in an absolute sense, that is, not only as "Jack is a good mate of Bill" but also as "Jack is a good mate." For example:

> Old Sam, born and reared in the bush, a good mate and bushman. (1968, OEDS)

As this example illustrates, being a "good mate" could be seen, in traditional Australian culture, as a standard of human value in general. This is also illustrated by the following nineteenth-century example, with a different syntactic frame:

> At this time I was mates with a young fellow called Jim Smith, a good enough lad as a mate. (1880, OEDS)

Clearly, being a "good mate" in that general, absolute sense is a matter of attitude to one's equals, whose existence one shares, and this attitude must involve more than readiness to help in misfortune. All the examples available are consistent with the idea that it involves also "solidarity and loyalty" in the sense of not wanting bad things to be done by anyone to one's "mate" as one doesn't want them to be done to oneself.[18] The expression *great mates* has similar implications. For example:

> An obelisk in the Jewish section of the Melbourne General Cemetery records the names of those who fought for Australia in the 1914 War. Many of them trained in the Faraday Street School cadets. They assimilated the lessons of patriotism and were great mates. (1974, Sydney *Morning Herald*, OEDS)

Praising a person as a "mate" (and, therefore, a fine human being) can also be done by means of other, more ad hoc chosen adjectives, as in the following example:

Poor old Joe! Too much courage and too little brain. . . . A grand mate, though. (1953, quoted in Wilkes 1978)

The word *mateship*, used in reference to an ideal, as well as a reality, points in the same direction.

This brings us to the following explication:

(my) mate
(a) everyone knows: many men think about some other men like this:
(b)   these people are people like me
(c)   these people are often in the same place as I
(d)   these people do the same things as I
(e)   these people do these things with me
(f)   the same things happen to these people as to me
(g)   I want to do good things for these people
(h)   when something bad happens to one of these people, it will be bad if I don't
       do something good for this person
(i)   I don't want bad things to happen to these people as I don't want bad things
       to happen to me
(j)   I don't want to say bad things about one of these people to other people
(k)   I don't want other people to say bad things about one of these people
(l)   I don't want other people to do anything bad to one of these people
(m)   these people think the same about me
(n) when men think like this about other men, they feel something good
(o) I think like this about this person

Component (a) of this explication shows that *mate* refers to a common pattern of social relations, typically linking men with other men, (b) reflects the egalitarian and collectivist character of this relationship, (c) refers to the companionship, (d) and (e) to shared activities, and (f) to the shared existential conditions. Component (g) refers to the willingness to help one's mates at all times, (h) to the obligation to help them in times of trouble, and (i) to identification with them in the face of misfortune. Components (j), (k), and (l) jointly show the assumptions of "solidarity" and "loyalty" with regard to the outside world, especially to anybody in authority. Component (m) shows the assumption of reciprocity. Component (n), which refers to the emotional dimension of the "mateship" relation, is formulated in such a way that it could cover not only something like personal affection but also something like a more general satisfaction in having this kind of bond with other men. Finally, component (o) reflects the fact that *mate* can refer to an individual as well as to a group.

Component (c) of the proposed explication might be questioned on the grounds that sometimes the frequent companionship may be in the past rather than in the present, but this is usually signaled by means of the adjective *old* ("an old mate of mine"), and in any case, the general frame given in component (a) signals that the conditions which follow refer to the prototype which defines the TYPE of relationship rather than every particular instance.

Having arrived at this final explication of *mate*, we are in a better position to assess the TAND decision to posit two distinct meanings (apart from "*mate*-partner"), *mate*$_2$

and *mate₃*. To this end, let us consider again the following two sentences, adduced by the TAND under the hypothetical meaning *mate₂*:

The boy had joined his mates in one of the little cemeteries on the Western front.

Seventeen of our mates were killed in the mining industry last year.

Is there any reason to regard such uses of *mates* as different in meaning from those illustrating the hypothetical meaning *mate₃*, as in the following sentence:

He's me mate. I gotta help 'im. (1977, Beilby)

The intention behind the TAND decision to separate the supposed meanings *mate₂* and *mate₃* is clear: *mate₃* is intended to apply to something like "personal friends," whereas *mate₂* (with all the examples in the plural) can refer to fellow-workers, fellow-sportsmen, or fellow-soldiers with whom one has been "thrown together" by life.

In the light of the foregoing discussion, however, I would argue that Australian culture makes no such distinction between "personal friends" and "impersonal mates" (in the sense of, for example, fellow-workers or fellow-soldiers). To draw such a distinction with respect to the word *mate* would mean to impose an alien perspective on Australian culture and Australian English. From the Australian cultural perspective, it is important that one's fellow-workers, or fellow-players, or fellow-soldiers are treated with the same commitment, solidarity, and loyalty with which good personal "mates" are treated.

Consider, for example, the following quote from an interview with the noted Australian footballer Paul Vautin, known as "Fatty":

Old mates—blokes who've known each other for 10, 20, 30 years, who've played together, got drunk together, been best man at each other's weddings—have thrown down the gloves and they're going for each other's throats. It's shocking. (Jamrozik 1995:36)

The "mates" whom Fatty is talking about are his fellow players from the Australian Rugby League—that is, people who have been "thrown together" by the circumstances but who are also drinking companions, people who enjoy each other's company and who are at the same time expected to be deeply committed to one another on a personal level.

Of course, one can always draw a distinction between one's "mates" in general and one's special "mates," or one's "best mates," as one can draw a distinction between one's "friends" in general and one's "best friends." But the word *mate* as such is no more polysemous in this respect than the word *friend* is. The nominal category *mate* is inclusive, and this very inclusiveness is culturally revealing. The same sentence can refer to special personal "mates" and to "mates" or "mateship" in a broader sense, without any distinction being made between the two, as in the following example:

Shearing to me is the mates I've made. . . . There's no greater mateship in any industry in Australia. (1984, *People Magazine* [Sydney], quoted in TAND)

In traditional Australian culture, "mateship" was expected to bind people not only with their "best mates" or their "great mates" but also with their fellow-miners, fellow-shearers, fellow-"diggers," fellow-soldiers, or fellow-footballers, and this expectation is one of this culture's most enduring and characteristic features.[19]

5.5 "Debunking" mateship?

Since the concept of 'mateship' has always been regarded as one of the main keys to Australian culture, it is not surprising that in their efforts to abolish the very notion of "Australian culture" many recent writers attack this concept first of all. I will illustrate this trend with two quotes, one from Donald Horne's *Ideas for a nation* (1989) and one from Elaine Thompson's *Fair enough* (1994). Horne's approach (mentioned earlier) is to dismiss the idea of mateship as something characteristically Australian:

> . . . by the end of the [nineteenth] century it [the word *mate*] had developed a special cultural form, in the noun "mateship," which was seen by many as Australia's decisive contribution to civilisation. The creation of this meaning was folkish, but it was also given intellectual popularisation by some of the professional bush cultists. It was nothing more than the idea of bonded (male) comradeship, but it was seen as having special Australian characteristics, given to it by the smell of gum-leaves. In the 1890s the word was also appropriated by the growing trades union movement, thereby giving nineteenth-century working-class consciousness a certain local flavour, and in the Great War it was appropriated by the Diggers, giving the camaraderie of soldiers a special Australian warmth that led its devotees to believe that their mateship was unique in the whole history of human sociability. (183)

In contrast to Horne, Thompson does see the idea of mateship as peculiar to Australia, but as "racist, sexist, ethnocentric, conformist and oppressive." "Mateship" thus becomes a whip with which Thompson belabors Australia's history and culture as a whole (with Donald Horne, on the cover, applauding):

> While the positive role of mateship in helping to create a powerful union movement should not be underestimated, neither should its shortcomings be overlooked. Because mateship was exclusive, it was not egalitarian but racist, sexist, ethnocentric, conformist and oppressive. These criticisms are hardly new, but the unattractive aspects of mateship were deeply embedded and part of mateship's defining characteristics. And they have ramifications for the way Australians have been portrayed by social commentators. (35)

> Australia was egalitarian *because* it was xenophobic and sexist. (252)

> Having done its best to destroy the indigenous cultures, Australian society has struggled to develop a distinct cultural identity out of an environment dominated by conservative, conformist, Anglo-oriented values. (215)

I hope this chapter shows that both Horne and Thompson are substantially wrong in what they say about mateship—Horne in dismissing it as a commonplace idea, and Thompson in presenting racism and sexism as its defining characteristics.

To begin with Thompson's charges, there are some words in English, as in many other languages, which do indeed unequivocally express racism and sexism. The well-known Russian word *černožopye* ('the black-arsed ones'), used with reference to Central Asians (cf. Wimbush & Alekseev 1982), offers a clear example of the former, as do English words such as *rice-eyes, slit-eyes, slant-eyes* (cf. Dean 1985); and obviously ethnic prejudice is reflected in English (Australian) words such as *wog, dago*, and *greaso*. As for sexism, the highly elaborated segment of Russian called *mat* (literally 'motherese') provides a particularly striking illustration, as do—on a much smaller scale—English words such as *bitch, doll*, and others. But there is nothing inherently racist or sexist about the words *mate* and *mateship*.

To say this is not to dispute the existence of either sexism or racism in the Australian past, or to deny any links between the ethos of mateship on the one hand and sexist and racist attitudes on the other. But it is simply incorrect to call sexism and racism "defining characteristics" of mateship.

As we have seen, the concept of 'mateship' does include (among others) the components 'these people are people like me' and 'men often think about other men like this'. But the component 'these people are people like me' can be interpreted more inclusively or more exclusively. It is not inherently racist or sexist, and this is why with changing social attitudes the use of *mate* could be increasingly extended to embrace migrants from Southern and Eastern Europe and from Asia. (It is also worth noting in this context the remarkable success of the Australian Freedom from Hunger's "A plate for a mate" project, which was run in Australian schools in 1991.)

As we have seen, the inherent semantics of *mate* does not preclude the possibility of extending the use of this word to women either, despite the male prototype inscribed into its meaning and perfectly understandable given the gender imbalance throughout much of Australia's history. (Thompson, incidentally, denies the existence of such an imbalance, on the grounds that there were many black women in the country—an argument which defies both logic and arithmetic.)

Horne asserts that there is nothing uniquely Australian in the idea of mateship. This misunderstanding may owe something to a tendency to assume that rough equivalents are exact synonyms. As we have seen, however, concepts such as 'mate', 'friend' and 'comrade' are very complex, and each such concept constitutes a unique configuration of several semantic components. Some of these components may occur in different languages, but the configuration as a whole is often unique. (For further discussion of Australian culture, see chapter 5.)

6. Conclusion

For a number of disciplines, such as sociology, psychology, anthropology, philosophy, it is important to understand how people categorize and conceptualize their relations with other people. In the abundant literature on the subject, however, human relations are often interpreted through the lens of one particular ethno-taxonomy, especially that embodied in the (modern) English language. This applies both to the more traditional works on "friendship" and to those within the new discipline of "interpersonal relations" (as, for example, in the "Sage series on close relationships"). The problem lies largely in the reification of English words such as *friend* and *friendship* and their unreflective use as descriptive tools and theoretical constructs in talking about people and human relations in general.

For example, in discussing what he calls "human friendships," which he compares with social relationships among non-human primates, Serpell insists that "mutual liking" is an essential feature of "friendship" (1989:116). But why should "mutual liking" be more important to human relations than, for example, mutual support, solidarity, loyalty, or shared experiences? Isn't the emphasis on "mutual liking" derived, unconsciously, from the modern English concept of 'friend'?

Consider also the following statements by another author, Allan (1979):

. . . friendship is a personal relationship in that it is seen as involving individuals and not as members of groups or collectivities. (38)

A second characteristic of friend relationships is that they are defined as voluntary. They are seen as consequent on the free choice and selection of each friend by the other. (40)

An assumption entailed in the idea that friendship is voluntary in that it is a relationship based on enjoyment. A friend is someone with whom you enjoy spending time and sharing activities. (41)

It is . . . a relationship . . . that exists simply because it is found to be enjoyable. (43)

All these statements reflect a perspective suggested to the author by the English word *friend*, in its modern usage. For example, as we have seen, the Polish word *koledzy*, the Russian word *tovariŝči*, and the Australian English word *mates* do not imply a "personal relationship, involving individuals as individuals, and not as members of groups"; yet the bond between *koledzy, tovariŝči,* or *mates* can be as strong, or stronger, than that between "friends."

The same applies to the voluntary, free choice of one's "associates." Even though "friends" can be chosen voluntarily, *koledzy, tovariŝči,* and *mates* are not "chosen," but this doesn't make these relationships any less important.

Finally, the idea that the most important human relationships outside the family are those based on "enjoyment" does not even apply to the traditional Anglo culture. For example, when Emerson wrote that "a friend is a person with whom I may be sincere" or that "better be a nettle in the side of your friend than his echo," he clearly didn't mean by "friend" an enjoyable companion. Nor does the key Russian term *drug* or the Polish term *przyjaciel* refer specifically to the idea of "enjoyable company." Clearly, the dimensions focused upon by Allan (1979) (and apparently supported by the comments of his respondents) are in fact those suggested by the modern English usage. They reflect the assumptions, expectations, and values of modern Anglo culture.

But the literature on human relations is also full of works which are not influenced by the meaning of English words such as *friend* and *friendship* and which are instead making distinctions unrelated to the normal usage—in English or in any other language. This is hardly preferable to analyses guided (if only unconsciously) by the English language.

Consider, for example, statements such as the following: "Deep friends love one another," and "the idea of deep friends not confiding in one another seems almost unthinkable" (Thomas 1987:217). What exactly are these statements about? The use of the English word *friend*? Presumably not, since *friend* implies neither love nor mutual confidences. The use of the expression *deep friends*? Presumably not that either, since in fact there is no such expression in English. (English speakers talk about "close friends," "old friends," "good friends," "great friends," or "best friends," but not "deep friends"). What are they about, then? If they are about human relations regardless of language and culture, then they seem to mean little more than that some people love one another and confide in one another—hardly an original observation.

Having made those initial statements about what he calls "deep friends," the author proceeds to make some terminological distinctions, singling out "friendships of pleasure," "friendship of convenience," and "companion friendship," and talks about these "kinds of friendship" created by his own arbitrary terminological decisions as if they were objective realities. For example, he states that "companion friendships are a manifestation of a choice on the part of the parties involved" (215).

But what is the point of making generalizations about categories that we have invented ourselves? The English language and Anglo culture do not distinguish between "friendships of pleasure," "friendship of convenience," and "companion friendship." On the other hand, the English language does embody the socio-cultural category of "friend," a category which deserves to be studied as a reflection of, and a key to, objectively existing Anglo culture.

Similarly, the fact that the Australian variety of English includes, additionally, a socio-cultural category of "mate" is an important empirical fact, providing evidence for specifically Australian patterns of social relations and specifically Australian cultural values. This evidence guides us toward some objective socio-cultural realities and allows us better to understand them. Such realities cannot be fully comprehended if sufficient attention is not being paid to language and, in particular, to key words such as *friend*, *mate*, *kolega*, *drug*, and *tovarišč*. To fully understand such words, however, we need to avoid reifying concepts supplied by our native language and to try to explore the relevant terms—including our own—from a universal, culture-in-dependent perspective.

Appendix

SUMMARY OF THE FORMULAE

*friend*₁
(a) everyone knows: many people think about some other people like this:
(b)   I know this person very well
(c)   I think good things about this person
(d)   I want this person to know what I think
(e)   I want this person to know what I feel
(f)   I don't want many other people to know these things
(g)   I want to do good things for this person
(h)   I know this person thinks the same about me

(i)   when I think about this person, I feel something very good
(j) I think like this about this person

friend₂
(a) everyone knows: many people think about some other people like this:
(b)   I know this person well
(c)   I want to be with this person often
(d)   I want to do things with this person often
(e)   when I am with this person, I feel something good
(f)   I think this person thinks the same about me
(g) I think like this about this person

(my) drug
(a) everyone knows: many people think about some other people like this:
(b)   I know this person very well
(c)   I think very good things about this person
(d)   I want to often be with this person
(e)   I want to often talk [say things] to this person
(f)   I know: I can say anything to this person
(g)   nothing bad will happen because of this
(h)   I want this person to know what I think
(i)   I want this person to know why I think this
(j)   I want this person to know what I feel
(k)   I want to do good things for this person
(l)   when something bad happens to this person,
             I can't not do something good for this person
(m)   I know: this person thinks the same about me
(n) when people think like this about other people, they feel something very good
(o) I think like this about this person

(my) podruga
(a) everyone knows: many women think about some other women like this:
(b)   I know this person very well
(c)   I have known this person for a long time
(d)   I think something good about this person
(e)   this person is someone like me
(f)   I have often been with this person
(g)   often, when I did some things,
             this person did similar things
(h)   often, when some things happened to me,
             similar things happened to this person
(i)   often, when I felt some things,
             this person felt similar things
(j)   when I am with this person, I feel something good
(k)   I know: this person thinks the same about me
(l) I think like this about this person

(my) prijatel'
(a) everyone knows: many people think like this about some other people:
(b)   I know this person well
(c)   when I am with this person, I feel something good

(d)   when I do something with this person, I feel something good
(e)   I think this person thinks the same about me
(f) I think like this about this person

(my) tovarišč₁
(a) everyone knows: people think about some other people like this sometimes:
(b)   these people are people like me
(c)   these people are in the same place as I
(d)   the same things happen to these people as to me
(e)   I don't want bad things to happen to these people as I don't want bad things to happen to me
(f) when people think like this about other people, they feel something good
(g) many men think like this about some other men
(h) I think like this about this person

tovarišč₂
(a) everyone knows: many people think about some other people like this:
(b)   these people are people like me
(c)   there are many people like this
(d)   these people want the same things to happen
(e)   these people want good things to happen to very many people
(f)   these people want bad things to happen to some other people   because of this
(g)   these people want to do many things because of this
(h)   I think something very good about all these people
(i)   when I think about these people, I feel something good
(j) I think about this person like this

(my) rodnye
(a) I think about these people like this:
(b)   these people are like a part of me
(c)   I am like a part of these people
(d)   it cannot be otherwise
(e) when I think about these people, I feel something very good

(my) koledzy
(a) everyone knows: many people think about some other people like this:
(b)   these people are people like me
(c)   I know these people well
(d)   I do many things in one place
(e)   these people are often in the same place
(f)   these people do the same things as I
(g)   I think these people think the same about me
(h) when people think like this about other people, they feel something good
(i) I think like this about these people

(my) colleagues
(a) I think about these people like this:
(b)   these people are people like me
(c)   these people do things of the same kind as I do

(d)   not many other people do things of this kind
(e)   I think something good about these people
(f)   I think these people know a lot about some things
(g)   because of this, these people can do things of this kind
(h) I think these people think the same about me

(my) przyjaciel/przyjaciołka
(a) everyone knows: many people think about other people like this:
(b)   I know this person very well
(c)   I think good things about this person
(d)   often when I think something, I can't say it to other people
(e)   I can say it to this person
(f)   I want this person to know what I think
(g)   I want this person to know what I feel
(h)   I think this person thinks the same about me
(i) I think like this about this person
(j) I don't think like this about many other people
(k) when I think about this person, I feel something very good

(my) znajomi
(a) everyone knows: many people think about some other people like this:
(b)   I know these people well
(c)   I don't want to say: very well
(d)   I can say things of some kinds to these people
(e)   I don't want to say things of some other kinds to these people
(f)   when I say things to these people, I often feel something good
(g)   I think these people think the same about me
(h) I think like this about these people

(X's) rodzina
(a) many people
(b) these people are like one thing
(c) because every one of these people is a mother, father, wife, husband, or child of
    another one of them
(d) X is part of this thing
(e) X's mother and father are part of this thing
(f) other people are part of this thing

X's family
(a) some people, not many people
(b) these people are like one thing
(c) because every one of these people is a mother, father, wife, husband, or child of
    another one of them
(d) X is part of this thing
(e) X's children are part of this thing

(my) mate₁
(a) everyone knows: many men think about some other men like this:
(b)   this person is someone like me
(c)   I have to do some things
(d)   I couldn't do them if another person didn't do them with me

(e)   I want to do them with this person
(f)   this person is often in the same place as I
(g)   this person does the same things as I
(h)   this person does these things with me
(i)   the same things happen to this person as to me
(j) I think like this about this person
(k) I know: this person thinks the same about me

(my) mate
(a) everyone knows: many men think about some other men like this:
(b)   these people are people like me
(c)   these people are often in the same place as I
(d)   these people do the same things as I
(e)   these people do these things with me
(f)   the same things happen to these people as to me
(g)   I want to do good things for these people
(h)   when something bad happens to one of these people,
           it will be bad if I don't do something good for this person
(i)   I don't want bad things to happen to these people
           as I don't want bad things to happen to me
(j)   I don't want to say bad things about one of these people to other people
(k)   I don't want other people to say bad things about one of these people
(l)   I don't want other people to do anything bad to one of these people
(m)   these people think the same about me
(n) when men think like this about other men, they feel something good
(o) I think like this about this person

Lexicon as a Key to Ethno-Philosophy, History, and Politics

"Freedom" in Latin, English, Russian, and Polish

The world has never had a good definition of the word
liberty.

Abraham Lincoln

1. 'Freedom'—a culture-specific concept

Most of the copious literature on the concept of 'freedom' has come from philosophers
of various sorts. To the best of my knowledge, there is hardly any serious linguistic
literature on the subject. Yet linguistic analysis of this concept could play a valuable
role. In particular, what is lacking in the philosophical literature is an analysis of
'freedom' and related concepts undertaken from a cross-linguistic perspective—an
analysis which would be able to reveal, in a rigorous and methodical way, the
similarities and the differences between concepts related to 'freedom' which have been
lexically encoded in different languages, and which are often assumed to be simply
identical.[1]

Philosophers, political scientists, and students of law are usually aware of the
untranslatability of more or less technical concepts such as 'bail', 'warrant', 'custody',
'solipsism', 'determinism', 'parliament', 'oath', and 'democracy'. There is, however,

125

much less awareness that nontechnical concepts such as those encapsulated in the English words *freedom, justice* and *truth* are also language-specific. An awareness is also lacking of the fact that words encode certain conceptualizations rather than any objective "pictures" of reality, or that the same situation or state of affairs can be differently construed (cf. Langacker 1987, 1990) for the purposes of linguistic encoding.

In the philosophical literature on freedom, the authors usually express their own views about freedom (or try to elucidate the views of some other philosopher or writer; see e.g. Johnson 1980). But a certain "view" is encoded in the very meaning of a word such as *freedom*. This view encapsulated in the meaning of a word constitutes an important social fact. It reflects the dominant outlook of a society and, to some extent, perpetuates that outlook. It is important, therefore, that in writing about topics such as freedom all authors should be able to disentangle their own view from the view embodied in language-specific lexical items such as *freedom* (English), *libertas* (Latin), and *svoboda* (Russian), that they should try not to allow their native language to colour their perceptions of the philosophical issues under discussion, and that they should try to reach in their discussion a language-independent philosophical perspective.[2]

From a linguistic point of view, it is particularly important that language-specific concepts encoded in key words such as *freedom, libertas,* and *svoboda* be accurately decoded and translated into a culture-independent semantic metalanguage which would make the similarities and the differences between them explicit.

In what follows, I am going to discuss the concept encapsulated in the English word *freedom* and several related concepts: 'libertas' (Latin), 'liberty' (English), 'svoboda' and 'volja' (Russian), and 'wolność' (Polish). In each case, I will try to reduce complex and language-specific notions to simple and universal concepts such as 'want', 'do', 'can', 'other', 'people', and 'good'.

2. Libertas

As pointed out by Wirszubski and many others, the Latin *libertas* "primarily denotes the status of a 'liber', i.e. a person who is not a slave"; and it implies "the negation of the limitations imposed by slavery" (1950:1). As a first approximation, then, the concept encoded in *libertas* can be explicated along the lines suggested by Cicero (Paradoxa Stoicorum; quoted in Lewis and Short 1962):

> quid est enim libertas? potestas vivendi ut velis
>
> 'because what is *libertas*? it is the ability to
>   live as you want to'

Obviously, nobody can live entirely "as they want," or do all the things that they want to do, because of the manifold limitations on human life. To be able to live as one wants to means to be in control of one's own life—as a *liber* was, and as a slave was not. But this "ability to live as you want" was not understood as any "freedom from restraints" or "the unqualified power to do whatever one likes" (Wirszubski 1950:7). It was seen as consistent with restraint, and it was often contrasted by Roman authors with *licentia*, the first being presented as moderate and restrained, the latter as immoderate and unconstrained. Two examples (from Wirszubski 1950:6):

> Illa vetus (Graecia) . . . hoc una malo concidit, libertate immoderata ac licentia contionum. (Cicero, Pro Flacco, 16)

> 'That old Greece . . . collapsed through that one weakness: an immoderate *libertas* or *licentia* of public gatherings.'

> Licentia plebis sine modo libertatem exercensis. (Livy, XXIII, 2, 1)

> 'The license of the common people, exercising their *libertas* without any restraint.'

In fact, the same Cicero who in one context defined *libertas* as *potestas vivere ut velis* ('being able to live as you want') in another stated that *libertas* consists in laws (*libertas in legibus consistit;* De Legibus, quoted in Wirszubski 1950:87).

Consider also the following sentence (from one of Cicero's letters, quoted in the *Oxford Latin Dictionary*):

> . . . sibi libertatem censent Graeci datam, ut Graeci inter se disceptent suis legibus. (Cicero, Epistulae ad Atticum)

> '. . . the *libertas* given to the Greeks, to decide things among themselves by their own laws.'

There is no question here of there being no restrictions on the Greeks' actions; what they want is to govern themselves. Interestingly, *libertas* of this kind can be GIVEN to them (as it could be given to a slave), so that they could become—within the bounds of what is possible—their own masters. The concept of 'libertas' doesn't imply a total absence of constraints on what a person can do, but only the ability to shape one's life, as far as possible, according to one's own wishes (that is, to be ruled by oneself rather than by somebody else).

The idea reflected in the Latin concept of 'libertas' appears therefore to be close to what Berlin (1969) calls (using the words *freedom* and *liberty* interchangeably) "the notion of positive freedom": "The 'positive' sense of the word 'liberty' derives from the wish on the part of the individual to be his own master. I wish my life and decisions to depend on myself, not on external forces of whatever kind. I wish to be the instrument of my own, not of other men's, acts of will" (131).

Charles Taylor (1982) makes the same point: "Doctrines of positive freedom are concerned with a view of freedom which involves essentially the exercising of control over one's life. On this view, one is free only to the extent that one has effectively determined oneself and the shape of one's life. The concept of freedom here is an exercise-concept" (213). If one doesn't live as one wants to it is because one lives as a slave—a slave of somebody else or, metaphorically speaking, a slave of circumstances. To have *libertas* means, essentially, not to be a slave to anybody or anything (cf. Johnson 1980):

Quae sit libertas? Nulli rei servire, nulli necessitati, nullis casibus, fortunam in aecquum deducere. (Seneca, Epistulae ad Lucilium; quoted in Stevenson 1958:723)

'What is freedom? It means not being a slave to any circumstance, to any constraint, to any chance; it means compelling Fortune to enter the lists on equal terms.' [Stevenson's translation].

In accordance with this discussion and illustrations, we could try to explicate the concept of 'libertas' as follows:

libertas (e.g., *X habet libertatem* 'X has freedom')
(a) someone (X) can think something like this:
(b)   when I do something I do it because I want to do it
(c)   not because someone else says to me:
      "you have to do it because I want you to do it"
(d) this is good for X

Components (b) and (c) show, roughly speaking, that one is one's own master and not a person under someone else's control, like a slave; and component (d) is needed to account for the positive connotations of the word, clear from nearly all the quotes adduced in large Latin dictionaries, such as, for example, Lewis and Short (1962). The presence of such positive connotations is also clear from common collocations such as *libertatem dare* 'to give freedom', *libertatem promittere* 'to promise freedom', *se in libertatem vindicare* 'to liberate oneself', and *favor libertatis* 'the gift of freedom'.

Taylor's idea of an "exercise-concept" applies to *libertas* in so far as this word could clearly be used to refer to actual behavior rather than to mere possibilities. To illustrate (examples from *Oxford Latin dictionary* 1968–1982):

summa libertas in oratione, multae facetiae (Cicero, Brutus)

'extreme *libertas* in speech, many jokes'

nimia libertas in adulescentia (Cicero, pro Caelio)

'excessive *libertas* in adolescence'

omnium rerum impunitam libertatem tenere (Cicero, De oratore)

'to maintain *libertas* in all things, with impunity'

tanta libertate verborum (Trebon, Epistulae ad Familiares)

'with such *libertas* of words (i.e. with such frankness, outspokenness)'

It might be suggested that *libertas* has more than one meaning and that the sentences adduced above do not exemplify the same meaning as Cicero's definition quoted at the outset. But even if one assumes that this is true, one will have to admit that the hypothetical second meaning is closely related to the first one:

(libertas₂)
(a) someone (X) can think something like this:
(b)   when I do something I do it because I want to do it
(c)   I don't have to think:
      "I can't do something because someone doesn't want me to do it"

3. Freedom

At first sight, the concept encoded in the English word *freedom* may seem to be identical with that encoded in the Latin word *libertas*. On closer inspection, however, certain interesting differences emerge. In fact, in several of the sentences with *libertas* quoted here, *freedom* could not be used, or would alter the meaning. For example, the phrase *freedom of speech* could not be used in the sense of "frankness," "outspokenness," or "poetic license" (and *freedom of words* would not be used at all); nor would one speak in English of **freedom maintained with impunity*. Similarly, one could not **exercise freedom*, as one could *exercere* ('exercise') *libertatem* (Acc.), as in the quote from Livy. In English, one can *exercise power* or *exercise one's rights* but not *freedom*. Furthermore, one could not always translate *freedom* as *libertas*. In particular, phrases such as *freedom from persecution* or *freedom from tyranny* (to be discussed in more detail below) could not be rendered as **libertas ab insectatione* or **libertas a dominatione*, because *libertas* didn't take "negative" ("privative") complements of this kind.

    The main difference between the two concepts relates to what might be called, loosely, a more "negative" orientation of *freedom*. This "negative" orientation can be interpreted in two different senses. First, it has to do with being able NOT TO DO things that one doesn't want to do; and second, with being able to do things that one wants to do WITHOUT INTERFERENCE from other people.

    The first aspect can be represented as follows:

freedom =>
if I don't want to do something I don't have to do it

There is no evidence whatsoever that a component of this kind was included in the Latin concept 'libertas', or that it is, or ever has been, included in the English concept of 'liberty' (even though the meaning of this last word has changed, as we will discuss later).

    The second "negative" aspect of *freedom* is highlighted in Isaiah Berlin's discussion of what he calls "the notion of 'negative' freedom." Unfortunately, as pointed out earlier, in Berlin's discussion the English words *freedom* and *liberty* are used interchangeably. This is confusing because these two words do not mean the same, and in fact what Berlin calls "the notion of 'negative' freedom" has become largely incorporated in the word *freedom*, whereas the word *liberty* in its earlier meaning was much closer to the Latin *libertas* and in its current meaning reflects a different concept, which is a product of the Anglo-Saxon culture. The polarization of the two concepts, 'freedom' and 'liberty', is in itself culturally revealing—a point which is lost if the two words are used interchangeably. Bearing this in mind, let us consider Berlin's explanation of "the notion of 'negative' freedom": "I am normally said to be free to the degree to which no man or body of men interferes with my activity. Political liberty in this sense is simply the area within which a man can act unobstructed by others. If I am prevented by others from doing what I could otherwise do, I am to that degree unfree" (1969:122–123).

    According to Berlin, the classical English political philosophers understood the notion of 'freedom' precisely in that sense. Berlin quotes in this connection Hobbes' statement: "A free man is he that . . . is not hindered to do what he hath the will to do" (123), and he attributes the same conception to Bentham, Locke, Adam Smith, and John Stuart Mill:

> . . . whatever the principle in terms of which the area of non-interference is to be drawn, . . . liberty in this sense means liberty *from*; absence of interference beyond the shifting, but always recognizable, frontier. . . . 'All the errors which a man is likely to commit against advice and warning are far outweighed by the evil of allowing others to constrain him to what they deem is good' (Mill). The defense of liberty consists in the 'negative' goal of warding off interference. (126–127)

It is interesting to note Berlin's emphasis on the preposition *from* ("liberty *from*"). In fact, the English word *liberty* does not take the preposition *from*, and apparently never did, whereas the word *freedom* does.[3] This syntactic property of the word *freedom*, which distinguishes it from *libertas* as well as *liberty*, provides evidence for the view that the new conception of what *'libertas/liberty'* should consist in led to the emergence in Anglo culture of a new concept: that encapsulated in the word *freedom*, as it is used in modern English. I would explicate the meaning of this concept as follows:

> *freedom*
> (a) someone (X) can think something like this:
> (b)   if I want to do something I can do it
> (c)   no one else can say to me: "you can't do it because I don't want this"
> (d)   if I don't want to do something I don't have to do it
> (e)   no one else can say to me: "you have to do it because I want this"
> (f)   this is good for X
> (g) it is bad if someone cannot think this

By positing this component, I do not wish to defend the view that words such as *libertas* or *freedom* present the states of affairs to which they refer as morally good. Certainly, English phrases and expressions such as *free of tax* and *free of tourists* don't imply any moral judgment, in the way words such as *kind, courageous, honest,* and *just* do. It is a mistake, however, to conclude from this (as e.g. Sommerville 1962 does) that the word *free* is free of any evaluative component. *Free* doesn't imply an absolute value judgment ('I think this is good'), but it does imply a value judgment relative to the experiencer ('I think this is good for X'). The collocation *free from Z* implies that Z is seen as something bad for the person X and that it is good for X to be "free" from it.[4]

Charles Taylor (1982) contrasts the "positive" and "negative" conceptions of (what he calls) *freedom* in terms of control actually exercised versus options. In contrast to "doctrines of positive freedom," "negative theories can rely simply on an opportunity-concept, where being free is a matter of what we can do, of what it is open to us to do, whether or not we do anything to exercise these options" (213).

The explications of the concepts *libertas* and *freedom* proposed here incorporate Taylor's distinction as well. The following component of *libertas*:

> when I do something I do it because I want to do it

refers to control which is actually exercised, whereas the corresponding components of *freedom*:

> (a) if I want to do something I can do it
> (b) if I don't want to do something I don't have to do it

refer to options which are open to us. What Taylor calls "the opportunity-concept" is accounted for in the first component above: 'if I want to do something I can do it'; but it is both the components above ((a) and (b)) which jointly account for what Taylor refers to as "options."

It is interesting to note in this connection Locke's comment: "In this then consists freedom, in our being able to act, or not to act, as we shall choose, or will" ("An essay concerning human understanding," quoted in OED). In essence, Locke's idea of "freedom" differs from Cicero's idea of "libertas" ("What is *libertas?* It is the possibility to live as you want to") precisely in the way suggested by the explications proposed in this chapter: *libertas* focused on doing things that one wants to do, whereas *freedom* focuses on being able to do things that one wants to do and not to do things that one doesn't want to do. The notion of "non-interference," stressed by Berlin, is spelled out in the components referring to other people ('no one else can say to me: you can't do it because I don't want this', 'no one else can say to me: you have to do it because I want this').[5]

In support of the explication of *freedom* proposed here I would draw attention, above all, to the syntactic fact mentioned earlier: in English one can speak not only of "freedom OF" or "freedom TO" (something desirable, e.g. freedom of action, freedom of trade, freedom to emigrate, and so on) but also of "freedom FROM" (something undesirable). The combination of *freedom* with the preposition *from* has been possible in English for centuries, but in modern English the range of nouns which can occur in this phrase has changed. For example, OED cites the following sentences illustrating this pattern:

> Though age from folly could not give me freedom,
> It does from childishnesse. (Shakespeare, 1606)

> Promising to the doers long life, health . . . , freedome from losses, and the like. (Purchas, 1614)

> The contemplation of our own freedom from the evils which we see represented. (Burke, 1756)

But in contemporary English, one would not speak of **freedom from folly, childishness, losses,* or *evils.* Nor would one speak of **freedom from illness, death, stupidity, injustice,* or *neglect.* On the other hand, one may very well speak of *freedom from persecution, harassment, oppression, tyranny, coercion, external control,* or *interruption,* as in the following sentence:

> This isolation, though it had, as Wittgenstein anticipated, 'great disadvantages,' was necessary if he were to enjoy the freedom from interruption he thought essential for his work. (Monk 1991:525)

The generalization appears to be this: *freedom from X* is felicitous if X refers to situations when other people do something to us, thus preventing us from doing what we want to do and what we think we have the right to do.

By a kind of rhetorical extension, *freedom from X* can also be used in situations when some condition prevents us from doing what we want to do and what we have the right to do, as in the case of *freedom from hunger* or *freedom from poverty*. Expressions of this kind constitute a kind of political statement: "Everyone has the right to do what they want to do and not to be prevented from it by X (hunger, poverty, etc.)." The implication is that hunger, poverty, and so on are social conditions IMPOSED on the sufferers by other people. *Freedom from illness* is not felicitous because it would imply that illness, too, is a social evil, imposed on some people by other people's actions or impardonable neglect. This point can be illustrated with Roosevelt's famous "four freedoms":

> In the future days . . . we look forward to a world founded upon four essential human
> freedoms. The first is freedom of speech and expression . . . The second is freedom
> of every person to worship God in his own way. . . . The third is freedom from want
> . . . The fourth is freedom from fear. (Quoted in OED)

Clearly, Roosevelt is speaking here of the social and political conditions which should be created in the "future world"; for example, his *freedom from fear* cannot be taken to refer to fear of death, or illness, it can only be interpreted as referring to fear of other people, born out of unjust social and political structures. As Locke (1690, quoted in OED) put it, "The modern spirit of liberty is the love of individual independence."

This "negative" semantics of *freedom* corresponds, then, to the ideal of "non-imposition," which is one of the major cultural themes in the Anglo world. It is not the ability to do whatever one wants that is a key Anglo ideal, because the supreme goal of individual rights is linked in this culture with a general recognition of other people's individual rights. It is "non-imposition" which is the key idea: "Maybe I can't do some things that I'd like to do, but at least no one else is going to prevent me from doing what I want and what I have the right to do." It is crucial to this conception that what applies to me applies also to everyone else: *freedom* is not just a privilege that some people may enjoy ('it is good for this person') but a universal right ('it is bad if someone can't think this'). The emergence of the concept of 'freedom' in the English language reflects the rise of this modern ideal; and the victory of *freedom* over *liberty* is a testimony to the shift in preoccupations and in values.

4. Liberty

The Statue of Liberty was once—and to many, still is—a symbol of America. Yet the ideal of "liberty" encoded in seventeenth- and eighteenth-century English appears to have quickly declined in America, as the need to struggle for this ideal came to be perceived as less pressing.

In 1788, George Washington wrote, "Liberty, when it begins to take root, is a plant of rapid growth" (quoted in Stevenson 1958:1104). In general perception, by the end of the eighteenth century, the plant of liberty had not only taken root in America but had grown so rapidly that Benjamin Franklin felt able to proclaim confidently, "The sun of liberty is set; you might light up the candle of industry and economy" (quoted in Stevenson 1958:1004).

But if the "sun of liberty" (in the old sense of the word) was set, the "sun of freedom" (in the modern sense of the word) was beginning to rise. The eighteenth-century *liberty* stood, rather like the Latin *libertas* (or the French *liberté*), for the opposite of slavery and oppression, and the rise of democracy in America has no doubt contributed to the decline of "liberty" as an ideal to be constantly struggled for (cf. Tocqueville 1953[1835–1840]). It seems reasonable to suppose that it has, consequently, contributed to the decline of the use of the word *liberty*, and to a narrowing of its meaning (to be discussed later). In support of the intuitive impression that the word *liberty* has declined in use, I will mention just two illustrative figures: in the corpus of Shakespeare's works, there are, roughly speaking, 100 occurrences of *liberty* per 1 million words, whereas in the modern COBUILD corpus, there are, roughly speaking, 100 occurrences of *liberty* per 10 million words, and if we discount the occurrences of *Liberty* with a capital L (as in "Liberty Road" or "Statue of Liberty"), it will be 100 occurrences of *liberty* per 20 million words.[6] The proportion of *liberty* to *Liberty* (100:122) is significant in itself, since names of places, landmarks, and institutions are often inherited from earlier times and often enshrine older concepts and ideals.

At the same time, however, the growth of individualism in both England and America and the spread of the philosophy of individual rights (documented by Berlin and others) have led, as we have seen, to the emergence and spread of a new concept of 'freedom', reflected in the English word *freedom* in the modern sense of the word, that is to say, a concept defined more in opposition to "interference" and "imposition" than to "slavery" or "oppression." Furthermore, the word *liberty* did not disappear from use altogether but underwent semantic change. If the word *freedom* focused, above all, on the rights of an individual to be "left alone" by other people, the word *liberty* became gradually specialized in "public rights," that is, in the rights of social groups, guaranteed by suitable political structures.

To appreciate this shift in the meaning of *liberty*, it is sufficient to ponder some older uses of this word, reflected, for example, in the following quotations:

So loving-jealous of his liberty (Shakespeare, *Romeo and Juliet*, quoted in Stevenson 1958)

Man's liberty ends, and it ought to end, when that liberty becomes the curse of his neighbours. (Frederic William Ferrar, *Ideal of nations*, quoted in Stevenson 1958)

The liberty of the individual must be thus far limited; he must not make himself a nuisance to other people.
(J. S. Mill, *On liberty*, quoted in Stevenson 1958)

I enjoy large liberty to round this Globe of Earth. (Milton, 1671, quoted in OED)

The difference between the modern English concept of 'freedom' and the older concept of 'liberty' is well illustrated by the difference in meaning between the two expressions: *freedom of speech* and *liberty of the tongue*, as in the following example:

John the Baptist, whom Herod had beheaded for the libertie of his tongue (John Knox, 1558, quoted in OED)

Freedom of speech emphasizes the fact that other people can't stop us from saying what we want to say. By contrast, *liberty of the tongue* emphasizes the fact that one says what one wants to say without taking other people's reactions into account. More precisely, *liberty* in that older sense can be explicated as follows:

liberty (older)
(a) someone (X) can think something like this:
(b)   if I want to do something I can do it
(c)   I don't have to think:
(d)   someone can say: "I don't want this"
(e)   I can't do it because of this

Other older examples of the use of *liberty* adduced by OED support an explication along these lines. Consider, for example, the following:

You have my full liberty [*freedom] to publish them. (Henry Fielding, *Tom Jones*, 1749)

In this sentence, *liberty* suggests something similar to permission, but in fact it is entirely compatible with the explication proposed above. The speaker is conveying the following message:

you can think something like this:
    if I want to publish them, I can do it
    I don't have to think:
        someone can think: 'I don't want this'
        I can't do it because of that

Needless to say, *freedom* cannot be used in a context of this kind. A few further examples:

Youthful men, who give their eyes the liberty of gazing. (Shakespeare, *Comedy of errors*, 1590, quoted in OED)

Here, too, *permission* (*to*) could be used instead of *liberty(of)*, but the meaning would clearly not be the same: *liberty* implies here, as in other contexts, that one does what one wants to do, without feeling constrained by other people's possible disapproval.

Bid him come in and wait for the liberty [*freedom] to talk. (Harriet Martineaux, 1833; quoted in OED)

Some particular matters, which I am not at liberty to report (Richard Steele, *Tatler*, no. 109, 1709, quoted in OED)

In this last example, it is particularly clear that *not at liberty* refers to the fact that one feels bound by what someone else may say and wish.

Similarly, the expression *to take the liberty* clearly refers to something that the agent wants to do, although someone else may not like it, and has nothing to do with anything that the agent has to do, or doesn't have to do.

> I will . . . take the liberty to give them . . . my opinion. (William Cobbett, 1818, quoted in OED)

The expression *to take the liberty* is one of the very few contexts in which the older *liberty* has survived. Generally speaking, the history of the English language has confirmed in a spectacular way the justice of Benjamin Franklin's statement that "the sun of liberty is set." In contemporary English, outside a few set phrases, *liberty* is confined, by and large, to political discourse, and it is usually used with respect to peoples rather than persons. To illustrate:

> The eyes of the world are upon you. The hopes and prayers of liberty-loving people everywhere march with you. (Dwight D. Eisenhower, Order to his troops, June 6, 1944, D-Day, quoted in Bloomsbury 1991)

> I would remind you that extremism in the defense of liberty is no vice. (Barry Goldwater, 1964, quoted in Bloomsbury 1991)

> In totalitarian states there is no *liberty* of expression for writers and no *liberty* of choice for their readers. (Aldous Huxley, quoted in Merriam-Webster 1972)

Above all, the possessive use of *liberty* (as in *man's liberty*, or *his liberty)* sharply declined. This sharp decline in the use of possessive modifiers can be illustrated with the following figures: in Shakespeare's corpus, 23% of all the occurrences of *liberty* have a possessive modifier (23 out of 83), whereas in the COBUILD corpus, only 5% do (12 out of 222, including *Liberty*). Even if we excluded all the examples of *Liberty*, the figure would still be considerably less than in Shakespeare's corpus (12 out of 100; 3 of these 12 being instances of the technical phrase *liberty of the subject*). Possessive modifiers suggest an individual right or privilege. If *liberty* tends not to take modifiers any longer, this suggests that the idea enshrined in it has come to be seen as a kind of absolute.

Thus, *liberty* has survived (barely) as a word for an abstract ideal, on a par, it would seem, with other words for abstract ideals such as *justice* and *brotherhood.*[7] Nouns of this kind tend to take no complements or prepositional phrases, or at least to be highly limited in this respect. For example, one can say, "John's honesty is not in question," but hardly, "John's justice is not in question" (although "God's justice" is still possible). Names of abstract ideals of this kind are usually restricted to rhetorical generalizations, such as the following:

> Of a truth, men are mystically united: a mysterious bond of brotherhood makes all men one. (Thomas Carlyle, *Essays*, quoted in Stevenson 1958)

The crest and crowning of all good,
Life's final star, is Brotherhood. (Edwin Markham, *Brotherhood*, quoted in Stevenson 1958)

Words of this kind appear to refer to some unquestionable value judgment, along the lines of "people say this is good" or "everyone knows this is good" (not just good for some particular person, but simply good). *Liberty* in its present rhetorical usage belongs to this category of concepts. Tentatively, it can be explicated as follows:

liberty (current)
(a) everyone can think something like this:
(b)   if I want to do something because I think it is good I can do it
(c)   no one can say: "this person can't do it because I don't want this"
(d) everyone thinks: this is good

Clearly, *liberty* in its present usage does not refer to a person's ability to act as they please with respect to anything whatsoever, no matter how trivial or selfish: the moral connotations of the word suggest that *liberty* has to do with everybody's inalienable right to do what they think is right and good ('if I want to do something because I think it is good I can do it'). As the seventeenth-century governor of Massachussets, John Winthrop, put it a long time before the word *liberty* narrowed its use to enshrine the ideal in question, "a liberty to do that only which is good, just, and honest" (quoted in Stevenson 1958).

5. The older meaning of *freedom*

It is important to point out that the meaning of the word *freedom* has changed, too, and that this word didn't always embody what Berlin calls the "negative conception of freedom." In older English, *freedom* appears to have meant something much closer to *liberty*, although the fact that the two words could be conjoined, as in the example below, seems to suggest that they never meant exactly the same:

They died for the Libertie and Freedom of their Cittie.
(Holden Sneton, 1606, quoted in OED)

To show the change which has taken place in the meaning of *freedom*, I will adduce several examples of the earlier usage (all from OED):

1. Alexander of Macedon . . . shall rule powerfully and with great freedom and absoluteness. (Bp. Hall, 1633)

In this sentence, *freedom* has nothing to do with any potential or actual interference from other people; rather, it refers to the fact that Alexander would do what he wanted to do without taking into account what other people might want him to do and without considering himself bound in any way by other people's wishes.

2. Hee would not permit Merchants and Sea-men to enjoy a freedom of that Sea . . . but at an extraordinairie rate. (Needham, 1652)

"To enjoy a freedom of that Sea" does not mean to be able to use it without interference from others, but to be able to use it and not to have to think that one cannot use it because someone who is in control of that sea may not want us to do so.

> 3. Having conferred on you the freedom of the library, he will not concern himself by observing how you use it. (Burton, 1862)

It might be suggested that in this last example *freedom* is used in the sense of "permission," but in fact this example does not differ significantly from the preceding one, where *freedom* is used IN COMBINATION with the word *permit* (and therefore cannot itself mean "permission"). Both examples (2 and 3) are compatible with the interpretation which says that someone can do what they want to do (with something) without having to worry that their action might be in conflict with the wishes of some person who is in control.

Essentially, the same applies to example 4, where the agent herself is under somebody else's control:

> 4. Let her alone to make the best use of those innocent Freedoms I allow her. (Otway, 1681)

In example 5, *freedom* is conjoined with *privilege*, which shows that here, too, what is involved is a "vertical" rather than a "horizontal" relation (that is, something closer to permission than to noninterference):

> 5. All Foreigners might freely come and reside in any Part of the Kingdom with the like Privileges and Freedoms as our selves. (W. Wood, 1719)

When the word *freedom* is applied to an animal, as in example 6, the implication usually is that the animal has no "master" (and not that it is not "imposed upon" or "interfered with"):

> 6. Neither age nor force
> Can quell the love of freedom in a horse. (Cooper, 1782)

The final two examples adduced below (7 and 8) may seem to be very different from the preceding ones, but in fact they can be explained in terms of the same semantic formula.

> 7. And laughed and joked with everyone . . . with the utmost freedom. (F. Darwin, 1887)

> 8. When officers do not eat or drink or take too many freedoms with the seamen. (J.S.C. Abbott, 1854)

These two examples appear to imply something like an absence of self-control, rather than the presence of control from somebody else. But it is not a matter of someone's being UNABLE to control themselves; rather, it is a matter of feeling that one doesn't HAVE to control oneself. Clearly, if one laughs and jokes "with the utmost freedom," there is no question of someone else's trying to stop one from doing what one wants to do but rather of one not having to think of what other people might say about our

behavior. Similarly, if an officer "takes freedoms with the seamen," there is no
question of somebody else's trying or not trying to stop the officer from doing so, but
rather of the officer not thinking of someone else's possible disapproval.

All these examples (1–8), therefore, different as they may seem, are compatible
with the following semantic formula:

> *freedom* (older)
> someone (X) can think something like this:
>   if I want to do something, I can do it
>   I don't have to think: I can't do it

This formula differs from that assigned to the older meaning of *liberty* in the absence
of the component 'someone can say: I don't want it'. In support of this distinction, I
would adduce the fact that *freedom* (earlier: *fredom*) could also be used in the sense
of "largesse," "generosity," "magnanimity." As C. S. Lewis points out, *The Franklin's
Tale* "gives us a sort of competition in *fredom* (magnanimity, generosity) and hands
over to the reader the problem 'which was the most free'" (1990:116). This use of
freedom is compatible with the component (A) 'I don't have to think: I can't do it' but
hardly with the more elaborate (B) 'I don't have to think: someone can say: I don't
want it'.

C. S. Lewis points also to an older use of the adjective *free* (*freo*) which (in my
view) is compatible with (A) but not with (B): "After her miraculous healing the blind
woman in the old version of Bede, who had been laid to the shrine by her maids, went
home 'freo on her own feet'" (1990:114). Having been cured and going home by
herself, the woman could plausibly think (A): 'I don't have to think: I can't do it'; but
there is no question here of other people's possible wishes (version B).

Of course, the meaning of the adjective *free* is one thing, and the meaning of the
noun *freedom* another. I admit that some aspects of the explication proposed here are
speculative, and I do not claim that it is necessarily entirely accurate. Be that as it may,
the examples adduced make it quite clear that the meaning of *freedom* has changed,
and that it has changed, roughly speaking, in the direction of "negative freedom" (in
Berlin's sense): clearly, the older meaning of *freedom* makes no reference to things
that one DOESN'T want to do, or to other people's potential or actual attempts to stop
us from doing what we want to do.

6. *Svoboda*

The Russian concept of 'svoboda' might seem at first glance to correspond exactly to
the English concept of 'freedom', especially in view of the fact that, unlike *libertas*,
or *liberty*, the word *svoboda* can take sometimes a "negative" complement corresponding, roughly, to the English *from*-phrase. For example:

> Soveršenno novoe dlja nego čuvstvo svobody ot prošedšego oxvatyvalo ego. (L.
> Tolstoy, *Cossacks*, quoted in SRJ)

> 'He was overcome by a completely new feeling of liberation from the past.' (Literally
> 'A feeling of *svoboda* [*freedom] from the past, completely new for him, came over
> him.')

Nikto tak ne nuždaetsa v svobode ot prizrakov, kak prostec, i nič'e osvoboždenie ne možet tak blagotvorno otozvat'sja na celom obščestve, kak osvoboždenie prosteca. (Saltykov, quoted in SRJ)

'Nobody needs *svoboda* [*freedom] from phantoms as much as the simple, uneducated man, and nobody's liberation can have a more positive influence on the whole society than that of the simple, uneducated man.'

But despite these superficial similarities, *svoboda* doesn't mean the same as *freedom*, and it embodies a different perspective on human life. The fact that even in the sentences adduced above, where *svoboda* takes the preposition *ot* 'from', it could not be rendered in English as *freedom* (as the asterisk on **freedom* indicates) provides evidence for this.

Furthermore, if *svoboda* often cannot be translated as *freedom*, *freedom* often cannot be translated as *svoboda*. For example, English expressions such as *freedom from interruption*, *freedom from interference*, or *freedom from harassment* could hardly be translated into Russian as **svoboda ot vmešatel'stva* or the like. To render *freedom from hunger* or *freedom from poverty* as **svoboda ot goloda* or **svoboda ot nuždy* is completely out of the question.

As a further example of a sentence where *svoboda* could hardly be rendered in English as *freedom*, consider the following:

Svoboda poezii v tom, čtoby ne stesnjat' svoego darovanija proizvol'nymi pretenzijami i pisat' o tom, k čemu ležit duša. (Černyševskij, quoted in SRJ)

'The *svoboda* [?freedom] of poetry consists in not restricting one's talent by arbitrary pretensions and in writing what one's heart desires.'

In this sentence, *svoboda* refers to the absence of self-imposed restrictions and pressures that limit the poet's spontaneity and ability to relax and to follow one's inspiration and desires.

It is interesting to note in this connection that *svoboda* can also be used in a somewhat different, though related, sense, as in the sentences below, where it suggests something like ease and relaxation (quotes from SRJ):

Volodja otvečal emu (učitelju) s svobodoj i uverennost'ju, svojstvennoj tem, kto xorošo znaet predmet. (L. Tolstoj)

'Volodja's answers to the teacher's questions were given with the ease [*freedom] and confidence of one who knows the subject well.'

Aeroplan letel protiv vetra. No s kakoj svobodoj, vpervye porazivšej menja, on obošel oblaka! (Kaverin)

'The aeroplane was flying against the wind. But with what startling ease [*freedom] it wound its way around the clouds!'

V manerax ego, i bez togo razvjaznyx, stala projavljat'sja i ta obyknovennaja za butylkoj svoboda, ot kotoroj vsegda nelovko stanovitsja trezvomu sobesedniku. (Gončarov)

'His manners, already casual, began to display that characteristic drunken ease [*freedom] which is always so disconcerting for the sober interlocutor.'

In all these sentences, the word *svoboda* refers to the manner with which some actions are performed. It could be argued that in sentences of this kind *svoboda* is used with a second meaning, different from the meaning it has, for example, in phrases such as *bor'ba za svobodu* 'struggle for freedom'. I think, however, that even if one accepts that *svoboda* is polysemous, one should still recognize the clues which the second sense offers to the primary meaning. The crucial aspect of *svoboda* highlighted by the secondary use of this word is something like "ease" or "relaxation." It is very significant in this respect that all Russian dictionaries define *svoboda* partly with reference to the words *stesnjat'* or stesnenie, from *tesno* 'tight', as if *svoboda* was, essentially, a "loosening" of some sort of material or psychological straitjacket. In the examples adduced in dictionaries, too, the words *stesnjat'* ('to constrain, to hamper') and stesnenie (noun) very frequently co-occur with *svoboda*, as if the two concepts were closely related. A few examples:

Nikto ne stesnjal moej svobody. Ja delal, čto xotel, osobenno s tex por, kogda rasstalsja s poslednim moim guvernerom-francuzom. (Turgenev, quoted in SRJ)

'Nobody restricted [*stesnjal*] my freedom [*svoboda*]. I did whatever I wanted, especially after the departure of my last French tutor.'

Učast' vaša rešena: ja vas ne stesnjaju . . . predostavljaju vam polnuju svobodu. (Pisemskij, quoted in SRJ)

'Your destiny has been decided: I'm not going to restrict you . . . I give you complete (full) freedom [*svoboda*].'

And one characteristic peasant-style example from Dal' (1955[1882])

Nikakoj svobodiški net, tesnjat vsem, otovsjudu.

'There is no *svoboda* [Dim.], they are squeezing [me, us] from all sides.'

One can't help thinking in this context of the much-discussed question of the importance of the traditional swaddling clothes in Russian culture. Some students of Russia have gone so far as to see in the centuries of almost universal use of swaddling clothes in Russian society a key to the understanding of the "Russian soul." For example, Erikson asks: "Is the Russian soul a swaddled soul?" (1963:388). To which he replies: "Some of the leading students of Russian character definitely think so" (cf. also Mead & Métraux 1953). Given these speculations, it is interesting to note that the Russian concept of *svoboda* fits remarkably well the image of a child unwrapped from its swaddling clothes and experiencing the pleasure of being able to move its limbs without any restrictions.

Unlike *libertas* or *freedom*, *svoboda* suggests a feeling of well-being, caused by the perceived absence of some pressure, some "squeezing," some tight, constraining bonds. It is interesting to note, in this context, the frequent collocation *dyšat' svobodno*, 'to breathe freely'. In English, *to breathe freely* would suggest that some obstacle to breathing (for example, a chicken bone) has been removed ("completely removed");

this would cause a relief but not an exhilarating sense of well-being. But in Russian, *dyšat'svobodno* suggests the image of some oppressive "straitjacket" being loosened, so that one's chest can freely expand ("fully expand") causing just that: an exhilarating sense of well-being.

The terms *completely* and *fully* have been contrasted advisedly in the last two sentences. The point is that *svoboda* has different collocations and different connotations than *freedom*. In particular, *svoboda* frequently occurs in the collocation *polnaja svoboda*, 'full *svoboda*', whereas **full freedom* is not felicitous in English: one can say *complete freedom*, but hardly **full freedom*. This difference between "full" *svoboda* and "complete" *freedom* is very significant because of the "positive" connotations of *full* and the "negative" of *complete*. One can speak, for example, of *full responsibility, full length, full blood*, or *full daylight*, but not of **complete responsibility, length, blood*, or *daylight*, and one can speak of *complete (*full) absence of, complete (*full) lack of, complete (*full) inability to*, and so on. *Freedom* can be "complete" because *complete freedom* suggests "complete absence" of interference, imposition, and so on. But *svoboda* is construed differently, as the following comment by the brilliant nineteenth century lexicographer Vladimir Dal' (1955[1882]) illustrates:

> *Svoboda*—svoja volja, prostor, vozmožnost' dejstvovat' po-svoemu; otsutstvie stesnen'ja, nevoli, rabstva, podčinenija čužoj vole. *Svoboda*—ponjatie sravnitel' noe: ona možet otnositsja do prostora častnogo, ograničennogo, k izvestnomu delu otnosjaščemusja, ili k raznym stepenjam ėtogo prostora, i nakonec k polnomu, neobuzdannomu proizvolu ili samovol'stvu.

> *Svoboda*—one's own will, boundless space (expanse), the possibility to act as one wants to; an absence of restrictions [*stesnenie*], slavery, subordination to someone else's will. *Svoboda* is a relative concept; it can refer to some particular, limited space, relevant to a given situation, or to different degrees of space, or, finally, to full, unbridled, arbitrary self-will.'

The connotations of "boundless space," broad, expandable space in which one can FULLY stretch, are strikingly present in *svoboda* and absent from *freedom* (though of course not incompatible with it).

All these considerations bring us to the following explication:

svoboda
(a) someone (X) can think something like this:
(b)   if I want to do something, I can do it
(c)   when I do something, I don't have to think:
      I can't do it as I want to do it because some (other) people do/say something
(d) X feels something good because of this

Component (c) accounts for the experiencer's sense that there are no external constraints on his or her actions, that there is no oppressive "straitjacket"; and component (d) spells out the resulting sense of exhilarating well-being. It is interesting to compare component (c) of *svoboda* with the corresponding component of *libertas*: 'when I do something, I do it because I want to do it, not because someone says to me: you have to do it because I want you to do it'. Clearly, the Latin concept focuses on not having a master (not being a slave), whereas the Russian one focuses on not sensing any external constraints. The corresponding English concept focuses, as we have seen, on options, and on the absence of interference from other people.

It might be suggested that the connotations of boundless space would be better accounted for if we assigned one additional "spatial" component to *svoboda*, along the lines of 'if I want to go somewhere I can do it'. I don't think, however, that this would be justified, given the fact that *svoboda* can also occur in phrases such as *svoboda pečati* ('freedom of the press') and *svoboda sovesti* ('freedom of conscience'). As we will see later, a "spatial" component will be assigned to another Russian word, *volja* (also translated into English as *freedom*), which cannot occur in such phrases. As for *svoboda*, the absence of any perceived constraints on one's actions (including movements) is, I think, sufficiently accounted for in component (c) of the explication: 'when I do something, I don't have to think: 'I can't do it as I want to do it (i.e. 'I can't do it the way I want to do it') because some people do/say something' and also in component (d) : 'X feels something good because of this'.

The cultural ideal enshrined in the Russian concept of 'svoboda' corresponds remarkably well to another well-known stereotype of the "Russian nature" (in addition to the "swaddled soul" stereotype), namely, the so-called *širokaja russkaja natura*, the 'broad Russian nature'. For example, Fedotov, in his article "Russkij čelovek" (The Russian character), describes the "broadness" (*širota*) of the Russian nature as the central feature of "Russianness" (1981:92).

The stereotype of a "broad Russian nature" suggests the image of a person who loathes restrictions, constraints, bonds of any kind, who feels the need to "spread out," to "overflow" any bounds like a flooding river. In fact, the elements, for example, wind, storm, or raging sea, provide another common image for *svoboda*, as in the following passages:

> Voda v gavani volnuetsja, šumit, budto serditsja na to, čto ee ogorodili krugom granitnymi kamnjami, lišiv svobody i prostora. (Novikov-Priboj, quoted in SRJ)
>
> 'The water in the port is breaking tumultuously and noisily as if it were angry at having been enclosed by granite stones and thus deprived of *svoboda* (?freedom) and space.'

In English, the notion of 'freedom' is not similarly linked with the elements, with boundless space, with "wild" behavior, with unconstrained breathing, with intoxicating freedom of movements. Rather, it is linked with individual rights, with private space, with being "left alone," with "privacy" and personal independence.

It is also interesting to note how many of the examples of *svoboda* adduced by large Russian dictionaries have to do with GIVING someone "full" *svoboda*, for example:

> [Dubrovskij] malo zanimalsja vospitaniem malen'kogo Saši, daval emu polnuju svobodu povesničat'. (Puškin, quoted in SRJ)
>
> 'Dubrovskij didn't do much to bring up little Saša, he gave him complete (literally "full") freedom to fool around as he liked.'

On skazal, čto ni na kom ne ženitsja, krome vas, . . . vam že on ostavil polnuju svobodu xot' sejčas ot nego otkazat'sja. (Dostoevskij, quoted in SRJ).

'He said that he wouldn't marry anybody except you; and at the same time he left you complete (literally "full") freedom to refuse him at any time, even right away.'

Examples of this kind suggest that *svoboda*, unlike *freedom*, can be seen as something that is arbitrarily GIVEN by another person (rather like the swaddling clothes being "arbitrarily" removed). This idea is not consistent with the notion of 'freedom', which crucially involves complete independence from other people. (At the most, someone may *let* you *have freedom*, that is, leave you alone, but hardly *give* you *freedom*, which would imply extreme dependence.)

While the "swaddling clothes" image helps to clarify the concept of 'svoboda', I would not join those who maintain that the traditional child-rearing practices should be seen as an explanation of the emergence of this concept. Much more plausibly, the semantic profile of *svoboda* can be linked with Russia's political history: the despotism of the tsars, the absence of democratic structures or an effective legal system applying equally to everyone, the importance of arbitrary power and the desirability of escape from that power, and so on (cf. Wittfogel 1963, Fedotov 1981, Solov'ev 1966–1970.)

It is worth recalling here the emphasis that many students of Russian history place on what they call "Russian antilegalism," "disparagement of law," "Russian legal nihilism," or "a deeply rooted tradition of anti-legal prejudice" (Walicki 1987:1). Often, comments of this kind are linked directly with remarks on the Russian "broad nature" and the Russian fear and hatred of "being cramped." For example, Weidle (quoted in Walicki 1987:10) wrote, "The largeness of soul on which a Russian prides himself gives him a feeling of being cramped when he is compelled to depend on rule of law."

Walicki quotes also (among many others) the remarks of the eminent nineteenth century Russian thinker Petr Chaadaev, "who saw his country as . . . strangely amorphous, lacking the discipline of forms, that is, the discipline of logic, of law, and of social conventions" (1987:11–12). The imagery used in such remarks seems to closely correspond to that linked with the notion of 'svoboda' (presence vs. absence of "forms," "constraints," "restraint," "discipline," and so on).

More than a century after Chaadaev made these remarks, another distinguished Russian writer, Andrej Amal'rik (author of the famous book *Will the Soviet Union survive until 1984?*) commented in the same vein:

Russkomu narodu, v silu li ego istoričeskix tradicij ili ešče čego-libo, počti soveršenno neponjatna ideja samoupravlenija, ravnogo dlja vsex zakona i ličnoj svobody—i svjazannoj s ètim otvetstvennosti. . . . Samo slovo "svoboda" ponimaetsja bol'šin- stvom naroda kak sinonim slova "besporjadok," kak vozmožnost' beznakazannogo soveršenija kakix-to antiobščestvennyx i opasnyx postupkov. (1978:43)

'Whether because of its historical traditions or for some other reason, the idea of self-government, of equality before the law and of personal freedom—and the responsibility that goes with these—are almost completely incomprehensible to the Russian people. . . . To the majority of the people the very word "freedom" is synonymous with "disorder" or the opportunity to indulge with impunity in some kind of anti-social or dangerous activity. (1970:31–32).

The published English translation of Amal'rik's work refers to "the very word 'freedom,'" but of course Amal'rik was talking about the Russian word *svoboda*, not the English word *freedom*.

The emphasis on the possible "anti-social" and "dangerous" effects of *svoboda* could conceivably indicate a new twist in the semantic history of this vital word, a twist which may have arisen in the Soviet era. But the general emphasis on the "anarchic" implications of this word is in keeping with the overall image of *svoboda* reflected in Russian thought and Russian literature.[8]

The semantic formula which I have proposed for *svoboda* is consistent with the (much-discussed) "anti-legal" bias of Russian culture. The component

> when I do something, I don't have to think:
> I can't do it as I want to do it
> because some (other) people do/say something

contrasts my own wishes with what "other people do or say." The opposition is not between my own wishes and someone else's wishes which that someone may seek to arbitrarily impose on me. Rather, it is an opposition between my wishes and the possibly cramping effect of "what some (other) people do or say," and "what some (other) people do or say" may include regulations of any kind, including legal norms.

The modern English concept of 'freedom' is not incompatible with restrictions and constraints; on the contrary, it suggests a perspective from which constraints imposed by the law can be seen as necessary to guarantee the inviolability of everyone's personal space (cf. Berlin 1969:127; see also Walicki 1984:226).

The Latin *libertas*, too, was seen as compatible with restrictions, although for different reasons. As Wirszubski put it, "*Libertas* is quite consistent with the dictates of the *disciplina Romana*, *mos maiorum*, and *instituta patrum*, because it is conceived of as a right and faculty, not of an isolated individual, but of the citizen in the organized community of the Roman State" (1950:8). But the Russian concept of 'svoboda', which evolved in a historical context very different from that of either England or Rome, does imply an enjoyable absence of constraints of any kind. In this respect, it is similar to another crucial Russian concept, 'volja', to which I will now turn.

7. *Volja*

As mentioned earlier, in addition to *svoboda*, Russian also has another word which can often be translated into English as *freedom*, but which encodes yet another concept: 'volja' (a word which also translates as *will*). In the nineteenth century, this word was used more broadly than now. For example, it was used in the slogan *zemlja i volja* (also the name of an organization) 'land and freedom'. Its nineteenth-century use is also illustrated in the words of the old song (quoted in SRJ):

> Za zemlju, za volju, za lučšuju dolju,
> Gotovy na smertnyj boj.

'For land, for freedom [*volja*], for a better life
We are ready to fight and to die.'

In contemporary Russian, however, the word *volja* would no longer be used in such contexts, having become restricted to life outside prison (and outside prison camps). The prison slang term *volnjaška*, common for example in Solzhenitsyn's novels, is clearly derived from that more narrow modern meaning of *volja*. *Volnjaški* (Pl.) are people who live in the world outside the prison system. The word reflected a prisoner's point of view (as the word *Gentile* reflects a Jew's point of view), and it conveyed a patronizing, superior attitude to the "free people," who were expected to be naive, untested, and weak, inferior to the tough and wise "zek."[9]

Fedotov (1981[1945]) describes the older concept of 'volja' in the following way:

> *Volja* is, above all, the possibility to live, or at least live for a while, just as one wants to, without feeling bound [*ne stesnjajas'*] by any social restrictions, not only chains. *Volja* is in conflict even with a person's equals, it is in conflict with the world. *Volja* triumphs either when one leaves the society for the limitless space of the steppe, or when one has power over society, when one can impose one's will over people, crushing any resistance. Personal *svoboda* requires respect for the *svoboda* of other people; but *volja* is always for oneself. It is not opposed to tyranny, because a tyrant is also a being endowed with *volja*. A brigand [*razbojnik*] represents the ideal of Muscovite *volja*, just as Ivan the Terrible represents the ideal of a tsar. Since *volja*, like anarchy, is impossible in a civilized society, the Russian ideal of *volja* finds its expression in a cult of the desert, of wild nature, of nomadic life, Gypsy life, wine, wild debauchery [*razgul*], passions oblivious of everything else [*somozabvenie strastej*], brigandry [*razbojničestvo*], rebellion, and tyranny. (183; my translation)

Fedotov, an emigré Russian writer (1886–1951) who only lived for a short time in the Soviet Union, regarded 'volja' as a concept more central to Russian culture than *svoboda*. It was *volja*, he suggested, that "the Russian people (*narod*) dreams and sings about, and that every Russian heart responds to. The word *svoboda* still feels somewhat like a translation of the French *liberté*. But nobody can deny the Russianness of *volja*. It is all the more essential to understand the difference between *volja* and *svoboda* as they sound to the Russian ear" (183; my translation).[10]

In contemporary Russian, however, *svoboda* is a much commoner and more central concept than *volja* (in the relevant sense). The frequencies of the two words cannot be compared directly because of the polysemy of *volja* (1. will, 2. freedom), but the relative frequencies of the adjectives *svobodnyj* and *vol'nyj* (198 versus 25, Zasorina 1977), speak for themselves. Moreover, the existence of the diminutive form *svobodiška* (as in the example from Dal's 1955[1882] dictionary quoted earlier) testifies to the salience of the concept of 'svoboda' in Russian folk culture, and not only in the culture of the Russian intelligentsia. Furthermore, if *svoboda* has ever sounded like a translation of the French *liberté*, it doesn't sound like that any more. In fact, Fedotov's own comments on *svoboda* (1981:183) make it clear that this word never corresponded exactly to *liberté*: "For a Muscovite, *svoboda* is a negative concept; it is a synonym of 'loosening of bonds' [*razpuščennost'*], impunity, lack of order and rigor of any kind [*bezobrazie*]" (my translation).

This description of *svoboda* tallies well with the analysis of the concept proposed in this chapter. But the French *liberté* does not have, and has never had, the connotations ascribed by Fedotov to *svoboda*. It has always been closer to the Latin *libertas* and to the English *liberty*; and it has never been a "negative concept" in either Fedotov's or Berlin's sense. Significantly, it has never been able to occur in "negative" collocations such as *freedom from* or *svoboda ot*. In fact, even the French adjective *libre* (whose range of use is wider than that of the noun *liberté*) differs in this respect from both the English adjective *free* and the Russian adjective *svobodnyj*. For example, *free to choose* translates into French as *libre de choisir*, *I'm leaving you free to do as you please* translates as *je vous laisse libre de faire comme bon vous semble*, but a *dust-free surface* is rendered as *une surface depoussierée* (literally 'a surface with the dust removed'), *area free of malaria* is rendered as *zone non touchée par la malaria* (literally 'an area not affected by malaria'), *we chose a spot free of tourists*, as *nous avons choisi un endroit sans touristes* (literally 'we have chosen a spot without tourists'), *free of tax* is rendered as *hors taxe* (literally 'outside tax'), and so on (examples from Collins-Robert 1983).[11]

Similarly, Russian phrases such as *mesta svobodnye ot lesa* 'places free from trees' or *nebo svobodnoe ot oblakov* 'a sky free of clouds' (both quoted in SRJ) could not be translated into French as **les lieux libres d'arbres* or **le ciel libre de nuages*.

Volja, as described by Fedotov, is of course very different from the Latin *libertas* and from the French *liberté*, but *volja*, too, represents a "positive" rather than a "negative" notion. Significantly, there has never been any **volja ot*, as there is *svoboda ot*, or *freedom from*. The etymological link between *volja* in the sense under discussion and *volja* 'will' was no doubt associated with a synchronic semantic link: the word implied that one could live "at will," do whatever one wanted to do. The nonstandard use of the word *volja* in the sense of "outdoors" points in the same direction: inside the house, one is restricted—not because one is forced to do things that one doesn't want to do but because one can't do certain things that one might want to do (move "freely" in different directions)—whereas outdoors, one can go wherever one wants to go.

Furthermore, *volja* (in the sense of *za zemlju, za volju* 'for land, for freedom') seems to have always referred to external circumstances, rather than to just any kind of *'liberté'*, and especially, to the freedom to go wherever one wants to. The opposite which *volja* brings to mind (even in the older sense of the word) is not so much *rabstvo* 'slavery' as *tjurma* 'prison', as in Lermontov's poem (quoted in SSRLJ): "Davnym-davno zadumal ja vzgljanut' na dal'nye polja, . . . uznat' dlja voli il' tjurmy na etot svet rodilis' my," 'I decided a long time ago to take a look at distant fields, and to discover whether we have been born into this world for freedom [*volja*] or for prison'.

The hypothesis suggests itself almost irresistibly that this strong link of *volja* with the freedom to go away (from the place where one is forcibly held) has its roots in the centuries-long institution of serfdom, which deprived the Russian peasant of the right to move to another area to live. To quote one historian:

> In this fashion serfdom kept creeping in until it established itself. It appeared originally in the form of compulsory service to the nobility, who in turn presumably served the state. Soon the peasant found it increasingly difficult to depart unless he escaped, and

in such case he violated the law and was liable to prosecution. Yet many peasants at the risk of severe punishment would contemplate escape. Once the serf gained his freedom, he turned into half-peasant, half-warrior. He faced the danger of being raided along the frontiers by Tartars or Turks or he went himself to raid the raiders. Whatever hazards this kind of life involved, there was one precious remuneration—the escapee was free; he was bound neither to the land nor to landlord; he was restrained by no law except the voluntarily accepted rules of the primitive democratic social order in which he now found himself. (Mazour 1962:74)

This is what *volja* was all about: the dream to escape from a place where one is held against one's will, to go wherever one wants to, and to live by one's own will, without restrictions. The prominent place of *volja* in Russian folklore (mentioned by Fedotov) supports the suggestion that this word embodies, above all, a peasant's point of view.

One more quote, referring to a later period in Russia's history (Peter the Great's reign):

The constant outflow of thousands and thousands who found life too hard to be borne was from this time perpetually on the increase. Peasants not registered in the census were regarded as fugitives, and fugitives were treated as criminals. Peter forbade the peasant to leave his squire's estate without a written permission which, if he went farther than twenty miles outside the district in which he lived, had to be shown to a government authority and countersigned. Members of a peasant family had no right to travel except with the head of the family, who was alone entitled to a passport; persons without passports were regarded as fugitives. The most frequent of all subjects of legislation were the regulations for man-hunts to recover such fugitives. (Pares 1955:250)

These links between *volja* and the mass phenomenon of peasant fugitives, recurring throughout Russia's history, explains, I think, why it was so easy for *volja* to develop its recent meaning of 'life outside prison' (or an idealized version thereof). In fact, both the older and the recent meaning of *volja* can be assigned the "spatial" component mentioned earlier: 'if I want to go somewhere I can do it'. But in the older meaning of *volja* (*volja₁*) this spatial freedom was contrasted with the presence of a "master" (or a landlord), whereas in the twentieth-century meaning (as the word was used in the Soviet era) it was contrasted with the lives of "other people" held forcibly in prisons (or labor camps) by some anonymous higher power. This can be represented as follows:

volja₁
(a) someone (X) can think something like this:
(b)   if I want to do something, I can do it
(c)   if I want to go somewhere, I can go there
(d)   no one can say to me:
      "you can't do it because I don't want this"
      "you can't go there because I don't want this"
(e) this is good for X

volja₂

(a) someone (X) can think something like this:
(b)   I am not like some other people
(c)   if I want to do something, I can do it
(d)   if I want to go somewhere, I can go there
(e)   other people can't do it because someone doesn't want it
(f) this is good for X

The very fact that words such as *volja* (or *liberty* or *freedom*) change their meaning in the context of broader changes in culture and society supports the view that the conceptions embodied in them are "something relative, historically produced and historically changing; something relatively autonomous, able to exert influence on historical events as a relatively independent factor, but not something predetermining these events" (Walicki 1987:14). At the same time, this close link between the meaning of words (especially cultural key words) and the broader historical changes makes the study of meaning highly relevant to the study of history, for the meanings of words provide evidence for historical processes and interpretations.

8. Wolność

In the words of a thirteen-year old Polish-English bilingual, the Polish word *wolność* means something "much more important" than the English word *freedom* does. The perspicacity of this intuitive judgment can be appreciated when one considers that *wolność* translates *freedom* in moral and political contexts, such as *the struggle for freedom* or *freedom of conscience*, but cannot be used to translate *freedom* in relatively "trivial" contexts, such as *freedom of movement*, *freedom of access*, and *freedom from interruption*. The connotations of *wolność* are primarily national, but the word has also a moral dimension: it brings to mind, above all, national independence, with the implication that national independence is a kind of moral absolute (always threatened, and always to be struggled for, at the cost of any personal sacrifices). It is interesting to note, in this connection, the first definition of *wolność* in the monumental *Dictionary of the Polish language* (SJP): " *wolność* 1. independence of one state (nation) from other states in both internal and foreign affairs; national independence, sovereignty." Personal "freedom" is presented by this dictionary as a separate and evidently less important meaning of the word: "2. the possibility, the right of unrestricted actions; personal independence, lack of restrictions."

I do not believe, however, that *wolność* is polysemous. In fact, even when used with respect to personal independence, this word retains its lofty character, and it can never be used with respect to any mundane, morally neutral "freedoms." "Freedoms" seen as relatively trivial would be referred to in Polish by means of the word *swoboda* (closer in meaning to the Russian *svoboda*, though by no means identical with it), not by means of the word *wolność*. For example, one could not replace *swoboda* with *wolność* in the following verse:

> Brysio młody wyje, szczeka, rwie się, dąsa
> i przeklęte więzy kąsa,
> i domaga się swobody!
> (Hertz, Bajki, quoted in SJP)

'Young Spot howls, barks, jumps, furiously tears
at his cursed ropes and demands freedom [*wolność].'

To the Polish "semantic ear," a dog's freedom doesn't have the "national and/or moral rights" ring which would justify the use of the word *wolność*.

Similarly, one would not use *wolność* in translating Pushkin's lines in *Eugene Onegin* referring to the enjoyable "freedoms" and relaxation of the life in the country:

Imeet sel'skaja svoboda
svoi sčastlivye prava.

'Country freedom possesses its happy rights.'
(Pushkin 1975:182)

Wolność brings to mind an oppressor and is normally associated with matters of "life or death" (especially death). As an extremely popular Polish song ("Red poppies at Monte Cassino") has it:

Bo wolność krzyżami się mierzy . . .

'Because *wolność* is measured by the number of crosses'
(i.e. crosses on the graves of those fallen in its defense)

(The reference is to the crosses on the graves of Polish soldiers fallen at the Monte Cassino battle in World War II.)

Nor can one speak in Polish of an *uczucie wolności* 'a feeling of *wolność*', as one can speak in Russian of a *čuvstvo svobody* or in English of a *feeling of freedom*: *wolność* is not a state which one could enjoy but an ideal, that is, something one wants (and has to struggle for).

The universalist character of the concept enshrined in the Polish word *wolność* is reflected in the syntax of this word, notably in its inability to take complements, whether of the negative type (*freedom from, svoboda ot*) or of the positive type (*freedom to*). (In this respect, *wolność* is similar, to some extent, to the present-day English *liberty*, but only to some extent.) From a Polish point of view, reflected in the Polish language, "wolność" is an absolute value, so the noun *wolność* can no more take limiting complements than nouns such as *sprawiedliwość* ('justice') or *honor* ('honor') do. Expressions such as *wolność od X* ('freedom from X') and *wolność do X* ('freedom of X, freedom to do X') are not unknown in Polish, but they are used only in philosophical literature, which often coins expressions in an artificial and arbitrary way, not in ordinary language.

Expressions such as *wolność sumienia* ('freedom of conscience'), *wolność wyznania* ('freedom of religion'), and *wolność słowa* ('freedom of speech') are fully acceptable, but here the modifier specifies a DOMAIN of freedom, rather than a concrete target of freedom. When the modifier specifies the target of freedom, the word *freedom* (or the word *liberté*) cannot be translated as *wolność*:

freedom to emigrate

la liberté pour emigrer

??wolność emigrowania, ?wolność do emigracji, ?wolność emigracji

I might add that the meaning of the word *wolność* which I have tried to explicate above differs from that which was encoded in the word *wolność* as it was used in the sixteenth or seventeenth century. For example, in the sixteenth century a writer could say:

> Tako daleko jako k temu mamy wolność, tego nie chcemy opuścić. (Ort Mac 64, quoted in Mróz-Ostrowska 1962:316)
>
> 'As far as we have freedom to do so, we don't want to fail to do it.'

But in contemporary Polish (where *k temu* 'to do so' would be rendered as *do tego*), one cannot say *wolność do tego. It seems obvious that the moral and public (national) character of the present-day meaning of this word has developed in the course of the last two centuries, during which Poland's history was dominated by uprisings, and other forms of struggle for national freedom. To quote the British historian Norman Davies:

> Before the notorious Partitions of 1773–95 the United Republic of Poland-Lithuania was at once one of the largest states, and the home of one of the most extraordinary cultures, of the continent. In the period since the partitions, the Poles have been engaged in an endless struggle for survival against the empires, ideologies, and tyrannies of Eastern Europe, sustaining a national crusade of wonderful tenacity. . . .
> In the Second World War it fell victim to Nazi and Soviet aggression, and was condemned to become the Golgotha of Europe. (1981: cover)

It is worth recalling in this context Marx's and Engels' condemnation of the first Polish Marxists for renouncing the struggle for Poland's independence (as a precondition of any other freedoms). Engels explained his and Marx's position on this point as follows:

> Every Polish peasant or worker who wakes up from the general gloom and participates in the common interest, encounters first the fact of national subjugation. This fact is in his way everywhere as the first barrier. To remove it is the basic condition of every healthy and free development. . . . In order to be able to fight one needs first a soil to stand on, air, light and space. (quoted in Walicki 1984:230)

During the last two centuries, then, the value of personal "freedom" became linked in the Polish consciousness with the value of national "freedom," and the "national rights" aspects of "freedom" came to the foreground, making the word unsuitable for use in "trivial" and morally neutral contexts, or in contexts referring to purely individual "freedoms" and rights, as in the following example:

> While acknowledging that restrictions on alcohol sales in Aboriginal communities will limit the absolute freedom of individuals, the report says indigenous people are "increasingly demanding the right to address the problem of alcohol abuse in their communities from a collective perspective." (*The Australian,* July 11, 1995)

At the same time, a reverse development seems to have affected the word *swoboda*. In the nineteenth century it was still possible to use this word in elevated contexts referring to political and national "freedom," as in the following lines by Adam Mickiewicz:

Witaj jutrzenko swobody!
Zbawienia za tobą słońce.

'Hail, dawn of freedom!
The sun of salvation comes in your wake.'

But in contemporary Polish, *wolność* rather than *swoboda* would be used in a context like this. The concept encoded in the Polish word *wolność* as it is used in ordinary language can, I think, be explicated along the following lines:

wolność
(a) everyone wants to think something like this:
(b)   when I do something I do it because I want to do it
(c)   not because someone says to me: "you have to do it because I want this"
(d) it is very bad if people in a country can't think this
(e) it is very good if people in a country can think this

In support of the suggestion that the concept of 'wolność' may invoke, specifically, something like the notion of 'country' ('place'), I would mention another highly characteristic Polish concept which has no exact equivalent in English or in other European languages: the concept of 'niepodległość, (roughly 'national independence'). This concept, too, has positive and "normative" associations, and it clearly distinguishes a country's, or a nation's, independence from all other kinds of independence, the general Polish word for independence being *niezależność*. (Of course, the meaning of the word *country* is quite complex, but I have used this word here to highlight this aspect of the culture-specific Polish concept 'wolność'. For other references to the concept 'country', see chapter 4.)

In the Polish concept of 'wolność', the public (national) and the individual element are fused together. This sui generis character of the Polish word *wolność* clearly reflects the historical experience of a country where the personal fate of an individual was inextricably linked with the fate of the nation, and where often, as the greatest Polish poet, Adam Mickiewicz, put it, "szczęścia w domu nie było, bo go nie było w ojczyźnie" ('there was no happiness at home, because there was no happiness in the homeland') (1955, II:109).

Since the vital personal "freedoms" came to be so inextricably linked together with public and national "freedoms" in the basic word *wolność*, "trivial personal freedoms" had to be pushed to the margin of the semantic field in question, finding expression in the marked word *swoboda*. The pair *wolność/swoboda* reflects a polarization of concepts, which set apart temporary and superficial circumstances of a person's life (*swoboda*) from a basic existential condition (*wolność*).

The Polish concept of 'wolność' has a normative character: it is not a matter of what one CAN think but of what one WANTS to be able to think (component [a]); it has also universalist character ('EVERYONE wants to think something like this'). It refers to an oppressor (component [c]), and it links oppression with conditions prevailing in a country (components [d] and [e]). It is not a personal ideal, but one which has both universal and "local" (national) overtones. Unlike the English *freedom*, it has nothing to do with "options," and unlike the Russian *svoboda*, it has nothing to do with ease, absence of constraints, or "feeling good." At the same time, it is not a purely intellectual ideal. There is something expressive, emphatic, almost hyperbolical about the word *wolność*. To account for these connotations, I have included the word *very* in components (d) and (e).

In the sixteenth and seventeenth century, when Polish nobility enjoyed privileges unheard of in most other European countries, these privileges were hailed, and usually referred to, as *Złota Wolność* 'the Golden Freedom'. (Davies [1981:207] calls the Polish-Lithuanian Commonwealth "The Paradise of the Nobility.") At that time, *wolność* did not stand for an ideal associated with struggle and sacrifice, but a privilege (for one stratum of the society) to savor and enjoy. But in twentieth-century Polish, *wolność* doesn't take the adjective *złota* 'golden' any more; over the last two centuries its connotations have become rather somber and heroic.

If, as Fedotov says, *volja* plays a key role in Russian culture as something that "every Russian heart responds to," similarly, *wolność* is a word to which every Polish heart responds (cf. Davies 1981, Garton Ash 1983, Benet 1953).[12] Only time will tell how long it will take for post-communist Poland to develop a new shared conception of "freedom" and for this to reshape the meaning of the word *wolność*.

9. Conclusion

Freedom does not stand for a universal human ideal. In fact, it doesn't even stand for a common European ideal, although European languages contain a family of related concepts centered on the idea that it is good for people to be able to do what they want to do. If we look further afield, even this vague common theme is often missing. For example, Australian Aboriginal languages appear to have no words corresponding even remotely to anything like *freedom*, *libertas*, *svoboda*, or *wolność*, presumably because the traditional Aboriginal way of life did not involve contrasts or conflicts which in the Western world led to the articulation of such ideals. In fact, even languages of complex modern societies such as Japan may have no words corresponding to something like *freedom*, or have them only as recent semantic and cultural loans, not at all entrenched in the commonly used lexicon. For example, in Japan the ideal of "freedom" appears to be culturally alien and not really consistent with the key Japanese values of *amae* ('loving dependence'), *enryo* ('nonassertiveness'), *on* ('infinite indebtedness to others'), or *giri* ('obligation to others'). (For a detailed analysis of all these concepts, see chapter 6.) In particular, the positive attitude to dependence, reflected in the concept of 'amae' (cf. Doi 1981), is seen as incompatible with a positive view of independence reflected in the modern Anglo concept of 'freedom'. Doi comments in this connection:

> The Japanese word *jiyū*, usually used to translate the English word *freedom* and other Western words of similar meaning, is of Chinese origin, but seems to have been used in Japan from an early date. . . . the word *jiyū*, judging from examples found in old Chinese and Japanese documents, often has, as Tsudo Sōkichi has pointed out, overtones that are to a certain degree critical. In this it is the exact opposite of "freedom" or "liberty," for which *jiyū* served as the translation following the Meiji Restoration but which in the West signify respect for the human being and contain no trace of criticism. For this reason the word *jiyū* has come in recent years to partake

in both its good, Western sense and its bad, Japanese sense, with a resulting extensive ambiguity in the concept itself. (84–85)

Drawing on Doi's discussion, another student of Japanese society elaborates:

> . . . to think about *amae* also means that we must look into the cultural meanings of *freedom* as understood in the United States and Japan. Here freedom is the freedom to choose—which implies a degree of personal isolation and autonomy. You should, ideally, choose on your own, apart from the concerns of others or their preferred choices for you. In Japan freedom is the freedom to be indulged, to do as one likes within the bounds of a permissive relationship. Other Japanese concepts of freedom do of course exist, especially since Western influence has pervaded the Asian culture. But our notion of freedom pushed to the extreme seems full of loneliness and pointless to a culture where human relationships are the major wellspring and end of the value system. *Amae* in contemporary Japan may no longer be the complete and explicitly reinforced source of meaning in life; to some extent it has been replaced by borrowed ideologies of a different sort of individualism, especially for young people before the responsibilities of marriage and family. But *amae* still represents a very important personal value. (White 1987:24)

Although certain aspects of Doi's discussion of both *freedom* and *jiyū* have been questioned by Dale (1986:61–62), Dale's criticisms do not affect the main point, that is, that in pre-Meiji times, the word *jiyū* had critical overtones, and that in modern usage, influenced by the use of this word as a translation equivalent of *freedom*, it is ambivalent rather than unambiguously positive like *freedom*.

Words such as *freedom, libertas, svoboda,* and *wolność* are not idiosyncratic lexical items any more than *amae* is. They embody different concepts, which reflect different cultural ideals. The emergence of such concepts in a given language can be understood only against the background of the culture to which this language belongs, and they provide precious clues to the understanding of that culture.

But to be able to elucidate such concepts, and to reveal the cultural ideals embodied in them, we need a language- and culture-independent semantic metalanguage, which can free us from the ethnocentrism that usually creeps into discussions based exclusively on one particular ethnic concept, such as that encoded in the English word *freedom*.

The boundaries of my language are indeed, as Wittgenstein put it, the boundaries of my world; for every natural language—English, Russian, Japanese, or whatever—defines the boundaries of a certain conceptual and cultural world. But the boundaries between conceptual and cultural worlds CAN be crossed. My language doesn't have to be my conceptual prison. But this conceptual liberation can be achieved, and a "free," universal perspective can be reached, only to the extent to which we are able to rely on a semantic metalanguage which is language-independent and founded on universal human concepts.

Appendix

SUMMARY OF THE FORMULAE
libertas
(a) someone (X) can think something like this:
(b)   when I do something I do it because I want to do it
(c)   not because someone else says to me: "you have to do it because I want
you to do it"
(d) this is good for X

(libertas2)
(a) someone (X) can think something like this:
(b)   when I do something I do it because I want to do it
(c)   I don't have to think: "I can't do something because someone doesn't want
me to do it"

freedom
(a) someone (X) can think something like this:
(b)   if I want to do something I can do it
(c)   no one else can say to me: "you can't do it because I don't want this"
(d)   if I don't want to do something I don't have to do it
(e)   no one else can say to me: "you have to do it because I want this"
(f) this is good for X
(g) it is bad if someone cannot think this

liberty (older)
(a) someone (X) can think something like this:
(b)   if I want to do something I can do it
(c)   I don't have to think:
(d)   someone can say: "I don't want this"
(e)   I can't do it because of this

liberty (current)
(a) everyone can think something like this:
(b)   if I want to do something because I think it is good I can do it
(c)   no one can say: "this person can't do it because I don't want this"
(d) everyone thinks: this is good

freedom (older)
someone (X) can think something like this:
    if I want to do something, I can do it
    I don't have to think: I can't do it
svoboda
(a) someone (X) can think something like this:
(b)   if I want to do something, I can do it
(c)   when I do something, I don't have to think:
        I can't do it as I want to do it
        because some (other) people do/say something
(d) X feels something good because of this

volja₁
(a) someone (X) can think something like this:
(b)   if I want to do something, I can do it
(c)   if I want to go somewhere, I can go there
(d)   no one can say to me:
          "you can't do it because I don't want this"
          "you can't go there because I don't want this"
(e) this is good for X

volja₂
(a) someone (X) can think something like this:
(b)   I am not like some other people
(c)   if I want to do something, I can do it
(d)   if I want to go somewhere, I can go there
(e)   other people can't do it because someone doesn't want it
(f) this is good for X

wolnosć
(a) everyone wants to think something like this:
(b)   when I do something I do it because I want to do it
(c)   not because someone says to me: "you have to do it because I want this"
(d) it is very bad if people in a country can't think this
(e) it is very good if people in a country can think this

Lexicon as a Key To History, Nation, and Society

"Homeland" and "Fatherland" in German, Polish, and Russian

1. Different "homelands," different "patriotisms"

Since many languages, especially European languages, have words denoting 'native country', the concepts embodied in these words may be assumed to transcend language boundaries. In fact, words that appear to match in this way often differ from one another in particularly telling ways, offering valuable insight into different national traditions and historical experiences. I will illustrate this general proposition by analyzing and comparing three key words of modern German and Polish: *Heimat*, *Vaterland*, and *ojczyzna*. For comparison, I will also include a cursory discussion of the Russian word *rodina*.

Despite the immense complexity of these concepts, which are laden with historical and cultural significance, in analyzing them I will rely almost exclusively on simple, universal concepts such as 'I', 'people', 'something', 'part', 'good', 'think', 'want', and 'feel'. I will, however, make three exceptions, by using, in addition to universals, the following three words: *country*, *born*, and *child*. These words, too, can be defined in terms of the universals, but to do so within the explications of such complex cultural concepts as *Heimat*, *Vaterland*, *ojczyzna*, and *rodina* would be confusing and counterproductive.

2. Heimat

Heimat is one of the most important words in the German lexicon and "has the resonance of what Raymond Williams called a 'key word.' Like his key words *industry*, *democracy*, *class*, *art*, and *culture*, *Heimat* came into its current usage at a certain juncture in German history and has remained in both an everyday and a more formally argumentative vocabulary ever since" (Applegate 1990:6).

There is an extensive literature on the concept of *Heimat*, which, for reasons of space, I could not possibly try to survey here. But what is particularly interesting about the long history of *Heimat*, and particularly relevant in the present context, is that despite its extensive use and manipulation in Nazi propaganda and its resulting "corruption" (Applegate 1990:4), *Heimat* survived the Nazi era, losing nothing of its emotive, social, or political power in German life. The little vignette from a civic gathering in the town of Pfalz in 1946 offered by Applegate illustrates this point very vividly:

> The new Landrat . . . pledged himself to "restor[ing] the well-being and future of the Heimat" in a spirit of forgiveness, repeating the word *Heimat* twelve times in a speech of five minutes. He concluded with a plea for "all of us to put our work at the service of the higher ideals of the people and the Heimat." The final speech of the evening was an emotional affirmation of Heimat on the basis of German collective life. (242)

Speaking of the word *Heimat* as something that gave coherence and purpose to the manifold activities which shaped the sense of distinctiveness and identity of the inhabitants of the town of Pfalz (in both the nineteenth and twentieth century), Applegate writes (emphasizing the untranslatability of the German words quoted):

> The Pfalz was the homeland; the Pfalz was Heimat. Out of *Heimatliebe* [love for *Heimat*] the Pfälzer undertook *Heimatpflege* [care for *Heimat*] and thought *Heimatgedanken* [*Heimat*-thoughts]. During his life, he might call himself a *Heimatkundler* ["*Heimat*-knower"] or simply a *Heimatler* ["*Heimat*-devotee," "*Heimat*-man"] and after his death his obituary would praise him for having truly loved his *Heimat*. (3)

Given the crucial importance of the concept of 'Heimat' in German culture, it would seem obvious that it is an important task of interpretive semantics to explicate its meaning and to show what exactly is unique about it and how it differs from its closest counterparts in other languages. But it has often been asserted that this task is simply not feasible. To quote Applegate once more:

> The term *Heimat*, one could argue, has entered into so many different discussions in such diverse areas of German society that it would be a great mistake to search for a solitary meaning, a single truth beyond all the white noise. And yet the ubiquity of the term and the deep emotionality of its appeal have proven irresistible temptations to interpreters in search of an essence for which *Heimat* is an expression. Their results have not always been enlightening. (4)

Applegate herself was clearly wary of all the past and ongoing efforts to capture the meaning of *Heimat* in something resembling a definition, and she decided instead to devote a book to the study of this elusive word. ("Instead of generating more definitions for a word that has collected so many, this study will investigate the history of the word itself, which in the case of *Heimat* means the history of a certain way of talking and thinking about German society and Germanness" [6]).

I agree that *Heimat* deserves a book-length study, or indeed a number of book-length studies. But it also deserves a definition, and if tangible changes in the meaning of this word can be documented, then it needs more than one definition. In what follows, I will propose, and try to briefly justify, a definition for the modern usage, exemplified in the two quotes:

> Heimat ist ja nicht nur dieses Stück Land mit seiner Enge und Abgeschlossenheit, dieser kleine und übersehbare Gegensatz von Welt und Ferne und Leben. Die Ströme und Bäche sind Heimat, die durchs Land gehen, die Wolken sind Heimat, wenn sie darüber hinziehen, und die Sterne . . . gehören dazu.
> (Rainer Maria Rilke, 1903, quoted in Füllerborn 1992:100)

> 'Heimat isn't merely this piece of land with its narrowness and seclusion, this small and surveyable antithesis of the world and distance and life. The streams and brooks are Heimat, the ones that move through the land, the clouds are Heimat, when they spread over and above it, and the stars . . . are part of it.'

> Von meinem Schreibtisch blicke ich über den Rhein in meine Heimat, das Elsaß, und wenn ich hinüberfahre, zücke ich an der Grenze, die seit 1918 wieder der Rhein bildet, einen französischen Paß.
> (René Schickele, 1933, quoted in Storck 1992:106)

> 'From my desk I look across the Rhine into my Heimat, the Alsace, and when I drive over there, at the border, which, since 1918, has again been the Rhine, I pull out a French passport '.

Trying to account for all the different aspects of *Heimat*, I would propose the following explication of this complex concept:

Heimat
(a) a place
(b) I was born in this place
(c) there are many places in this place
(d) when I was a child I lived in these places
(e) I felt something good when I lived in these places
(f) I felt that nothing bad could happen to me
(g) I can't feel like this in any other places
(h) because of this, when I think about these places I feel something good
(i) I think something like this when I think about these places:
(j)   these places are not like any other places
(k)   I was like a part of these places when I was a child[1]
(l)   I can't be like a part of any other places
(m)   this place is like a part of me
(n) (I know: some other people think the same when they think about these places)
(o) (I think these people feel the same when they think about these places)
(p) (when I think about these people, I feel something good)

Component (a) indicates that *Heimat* is a "place"—not necessarily a "country," as, for example, *Vaterland*, *ojczyzna* (Polish), or *rodina* (Russian), to be discussed below, but simply "place." It is not a small place like a garden or even a village; there are many places in this place (component [c]); but it is small enough to have a human measure, so that a person, and indeed a child, can not only be aware of these many places but feel like a part of them (component [k]).

Component (b) ('I was born in this place') may be questioned on the basis of various personal statements by people who were raised, but not born, in what they regard as their "Heimat." For example, Iring Fetscher (1992) regards Dresden as his "Heimat," although he was born, he says, in Württemberg:

> Ich kann mich noch ganz gut daran erinnern, daß ich als etwa Vierzehnjähriger das Aufsatzthema gestellt bekam: "Kann denn Großstadt Heimat sein?" "Denn" ließ auf eine womöglich negative Antwort schließen. Ich entschloß mich aber—aus Überzeugung—die Frage mit "ja" zu beantworten. Die Kunst und Barockstadt Dresden mit ihren engen Gassen und verlockenden Antiquariaten war für mich—auch wenn ich, in Württemberg geboren, von zwei süddeutschen Eltern stammend, in Dresden nur "aufgewachsen" war—Heimat.(17)

> 'I still remember clearly, when I was fourteen, having to write an essay on the topic: "Can a large city ever be Heimat?" "Ever" seemed to prompt a negative answer. Nevertheless, I decided—from conviction—to answer the question with "yes." The Baroque city Dresden with its narrow lanes and alluring secondhand bookshops was for me—even if I, born in Württemberg, of South German parentage, had only "grown up" in Dresden—Heimat.'

But although statements of this kind are quite common, arguably they are based on a metaphorical extension. Perhaps, for Fetscher, Dresden was LIKE *Heimat* (even though it is a big city and even though he wasn't born in it); subjectively, for him Dresden was what *Heimat* was for other people. If a big city could normally be seen as someone's *Heimat* in the literal sense of the word, school essays topics raising such a possibility for discussion would not be set.

It is possible for people to develop *Heimatsgefühle*, 'Heimat-feelings' for places other than those where they were born, of course, as one can develop "maternal feelings" for people who are not our children, but this means that one can develop for a new place feelings LIKE those normally associated with a *Heimat*, not that the new place becomes the *Heimat* (in a literal sense of the word).

One must agree with Fetscher, nonetheless, that the link between *Heimat* and childhood is stronger and more important than that between *Heimat* and a mere birthplace, and, in particular, that *Heimat* suggests something like nostalgia for childhood and for the special, unrecoverable, happiness which can be associated with it:

> Freilich gilt das nur für die, denen ein günstiges Schicksal ein Mindestmaß von kindlicher Geborgenheit und Heimat zuteil werden ließ.

> 'Of course this can only be applied to those whom a favorable destiny granted a minimum of security and *Heimat* as a child.'

In the explication proposed here, the special links between *Heimat* and childhood are reflected not only in the component (d) ('when I was a child I lived in these places'), but also in the evocation of childhood happiness in (e) ('I felt something good when I lived in these places'), in the nostalgic components (g), (l), and (m), ('I can't feel like this in other places', 'I can't be like a part of any other places', and 'this place is like a part of me'), and also in the causal link between one's love for one's *Heimat* and the childhood connection, component (h), ('because of this, when I think about these places I feel something good'). Component (f) seeks to capture the idea that in one's *Heimat* one feels "geborgen," that is, roughly speaking, safe (as in one's mother's arms).

The idea of childhood "belonging" associated with *Heimat* is reflected in the components (d) and (k) ('. . . I lived in these places', 'I was like a part of these places'), and the notion that *Heimat* referred to "something lost" and "only available to the memory" (debated, for example, by Heinrich Böll, Günther Grass, and Norbert Blüm, among others, in the 1970 Hessen radio discussion related in Applegate 1990:4–5), corresponds to components (g) and (l) ('I can't feel like this in other places', and 'I can't be like a part of any other places'). Component (m) suggests that, to some extent, a person's *Heimat* "defines" that person, that it is a part of his or her personal identity.

But the nostalgic ring of *Heimat* doesn't have to be interpreted exclusively in terms of childhood. The quote from Rilke adduced above is very characteristic in this respect, with its triple contrast between *Heimat* and *Leben* ('life', which takes us away from childhood in time), *Ferne* ('far-away-ness', distance, being far away from familiar places to which one once belonged), and *Welt* ('the world', that is, abstract social and political entities which come to replace the emotional security of one's local community).

Applegate (1990:11) is no doubt right when she points out that "in reality, of course, Heimat's nostalgic evocation of a closed and close-knit community reflected its replacement by these larger and less personal forms of political and territorial belonging"; in other words, she is right in linking the modern concept of 'Heimat' with the changes in the German national consciousness brought about by the formal unification of Germany in 1871 under Prussian leadership. The very fact that the word *Heimat* preserved its key position in the German cultural lexicon, beside the "larger" concept of 'Vaterland' ('fatherland', to be discussed below), supports the claim implicit in the title of Applegate's book, *A nation of provincials: The German idea of Heimat*, and gives credence to statements such as the following:

> The idea of Heimat potentially embraced all of Germany, from its individual parts to its newly constituted whole. It offered Germans a way to reconcile a heritage of localized political traditions with the ideal of a single, transcendent nationality. Heimat was both the beloved local places and the beloved nation; it was a comfortably flexible and inclusive homeland, embracing all localities alike. (11).

> For the incomplete nation of 1871, the invented traditions of the Heimat bridged the gap between national aspiration and provincial reality. These efforts [toward national integration on the basis of regionalism] might be called federalist, in the sense that Heimat enthusiasts celebrated German diversity. They supported national cohesion without necessarily showing any enthusiasms for its symbols or for its agents, Prussia and the national government. (13).

Unlike *Vaterland* (to be discussed below), *Heimat* does not refer to a nation, but arguably its perspective is not purely individual either; perhaps the warm glow of this word ("Bei dem Wort Heimat wird uns allemal warm ums Herz," 'the word *Heimat* gives us always a warm feeling in the heart', Fetscher 1992:15) extends in some way to the people who share our *Heimat* with us. To canvas this possibility, I have tentatively included in the explication of *Heimat* three additional components, (n), (o), and (p), for further consideration.

The widening of the use of *Heimat* after 1871 did not necessarily mean a semantic change. Applegate's (1990) observation, "The evolution of *Heimat* as a concept followed the shifting hierarchies of belonging, from hometown to territorial state to nation" (13), can be accepted as a comment about changes in the socio-political psychology rather than in the semantic structure of *Heimat*. Common twentieth century uses of *Heimat*, such as that in the "Russland Lager-Lied" (a song of German captives in a Russian camp, dating from 1945 or later) seem quite compatible with the explication proposed here:

> Und wir ale hir in Rusland haben eine Bitren Schmertz
> und wir dachten oft in Stielen es zereist unz nur das Herz
> den die Mutter in der Heimadt Vater und Bruder an der Front
> und wir sind so arm aleine unter dem ferlassen Folk.
> (quoted in Greverus 1972:452; spelling as in the original)

> 'And we all here in Russia have a bitter pain,
> and we often thought that it would tear our hearts,
> our mothers in the homeland [*Heimat*], fathers and brothers on the front,
> and we are so miserable alone among this abandoned people.'

It is interesting to note in this connection that it is the word *Heimat*, not *Vaterland*, which typically occurs in the songs of captivity, whereas in the "fighting songs," as well as the "corporation songs" *(Burschenlieder)*, it is typically the word *Vaterland*, to which we will turn next.

3. Vaterland

Vaterland (roughly 'fatherland') has for a long time been another extremely important word in the German lexicon. The fact that the Grimms' (1956[1886]) *Deutsches Wörterbuch* (German dictionary) lists as many as thirty compounds (and derivatives) built upon this word provides telling evidence for this. A volume of German poems and songs (Harzmann 1930, henceforth referred to as H) contains several dozen examples. Characteristically, *Vaterland* occurs twice in the German national anthem:

> Einigkeit und Recht und Freiheit
> Für das deutsche Vaterland!
>
> . . . .
> Blüh in Glanze dieses Glückes
> Blühe deutsches Vaterland!

> 'Unity and justice and freedom
> for the German Fatherland!
>
> . . . .
> Blossom in the brilliance of this happiness
> Blossom German Fatherland!'

The Grimm dictionary offers the following definition: "Land, worin mein Vater lebte, als welchen Landesangehörigen ich mich betrachte; oft zusammenfallend mit Geburtsland, doch ist dies nicht nötig" ('The country where my father lived, the country to which I believe I belong; often concides with the country of birth, but this is not essential').

The more recent Brockhaus Wahrig dictionary (*Deutsches Wörterbuch* 1981) gives the following: "Land, in dem man geboren und/oder aufgewachsen ist, Heimat(land)" ('country where one was born and/or where one grew up, one's "Heimat", the country which is one's Heimat'); and Duden (1981): "Land, aus dem man stammt, zu dessen Volk, Nation man gehört, dem man sich zugehörig fühlt, Land als Heimat eines Volkes" ('the country from which one originates, to whose people, nation one belongs, where one feels one belongs, the country therefore as Heimat of a people').

All these definitions contain useful elements, but none provides an adequate explication.

3.1   *Vaterland* as a superordinate entity

To begin with, let me adduce two classic quotes from early nineteenth-century poetry, one from Ernst Moritz Arndt's famous poem "Was ist des Deutschen Vaterland?" quoted in Fetscher (1992:20), and one from Heinrich von Kleist's "Catechism of a German," also quoted in Fetscher (22):

> Was ist des Deutschen Vaterland?
> Ist's Preußenland, ist's Schwabenland?
> Ist's, wo am Rhein die Rebe blüht?
> Ist's, wo am Belt die Möwe zieht?
> Oh, nein, nein, nein!
> Sein Vaterland muß größer sein!
> (Arndt)

> 'Which is the Fatherland of the German?
> Is it Prussia, is it Swabia?
> Is it where the vines grow on the Rhine?
> Is it where seagull roves the Belt?
> Oh, no, no, no!
> His Fatherland must be bigger than this!'

> Frage: Sprich, Kind, wer bist Du?
> Antwort: Ich bin ein Deutscher.
> Frage: Ein Deutscher. Du scherzest. Du bist in Meißen geboren.
> Antwort: Ich bin in Meißen geboren, und das Land, dem Meißen angehört, heißt Sachsen, aber mein Vaterland, das Land, dem Sachsen angehört, ist Deutschland, und dein Sohn, mein Vater, ist ein Deutscher.
> (Kleist)

> 'Question: Speak, child, who are you?
> Answer: I am a German.
> Question: A German. You are joking. You were born in Meissen.

Answer: I was born in Meissen, and the country to which Meissen belongs, is Saxony, but my Fatherland, the country to which Saxony belongs, is Germany, and your son, my father, is a German.'

As these quotes suggest, *Vaterland*—in contrast to *Heimat*—referred from early on to a country, seen at least implicitly against the background of other countries (there are many different *Länder* 'countries', and one of these *Länder* is one's *Vaterland*).

The psychological size of a *Vaterland*, then, was from the start much larger than that of a *Heimat*: if for *Heimat* the point of reference, and standard of size, was provided by individual human experience, *Vaterland* could include many *Heimat*'s, because its implicit point of reference was not experiential but political, with a particular emphasis on the unity of a large abstract entity, seen against the background of a number of smaller local entities (as made clear in Kleist's "Catechism of a German" and in Arndt's poem).

These considerations lead us to the following initial (highly incomplete) explication:

Vaterland (incomplete)
a country
I am like a part of this country
there are many places in this country
these places are like one big thing

3.2 High regard, love, and pride

From early on, one's *Vaterland* was a country to which one felt one "belonged," a country which one loved, and a country which one held in high regard. Both the love and the high regard for the *Vaterland* are clearly reflected in Klopstock's (1770) "Vaterlands lied":

> . . . Ich bin ein deutsches Mädchen! Mein gutes, edles, stolzes Herz / schlägt laut empor / Beim süssen Namen Vaterland! So schlägt mir einst beim Namen / Des Jüngling's nur, der stolz wie ich / Aufs Vaterland / Gut, edel ist, und Deutscher ist! (quoted in Greverus 1972:291).

> '. . . I am a German girl! My good, noble, proud heart / beats loudly / at the sweet name Fatherland! as it beats only at the name / of [my] young man, who, like I, is proud of / the Fatherland / and who is good, noble, and a German!'

The common compound *Vaterlandsliebe* 'love for the Vaterland' supports the emotional component of this word, as do recurring phrases such as *das liebe Vaterland* 'the beloved Vaterland' and *das teure Vaterland*, 'the dear Vaterland' (e.g. "ein dreifach Hoch dem Lieben Vaterlande" (Engelhardt 1818) 'three cheers for the dear Fatherland' in Harzmann 1930:51), and recurring oaths promising faithful love, e.g.:

> treue Liebe bis zum Grabe
> Schwör ich dir mit Herz und Hand
> Was ich bin und was ich habe
> Dank ich dir, mein Vaterland

'Faithful love to the grave,
This I swear to you with my heart and hand
What I am and what I have
I must thank you for, my Fatherland'

Among the frequently declared "good feelings" for the *Vaterland*, the most common ones are love, devotion, pride, high regard, honor, "fire" (burning love), gratitude, filial piety, and religious devotion. The words which most frequently recur in combination with *Vaterland* are *Liebe* ('love'), *Ehre* ('honor'), *stolz* ('proud'), *ergeben* ('devoted'), *Dank* ('thanks'), *heilige* ('holy', 'sacred'), *Glut* ('burning in the heart') and *heil*! Some examples:

Ehre des Vaterlandes Fahnen
(Bardill, 1820, H 18)

'Honor to the flags of the Fatherland'

Heil dir, mein Vaterland!
(J.L. Haupt, H 57)

'Hail to thee, my Fatherland!'

Wir schwören neu mit Herz und Hand:
Kein Drohen soll, kein Gleissen,
Die Glut für Recht und Vaterland
Uns aus dem Herzen reissen.
(Heinrich von Treitschke, H 209)

'We swear anew with heart and hand:
No threats, no glittering promises, can
Purge the fervor for justice and Fatherland
From our hearts.'

The expression of love and *Ehre* for the *Vaterland* is habitually linked with praise, with the *Vaterland* being described as the best country, the most beautiful one, a great one, and ascribed majesty and "highness":

... des Vaterlandes Majestät!
(E. A. Arndt, 1915)

'... the Fatherland's majesty!'

Das höchste, was wir kennen, ist teutsches Vaterland
(Karl Reh, 1815, H 67)

'The highest thing that we know is the German Fatherland'

Nicht mit dem Schläger in der Hand ...
Dient ihr dem grossen Vaterland ...
(Christoph Schneider, 1867, H 332)

'It is not with the sword in the hand ...
that you serve the great Fatherland ...'

Und deine Kinder gingen Hand in Hand
Und machten dich zum grössten Land auf Erden,
Wie du das beste bist, o Vaterland!
(Konrad Krez, 1875, H 200)

'And your children walked hand in hand
and made you the greatest country on earth,
just as you are the best, Fatherland!'

Mein heil'ges deutsches Vaterland! (Walter Fler, 1914, H 372)
'My holy German Fatherland!'

The habitual praise of the *Vaterland* as a country exceptionally good, beautiful, virtuous, faithful, great, and generally uniquely praiseworthy, is well documented in the chapter on "Vaterlandspreis" in Greverus (1972).

On the basis of these considerations, we can expand our initial explication as follows:

Vaterland (incomplete)
a country
I am like a part of this country
there are many places in this country
these places are like one big thing
when I think about this country, I feel something good
I think very good things about this country
I think something like this when I think about this country:
    this country is not like any other country
    no other country is like this country

The combination of the two components 'this country is not like any other country' and 'no other country is like this country' may seem redundant, but I think it is probably needed to account for both the perceived "uniqueness" of the *Vaterland* and the ego's pride in it (and apparent sense of superiority).

3.3   *Vaterland* and nation

Is *Vaterland* a country of birth?

As we saw earlier, the Grimm dictionary (1956[1886]) insists that one's *Vaterland* is not necessarily one's birth-country, and it is true that the word can be applied much more readily to people's "adopted" countries than *Heimat*, or *homeland*, can.[2] The fact that the Volga Germans (born in Russia) could readily refer to Germany as their *Vaterland* (though not their *Heimat*), too, suggests that *Vaterland* is not necessarily conceived of as the country of birth. In any case, it is certainly clear that *Vaterland* doesn't have, and has never had, the special sentimental link with childhood that *Heimat* does.

On the other hand, from early on *Vaterland* implied a link with other people "belonging" to the same country. In fact, Duden's quasi-definition of *Vaterland* as "Land als Heimat eines Volkes" ('a country seen as the *Heimat* of a people') is correct, I think, in contrasting the individual perspective of *Heimat* with the collective perspective of *Vaterland*.

This collective perspective of *Vaterland* is linked with its emphasis on unity (against the background of diversity). The most characteristic and common collocation of *Vaterland* is *das deutsche Vaterland* 'the German *Vaterland*'. Although the Polish word *ojczyzna* is also nation-oriented, it normally cannot be used in a similar collocation: *polska ojczyzna* 'the Polish *ojczyzna*' (nor does the Russian word *rodina* occur in the collocation *russkaja rodina* 'the Russian *rodina*'). The first two lines of the German national anthem, quoted earlier ("Einigkeit und Recht und Freiheit für das deutsche Vaterland") are very characteristic in the way they link the "Germanness" of the Vaterland with its unity (against the implicit diversity of the local Heimat-s, which are Prussian, Saxon, Schwabian, or whatever). The phrase *das deutsche Vaterland* reflects both the collective, nation-oriented character of the concept 'Vaterland' and its emphasis on unity over and above diversity.

Trying to account for the collective, nation-oriented character of *Vaterland*, we may start by adding to our initial explication the following further components:

> many other people think the same when they think about this country
> these people feel the same when they think about this country
> all these people are like one thing
> I am part of this thing

Quotes such as the following ones support these components very clearly:

> Wir fühlen alle uns als Brüder
> Und drücken froh die Bruderhand,
> Denn wir sind einer Kette Glieder,
> Uns eint das deutsche Vaterland!
> (L. Mesunius, 1859, H 215)

> 'We all feel as brothers would
> and gladly squeeze the fraternal hand,
> Because we are the links on a chain,
> United by the German Fatherland!'

> Und wir haben alle ein Vaterland
> Dem wollen wir leben und sterben.
> (J. L. Haupt, H 52)

> 'And we all have a Fatherland,
> for which we want to live and die.'

> Was wir ersehnt, erstrebt seit langen Jahren:
> Des deutschen Vaterlandes Einigkeit.
> (Otto Haupt, H 257)

> 'What we have long yearned and striven for:
> The unity of the German Fatherland.'

> Stets frei und einig erschaue
> Das deutsche Vaterland!
> (Richard Dehe, 1907, H 271)

'Always freely and unitedly look upon
the German Fatherland!'

An early example of a sentence equating 'Vaterland' with 'nation' is the following:

es ist wahr, ich bin ein fürst wolbekannt
in deutscher nation, mein vaterlant.
(Schede, quoted in Grimm 1956[1886]).

'It is true, I am a well-known prince in the German nation, my Fatherland.'

The fact that the expression *Vaterlandsverräter* 'betrayer of the Vaterland' was in use in the first half of the nineteenth century points in the same direction, as one betrays people rather than a place. For example, Heine wrote this in the preface to his poem "Deutschland, Ein Wintermärchen" (Germany, a wintertale):

Ich höre schon ihre Bierstimmen: du lästerst sogar unsere Farben, Verräter des Vaterlands, Freund der Franzosen, denen du den freien Rhein abtreten willst!

'I can already hear their beer-voices: you even scoff at our colors, traitor of the Fatherland, friend of the French, for whom you will give up our free Rhine!'

3.4 Duty and service

Also linked with *Vaterland* from early on were ideas of duty, unconditional service, and obedience:

was Vaterlandspflicht fordert, kann der Ehre nicht schwer sein. (W. F. Mayern, 1787, quoted in Grimm 1956[1886]).

'what the duty toward the Vaterland demands cannot be a burden for the honor.'

Nineteenth-century German poetry offers plentiful examples of sentences where *Vaterland* is associated with boundless duty and service. The metaphor of "sonhood" is particularly characteristic in this regard: the *Vaterland* is not so much the country *of* one's father, as suggested in the Grimm dictionary, as the country which *is,* symbolically, one's, and one's nation's, father, a father whom one must love, revere, serve, and obey. The twin phrases *Vaterlands Söhne* and *Söhne des Vaterlandes* 'the sons of the *Vaterland'*, very common in German poems and songs, are particularly characteristic in this regard. For example:

Vaterlands Söhne! traute Genossen!
(A. L. Follen, 1817, H 85).

'Sons of the Fatherland! Beloved comrades!'

Lernt frei des Trugs, Ihr Söhne des Vaterlands
In Wort und tat verteidigen . . .
(E.C.F. Krauss, 1820, H 45)

'Learn free of deceit, you sons of the Fatherland, defend, in word and deed . . .'

Gruss dir, Panier voll Wunderschöne,
Dass mahnend alter deutscher Pracht
Jüngst unsres Vaterlandes Söhne . . .
(T. Kellenbauer, 1862, H 205)

'Greetings to you, banner depicting the most beautiful,
Recalling old German splendor
to the youngest of our Fatherland's sons . . .'

Vaterland, Vaterland, du sollst nimmer wanken:
Als deine Söhne stehen wir . . .
(P. Kaiser, 1818, H 66).

'Fatherland, Fatherland, you will never falter:
We stand behind you as your sons . . .'

But even more revealing than the common metaphor of 'sonhood' is the ubiquitous syntactic frame *für das Vaterland* 'for the *Vaterland*' (or *fürs deutsche Vaterland*, 'for the German *Vaterland*'), often in the imperative mood, or combined with modal verbs such as soll 'should', and often with an exclamation mark, indicating an emotive and/or 'imperative' component. For example:

. . . Dann Brüder folget mir, schwinget das Kreuzpanier.
Fürs Vaterland!
(Ch. v. Buri, 1819, H 70)

'. . . Then brothers follow me, wave the banner of the cross
For the Fatherland!'

Für Freiheit, Ehre, Vaterland
Soll unser deutsches Schwert stets blitzen ...
(Bunderlied, 1810, H 4)

'For freedom, honor, Fatherland,
our German sword must always flash. . .'

Ritual military formulae involving Vaterland, such as the nineteenth-century Prussian formula "Für König und Vaterland," and the Nazi formula "Für Führer und *Vaterland*" (cf. Klemperer 1946:135), are also worth noting in this context. Their elliptical nature highlights the unspoken link between what people WANT to do for the *Vaterland* and what they SHOULD or HAVE TO do for it.

Similarly vague or unspecified in their modal force are imperative appeals such as the following:

Für Freiheit, Vaterland und Ehre
Bleib' stets gezückt das deutsche Schwerdt!
(G. D. Roller, 1828, H 73)

'For freedom, Fatherland, and honor
Always remain poised, German sword!'

The frequent combination of the three nouns *Vaterland*, *Freiheit*, and *Ehre* (*Vaterland*, freedom, and honor), usually in a modal, volitional, and emotive context, highlights the status of *Vaterland* as an ideal (something supremely good that one wants and should do something for—almost anything that might be required), rather than a descriptive term comparable to the English *native country* or *homeland*. This status of *Vaterland* is emphasized, in particular, in the common phrases such as *Tod fürs Vaterland* ('death for the *Vaterland*'), *sterben fürs Vaterland* ('to die for the *Vaterland*'), *sterben and leben fürs Vaterland* ('to die and to live for the *Vaterland*'), and *leben und streben für Vaterland* ('to live and to strive for the *Vaterland*'), always in an exalted modal context. For example:

Vaterland, dir nur ergeben
Wollen wir sterben und leben!
(E. Barbili, 1820; H. 18)

'Fatherland, devoted to you alone
We wish to die and live!'

Das höchste das wir kennen ist teutsches Vaterland,
Das schönste das wir nennen ist Tod fürs Vaterland
(K. Reh, 1815, H 67)

'The highest thing that we know is the German Fatherland,
The most beautiful thing that we can think of is death for the Fatherland'

Lass Kraft mich erwerben
In Herz und in Hand,
Zu leben und zu sterben
Fürs heilge Vaterland!
(H. F. Massman, 1820, H 101)

'Let strength win me over
with heart and with hand,
to live and to die
for the holy Fatherland!'

Ich hab mich ergeben
Mit Herz und mit Hand
Dir, Land voll Lieb und Leben,
Mein deutsches Vaterland!
(H. F. Massmann, 1820, H 101)

'I have yielded
with heart and with hand
to you, land full of love and life,
my German Fatherland!'

If not used in combination with the preposition *für*, the word *Vaterland* frequently occurs in the dative case, with similar implications:

Dem Vaterlande unser Gut und Blut!
(S. Höch, 1859, H 214)

'For the Fatherland our possessions and our blood'

Among the most characteristic verbs which occur with *für* or with the dative case, with similar implications, are *(sich) opfern* 'sacrifice oneself' and *sich weihen* 'devote oneself':

Ich bin ein Glied der heil'gen Schar,
Die sich dir opfert, Vaterland
(W. Flex, 1914, H 373)

'I am a member of the holy troop,
who offer themselves to you, Fatherland.'

weihte mich zu scharfer Wehre
Für das deutsche Vaterland!
(H. Vogt, 1924, H 328)

'I devote myself to keen struggle
for the German Fatherland!'

Heil dir, mein Vaterland!
Noch gibt es Herzen, welche für dich schlagen,
Die für dich glühn in hoher Liebesglut,
Die alles für die guten Sachen wagen,
Die freudig opfern all ihr Gut und Blut.
(J. L. Haupt, H 57)

'Hail to thee, my Fatherland!
There are still hearts that beat for you,
that glow for you with the fire of love,
that risk everything for the noble cause,
that sacrifice all their possessions and blood happily.'

Die grossen Volkes Söhne all
Sie reichen sich die Hand
Und weihn bei unsres Liebes Schall
Sich neu dem Vaterland
(W. Kleefeld, 1899, H 255)

'The sons of the great people
all give each other their hands
and offer themselves afresh to the Fatherland
at the sound of our love.'

The word *dein* 'yours', too, is often used in a sense similar to 'offering oneself', for example:

Dein in Leben, dein in Sterben,
Ruhmbekranztes Vaterland!
(R. Baumbach, 1878, H 260)

'Yours in life, yours in death,
Glorious [literally 'crowned with glory'] Fatherland!'

Finally, one further characteristic quote which spells out quite explicitly the idea that one belongs not to oneself but to the *Vaterland:*

Du darfst dir selbst nicht angehören,
Dein Alles gilt dem Vaterland,
Nicht eh'r zu ruhen musst du schwören,
Als bis es frei und gross erstand.
(A. Börner, 1926, H 411)

'You must not belong to yourself,
Your all is deemed the Fatherland's,
You must swear not to rest
Until it is created free and great.'

In songs devoted to *Vaterland,* which can be regarded as a genre of its own (*Vaterlands-lieder*), the loving praise of the *Vaterland* is often combined with promises to defend it, and with threats against its enemies. The words used most often in this connection include verbs such as *verteidigen* 'defend', *hüten* 'guard', *schützen* 'protect', *kämpfen* 'fight (for)', *streiten* 'fight for', and *retten* 'save', and the corresponding nomina agentis, especially in the plural, such as *Retter, Schützer,* and *Streiter*:

... Da stoben, wie Wetter, wie Wirbel im Meer
Des Vaterlands Retter, Teuts Söhne daher
(1808, H 3)

'... There raged, like the weather, like storms on the sea,
The saviors of the Fatherland, the sons of the Teuton.'

Wir stehn in des Lebens Morgenglanz,
Die kommenden Hüter des Vaterlands.
(H. F. Massman, 1817, H 69)

'We stand in the morning-glow of life,
the coming guardians of the Fatherland.'

Doch umschlingt uns alle Ein Bruderband,
Alle Streiter dem Einen Vaterland
(H. F. Massman, H 69)

'And still we are entwined by one brotherly tie,
All warriors for one Fatherland.'

It appears that the word *Vaterland* gradually changed its tone from purely emotional (as in Klopstock's "Vaterlandslied" quoted earlier) to moral, so that patriotic duty and obligation became absorbed from common contexts into the meaning of the word itself. Thus, at some points of its history, *Vaterland* came to embody a categorical moral imperative, and given the collective orientation of the word, the moral imperative had a collective character, too, implicitly appealing to shared values and shared obligations.

This is highly consistent with Leo Weisgerber's observation (made in the context of a discussion of the formula *Volk und Vaterland,* 'the people and the Vaterland') that "im Gedanken des Vaterlandes stand nicht die ausübende Macht, sondern der Schutz vor fremdem Eingriff zu im Vordergrund" (1959:262) ('in the idea of *Vaterland* it was not so much power as defense against an attack from outside that was most prominent').

The *Vaterland* was seen as something to be defended, protected, served, fought for, and, if need be, died for (and not only by an individual but by all its "sons")—and also as "someone" to be obeyed. Thus, we may suggest further semantic components of *Vaterland* along the following lines:

> this country is like a person
> this country did many good things for me
> I want to do good things for this country
> I think that if this country wants me to do something I have to do it

The first two ('wanting') components are supported by explicit 'wanting' statements such as the following:

> Wahret es treu!
> Vaterland, dir nur ergeben
> Wollen wir sterben und leben!
> Teutschland sei frei!
> (E. Barbili, 1820, H 18)

> 'Guard it faithfully!
> Fatherland, loyal to you
> we wish to die and live!
> Germany, be free!'

The component 'if this country wants me to do something . . .' is supported by very frequent mentions of the *Vaterland* "calling" (*rufen, Ruf*). For example:

> Das ruft, das ruft mein Vaterland!
> (W. Roll, 1853, H 213)

> 'There calls, there calls my Fatherland!'

> Wir dauern aus und können mutig ringen,
> Wenn es der Ruf des Vaterlands gebeut!
> (K. Hinkel, 1815, H 27)

> 'We persevere and struggle bravely
> If the call of the Fatherland demands it!'

The component 'I have to do it' (and its extension: 'I think all these people think the same') is supported by frequent mentions of "oaths" and "swearing," as well as references to the *Vaterland's Gebot's* ('orders', 'commandments').

> Hier war's, in dieser Halle,
> Da hoben sie fromm die Hand,
> Die männlichen Burschen alle,
> Zum Schwur fürs Vaterland
> Zu retten, was verloren . . .
> (R. Dehe, 1907, H 270)

'It was here, in this hall,
where reverently raised their hand,
all of the manly lads,
an oath for the Fatherland,
to save what was lost . . .'

Auf denn es sei: Vaterland, treu
Leb ich dir immerdar, steh ich zur frommen Schar,
Die so in Not wie Tod höret Dein laut Gebot:
Hurra juch hei!
(Ch. Buri, 1819, H 70)

'So forward, Fatherland,
I remain faithful to you forever, I stand by the reverent troops,
who, whether in need or death, clearly hear your command:
Hurrah hurrah hurray!'

The moral imperative may explain, to some extent, the power that this word is said to have exercised in Germany in wartime:

. . . wenn wir die Gefallenen der beiden letzten Kriege fragen würden—ihre Briefe,
die ja veröffentlicht sind, erlauben uns diese Frage—wenn wir sie fragen würden, was
ihnen nahe gewesen sei und ihnen die Kraft zu ihrem Opfer gegeben hat, dann
antworten sie einmütig mit diesen Räumen und Gestalten, die das Wort "Vaterland"
umschliesst.
(Ihlenfeld 1966:55)

'. . . if we were to ask the fallen soldiers of the last wars—their letters, which have
been published, permit us this question—if we were to ask them, what was close to
them and what gave them the strength for their sacrifice, they would unanimously
answer in ways that encompass the word *Fatherland* (*Vaterland*).'

I think the proposed explication of this word makes it clear how this word could have been put to use by the Nazi propaganda and rhetoric; one doesn't need to postulate a semantic change due to "a misuse of the word and of its original meaning" ("Mißbrauch des Wortes und seines ursprünglichen Gehaltes," Ihlenfeld 1966:48). Two examples from the time of World War II illustrate this point. First, a few lines from a 1940 song by a German teacher and poet from Bessarabia evacuated (with other Bessarabian Germans) to Germany:

Es trübet sich der Blick / Doch führet uns des Schicksals Hand / Ihr Brüder, welch
ein Glück / Ins grosse, deutsche Vaterland / Ins Heimatland zurück. (Greverus
1972:210)

'Our countenance clouds over / But the hand of destiny leads us / Brothers, what luck
[or: happiness] / to return to the great, the German Fatherland / Back to the Heimatland.'

And another example, a fragment of a World War II song from a camp for German prisoners of war (from a handwritten collection, hence the misspellings):

Wir haben viele viele Freiheits Kämpfer
sie wollen Kämfen fir ihres Treues Vaterland.

Das Schiksal wolte Nicht das wir das Ziel erlangen
wir sind verlassen haben keine Heimadt mehr. (Greverus 1972:441)

'We have many many fighters for freedom
they want to fight for their faithful Fatherland.
Fate did not want us to reach our goal
we are deserted and have no *Heimat*.'

3.5   *Vaterland* in postwar Germany

Commentators have noted that in post-war Germany many people have avoided using the word *Vaterland* altogether, because of its Nazi associations.

As Thielike put it, "Wir verfügen weithin nicht über die Freiheit, unbefangen und unbekümmert ein Wort wie 'Vaterland' überhaut in den Mund zu nehmen" (1962, quoted in Ihlenfeld 1966:55) ('We do not feel free to say aloud a word like "Fatherland" without inhibition'). Similarly, Ihlenfeld himself writes: "für uns Deutsche [ist] dem Gedanken ans Vaterland nun auch eine kaum überwindliche Schwermut eingetan und steht gegen jeden unbefangenen, jeden unreflektierten Gebrauch des Wortes" (52), ('for us Germans the thought of Fatherland is laden with a barely surmountable melancholy, and it stands against every careless, against every unreflecting usage of the word').

It is interesting that the word *Volk* was apparently not affected (to anything like the same degree), despite the fact that it, too, was used extensively in the Nazi propaganda. On a smaller scale, *Heimat*, too, was used by the Nazis ("In the writings of the Nazi ideologues of the 1930s, Heimat became simply one more term among many that revolved around the central themes of race, blood, and German destiny"; Applegate 1990:18), and yet, as mentioned earlier, *Heimat* survived the Nazi period unsullied. One can speculate, therefore, that if *Vaterland* became for many people in Germany an almost unusable word (especially for younger people, cf. Ihlenfeld 1966:48: "Eine so vaterlandsmüde Jugend wie die heutige hat es in Deutschland wohl noch nie gegeben." 'There has probably never been a young generation so weary of *Vaterland* as the one today in Germany.') this was due to the interaction between its use in the Nazi era and its inherent content, and not to the Nazi use alone. It seems to me that the moral-national imperative inherent in its meaning ('when this country wants me to do something I have to do it', etc.) accounts for the strong rejection of the word *Vaterland* in post-war Germany.

Not infrequently, contemporary German writers (and speakers generally) use *Vaterland* ironically:

Fein, und [sie] fahren auf Auktionen, um wertvolle Kruzifixe fürs Vaterland zu retten, denken nicht an das Blut, den Schweiss, die Scheisse, aus denen ihr Geld gemacht wird. (Böll 1980:121)

'All right then, they go along to auctions, to rescue valuable crucifixes for the *Vaterland*, and do not stop to think of the blood, sweat, shit, from which this gold is made.'

Nonetheless, *Vaterland* does still play an important role in public discourse;[3] and it is important to understand what exactly it means in this discourse in Germany. Thus,

West German President Gustav Heinemann called Germany "ein schwieriges Vater-land" ('a difficult Vaterland') in his inaugural address in 1969:

> Es gibt schwierige Vaterländer. Eins davon ist Deutschland. Aber es ist unser Vaterland. Hier leben und arbeiten wir. Darum wollen wir unseren Beitrag für die Menschheit mit diesem und durch dieses Land leisten.

> 'There are difficult Fatherlands. One of these is Germany. But it is our Fatherland. This is where we live and work. Thus we want to make our contribution to humanity with this and through this country.'

According to my German informants, one cannot speak of a *schwierige Heimat* ('difficult *Heimat*'), and it would hardly make sense to speak in English of a "difficult homeland." Presumably, it is not places themselves which are difficult but rather the obligations and responsibilities (as well as collective memories) associated with them.

The expression *schwieriges Vaterland* has since become a set phrase in German public discourse, as the title of a book by German political scientists Martin and Sylvia Greiffenhagen *Ein schwieriges Vaterland* (1979) illustrates. The special supplement of the *Spiegel* magazine (*Der Spiegel Dokument,* March 2, 1994), entitled "Zwei Vaterländer?" (Two fatherlands?), in which the word *Vaterland* is used several times, illustrates the enduring importance of this concept in German life (as well as its painful web of associations). This special issue is so relevant to the present topic that it deserves to be quoted at some length:

> Ein schwieriges Vaterland: dabei dachte man bis 1989 an historisch teilweise weit zurückliegende deutsche Ungereimtheiten wie die Spannung zwischen vielen Staaten in einem deutschem Vaterland, die verspätete Nation unter Weitergeltung vordemokratische Strukturen, die patriotischen Turbulenzen der Weimarer Republik, die blutige Diskreditierung des Begriff's Vaterland durch Hitler, und nach dem Krieg neue Schwierigkeiten, nicht nur mit dem Verhältnis von Staat und Nation. Un-terschiedliche politische Kulturen machen es schwer, umstandslos vom deutschen Vaterland zu sprechen.

> 'A difficult *Vaterland*: until 1989 this made one think about the abnormalities of the German past (some stretching far back in history), such as the tension between many states in one German *Vaterland*, a belatedly emergent nation still under the influence of predemocratic structures, the patriotic turbulences of the Weimar republic, the blood-soaked discrediting of the concept *Vaterland* under Hitler, and after the war, new difficulties, and not only those involving the relationship between the state and the nation. Different political cultures make it difficult to speak of a German *Vaterland* in general.'

The article concludes, with reference to the difficulties of post-unification Ger-many: "Deutschland ist auf neue Weise ein schwieriges Vaterland geworden" (7) ('Germany has become a difficult *Vaterland* in a new way'). In a similar vein, one could also say that although the word *Vaterland* tends now to be used self-consciously, ironically, or as a kind of shared historical allusion, it is still a key concept, albeit in a new way.

3.6   Summary: a full explication of *Vaterland*

Anticipating my discussion of the Polish key concept 'ojczyzna', I have indicated the components of *Vaterland* which are also included in the explication of *ojczyzna* (marking them with the sign "= 0"), as well as the components of *Vaterland* which do not have their counterparts in the explication of *ojczyzna* (marking them with the sign "≠0").

I haven't similarly indicated the components shared by *Vaterland* and *Heimat* because hardly any components included in both these concepts have exactly the same form (although there are several identical subcomponents).

Vaterland

(a) a country	= 0
(b) I am like a part of this country	= 0
(c) when I think about this country, I feel something good	= 0
(d) I think something like this when I think about this country:	= 0
(e) this country is not like any other country	= 0
(f) it is a very good country	≠ 0
(g) other countries are not like this country	≠ 0
(h) this country is like a person	= 0
(i) this country did many good things for me	= 0
(j) I want to do good things for this country	= 0
(k) if this country wants me to do something, I have to do it	≠ 0
(l) many other people think the same when they think about this country	= 0
(m) these people feel something good when they think about this country	= 0
(n) these people are like one thing	= 0
(o) I am like a part of this thing	= 0

4. *Ojczyzna*

Ojczyzna (etymologically derived from *ojciec* 'father', but in meaning, roughly, 'homeland' or 'motherland') is, or at least has been for two hundred years, one of the most central concepts in Polish culture. According to the sociologist Antonina Kłoskowska, it constitutes "a synthesis of the central values of this culture" (1991:52–53). As the Czech linguist Damborsky (1993) has noted, the traditional "definition" of Polishness in the neighboring Czech lands is given in the three-word slogan "Bóg, honor, i ojczyzna" ('God, honor, and *ojczyzna*').

A great deal has been written in Poland about the concept of 'ojczyzna' and its role in Polish history and literature. (For an excellent recent account of this literature, see Bartmiński, 1993b).[4] What is crucial from the present point of view, however, is not so much different views about *ojczyzna* which have been expressed (whether in literature, in public debate, or in opinion surveys) as the meaning of the word as such. As Bartmiński (1989:166) says, an explication of the concept 'ojczyzna' should show the collective consciousness articulated in the Polish language (that is, in the meaning of the word *ojczyzna* itself).

Ojczyzna is an old word, well attested in Polish literature from the sixteenth century onward. But it was only in the nineteenth century, after Poland was partitioned between Russia, Prussia, and Austria, that the word became highly prominent in Polish literature and everyday life (as reflected in letters, diaries, memoirs, and so on) and that it developed into a veritable *sacrum narodowe* ('national sacred treasure'), as Bartmiński (1989:165) put it. Throughout the nineteenth century (a century of repeated uprisings and unsuccessful attempts to regain freedom and national independence), the salience of this word steadily grew. When finally Poland did regain its independence after World War I, this growth was apparently arrested (cf. Taborska 1993), but it received a new impetus under the Nazi occupation of World War II. During the communist era, the word ojczyzna was the subject of political manipulation and propaganda and in the general perception became corrupted. But when in 1982, after martial law was declared in Poland and thousands of Solidarity activists were imprisoned, Father Jerzy Popiełuszko (murdered in 1984 by the political police) introduced his famous monthly *msze za Ojczyznę* ('masses for the *ojczyzna*'), the word *ojczyzna* regained a pure ring and was able to act as a rallying cry for the great majority of the nation active in, or sympathetic to, the Solidarity movement. A central feature of those masses were the homilies delivered by Father Popiełuszko, in which the key word, returning again and again, was *ojczyzna* (cf. Popiełuszko 1992).

It was only after the final demise of communism and the re-emergence of an independent Poland that the word *ojczyzna*—though still present in the political language—began to lose its central role in Polish life epitomizing Polish attitudes and Polish concerns (cf. Kloskowska 1993).

What, then, does a phrase like *msze za ojczyznę* 'masses for the *ojczyzna*' mean? Translations such as "masses for the native country," or "masses for the homeland," are inaccurate; and a German translation such as *Messen für das Vaterland* is downright dangerous, not only because of the possible Nazi connotations of *Vaterland* but also because of the significant semantic differences between *ojczyzna* and even the pre-Nazi (as well as post-Nazi) *Vaterland*.

Simplifying things considerably, we could say that if one's *Vaterland* is like a wonderful father who can demand things from one and whom one must willingly obey, *ojczyzna* is like a beloved mother who doesn't demand anything but who has suffered a great deal and whom one would want to protect from further misfortunes, fully expecting and accepting the need for self-sacrifice.

Before turning to a more detailed discussion of *ojczyzna*, it should be pointed out that in addition to the mainstream usage there was also a regional usage, well known from Polish literature. Adam Mickiewicz's great classic "Pan Tadeusz" (first published in Paris in 1834) starts with words that every Pole knows by heart:

> Litwo, ojczyzno moja! Ty jesteś jak zdrowie!
> Ile Cię trzeba cenić, ten tylko się dowie,
> Kto Cię stracił.

> 'O Lithuania, my homeland [*ojczyzna*]! You are like good health.
> Only he can value you fully who has lost you.'

When Mickiewicz, the leading Polish political exile, writing about Poland, in Polish, and for Poles, called "Litwa" (Lithuania) his *ojczyzna,* he was using this word in a sense similar to that of the German *Heimat*. He meant, roughly speaking, the places where he lived as a child, where he felt at home as a child, where his family lived, and where his life had its roots. In addition, the word had a strong emotional component (like *Heimat*).

But Mickiewicz himself used the word *ojczyzna* also in the other, broader sense, as when he dedicated his drama *Dziady* (Forefathers' eve) to his friends who had similarly been exiled and who died for *ojczyzna*, as "martyrs for the cause of the nation":

Świętej pamięci Janowi Sobolewskiemu, Cyprianowi Daszkiewiczowi,
Feliksowi Kółakowskiemu, spółuczniom, spółwięźniom, spółwygnańcom,
za miłość ku ojczyźnie prześladowanym, z tęsknoty ku ojczyźnie
zmarłym, w Archangielu, na Moskwie, w Petersburgu, narodowej sprawy
męczennikom, poświęca autor.

'To the sacred memory of Jan Sobolewski, Cyprian Daszkiewicz, and Feliks Kółakowski, fellow-students, fellow-prisoners, fellow-exiles, who were persecuted for love of homeland [*ojczyzna*] and died pining for it in Archangel, Moscow, and Petersburg, martyrs to the national cause, I dedicate this work.'

In this dedication, *ojczyzna* does not refer to beloved local places, like *Heimat*, but to a beloved country; and it is closely linked with the notion of 'naród', 'nation'. In this respect, it can be compared to *Vaterland*. It can still be compared to *Heimat*, however, in its nostalgic perspective, reflected in particular in the untranslatable phrase "z tęsknoty ku ojczyźnie zmarłym," roughly, 'who died out of nostalgia for the *ojczyzna*'.

But Polish doesn't have two words which are comparable to *Heimat* and *Vaterland*; it has just one—*ojczyzna*—whose meaning differs from that of either *Heimat* or *Vaterland*, although it shares some components with both. In the mainstream modern sense, *ojczyzna* (like *Vaterland* or *homeland*) refers to a country among other countries, that is, to a unique member of a broader category of lands viewed as separate entities. Since this word acquired its modern identity and became a key word in Polish at a time when there was no Polish state, it did not refer to a political entity. On the other hand, it had a clear historical, as well as geographical dimension (linked with strong emotional and moral content). This historical aspect of *ojczyzna* constitutes one of its most characteristic features (differentiating it from, for example, *homeland*, *Heimat*, *Vaterland*, or the Russian *rodina*). The disasters that happened to Poland between the first partition (1772) and the national "resurrection" (1918) left their imprint on the very meaning of this crucial word.

4.1   *Ojczyzna*—the country of birth?

The nineteenth-century poet Maria Konopnicka has left us the following poetical definition of *ojczyzna* :

Ojczyzna moja—to ta ziemia droga,
Gdziem ujrzał słońce i gdziem poznał Boga.

'My *ojczyzna*—is that dear land,
where I [first] saw the sun and where I got to know God.'

In a similar vein, the *Dictionary of the Polish language* (SJP) defines *ojczyzna* as "the country where one was born and which is the country of one's fellow-countrymen [*rodacy*]." But does a person's *ojczyzna* need to be their country of birth? The answer is not as straightforward as it seems, in view of the existence of phrases such as *druga* ('second') *ojczyzna* or *przybrana* ('adopted') *ojczyzna*. In my view, however, all uses of *ojczyzna* with respect to countries other than one's country of birth have to be regarded as metaphorical, and phrases such as *przybrana ojczyzna* should be interpreted as sui generis abbreviations along the following lines: "an adopted *ojczyzna*" is a country which is not one's *ojczyzna* but which one thinks of as if it were one's *ojczyzna*.

Personal identification ('I am like a part of this country') appears to be more important for this concept than the mere fact of birth ('I was born in this country'); nonetheless, the idea of 'origin' is important, too. This is supported by the fact that *ojczyzna* can be used metaphorically in the sense 'country of origin of something' (e.g. China is the *ojczyzna* of silk); and also that the adjective *ojczysty* (as in the phrase *ziemia ojczysta* 'the land, earth of one's *ojczyzna*') can only refer to the country of origin, not to any "adopted *ojczyzna*." The very close conceptual link between *ojczyzna* (despite its etymology) and *mother* (confirmed, for example, by the common phrase *łono ojczyzny,* 'womb/bosom of the *ojczyzna*') points in the same direction. (The notion of a 'father figure' refers to a special kind of relationship which can extend well into a person's adulthood, but a 'mother' is above all a point of origin, a 'body' from which one has emerged at the beginning of one's life journey and which, one might add, represents the archetypal security of the womb. For Poles for nearly two centuries, the nostalgia for the lost *ojczyzna* was linked symbolically with that archetypal image. To quote Mickiewicz again:

Panno Święta, co Jasnej bronisz Częstochowy . . .
tak nas powrócisz cudem na ojczyzny łono.

'Holy Virgin, who have defended the Holy Mountain of Częstochowa . . . you will bring us back miraculously to the womb/bosom of the *ojczyzna*.

In this respect, then, (the link with one's "point of origin") *ojczyzna* is closer to the German *Heimat* than to *Vaterland*; and I have posited the component 'I was born in this country' for *Heimat* and for *ojczyzna* but not for *Vaterland* (although *Heimat* doesn't have the same strong link with 'mother' that *ojczyzna* has).

On the other hand, there is no evidence that *ojczyzna* has the same link with the world of childhood as *Heimat* does. Nor does it necessarily imply happy memories of a safe haven. Consequently, I have not posited for *ojczyzna* either of the two "childhood components" postulated for *Heimat*: 'when I was a child, I was like a part of these places', 'I felt something good when I was like a part of these places'.

But there are other links between *ojczyzna* and *Heimat*. In a sense, both *Heimat* and *ojczyzna* oppose one's own place to "foreign," "alien" places, places where one must feel like a stranger. In the case of *ojczyzna*, this contrast between being "at home" and being "a stranger among strangers" is highlighted by the lexical opposition between the two rhyming words: *ojczyzna* and *obczyzna* (from *obcy* 'alien' or 'stranger'). *Obczyzna* means, roughly, 'a land of strangers, where one is a stranger oneself', and this very contrast highlights the special quality of *ojczyzna* as a place uniquely and irreplaceably "one's own," the only place where one can truly "belong." Two examples:

Zmuszeni byli emigrować na obczyznę w poszukiwaniu chleba.
(Życie Literackie, 1954, SJP)

'They were forced to emigrate to foreign lands in search of a livelihood.'

Wolę wszelką nędzę znosić jak królową być w obczyźnie.
(Damroth, 1922, SJP)

'I would prefer any misery to being a queen in a foreign land.'

To portray this aspect of *ojczyzna*, I have posited the component 'I can't be like a part of any other country'. In the case of *Heimat*, the analogous components read: 'I was like a part of these places when I was a child' and 'I can't be like a part of any other places'; they are therefore childhood-oriented. By implication, the uniqueness and irreplaceability of one's *Heimat* places have a great deal to do with the uniqueness and unrecoverability of one's childhood. But in the case of *ojczyzna*, the uniqueness of one's link with the country where one was born lies elsewhere: largely in the perceived uniqueness of this country's history and in the solidarity with the other people born in the same country and caught in the same history (with the resulting memories, feelings, and obligations).

The importance and strength of the link among the people belonging to the same *ojczyzna* is manifested in the specifically Polish word *rodacy* ('beloved countrymen'), included in the SJP definition of *ojczyzna* quoted earlier. On the surface, this word seems to correspond to the English word *fellow-countrymen*, or to the French word *compatriotes*, but in fact it means much more. It implies that people who belong to the same *ojczyzna* share so much (through their love of that *ojczyzna* and through their participation in the same history) that they can be expected to love (or at least, feel something very good for) one another. One characteristic (and very famous) quote:

Zwyciężonemu za pomnik grobowy zostaną suche drewna szubienicy, za całą sławę krótki płacz kobięcy i długie nocne rodaków rozmowy. (Mickiewicz).

'The vanquished shall have as his only monument the dry wood of the gallows, as his only fame, a woman's brief lament, and the lengthy nocturnal discussions of his fellow countrymen [rodacy]'.

It is interesting to note that while Russian has a "loving word" for members of one's family and household (*rodnye*; see chapter 2, section 3), Polish links an expectation of mutual love with belonging to the same *ojczyzna* (in the word *rodacy*).

The link between 'country' and 'nation', which lies at the heart of *ojczyzna*, is also characteristic of *Vaterland*, but the link between *ojczyzna* and *rodacy* ('one's own people'), as well as the contrast between *ojczyzna* and *obczyzna* (alien places), are peculiarly Polish.

These considerations lead us to the following partial explication:

ojczyzna (incomplete)
a country

I was born in this country
I am like a part of this country
I can't be like a part of any other country
this country is like a part of me
many other people think the same when they think of this country
when I think about these people, I feel something good

The close links of *ojczyzna* with history and with the notion of a 'nation' will be explored in the subsequent sections of this chapter and will be portrayed in further parts of the explication.

To account for this expectation of a strong emotional bond between people belonging to the same *ojczyzna*, I have included in its explication the component 'when I think of these people, I feel something good'. While it would be hard to quote any direct evidence for including a component of this kind in the explication of the word *ojczyzna* (in contrast to *rodacy*), it is interesting to note that in the 1991 survey of responses to the word *ojczyzna* (Kloskowska 1993), a large number of interviewees responded in a way linking this word with a strong bond among people belonging to the same *ojczyzna*. For example, when asked, "What would you call people who have the same *ojczyzna* as you?" as many as 9% replied: *bracia* ('brothers'), and all the replies using a kinship term (including *rodzina* 'family') in connection with *ojczyzna* reach 48%.

Summing up the results of the survey, Kloskowska notes that the following elements emerged in the responses as the most prominent ones: "a feeling of roots, belonging, being conscious of sharing in the history of a strongly bonded collectivity, not being a stranger in an alien place" (54). Remarks of this kind highlight the 'solidarity' aspect of *ojczyzna* (manifested directly in the word *rodacy*), an aspect contrasting with the more individualistic character of *Heimat*.

The link between 'country' and 'nation', which lies at the heart of *ojczyzna*, is also characteristic of *Vaterland*, but the link between *ojczyzna* and *rodacy* ('one's own people'), as well as the contrast between *ojczyzna* ('one's own country) and *obczyzna* ('alien places', 'places of exile') is characteristically Polish.

4.2   A collective memory of the past martyrology

In modern usage, the concept 'ojczyzna' is closely associated with concepts such as 'death', 'suffering', 'martyrdom', 'loss', 'exile'. Mickiewicz's dedication linking *ojczyzna* with death, persecution, exile, nostalgia, and martyrdom is quite characteristic in this respect. The beginning of a well-known poem by another romantic poet, Juliusz Słowacki, is also very characteristic:

O! nieszczęśliwa! O! uciemiężona
Ojczyzno moja.

'O, homeland [*ojczyzna*]! How unhappy, how oppressed!

A few more characteristic examples (quoted in Bartmiński 1993b):

A ja wszędy w tej krainie Widzę jedną wielką bliznę,
jedną moję cierpiącą Ojczyznę!"
(Słowacki)

'And everywhere in this land I see one great scar, my suffering homeland [*ojczyzna*]!'

Kto zostanie, niech już nad grobem ojczyzny nie płacze. (Norwid)

'Let the survivor not weep over the gravestone of the homeland [*ojczyzna*].'

czas niedaleki, W którym ojczyznę, matkę naszą biedną z grobu wyniesiem—by żyła
na wieki (Gaszyński)

'the time is not far distant when we will raise our homeland [*ojczyzna*], our poor
mother, from the grave—that she may live forever.'

gorycz wyssana ze krwi i łez mej ojczyzny. (Mickiewicz)

'a bitterness sucked from the blood and tears of my homeland [*ojczyzna*].'

Ojczyzny mojej stopy okrwawione
Włosami otrzeć na piasku upadam. (Norwid)

'I fall to the sand to wipe the bleeding feet of my homeland [*ojczyzna*] with my hair.'

As Bartmiński has documented, in Polish literature (especially in poetry), *ojczyzna*
typically co-occurs with words such as *cierpiąca* 'suffering', *bolejąca* 'in great pain',
płacząca 'weeping', *nieszczęsna* 'unhappy', *biedna* 'poor', or occurs in collocations
such as "the blood and tears of my *ojczyzna*," "the grave of my *ojczyzna*," "my *ojczyzna*
is dying," "the death of the *ojczyzna*," and "the sorrow of the *ojczyzna*," and the like.

Maria Janion (1979) makes the following generalization about *ojczyzna* in Polish
romantic poetry:

> *Ojczyzna* was presented as a person, sometimes dead, sometimes in a coma, some-
> times mortally wounded, a person who requires urgent help, for whom one must leave
> everything and whom one must never forget. The fact that she appeared as someone
> helpless, unhappy, tormented, martyred, wronged, evoked in the romantic poets a
> sense of solidarity and love, and a yearning to come to her rescue. (46–47)

The sorrowful, painful connotations of *ojczyzna*, so characteristic of romantic
poetry, are by no means confined to the romantic period: they are detectable in most
uses of the word throughout the nineteenth and twentieth century. To quote just one
characteristic late twentieth century example (from a poem by Tadeusz Różewicz):

no początku ojczyzna
jest blisko
na wyciągnięcie ręki
dopiero później rośnie
krwawi
boli
(Bartmiński 1993b)

'at first the homeland [*ojczyzna*]
is near at hand

only later does it grow
bleed
ache'

The writer Marian Brandys (quoted in Bartmiński 1993b), observed that he had used the word *ojczyzna* only once in his life, in September 1939, when he was suffering an acute sense of defeat. He asked his colleagues then: "What will happen to our *ojczyzna*?"[5] Consider also the following definition of *ojczyzna* offered in a 1989 survey of views on this subject: "Historia, wspólnota dążeń i cierpień" ('history, an awareness of shared goals and sufferings'). I doubt very much whether "sufferings" would be mentioned by anyone in a similar survey of opinions on *Vaterland* or *Heimat*.

In the eighteenth century, *ojczyzna* could still co-occur with adjectives such as *wesoła* 'merry, cheerful', as in the quote below:

Ten się ojczyzny zwać synem prawdziwym . . . może, który . . . Wesół z wesołą, z płaczącą się smuci. (Naruszewicz, quoted in Bartmiński 1993b).

'Only he can be called a true son of the motherland [*ojczyzna*] who makes merry when she makes merry, and laments when she laments.'

But in modern Polish, combinations of this kind are felt to be incongruous and are instinctively avoided. Characteristically, the typical modern collocations listed under *ojczyzna* in Skorupka's (1974) phraseological dictionary of the Polish language are *bronić ojczyzny* 'defend the *ojczyzna*', *polec, przelewać krew, umrzeć, walczyć, zginąć za ojczyznę, w obronie ojczyzny* 'be killed for, shed one's blood for, die for, struggle for, perish for the *ojczyzna*', and finally *służyć ojczyźnie* 'serve the *ojczyzna*' (with strong implications of self-sacrifice). This is of course similar to the phraseology of *Vaterland,* but only in its "negative" subset (see later).

Positive collocations such as *wolna ojczyzna* 'free *ojczyzna*' are possible, but they imply something like "finally liberated," "finally free," so they, too, refer to past disasters. The following lines from a poem by Leopold Staff (written shortly after Poland regained its independence in 1918, quoted in Bartmiński 1993b) are very characteristic in this regard:

Ojczyzno nasza, Matko bolesna . . .
Nad tobą świeci wolna Kopuła!

'O homeland [*ojczyzna*], mother of sorrows,
The dome of freedom rises above you.'

Similarly, Słonimski, another twentieth-century poet, wrote:

Ojczyzna moja wolna, wolna . . .
Więc zrzucam z ramion płaszcz Konrada . . . (SJP)

'My *ojczyzna* is free, free . . .
So I cast away [from my shoulders] the cloak of Konrad'[6]

Admittedly, there are contexts where reference to "bad things" (past misfortunes) may seem to be entirely missing. The title of a geography textbook published in independent (recently liberated) Poland in the 1920s (*Nasza ojczyzna* 'our *ojczyzna*') may be a case in point. I would argue, however, that even a title of this kind can be said to contain implicit allusions to past misfortunes. In this context, the implicit message can be reconstructed as follows: 'this is our country; we should know it; many bad things have happened to this country; we don't want bad things to happen to this country; we want to do good things for this country; we think good things can happen to this country now'.

Even the phony, propaganda phrase *nasza socjalistyczna ojczyzna* 'our socialist *ojczyzna*' used in official language under the communist regime, sounded as if it implicitly referred to an unhappy past overcome by the glorious present.

Many collocations characteristic of *ojczyzna* are, as we have seen, also characteristic of *Vaterland* (e.g. both frequently occur in frames such as "to die for, to fight for, to defend"). But *Vaterland* is also frequently used in combinations with adjectives such as *grosses* 'great' and *schönes* 'beautiful', or with the verb *blühen* 'to flourish' (as in the German national anthem). By contrast, *ojczyzna* is not normally described as *wielka* 'great' or *piękna* 'beautiful', and the optative phrases involving *ojczyzna* have typically referred to *zmartwychwstanie* 'resurrection' rather than to blooming or flourishing.

One of the most characteristic examples in this respect is a line from a hymn, frequently sung in the past in Polish churches:

Ojczyznę wolną racz nam wrócić Panie!

'O Lord, give us back a free *ojczyzna*!'

In communist times, this line sounded like an act of political defiance (and was meant as such), of course, and the regime demanded that it be replaced with a more *bien pensant* version:

Ojczyznę wolną pobłogosław Panie.

'O Lord, bless our free *ojczyzna*.'

But even in the official version the phrase *ojczyznę wolną* (literally 'a free *ojczyzna*'), sounded like a reference to past misfortunes; in the authentic version, as normally sung in Poland, the reference was of course to present, as well as past, misfortunes.

Unlike the German word *Vaterland* or the Russian word *rodina*, *ojczyzna* is not the kind of word which could be used in vigorous, triumphant, marching songs; it is too poignant, too solemn, too pain-infused a word for this kind of context. It is also interesting to note that while the German phrase *sterben fürs Vaterland* 'to die for the *Vaterland*' has common counterparts in the Polish phrases *zginąć za ojczyznę* and *polec za ojczyznę*, the phrase *leben und sterben für Vaterland*, 'to live and to die for the *Vaterland*' does not. *Ojczyzna* was associated far more with dying than with living.

Similarly, there is no tradition of special songs associated with *ojczyzna*, as there was a special genre of *Vaterland-lieder* in Germany. Patriotic Polish songs, of which there are a great many, normally seemed to avoid the word *ojczyzna*, common as it was in lyrical and rhetorical poetry. In particular, fighting songs typically used the word *Polska* 'Poland' rather than *ojczyzna*. All these facts suggest a unique semantic component of *ojczyzna*, which I would tentatively formulate as follows: 'many bad things happened to this country'.

A recent article on the use of the word *Vaterland* (Kleine-Brockhoff et al. 1989) mentions a huge restaurant in prewar Berlin whose name was "Das Haus Vaterland," and one of my German informants recalls a café in Munich called "Vaterland." But according to all my Polish informants it is inconceivable that a Polish restaurant should be called "Ojczyzna." "Polska," "Polonia," "Patria," yes, but never *ojczyzna*. In fact, some older informants (World War II veterans in their seventies and eighties) got quite upset at the idea, which sounded to them like sacrilege or mockery. I believe that reactions of this kind support the references to "bad things" in the explication of *ojczyzna* proposed here.

It is worth mentioning in this connection another famous passage from a poem by the early twentieth-century poet Jan Kasprowicz:

Rzadko na moich wargach, niech dziś ma warga to wyzna
Jawi się krwią przepojone, najdroższe słowo ojczyzna.

'Seldom on my lips there appears,
let my lips confess it today,
the bleeding, beloved word *ojczyzna*.'

The reticence confessed here by Kasprowicz is of course something quite different from the reluctance to use the word *ojczyzna* reported in contemporary opinion surveys. Apparently, to most young people in contemporary Poland the word *ojczyzna* is no longer relevant and doesn't correspond to their present concerns. But for Kasprowicz, the word WAS relevant; but it was too sacred and too pained ("bleeding" or "soaked in blood") ever to be used irreverently.

Discussing the concept 'ojczyzna' and its closest counterparts in other European languages, Bartmiński (1993b) writes that perhaps the most characteristically Polish attitude is that "which accepts as the most basic value national freedom [*wolność*] and independence [*niepodległość*] and which deduces from this a set of obligations of the individual towards the nation."

The words *wolność* 'freedom' and *niepodległość* 'national independence' used in this passage identify key Polish cultural concepts that have no exact equivalents elsewhere. *Wolność* is not so much 'freedom' as, above all, 'national freedom', and *niepodległość* is not simply 'independence' but 'national independence' (cf. chapter 3). Both these words reflect the historical experience of a nation for whom national freedom and independence could not be taken for granted but had to be constantly fought for. Thus, both these words carry echos of a collective memory of national subjugation—that is, of 'bad things that happened to this country', with the concomitant protestation 'I (we) don't want bad things to happen to this country'. The concept 'ojczyzna' bears the imprint of the same concerns.

4.3   The moral aspect of *ojczyzna*

The collective memory of "bad things" which have happened to this country (personified as a suffering mother) leads to a desire for this country to be protected from similar "bad things" in the future:

> I don't want bad things to happen to this country

This, in turn, invites an attitude of self-sacrifice:

> I want to do good things for this country
> if I feel something bad because of this,
> I don't want not to do these things because of this

In the surveys of views on *ojczyzna* reported on by Kloskowska (1993), several respondents quote the nineteenth-century poet Norwid's poetic definition of this concept:

> Ojczyzna to jest wielki zbiorowy obowiązek.

> 'the homeland [*ojczyzna*] that is our great, our collective duty.'

As we have seen, the German word *Vaterland*, too, has come to have a moral dimension, which it didn't have in its earlier usage. It implies duty, as well as pride. But the duty it implies is not so directly linked with the idea of 'sacrifice' as the duty *ojczyzna* implies. Rather, it is a duty to obey ('if this country wants me to do something, I have to do it'). Typically, *Vaterland* CALLS (its "sons"), whereas *ojczyzna* weeps, suffers, dies, sheds blood and tears (and silently EXPECTS her "children" to respond). Both concepts imply a moral imperative "to do good things for one's country," but *Vaterland* suggests a "have to" modality, whereas *ojczyzna* suggests a "want to" attitude (combined with an additional element of 'it would be bad if I didn't'). Furthermore, *ojczyzna* is additionally skewed toward something like a willingness to suffer:

> if I feel something bad because of this,
> I don't want to say: 'I don't want this'

The only proverb cited in the monumental *Dictionary of the Polish language* (SJP 1958:898) under *ojczyzna* is this: "miłe blizny dla ojczyzny" ('scars [incurred] for the *ojczyzna* gladden the heart'). Certainly, the rhyme *"ojczyzna—blizna"* ('*ojczyzna*— scar') is one of the most hackneyed rhymes in the Polish language. The link between *ojczyzna* and something like an expectation of selflessness and sacrifice is supported by the frequently expressed notion that *ojczyzna* is not necessarily a place where one can expect "good things" to happen to one. One characteristic example is provided by the first line of Mickiewicz's satirical poem "Pan Baron":

> Gdzie dobrze tam ojczyzna.

> 'where things go well [or: where one is well off] there is (one's) *ojczyzna*.'

As Bartmiński (1993b) pointed out, in a different context Mickiewicz reverses this satirical statement:

Tam ojczyzna, gdzie źle.

'*Ojczyzna* is the place where you are not well off
[where bad things happen to you].'

Furthermore, *ojczyzna* implies not only a moral imperative to 'do good things' for one's country (to serve it, to defend it, to fight for it) but also a moral imperative to love this country (to 'feel something good' for it). Bartmiński links this aspect with the symbolic identification of *ojczyzna* with 'mother': "The ethical requirement to love one's *ojczyzna*—like the ethical requirement to love one's mother—doesn't need any justification" (1989:171). Hence the need for the semantic component: 'if I didn't feel something good for this country, this would be very bad'.

The ethical requirement to love one's country and to identify with it is so strong in Polish culture that it has found its direct expression in the Polish lexicon, in the form of the special verb *wynarodowić się*. Derived from *naród* 'nation', this verb refers to the process whereby an individual loses (or sheds) his or her identification with the Polish nation. The word is strongly pejorative and implies something like 'treason', 'crime', 'disgrace'. Frequently, this word was used with reference to persons who married a Russian or a German and as a consequence lost their Polish national consciousness and their emotional allegiance to Poland and Polish culture (and were ostracized for their "treason"). It was also frequently used of Polish emigrants who became so absorbed in the life of their new country of residence that they lost (or shed) their Polishness. For example:

Ojcowie rodzin stwierdzali z bólem, że dzieci się wynaradawiają i że za parę lat nie będą mogli do nich po polsku przemówić. (Wiktor, 1951, SJP)

'Fathers found with grief that their children were losing their nationality and that in a few years' time they wouldn't be able to speak to them in Polish.'

Clearly, the word *wynarodowić się* reflects a specifically Polish historical experience, the pressure many felt to give up their Polish identity—and the unqualified condemnation of those who gave in to such pressure.

The threat to Polish national identity from neighboring powers, especially Russia, led many Poles to political emigration or exile. Interestingly, this fact, too, found its lexical expression, leading to the emergence of a special new meaning of the word *kraj*: (1) country; (2) the country (Poland), seen from the perspective of Poles forced to live outside it . For example:

Tęsknię do kraju. (Słonimski, 1951, SJP)

'I miss (ache for) [my] country.'

I prawdziwie głosem psa takiego zawyć był gotów z tęsknoty za krajem. (Berent, 1937, SJP)

'And he was genuinely ready to howl like a dog from nostalgia for [his] country.'

(Cf. also the expression *Armia Krajowa* 'Home Army', which was the name of the Polish army fighting against Nazi Germany on Polish soil, in contrast to the Polish forces fighting Hitler outside Poland, *krajowa* being an adjective derived from *kraj* in sense 2 of the word.)

In a sense, the word *kraj*, which implicitly recognizes and legitimizes the need for many Poles to live abroad, could be said to be in semantic opposition to *ojczyzna*. It implies that Poland as the *ojczyzna* of the Polish nation extends beyond a certain geographical territory (*kraj*, the country sensu stricto), but includes also (in a spiritual sense) all those fighting, or working, or simply pining for Poland outside its geographical boundaries.

Thus, both these uniquely Polish concepts—'wynarodowić się' and 'kraj' (as well as 'obczyzna' and 'rodacy', discussed earlier)—closely reflect Polish historical experience and the specifically Polish response to that experience. The concept 'ojczyzna' belongs to the same cluster of concepts.

4.4   *Ojczyzna* as culture and tradition

Bartmiński (1993b) writes:

> Undoubtedly the most characteristic and unique aspect of the Polish understanding of *ojczyzna*, brought about by Poland's history in the last two centuries, consists in a special emphasis on the role of culture, stronger than elsewhere, either in the East or West. This emphasis on culture subsumes literature and art, language and customs, and also an ethical program with a strongly developed patriotic ethos. The institution of the state is seen in this context as secondary. In Poland, after the collapse of the first Republic [in 1795], the notion of '*ojczyzna*-state' had no chances of continuation.

Intuitively, the idea that *ojczyzna* gives special attention to culture and tradition seems correct, and it can certainly be supported with numerous quotes from Polish writers and thinkers, as well as recent sociological data. But can it be supported with linguistic evidence as well?

In some measure it can. In particular, interesting light is thrown on this question by the use of the highly emotional adjective *ojczysty*, derived from *ojczyzna*. This adjective occurs in a rather limited set of collocations, which include, above all, the following: *język ojczysty* ('native language'), *mowa ojczysta* (roughly, the same, but more emotional and rhetorical), *dzieje ojczyste* ('the past history of one's native land', emotional and rhetorical), *kraj ojczysty* ('native country'), and *ziemia ojczysta* ('native land'). (SJP cites also *historia ojczysta* 'Polish history' and *prawa ojczyste* 'the laws of one's native land'.)

In trying to elucidate the special value of the adjective *ojczysty*, it is particularly instructive to compare the following two, roughly synonymous, expressions: *ziemia ojczysta* and *ziemia rodzinna* (both roughly 'one's native land'). The difference is that *rodzinna* (derived from *rodzina* 'family') reflects an individual's point of view (like *Heimat*), whereas *ojczysta* suggests something treasured by a collectivity, that is, the nation as a whole (and by the individual as a member of that collectivity, participating in its shared values).

Thus, the collocations with the adjective *ojczysty* suggest the following further semantic components of *ojczyzna* itself:

(a) these people are like one thing:
(b) these people say things in the same way
(c) these people do many things in the same way
(d) these people think about many things in the same way
(e) these people often feel in the same way

Component (b) suggests a unity of language (and ways of speaking), (c) a unity of customs and, more generally, way of life, (d) a body of shared beliefs and attitudes, and (e) a pool of shared emotions and sentiments. Taken together, these additional components imply a high measure of cultural homogeneity, including linguistic unity.

It would be easy to adduce quotes from Polish literature which seem to undermine these postulates by linking *ojczyzna* with cultural plurality, universal ethics, human solidarity independent of language and creed, and so on. The most famous example of this kind is furnished by Antoni Słonimski's poem, "Ten jest z ojczyzny mojej" ('He is from my *ojczyzna*'):

> ... Ten, który wszystkim serce swe otwiera
> Francuzem jest, gdy Francja cierpi, Grekiem,
> Gdy naród grecki z głodu obumiera,
> Ten jest z ojczyzny mojej, jest człowiekiem.
> (Słonimski 1964:457)

> 'He who opens his heart to all,
> Is a Frenchman when France suffers, a Greek
> When the Greek nation is dying of hunger,
> He is from my *ojczyzna*. He is a human being.'

It should be recognized, however, that utterances of this kind have a polemical character and that they implicitly oppose a higher, universal ideal to the national ethos reflected in the concept 'ojczyzna' as it is. They do not seek to explicate the concept of 'ojczyzna' but to propose something that could supersede it. In fact, therefore, utterances of this kind not only do not undermine the case for including the additional components sketched above but lend further support to them.

4.5 *Ojczyzna*—the country of ancestors?

In Polish literature and thought, the notion of 'ojczyzna' is often explained with reference to ancestors. For example, Karol Libelt (1967 [1844]), in a classic treatise on the subject, says that *ojczyzna* is, first of all, one's native land, and secondly "it is one people, one stock, one tribe, from which our parents have emerged, and of which we are a part ourselves" (9).

Characteristically, many literary and everyday definitions of *ojczyzna* include the word *groby* 'graves', apparently not only with reference to past misfortunes (uprisings, battles, etc.) but also with reference to earlier generations. To quote just one example from the 1991 survey of opinions (Kloskowska 1993): "*Ojczyzna* is the place where one can always find brotherly affection, perhaps it doesn't even have to be a place, what matters is the atmosphere, and in particular, the graves of the ancestors, places looking at which I become conscious of history" (54).

It should also be pointed out that while the etymological link between *ojczyzna* and *ojciec* 'father' is no longer synchronically valid (since *ojczyzna* is certainly not thought of as "the country of one's father"), there is still a perceived link between *ojczyzna* and *ojcowie*, the plural of the word for 'father', which can also mean 'our ancestors'. If one defined *ojczyzna* as *ziemia ojców* 'the land of our ancestors', this would probably be accepted by many native speakers as intuitively quite plausible, and the morphological link between *ojczyzna* and *ojcowie* (in the sense 'ancestors') would be perceived as synchronically valid.

To account for the semantic link between *ojczyzna* and past generations, I have tentatively included in the explication of this word the following components: 'before this time, for a long time many other people were like a part of this country' and 'I am like a part of all these people'.

4.6   Summary: a full explication of *ojczyzna*

To facilitate comparison between *ojczyzna* and *Vaterland*, I have marked the components shared with *Vaterland* with the sign "=V", and those absent from the explication of *Vaterland*, as "≠V":

ojczyzna

(a)	a country	= V
(b)	I was born in this country	≠ V
(c)	I am like a part of this country	= V
(d)	I can't be like a part of any other country	≠ V
(e)	this country is like a part of me	≠ V
(f)	when I think about this country, I feel something good	= V
(g)	if I didn't, this would be very bad	≠ V
(h)	I think something like this when I think about this country:	= V
(i)	this country is not like any other country	= V
(j)	this country is like a person	≠ V
(k)	many bad things happened to this country	≠ V
(l)	I don't want bad things to happen to this country	= V(?)
(m)	this country did many good things for me	= V
(n)	like a mother does good things for her children	≠ V
(o)	I want to do good things for this country	= V(?)
(p)	if I feel something bad because of this I don't want not to do these things because of this	≠ V
(q)	many other people think the same when they think about this country	= V
(r)	these people feel something good when they think about this country	= V
(s)	these people are like one thing	= V
(t)	I am like a part of this thing	= V
(u)	these people say things in the same way	≠ V
(v)	these people do many things in the same way	≠ V
(w)	these people think about many things in the same way	≠ V
(x)	these people often feel in the same way	≠ V
(y)	when I think about these people, I feel something good	≠ V
(z)	these people are like a part of this country	≠ V
(ż)	before this time, for a long time many other people were like a part of this country	≠ V(?)

(ż) I am like a part of all these people   ≠ V
(ż) in many ways, I am like these people   ≠ V

5. Rodina

Russian has not one but three words which could be loosely glossed as "homeland" and which could be compared with *Vaterland* and *Heimat* and *ojczyzna*. These words are *rodina*, *otečestvo*, and *otčizna*. Of the three, however, only one— *rodina*—is used frequently and can be regarded as one of the Russian key words. (For example, in Zasorina's 1977 corpus based on 1 million running words, *rodina* has a frequency of 172, whereas *otečestvo* has only 30, and *otčizna* 2.)

In a recent article, "The road to the spiritual regeneration of Russia," published in the Russian emigré periodical *Russkaja mysl'*, the Orthodox priest Viktor Potapov (1993:7) uses all three words: *rodina*, *otečestvo*, and *otčizna*, each in a different context:

Tol'ko v cerkvi možno poljubit' svoju rodinu i svoj narod podlinno xristjanskoj ljubov'ju.

'Only in the Church can one come to love one's *rodina* and one's nation with a genuinely Christian love.'

Pravoslavnaja cerkov' odobrjaet nacionalizm . . . esli on napravlen na zaščitu Otečestva ot vnešnej agressii.

'The Orthodox Church approves of nationalism if it is directed towards defending the *Otečestvo* from outside aggression.'

Tol'ko zabota o nebesnoj Otčizne pomožet nam obustroit' zemnuju otčiznu na xristianskix načalax.

'Only a concern for the heavenly *Otčizna* will help us to rebuild our earthly *otčizna* on Christian foundations.'

In another recent article published in the same periodical (cf. *Russkaja mysl'*, 1993:12), Viktor Volkov, a Russian writer born in France (of emigré Russian parents), was asked where his rodina was. The writer replied that he felt fully French, although he didn't have a single drop of French blood, and fully Russian, although until very recently he had never been in Russia, and he summed up: "One could say that France is my *rodina*, but Russia is my *otčizna*."

Though obviously far from sufficient, these few examples do illuminate some of the differences between the three concepts. In particular, they highlight the "ideal" character of *otčizna* (as, so to speak, a place of one's dreams) and the "real" character of *rodina* (as a place where one was actually born). They also highlight the "personal" character of *rodina* (as a country where one was born) and the impersonal, socio-political character of *otečestvo* (not only a country but also a state). The quotes also illuminate the differences in expected attitudes: *rodina* is, roughly speaking, a country to which one is emotionally attached, *otečestvo*—a country toward which one has obligations, and *otčizna*—a mythical country for which one yearns.

In surveys conducted recently among Xar'kov university students exploring their understanding of *rodina* (cf. Antipenko & Karnaušenko 1993), the great majority (72%) defined *rodina* as the country (or territory) where one was born. In addition, many respondents mentioned the "familiar" character of *rodina*, as a place where everything is "rodnoe, blizkoe, ponjatnoe i privyčnoe" (that is, roughly speaking, near to one's heart, close to one's heart, understandable, and accustomed). The untranslatable adjective *rodnoj* (neuter form *rodnoe*), cognate with *rodina*, is particularly significant here: it is derived from *rodit ́(sja)* 'be born', and it implies strong emotional ties based on blood, on common origin, on "belonging together."

Like the Polish word *ojczyzna*, *rodina* is also strongly associated with the image of 'mother', and the phrase *rodina-mat'* 'mother-*rodina*', is a common collocation.

It might be added that *rodina* has also a second meaning, referring (like *Heimat*), to the places where one was born and where one was a child, rather than to a country as a whole. *Rodina* in that local sense, too, is semantically (as well as etymologically) linked with the adjective *rodnoj* (cf. chapter 2, section 3). The two meanings (roughly [1] native country, [2] native places) are synchronically distinct, and, for example, the collocation *rodina-mat'* can only refer to the 'native country', never to 'native places'; but they share a number of components, and, in particular, they both imply familiarity, warmth, and a unique emotional well-being reminiscent of that associated with *Heimat*.

All these considerations lead us toward the following explication of *rodina*:

rodina
(a) a country
(b) I was born in this country
(c) I am like a part of this country
(d) I couldn't be like a part of any other country
(e) when I think about this country I feel something good
(f) I think something like this when I think about this country:
(g)   this country is like a person
(h)   this country does good things for me, like a mother does good things for
       her children
(i)   I know everything in this country
(j)   I am like other people in this country
(k)   when I am in this country, I feel something good
(l)   I couldn't feel like this in any other country

Like *ojczyzna*, *rodina* refers to the country of one's birth. Like *ojczyzna*, it implicitly likens the country to a mother, and it implies a unique emotional bond. Unlike *ojczyzna*, however, and unlike *Vaterland*, *rodina* does not embody a moral imperative. Admittedly, phrases such as *rodina zovet* ('*rodina* is calling') have often been used in Russian public discourse (especially in Soviet propaganda),[7] but the imperative to serve, to defend, or to die for has not become embodied in the very meaning of the word *rodina*. As mentioned earlier, an imperative of this kind has become embodied in the (modern) meaning of the less common word *otečestvo* (as in *velikaja otečestvennaja vojna* 'the great patriotic war, which everyone has to take part in'), but not in that of *rodina*.

For this reason, I suggest, *rodina* can be used much more widely than *otečestvo*; and also, more widely than either *ojczyzna* or *Vaterland*. For example, one can readily use it in Russian phrases such as *vernut'sja* na rodinu 'to return to one's *rodina*', or *pobyvat'* na rodine, 'to spend some time in one's *rodina*'(both listed, for example, in the Russian phraseological dictionary edited by Denisov & Morkovkin [1978]). But one could not use *ojczyzna* (or *Vaterland*, not to mention *otečestvo*) in such phrases, at least not in ordinary language, and while nineteenth-century poetry does furnish examples of such phrases, as in Słowacki's line, "Bo kiedy Zośka do ojczyzny wróci" ('because when you, Zośka, return to the *ojczyzna*'), in contemporary language examples of this kind would be seen as poetic and archaic exceptions.

Consider also the following sentence from a recent interview with Aleksander Solzhenitsyn published, incidentally, in a column entitled "Vesti s rodiny" ('News from the *rodina*'):

> . . . ja skazal, čto Sovetskij Sojuz razvalitsja nepremenno. . . . Gorbačev ėtogo perenesti ne mog, potomu čto nadejalsja soxranit' Sovetskij Sojuz. Poėtomu moja stat'ja, xotja ona uže suščestvuet tri goda, ešče ne obsuždalas' na Rodine po-nastojaščemu. (Solzhenitsyn 1993:2)

> 'I said that the Soviet Union would definitely disintegrate. Gorbachev couldn't bear this prospect, still hoping to preserve the Soviet Union. Because of this, my article, which has been in existence for three years, has not yet really been discussed in the country [Rodina].'

It seems almost inconceivable that the German word *Vaterland* or the Polish word *ojczyzna* should be used in such a context (or, for that matter, in the title of a similar magazine column) in contemporary language.

Ojczyzna and *Vaterland* do not refer to real countries with some additional emotive components; rather, they refer, in their different ways, to certain ideals, and to certain moral obligations (with the stress on something like obedience in *Vaterland* and on something like sacrifice in *ojczyzna*). This is the main reason, I suggest, why casual references to a stay in one's *Vaterland* or *ojczyzna* sound either incongruous or ironic, whereas similar references to *rodina* are fully acceptable.

The "obligation-free" character of *rodina* gives a specific tone to the "mother-image" associated with this word. If *Vaterland* evokes the image of a stern father who must be not only loved but also obeyed (by his grown-up sons, *Vaterlands Söhne*), and if *ojczyzna* evokes the image of a beloved mother who has suffered and for whom her (grown-up) children (not necessarily sons) must be willing to make sacrifices, *rodina* evokes an image of a loving mother who does good things for her (small) children and who doesn't expect anything in return. She is a warm and indulgent mother figure, associated, so to speak, with milk rather than blood (recall the quote from Kasprowicz), and with *svoboda* (a Russian key word usually translated as *freedom*, but in fact implying a lack of all restraints, cf. chapter 3, section 6) rather than obligations. My *rodina* is a country where I can feel good (as one can feel good in one's mother's arms) rather than constrained or called upon to do something. (As mentioned earlier, there is a clear contrast in this respect between the central Russian concept of *rodina* and the more marginal concept of *otečestvo*).

As I have argued in chapter 3, section 8, the Polish word *wolność* is strongly associated with a struggle for national independence, whereas the Russian word *svoboda* is associated with a yearning for the absence of all restraints and has a slightly anarchic ring to it. The semantic differences between *ojczyzna* and *rodina* are consistent with those between *wolność* and *svoboda*. On the other hand, the semantics of *Vaterland* is consistent with the German national ethos reflected, in a small way, in the German tautology *ein Befehl ist ein Befehl* 'an order is an order', which, not surprisingly, has no counterpart in either Polish or Russian.

Another reason why *rodina* can be readily used in phrases such as "return to . . ." or "spend some time in . . ." whereas *Vaterland* and *ojczyzna* can't is that the latter two words both refer to a nation, as well as to a country, whereas *rodina* does not seem to do so. Despite the huge differences in the German and Polish historical experience, and in the nature of German and Polish nationalisms, one could say that both *Vaterland* and *ojczyzna* have been, historically, banner words of nationalism, *Vaterland* of German nationalism and *ojczyzna* of Polish nationalism. But *rodina* has not been, historically, a banner word of Russian nationalism.

In some ways, then, *rodina* is more similar to *Heimat* than it is to either *Vaterland* or *ojczyzna*. It is, one might say, descriptive and emotive; it is focused more on biography and geography than on history or politics; and it embodies sentiment rather than pathos or appeal. It implies a love based on familiarity and "belonging," without an associated moral imperative (although, unlike *Heimat*, it can also be used in highly ideological contexts, such as *izmena rodine* 'state treason', an article of the criminal code).

Unlike *Heimat*, *rodina* (in its main meaning) refers to the country as a whole and not just to one's own "native places"; it does not, therefore, imply any "local patriotism," as *Heimat* does, and it doesn't celebrate political or cultural diversity. It implies an emotional identification with either Russia or "the Russian empire" (the country of the Russian language) and perhaps even reflects a pride in the vastness of the native country. The phrase from the Soviet national anthem *neob"jatnoj rodiny svoej* '(of) one's vast, boundless *rodina*' does seem to ring true in this respect, despite the false, propaganda-based tone of the song as a whole.

Trying to pinpoint the differences between the Russian concept of *rodina* and the Polish concept of *ojczyzna*, it is instructive to compare the collocations of the Russian adjective *rodnoj*, cognate with (and synchronically related to) *rodina*, with those of the Polish adjective *ojczysty*, cognate with (and synchronically related to) *ojczyzna*:

Russian	Polish	English glosses
rodnoj jazyk	*język ojczysty*	native language
rodnaja strana	*kraj ojczysty*	native land
rodnaja zemlja	*ziemia ojczysta*	native "earth"
rodnaja mat'	**matka ojczysta*	one's own mother
*rodnaja istorija	*dzieje ojczyste*	history of one's country

(In older Polish usage, one could also speak of *obyczaje ojczyste* and *prawa ojczyste* 'customs and laws characteristic of one's native country', whereas similar collocations including the Russian word *rodnoj* seem unthinkable.)

Differences of this kind support the idea that *rodina* implies an emotional identification with one's native country in terms of what is experientially given, that is, the land and the language, with no reference to history, whereas *ojczyzna* implies also a strong sense of identification with one's country's history and traditions.

The fact that in Russian the same adjective *rodnoj* can be combined with the words for land, language, and mother is consistent with the impression that *rodina* (the land where Russian language is spoken) is felt to be very much like a mother. In Polish, the emotionally charged adjective *ojczysty*, derived from *ojczyzna*, cannot be combined with any kinship terms, and as mentioned earlier its orientation is clearly national, not personal.

These differences in collocations suggest that although both *rodina* and *ojczyzna* are somehow linked in speakers' consciousness (or subconsciousness) with the image of a mother, in the case of *rodina* this link is more direct. *Rodina* is like a mother in an emotional sense, as something or someone in whose arms one can take refuge (no matter what life's sufferings may be); but *ojczyzna* is like a mother in a more axiological sense, someone/something of infinite value to whom one owes one's national identity and for whom one should be ready to make sacrifices.

6. Conclusion

Every society has its own key words. Some of these key words are so obviously unique that they are commonly quoted in the original: for example, *kolxoz, gulag, kibbutz, kamikaze*. Others, however, which are also bound to a particular culture and society, appear to have counterparts in other languages. And thus, for example, dictionaries and translators readily equate *Vaterland, ojczyzna*, and *rodina*. Matching words which are superficially similar but in fact profoundly different is a procedure which may seem at times unavoidable but which is nonetheless deeply misleading. In-depth cross-cultural studies can help to reveal the true individuality of such concepts, as well as the links between them, and the natural semantic metalanguage, based on universal semantic primitives, provides the necessary conceptual tools.

Appendix

SUMMARY OF THE FORMULAE
Heimat
(a) a place
(b) I was born in this place
(c) there are many places in this place
(d) when I was a child, I lived in these places
(e) I felt something good when I lived in these places
(f) I felt that nothing bad could happen to me
(g) I can't feel like this in any other places
(h) because of this, when I think about these places I feel something good
(i) I think something like this when I think about these places:
(j)   these places are not like any other places
(k)   I was like a part of these places when I was a child
(l)   I can't be like a part of any other places

(m) this place is like a part of me
(n) (I know: some other people think the same when they think about these places)
(o) (I think these people feel the same when they think about these places)
(p) (when I think about these people, I feel something good)

Vaterland
(a) a country	= 0
(b) I am like a part of this country	= 0
(c) when I think about this country, I feel something good	= 0
(d) I think something like this when I think about this country:	= 0
(e) this country is not like any other country	= 0
(f) it is a very good country	≠ 0
(g) other countries are not like this country	≠ 0
(h) this country is like a person	= 0
(i) this country did many good things for me	= 0
(j) I want to do good things for this country	= 0
(k) if this country wants me to do something, I have to do it	≠ 0
(l) many other people think the same when they think about this country	= 0
(m) these people feel something good when they think about this country	= 0
(n) these people are like one thing	= 0
(o) I am like a part of this thing	= 0

ojczyzna
(a) a country	= V
(b) I was born in this country	≠ V
(c) I am like a part of this country	= V
(d) I can't be like a part of any other country	≠ V
(e) this country is like a part of me	≠ V
(f) when I think about this country, I feel something good	= V
(g) if I didn't, this would be very bad	≠ V
(h) I think something like this when I think about this country:	= V
(i) this country is not like any other country	= V
(j) this country is like a person	≠ V
(k) many bad things happened to this country	≠ V
(l) I don't want bad things to happen to this country	= V(?)
(m) this country did many good things for me	= V
(n) like a mother does good things for her children	≠ V
(o) I want to do good things for this country	= V(?)
(p) if I feel something bad because of this I don't want not to do these things because of this	≠ V
(q) many other people think the same when they think about this country	= V
(r) these people feel something good when they think about this country	= V
(s) these people are like one thing	= V
(t) I am like a part of this thing	= V
(u) these people say things in the same way	≠ V
(v) these people do many things in the same way	≠ V
(w) these people think about many things in the same way	≠ V
(x) these people often feel in the same way	≠ V
(y) when I think about these people, I feel something good	≠ V
(z) these people are like a part of this country	≠ V

(ź) before this time, for a long time, many other people were like a part of this
    country   ≠ V(?)

(ż) I am like a part of all these people   ≠ V

(ż) in many ways, I am like these people   ≠ V

rodina

(a) a country

(b) I was born in this country

(c) I am like a part of this country

(d) I couldn't be like a part of any other country

(e) when I think about this country I feel something good

(f) I think something like this when I think about this country:

(g)   this country is like a person

(h)   this country does good things for me, like a mother does good things for
        her children

(i)   I know everything in this country

(j)   I am like other people in this country

(k)   when I am in this country, I feel something good

(l)   I couldn't feel like this in any other country

Australian Key Words and Core Cultural Values

1. "Australian culture"

If Russian culture is epitomized by three untranslatable Russian words *duša* (roughly 'soul'), *sud'ba* (roughly 'fate'), and *toska* (roughly 'yearning/melancholy') (see Wierzbicka 1992b), and Japanese culture by such untranslatable words as *amae*, *giri*, *on*, *wa*, *enryo*, *seishin* and *omoiyari* (see chapter 6), traditional Australian culture is reflected, above all, in the word *mate* (cf. chapter 2, section 5). As I will try to show in this chapter, it is also reflected in such characteristically Australian speech act verbs as *dob in*, *chiack*, *yarn*, *shout*, and *whinge* (some of them, notably *chiack*, now archaic and replaced by various other verbs in the speech of the younger generation), and also in a number of characteristic Australian "*b*-words," including, in particular, *bloody*, *bastard*, *bugger*, and *bullshit*.

Before turning to detailed discussion of these words, however, some remarks of a more general nature are in order. If "culture" is indeed, as some contend, a "perilous idea" (cf. Wolf 1994), to put a case for "Australian culture" is particularly risky. Since Australia can now be described as a multicultural society, the very phrase "Australian culture" (in the singular) is often perceived as jarring, incoherent, even reactionary. What Australian culture? There are many cultures in Australia—Greek culture, Italian culture, Vietnamese culture, and so on, and since this diversity of cultures can be seen in a positive light, references to "Australian culture" in the singular tend to be scrupulously avoided. To quote one example: "Australia's multicultural society has given our isolated continent a global perspective. The diversity of views, languages, cultures, and attitudes, and the variety of religions and foods, has produced a unique and complex society" (Chryssides 1995:viii).

There is no doubt a great deal of truth in such statements, but it is not the whole truth. If we look at the evidence from language, diversity is not the only unique feature of the Australian experience. No matter how one values Greek, or Vietnamese, or Chinese culture in Australia, one can hardly say that any one of these cultures is a uniquely Australian creation. On the other hand, what applies to Greek, Vietnamese, or Chinese culture in Australia applies neither to Australian Aboriginal culture(s) nor to Anglo-Australian culture: judging by the evidence of language (if nothing else), these latter cultures are indeed unique to Australia.

The unique character of Australian Aboriginal culture(s) is now generally acknowledged. Some writers go so far as to claim that there is "a belated but growing acknowledgment of the centrality of Aboriginal culture to the way Australians as a whole think of themselves" (Dobrez 1994:i), apparently on the assumption that among many cultures represented in Australian society, Australian Aboriginal culture is the only one with a local origin ("it must be evident that any notion of Australianness which sources itself to a heritage of a non-local origin is bound to remain problematical" [i]).

But while it is true that Australian Aboriginal culture, expressed most clearly in Australian Aboriginal languages, "sources itself," as Dobrez put it, "to a heritage of a local origin," so does Anglo-Australian culture, expressed most clearly in Australian English. But this is a fact that many Australian intellectuals would apparently rather forget, or deny. Proud as they are of Australia's unique multicultural diversity, they seem ashamed of the prevailing attitudes and values that defined Anglo-Australian culture over the last two centuries. Since these attitudes and values are reflected in Australian English, as it took shape during those two centuries, they also appear to be ashamed of Australian English and intent on repudiating it. The "debunking" of concepts such as 'mate' and 'mateship' features prominently in these endeavors, as does also the "debunking" of Australian classics such as Russel Ward's (1958) *The Australian legend* (in which words of this kind play a significant role): "Discussion of culture inevitably raises the question of 'national identity' . . . it goes without saying that the old rural myths, expressed most succinctly in Russel Ward's *The Australian Legend* (1958), at one time hotly debated, have been exposed as male chauvinist, racist and historically flawed" (Headon, Hooton & Horne 1995:xiv).

The Anglo-Australian past is rejected, and those who still argue for the reality of Anglo-Australian culture are likely to be accused of "cultural racism" (cf. e.g. Headon, Hooton, & Horne 1994: xiv). Australia's history is now frequently presented as "a smorgasbord of national identities and pasts," and multiculturalism is backdated to at least 1788, in an effort to retrospectively erase, or downgrade, Anglo-Australian culture as a basis of the past (white) Australian identity. As Carter points out, "Australia, it is claimed, has always been multicultural" (1994:71).

This is one vocal stream in the current debate: repudiating the past by extolling diversity and denying any underlying cultural unity—both in the present and in the past. But this is not the only one. Other voices, while recognizing and praising diversity, are still prepared to talk about "unity in diversity," although the content of this unity is seldom spelled out. For example, Mackay (1993) writes: "The Age of Redefinition has put Australians' sense of unity to the test. However unattractive or unrealistic it may now seem, we had a strong sense of homogeneity in Australian society up until the early 1960s. From then on, we have been placing increasing emphasis on diversity" (291).

Mackay adds, somewhat wistfully: "Presumably, there is something more to being an Australian than simply living in Australia" (291), and he points to the need to clarify "the concept of 'unity in diversity,'" and to the fact that "ultimately, the sense of community—regardless of the diversity which it embraces—depends on a fundamental unity: shared culture, shared values, shared ideals" (290).

I would argue that shared values, shared ideals, and shared attitudes are reflected in shared language. In Australia, the shared language is English—Australian English—a language whose continuity and change documents the continuity and change in Anglo-Australian culture.

Not only is Australian English every bit as real as the Greek, or the Italian, or the Vietnamese languages spoken in Australia, but it is the only language, apart from the Australian Aboriginal languages, which is part of the local heritage, and the only language which documents, and passes on, the attitudes and values which bind the population of Australia together.

A photograph of three opera singers ("The Three Tenors") taken by Helen Chryssides during a rehearsal for the "Viva Italia!" concert in Melbourne and included in her book *A Different light: Ways of being Australian* (1995:205) illustrates this central role of Australian English in the "multicultural Australia." Chryssides herself is of half-Polish half-Greek background, the concert celebrates Italian culture, the three musicians are Chinese, but the big sign displayed on the T-shirt of one of them reads "G'day Mate!" Despite all the transformations which have taken place in Australian society, it is still expressions like *G'day mate* that provide symbols of Australian unity and cultural continuity (whereas new words and expressions such as *pizza and video night, tabouli, Vietnamese spring rolls*, and *Big Mac* provide evidence of diversity and change).

Shared material culture, including spaghetti and Big Macs, is an important unifying force, and shared words such as *spaghetti* and *Big Mac* reflect this. But a shared ethos (historically shaped and historically changing but not completely fluid) is even more important, and aspects of Australians' shared ethos are both documented and passed on to the future generations of Australians (wherever their parents come from) via Anglo-Australian words and expressions such as *mate, good on ya, dob in, whinge, no worries*, and *bullshit* (in the special, Australian sense of the word, to be discussed below).

The sharp attacks leveled at Russel Ward's (1958) classic *The Australian legend* epitomize the widespread tendency to repudiate the Anglo-Australian past in general, seen almost exclusively in terms of "immoral behaviours [such] as sexism and racism" (Carter 1994:6). Dobrez (1994:vii) calls Ward's thumbnail sketch of the "typical Australian" "celebrated—now infamous," even though, as he points out himself, "Ward emphasizes that he is dealing with a 'national *mystique*'" ("National character is . . . a people's idea of itself," quoted in Dobrez 1994:vii).

In his article on Australia's cultural heritage, Taylor (1994) writes warmly of "things we want to keep":

> Over the past twenty years or so there has been a remarkable shift in attitude by Australians to their history and linked with this the implication that there is a cultural heritage worth both protecting and cherishing. Australians at large have discovered that we do have a history and national culture that promote a sense of identity and Australianness. (26)

But when it comes to specifying what this "fascinating and fertile cultural inheritance" (33) consists in, Taylor focuses on places, monuments, and what he calls "cultural landscapes": "grandiose homesteads and urban splendours, the Aboriginal wonders of Kakadu, or the Sydney Opera House, . . . the memories of European exploration, convict settlements, . . . gold mining, . . . and urban areas with rich social tapestry."

An awareness seems to be lacking that Australian English, too, belongs to Australia's unique heritage, and that while of course not everything in this heritage can, or ought to, be preserved, it all needs to be understood, and both its outdated and its still thriving aspects need to be recognized for what they are: a key to Australia's history and an important factor in national identity.

Words are a society's cultural artifacts. Boomerangs may become obsolete, but students of Australia's Aboriginal culture can hardly afford not to take an interest in the functions, and meanings, of boomerangs; and likewise they can hardly afford to ignore key words for emotions or interpersonal relations in Australian Aboriginal languages (cf. e.g. Myers 1986, Goddard 1991, Harkins 1994). Similarly, students of non-Aboriginal Australian culture must take an interest in Australian homesteads, ironwork verandas, goldmining equipment, and household utensils, and in Australian conceptual artifacts such as *mateship, dobbing,* and *whingeing* (to be discussed below in detail). Even abbreviations such as *mozzies* and *maggies* or *sickie* and *compo* (for *mosquitoes, magpies, sick day,* and *workers'compensation,* respectively) are significant cultural artifacts, alongside names like *Bazza* (for *Barry*) and surnames like *Richo* (for *Richardson*); or characteristic Australian interjections (*good on ya, no worries, right-o, good-o*), Australian swearwords, and so on. Even such seemingly humble elements as these reflect, and pass on, characteristic Australian attitudes and values (for detailed analysis, see Wierzbicka 1986, 1991a, 1992b).

For example, the words *dob in* and *dobber* reflect the Australian cult of loyalty and solidarity—not only male solidarity—especially solidarity vis à vis authorities, and the words *whinge* and *sook* reflect the Australian cult of toughness and resilience.

The word *larrikan* (defined by the *Shorter Oxford English dictionary* [1964] as "the Australian equivalent of the 'Hoodlum' or 'Hooligan'") expresses a positive evaluation of irreverent wit and defiance of social norms and conventions.

The word *Aussie* (noun and adjective) expresses the capacity of "traditional Australians" for combining an attachment to their country and pride in it with a self-deprecating dislike of pathos, pomposity, and "big words"; it also reflects some important aspects of the traditional Australian self-image, with an emphasis on being brave, tough, practical, good-humoured, and cheeky.

The colloquial Australian collocation (and exclamation) *fair go,* elaborated as *fair crack of the whip* or *fair suck of the sauce bottle* and solemnly defined by *The Australian national dictionary* as "an equitable opportunity; a reasonable chance" reflects the traditional Australian spirit of tolerance and respect for "equal opportunity" and fair play.

The expression *good on ya* (which implies admiration for the addressee's attitude and not necessarily for achievement or success) reflects the value placed on attitudes rather than on success or achievement as such.

The response words *goodo* (*good-oh*) and *righto* (*right-oh*, *rightio*), whose very meaning signals a good-humored willingness to cooperate on an equal footing, reflect the value placed on egalitarian relations and on a relaxed atmosphere in social interaction; and so does the traditional Australian greeting *g'day* (inherently good-humored and egalitarian, unlike *good morning*). Similarly egalitarian and good-humored are other Australian greetings and friendly queries such as *how ya going?*, *how is it going?*, and *how ya going, mate, all right?*

The exclamation *you bloody beauty* reflects among other things the Australian value of anti-sentimentality, as does the use of the word *bastard* to express positive feelings.

Australian names such as *Tez*, *Tezza* (for Terry), *Bazza* (for Barry), and *Shaz*, *Shazza* (for Sharon) reflect the traditional Australian combination of values: solidarity, equality, and anti-sentimental ("rough") affection.

Words and expressions such as these are often dismissed as unworthy of serious attention, but in fact they are important witnesses for cultural realities now frequently denied and attacked as "stereotypes." The meanings encapsulated in such words and expressions are a contribution to the universal human repertoire of forms of thought and feeling; they are works of that "creative human spirit" which, as Johann Gottfried Herder put it two hundred years ago, everywhere "reinvents itself" in new forms. The words *spaghetti*, *moussaka*, and *tabouli* as they are currently used in Australia reflect the diversification of Australian life at the turn of the century, but neither these words nor their meanings are specifically Australian cultural creations.

2. Australian speech act verbs

2.1 Chiack (chyack)

The Australian English word *chiack*, allegedly derived from "'the cockney pronounciation of 'cheek'—impudent badinage" (Bulletin 1898, quoted in TAND 1988), refers to a characteristically Australian form of social interaction and reflects a characteristically Australian form of humor. (The word is highly colloquial, and since it belongs, essentially, to spoken rather than written language, its spelling is variable.) Essentially, "chiacking" consists in saying something bad about the addressee for shared fun. Traditionally, Australians themselves have been inclined to see "chiacking" as one of their favorite national pastimes and forms of entertainment. Most examples of this word cited by either Wilkes (1985[1978]) or TAND (1988) refer in fact to a habitual, rather than occasional, activity of "chiacking." (Unattributed examples from this chapter are from TAND.) In examples from these sources, Dawes (1943) talks about the "Australian passion for handing out *chiack*," and Hardy's (1971) reference to *the old chiack* indicates that "chiacking" is very much part of the familiar (and positively viewed) Australian way of life:

> Hullo, hullo, Chilla said, always a bit too keen on the old chiack, especially when it came to Tich's unsuccessful carryings on with the female of the species. (Hardy 1971)

Other characteristic examples cited by TAND include the following:

My mates chyacked me all night. (Australasian Printer's Keepsake, 1885)

Diggers of the Yarra tribe . . . like to chiack the Cornstalk variety about our "arbour." (Aussie 1919)

They whooped, they made ribald noises, they chyacked one another. (S. Campion 1944)

They chyacked their sissy mates and their sisters who were forced to attend late afternoon dancing classes. (R. McKie 1977)

As these examples indicate, "chiacking" is closely associated with the Australian idea of 'mateship': it is usually done among "mates," and it is often done reciprocally, and if not reciprocally among mates, then collectively with mates (cf. chapter 2, section 5). Usually, the men speak one at a time, making negative remarks about the addressee, while the other men are laughing, so that a group of mates constitutes both a group of participants and an audience, as in the following examples from Wilkes (1978):

They're always a-poking borack an a-chiackin' o' me over in the hut! (J. A. Barry 1893)

There were several pretty girls in the office, laughing and chiacking the counter clerks. (Henry Lawson 1896)

Don't walk about - it's tirin'; stand at street-corners and spit—besides that ther best place ter see life and chyack the girls. (Henry Fletcher 1908)

The milk-carters . . . sloshed the milk into the cans, chyacked Dolour about her goggles, and charged out again. (Ruth Park 1948)

The rowdy bodgie youths kept seats near this group, chiacking the buxom, brassy-haired waitress as she rushed around with a tray-load of dishes and lively back-chat. (K. S. Pritchard 1967)

"Chiacking," then, is very much a shared entertainment, which both expresses and promotes the feeling of "mateship" among those who jointly engage in it. It is definitely a pleasurable activity, associated with laughter, rowdiness, noise, and good humor. The following examples (from the same sources) highlight this aspect of "chiacking":

Pleasant chi-ack in the billets (Action Front 1940)

They served out hot tea and in a few moments grumbling gave place to "chiacking"; criticism that a few moments ago had been edged was now good-humoured. (R. H. Knyvett 1918)

Thus ended the relief of Rustenburg, in cheers and laughter and chyacking and sleep. (S. Campion 1944)

The groomsmen all red in the face and looking as if they would choke in their stiff white collars, rocked the whole congregation with a desire to chuckle and chiack. (K. S. Pritchard 1948)

They were a vociferous crowd, ruggedly vocal in a loud, chiacking anticipation of the heady joys to come. (E. Lindall 1964)

Other types of humour—chyacking and leg-pulling, sardonic anecdotes, jolliness and exuberance. (Donald Horne 1967)

Though pleasurable for those who engage in it, the activity of "chiacking" is by no means always pleasurable for those who are the victims of it. Nonetheless, it is never hostile, and it is expected that it will be borne with good humor (examples from TAND 1988):

Ironbark's face was red by this time with all the chyacking he got from the blokes. (D. Stivens 1955)

Next day at lunchtime I got the same chyacking treatment from Gordon's brother Frank. (B. Heslin 1963)

I was always civil to the chaps, for all the chyacking they gave me. (W. H. Suttor 1887)

Tommy Bent . . . was a victim of most of the "chyacking." (Gadfly 1906)

When their chiacking got too much I would go out and talk to the turkeys. (M. Eldridge 1984)

What does it mean, then, to *chiack* somebody? I propose the following analysis of this concept:

chiack (e.g. X was chiacking Y)
(a) for some time, X was saying some bad things about person Y
(b) X wanted Y to hear it
(c) X was saying these things as people say bad things about someone
(d) when they think something like this at the same time:
(e)   I want to say these things about this person
(f)   because I want people here to feel something good
(g)   not because I want this person to feel something bad
(h)   I can do it because this person is someone like me
(i) people think: men feel something good when they can do this with other men

Although *chiacking* involves saying something bad about the addressee (component [a]), the speaker clearly indicates that it is done for pleasure and fun (component [f], and that it is devoid of any hostile or malicious intent (component [g]). Components (f) and (i) indicate that *chiacking* is always seen as a collective activity, whether it is reciprocal (between two people) or done by a group of people (about someone else), component (i) shows also that it is primarily, though not exclusively, a male activity (done from man to man, or by a group of men), and component (h) implies "solidarity" and egalitarianism.

The concept of 'chiacking' reflects some of the most characteristic features of traditional Australian culture: sociability, "mateship," enjoyment of joint activities with one's mates (including idle activities, such as drinking), male solidarity and male togetherness, associated with displays of "toughness" and "bad language," and so on.

The concept of 'chiacking' reflects also the traditional Australian preference for saying "bad things" rather than "good things" about people in general and about the addressee in particular—not because one thinks "bad things" about them or feels "bad feelings" toward them but because of the cultural ideals of roughness, toughness, anti-sentimentality, anti-emotionality, and so on.

The link between "saying something bad" and "feeling something good" is particularly characteristic. It is a link which is also manifested in the typically Australian phenomenon of friendly insults ("G'day ya old bastard!"; cf. Taylor 1976), in the tendency to express enthusiasm by means of swearwords ("you bloody beauty!"), in the lack of offensive connotations linked with words such as *bugger* ("poor bugger"), *crap*, *bullshit*, and so on. (For detailed discussion, see section 3 of this chapter.)

> The interesting thing about the Australian attitude to human relationship is the special forms it has to take to avoid coming into conflict with our basic antipathy towards the public expression of sentiment and emotion. Because we are unsentimental and cynical towards the emotions, Australians have to express their social affection in some way which is not on the face of it self-revealing. Thus, there has evolved the principle of 'rubbishing' your mates and *chayacking* the stranger. In an atmosphere of reciprocal banter or 'rubbishing' Australians can express mutual affection without running any risk of indecently exposing states of feeling. (Harris 1962:65–66; emphasis added)

Renwick (1980) remarks that "with regard to personal characteristics, Australian men and women are friendly, humorous, and sardonic (derisive, disdainful, and scornful)" (22–23). They "express negative feelings and opinions about both situations and people, sometimes about people they are with." They have a tendency "to be personally evaluative and to express negative reactions" (29). In particular, negative remarks play an important role in Australian humor. Renwick observes that "Americans sometimes feel that Australians' humor is . . . disrespectful, harsh, and offensive," and he advises Americans as follows: "Stand ready, in a relaxed manner, to be tested. The Australian may challenge you and probe to see if you are a person of substance, someone with a backbone, some steel inside, some depth and character. Practice testing and sparring with the Australian yourself. Develop personal resilience. Don't be put off by derisive comments, undercutting, and cynicism" (33).

These comments, and this advice, show deep insight into the traditional Australian ethos—an ethos reflected with particular clarity in the Australian concept of 'chiacking'. The fact that this key word is now disappearing from Australian speech, so that younger Australians are often unfamiliar with it, reflects some of the changes which this culture is undergoing. As pointed out by many observers of the Australian scene, since World War II there has been a considerable shift in Australia from traditional working class values to middle class values. For example, McGregor (1981) reports that according to Gallup polls taken over the past few decades the proportion of the Australian population identifying themselves as working class has declined markedly, while the proportion identifying as middle class has correspondingly increased. The decline of the use of key Australian words such as *chiacking* (and also *yarn* and *shout*, to be discussed later) reflects these broader social changes. In particular, while *chiacking* is still a common Australian activity, the concept of 'chiacking' is already losing some of its salience in contemporary Australian culture.

2.2 *Yarn*

Yarn (which can be used in Australia as either a noun or a verb) is another important Australian word, referring to something like a chat or a talk, but embodying a characteristically Australian way of looking at the activity in question. It is typically used in the phrase *to have a yarn*; for example (all examples from TAND 1988):

> They asked the Buxtons to come over to their camp, and have a "yarn." (J. Bonwick 1870)

> He used to delight in going to travellers' camps to have a 'yarn' with them. (M. A. McManus 1913)

As these examples indicate, "having a yarn" is often seen as a form of pleasurable sociability. The expectation that "yarns" generate "good feelings" is reflected in the common collocation *a good yarn*, which implies a satisfying as well as fairly lengthy (and leisurely) verbal exchange:

> You are questioned all about home, what brought you out, and all such questions, until what is termed in the colony a good yarn is over, you may then be asked to have a nobler. ("Eye Witness" 1859)

> He says he doesn't really want to do any sort of interview, but it doesn't take long to see that deep down, the man likes a good yarn. (Sydney *Morning Herald* 1986)

Yarn as a verbal exchange should be distinguished from *yarn* as a kind of long tale "spun" out of facts and fantasy for the purpose of companionship: to *have a yarn* is not the same as to *spin a yarn*—another favorite Australian speech genre of "the olden days." But the slow, relaxed nature of the *yarns* that people *spin* (or used to *spin*) highlights the unhurried, relaxed nature of the *yarn* that one can *have* with someone else.

Although a "good yarn" (with someone) is normally a long one, a short "yarn" is also seen as enjoyable, provided that it is leisurely, unhurried, and without a rigidly imposed temporal boundary. This is reflected in the common collocation *a bit of a yarn*. For example:

> There they all stood and had a bit of a yarn before they came home. (A. A. Smith 1944)

The pleasurable, sociable, and unhurried character of "yarning" is highlighted in the following examples:

> The manager received me with open arms, and we "yarned" far into the night over the old country. (A. W. Stirling 1884)

> I thought it glorious fun smoking our cigars and yarning until overcome by our long drive, we both fell asleep. (S. S. Junr 1868)

But "yarning" is not an idle activity undertaken solely for pleasure and devoid of any serious meaning:

> By "yarning," dear reader, I don't mean mere trivial conversation, but hard, solid talk. (M. Clarke 1896)

"Yarns" differ in this respect from "chats," which are also exercises in pleasurable sociability but which, by definition, play down the significance of the exchange. *Chatting* can be idle, but *yarning* is not seen as idle, whatever the topic, because it suggests a serious need for human contact and for human communication. The following example illustrates well this aspect of *yarn*:

> Some of me old mates from the bush turned up for a beer and a yarn. (A. Buzo 1986).

Certainly, the phrase *a beer and a yarn* stands here for two enjoyable activities undertaken for pleasure. But the sentence also illustrates well the special importance of such activities in the Australian context, where the distances, the isolation, and the loneliness used to create a special need for human contact, human warmth, and human communication going far beyond the casual, lightweight sociability characteristic of a *chat*.

Like 'chiacking', 'yarning' and 'having a yarn' are concepts with masculine associations. This is another dimension of contrast between a *yarn* and a *chat;* in Australia, men used to, traditionally, have "a beer and a yarn" (with their "mates"), whereas "ladies" would usually have a "cuppa" (a cup of tea) and a "chat." These different gender associations may have something to do with different expectations with regard to "verbal economy": the concept of 'chat' implies "chattiness," that is, a facility with words, an uninterrupted and easy verbal flow between two people; by contrast, the concept of 'yarn' implies a terseness and a background of silence, of isolation, and of a real need for a verbal exchange as a form of scarce human contact (one could *chat* with one's neighbours every day but one could hardly *yarn* with them every day).

This need for "congenial fellowship" (especially male fellowship) reflected in the concept of 'yarn' is highlighted in the following example (reflecting also other, less appealing, features of the Australian "bush ethos"):

> It's hard work sinking bores, and after a few months on your own, with no one but a couple abos [Aborigines, derogative] to yarn to, you've gotta get stinkin' [drunk] once in a while. (J. Marshall 1962)

Both the similarity and the difference between the concepts 'yarn' and 'chat' can, I think, be accounted for in the following pair of explications (the first of which constitutes a revised and expanded version of the explication posited in my 1987 book *English speech act verbs: A semantic dictionary*):

> *chat* (e.g. X had a chat with Y)
> (a) for some time, X was saying some things to Y
> (b) as people say things to someone
> (c) when they think something like this at the same time:
> (d)   I want to say some things to this person

(e)   not because I want this person to know something
(f)   I think this person wants the same
(g)   I think this person will say some things to me during this time
(h)   I think I will feel something good because of this
(i)   I think this person will feel the same

yarn (e.g. X had a yarn with Y)
(a) for some time, X was saying some things to Y about some things
(b) as people say things to someone
(c) when they think something like this at the same time:
(d)   I want to say some things to this person about some things
(e)   I want to do it for some time, not a short time
(f)   I think this person wants the same
(g)   I think this person will say some things to me about these things during this
      time
(h)   I think I will feel something good because of this
(i)   I think this person will feel the same
(j) people think: it is good if men can do this from time to time with other men

The differences between these two explications can be summarized as follows: *Chat* has a "trivializing" (ostensibly at least, noninformative) component (e), which would not be compatible with the more serious intent of *yarn*. Component (g) of *chat* implies reciprocity, and it does not imply any continuity of topic; and component (d) suggests a desire for something like sociability rather than for an exchange focused on a particular topic or topics. By contrast, components (a), (d), and (g) of *yarn* do suggest a certain continuity of topic and an interest in a particular topic or topics. Furthermore, *yarn* suggests an "unhurried" attitude (component [e]) to talk, and an importance attached to occasional togetherness and companionship.

All in all, the characteristic Australian concept of 'yarn' (which coexists in Australia with the pan-English 'chat') points, indirectly, to the need for something like "mateship," to the importance of shared activities, to the emphasis on human relations rather than on productivity or achievement of external goals, and to the relaxed attitude to time.

Renwick (1980), among many others, describes the pace of life in Australia as relatively slow (at least in comparison with America): people tend to be less "task-oriented" and "future-oriented," to have a more relaxed, "day-to-day" orientation, to want to enjoy life and enjoy being with others, and to be more interested in personal relationships than in productivity. Of course, these are "stereotypes," but these stereotypes are consistent with linguistic evidence provided, for example, by oft-discussed traditional Australian expressions such as *she'll be right* or *no worries* or the difference between the wide range of use of the "have-a-V" construction (e.g. "to have a kick of the footie") in Australian speech and the wide range of the "take a V" construction (e.g. "to take a walk") in American English (for discussion, see Wierzbicka 1986). The characteristically Australian concept of 'yarn', too, reflects and documents these traditional attitudes. Like the concept of 'chiacking', the concept of 'yarning' is losing its salience, and the word *yarn* is losing ground in Australian English, but it has not gone out of use yet, as the following recent example (from the speech of a man in his twenties) illustrates:

... with Harrigan and his ilk you can have a yarn with them if you aren't happy with something and they'll hear you out—and if you do swear or curse a decision then they are smart enough to realize it's not personal; they understand it's just a player letting off some steam. (Daley & Clyde 1995:118)

2.3 Shout

'Shouting' is another specifically Australian concept, standing for an activity which from early on in the Australian history established itself as one of the most character-istic national customs, remarked on by many observers. For example (from TAND 1988):

Nearly every one drinks, and the first question on meeting generally is, "Are you going to shout?", i.e. stand treat. (W. Burrows 1859)

'A shout', in the parlance of the Australian bush, is an authority or request to the party in waiting in a public-house to supply the bibulous wants of the companions of the shouter, who of course bears the expense. (C. Munro 1862)

Of all the folly that has ever beset a community, that of shouting has held the ground the longest, and is the most absurd. (Bell's Life in Sydney 1864)

He viewed this 'shouting' mania with disgust. (Bulletin [Sydney] 1892)

As many examples cited by TAND clearly indicate, *shouting* is definitely linked in Australia with the idea of generosity, and it often is (or was) asymmetrical, as when a man with money "shouts" drinks for the moneyless "hands" or even for bystanders:

Most peculiar thing to me as the night wore on, and yarn after yarn went around, the old bloke always shouted, and for all hands each time. (Western Champion 1894)

At our approach four miserable derelicts left the stool on the verandah and slouched into the bar on the prospect of a 'shout'. (F. J. Brady 1911)

In the relatively noncompetitive and egalitarian Australian society, "shouting" was one domain where one could be freely competitive—competing with other people, as it were, in generosity and in the spirit of companionship:

In the Westralian mining towns ... man's class is decided by the number he shouts for. .... To shout for the room is common, to shout for the "house" nothing extraor-dinary, and if the shouter is "brassed up" at all, he says: "Call in them chaps outside." (Bulletin [Sydney] 1909)

He was also of that species of good Aussie mixers who, if someone 'shouted' a round, would forthwith plonk down a handful of silver to indicate payment for the next round before anyone could raise the first glass. (S. Hope 1956)

At the same time, however, the activity "shouting" was traditionally associated with expectations of reciprocity and turn-taking:

It is drink, drink, all day, and swim in it at night. Everyone you meet will 'shout', and you have to 'shout' in return. (Demonax 1873)

> You wouldn't expect a man to leave before his shout would you Ben? (M. Paice 1978)

The expected reciprocity of "shouting" highlights the link which this concept has with the key Australian value of "mateship"; and the words *shout* and *mates* frequently occur together:

> The unbreakable custom that if four or five mates grouped together one started to buy all the drinks, but in the circle everyone had to have his turn. (H. O. Tesher 1977)

The expectations of reciprocity and turn-taking appear to imply a mutuality and an equality which is hard to reconcile with the frequent asymmetry of "shouting" illustrated earlier. Trying to solve this apparent paradox I would propose that reciprocity and turn-taking constitute a social convention associated with "shouting" but are not a necessary part of the concept itself. On the other hand, the idea of drinking companionship (male companionship) is part of the concept: even in those cases when "shouting" constitutes a one-sided treat and a display of one-sided generosity the notion is still there that it is good and pleasurable for a man to drink with other men and that on such occasions it is good to "do things" for one's companions and to identify one's own interests with theirs. Thus, although "shouting" can be done by one individual, it is still analogous to "chiacking" and to "yarning" in its celebration of relaxed male companionship, and male solidarity ("mateship"). The following example illustrates clearly this importance of male companionship and solidarity over and above any strict reciprocity:

> All Merr's mates shouted him at the pub for a week. (A. Garve 1968)

Thus, the idea of a "shout" implies not just one invitation to shared drinking but a sequence of such invitations (typically, a sequence of "rounds"), and it strongly suggests reciprocity and turn-taking without, however, precluding one-sided generosity on the part of one particular person. The overall meaning of *shout*, then (in its older meaning linked specifically with drinking) can be portrayed as follows:

*shout*₁ (e.g. X shouted a round for everyone)
(a) X said something like this:
(b)   I will have a drink now
(c)   I want everyone else to have a drink at the same time
(d)   I will pay for this
(e) X did it as men often do when they are with other men
(f) people think: it is good if men do this with other men
(g)   it is good if one person does it after another person
(h)   when men do this, they feel something good because of this

Components (b), (c), and (d) jointly highlight the "shared activity" aspect of "shouting," component (e) shows that "shouting" was a kind of social ritual, (f) highlights the positive view of this ritual inscribed in the word itself (a view not necessarily shared by outsiders), and (h) reflects the male orientation of this ritual.

To "shout" means, so to speak, to participate in an ongoing discourse in which men repeatedly "shout" for other men. This implies an expectation of turn-taking but does not imply a need for strict reciprocity—a fact highlighted by what TAND (1988) rightly describes as an extended ("transferred and figurative") sense of this word (roughly "treat offered to someone else"). For example:

The governor shouted heavy, and gave us all an excellent feed. (N. Earle 1861)

I'll shout a trip (first-class) for him from Sydney to Narrandera (Bulletin [Sydney] 1896)

Once or twice a year I 'shout' the boys of an orphanage to the pictures. (R. Comm. Moving Picture Industry 1927)

It's Saturday, and I was wondering if you'd like to have dinner there. It'll be my shout. It goes on the expense account. (D. Middlebrook 1975)

But even this kind of one-sided *shout* has implications of shared pleasure, as well as of generosity: a person who *shouts* a treat for someone else fully expects to share in the target person's enjoyment (if only by enjoying their enjoyment) and thus shows a generous and friendly spirit. (The last example above shows a somewhat jarring mixture of attitudes and reflects a modern corruption of the pioneer ideal.)

What is truly important about the concept of 'shouting' is the idea of being generous with other people in the spirit of solidarity and congenial (male) fellowship. There is no stress on reciprocity in the sense of "repayment of a debt" (as it is said to be the case with the Japanese concepts 'on' and 'giri', cf. Lebra 1986). One is obliged to drink, to share in the companionship, and to enjoy a relaxed atmosphere of generosity and group identification, rather than necessarily "repay" the treat to the very person who has provided it. Reciprocity is at the most hinted at by a general expectation that the recipient would want to do the same (perhaps some other time, with some other people). Accordingly, I have posited for *shout*$_2$ the component 'I think it is good if people say this to other people', which echoes the last component of *shout*$_1$: 'people think it is good if men do this with other men'.

shout$_2$ (e.g. X shouted Y a trip to Sydney)
(a) X said something like this to someone:
(b)   I want to do something good for you
(c)   I will pay for this
(d) people think: it is good if people say this to other people
(e)   when people do this, they feel something good because of this

It should be noted that this second, extended sense of *shout* is in fact growing in use, while the primary sense is declining (together with the social tradition which gave rise to it, and with the social and cultural conditions associated with it).

2.4 Dob in

If the words *chiack*, *yarn*, and *shout* can be said to affirm and celebrate "mateship" and "congenial fellowship" in a positive way, *dob in* (described by the Supplement to OED as "Australian slang") can be said to affirm it and celebrate it as it were in a negative way—by condemning, with contempt, anyone who betrays it.

TAND (1988) defines the meaning of the expression *dob in* as "to inform upon, to incriminate." But this is not an improvement on the earlier description offered by the Supplement to OED: "to betray, to inform against." The notion of "betraying" constitutes a crucial difference between the specifically Australian concept of 'dobbing' and the pan-English concept of 'informing'. On the other hand, the description "Australian slang" offered by the OED Supplement is misleading: in Australia, *dob in* is not slang (restricted to some particular social group), it is simply part of common everyday language, a word which is (still) in general use and which is clearly one of the key words in Australian English.

O'Grady (1965) comments in this connection (using the word *dob in*): "Australians are noted for a deep-seated reluctance to report any fellow-citizen to anyone in a position of authority. Police, bosses, foremen, wives, etc. must do their own detecting. Anybody who 'dobs in' anybody else is a 'bastard'—in the worst sense of the word" (34).

Similarly, Baker (1959) mentions "a totally unforgiving attitude towards 'rats', 'scabs' and betrayers in general" among the most distinctive features of the "Australian character" (15). "The essence of the tradition is loyalty to one's fellows, and the strength of its appeal may be seen in the restraining power of the term 'scab' in an Australian union" (Crawford 1970:137). According to Ward (1958, quoted in Crawford 1970:135), "the combination of loyalty to one's fellows with disrespect towards superior orders [and the] enduring disrespect for authority [may be] traced back to the convicts" (cf. chapter 2, section 5).

All this is reflected very clearly in the key word *dob in*. Some examples (from Wilkes 1978 and TAND 1988):

> You said you'd go to the police and dob him in unless he coughed up. That's the story isn't it? (Judah Waten 1957)

> A couple of the Indonesian p.o.w's have dobbed us in. Told the Nips everything. (R. Braddon 1961)

In these two examples, *dob in* could be in principle replaced with *inform on* (though not without a significant change in meaning). In the examples which follow, however, *inform on* could hardly be used at all, since it is not used with respect to strictly personal relations (such as, for example, family relations):

> Helen stuck on a real act and dobbed me in to Mum, screaming about how I had busted her best doll on purpose. (P. Barton 1981)

Unlike *inform on*, *dob in* is derogatory and contemptuous: *dobbing* is something a decent person cannot possibly do.

> I shut up and let Ray take all the credit. Couldn't dob him in, could I? (J. O'Grady 1973)

> You bitch! Go and dob me in because I gave you a bit of a shove! (Williamson 1972)

> But you feel such a rat to tell on her. To dob her in. (H. F. Brinsmead 1966)

If one believes that in some cases the circumstances do require reporting someone (for example, a drug pusher) to the authorities, the concept of 'dobbing' can be a powerful obstacle which has to be overcome:

> In 1992, I put my face to the New South Wales police force's 'Operation Noah' campaign, encouraging the public to phone their local station or a central command post to dob in a drug pusher. I am very anti-drugs. Many believe 'dobbing' is a very un-Australian thing to do, but I had no qualms endorsing such a project because I believe drugs such as marijuana, cocaine, speed, LSD, crack and all the rest of it can take an evil grip on your life. (Daley & Clyde 1995:170)

The noun *dobber* is equally or even more contemptuous and derogatory than the verb *dob in* (as is also the now obsolete *cobber-dobber*, from *cobber* 'mate'):

> Don't look at me, you bastards! I'm no bloody dobber! (J. Powers 1973)

> The expression 'dobber' was one that I knew implied contempt and was apt to be applied to tale-bearers and informers. (G.A.W. Smith 1977)

One further difference between *inform on* and *dob in* is that the latter implies that the agent is definitely hurting the person spoken of, whereas the former does not necessarily imply that. In *informing*, the stress is on the transmission of (potentially damaging) information, not on interpersonal relations between the speaker and the person spoken of, but in *dobbing in*, the stress is on interpersonal relations. This semantic difference between the two verbs is reflected in a syntactic one. *Dob in* treats the victim as a direct object ('to dob someone in') and thus suggests that the agent is "doing something to" the person dobbed in. By contrast, *inform on* treats the victim as an oblique object (one cannot "inform someone on"); this suggests that the agent of *informing* is not necessarily "doing something to" the person informed on.

It is interesting to note in this connection that *dob*, too, can be used with the particle *on*, and that *dob on* is closer semantically to *inform on* than *dob in* is. *Inform on*, *tell on*, and *dob on* all suggest intentional transmission of damaging information without implying that serious harm has already been done, as *dob in* does. At the same time *dob on*, which appears to be used mainly by schoolchildren, shares with *dob in* its contemptuous and derogatory character: evidently, the general Australian contempt for those who break group solidarity and who attempt to side with the authorities against fellow "subordinates" is an important part of the Australian school ethos, as well as of the Australian ethos in general.

I will not try to propose here an explication of *dob on*, interesting as it is, focusing instead on the more basic concept *dob in*, used widely right across the whole of Australian society.

dob in (e.g. X dobbed Y in)
(a) X said something like this to Z about Y:
(b)   I want you to know that Y did something bad
(c) X knew:
(d)   X is someone like Y
(e)   Z is not someone like Y
(f)   Z can do bad things to someone like Y

(g) people think: if someone does something like this, it is very bad
(h) people feel something bad when they think about things like this

The crucial pattern of interpersonal relations is reflected in the components (d), (e), and (f): since the dobber is a person like the "dobbee" (needless to say, not a real word), whereas the addressee is not, the dobber is breaking the solidarity of people expected to identify with one another. Furthermore, since the addressee is not only an outsider but actually represents "the authorities" (component [f]), this breaking of solidarity of equals is likely to be seen (in Australia) as particularly contemptible (components [g] and [h]).

It is worth noting that *dob in* has also another meaning in Australia: roughly, doing a bad turn to a "mate" by "volunteering" for something on his or her behalf. This meaning is related to the first one insofar as it implies saying something about a "mate" to a person in charge, causing something bad to happen to the "mate," and thus violating the expectation of loyalty and mutual support. The main difference between the two meanings consists in the fact that in one case one says something bad about the mate, whereas in the other one says something unfounded and embarrassing (with possible "bad" results): namely, that s(he) is willing to do something which in fact s(he) is not.

2.5 Whinge

Whinge (roughly 'complain' or 'whine') is clearly one of the key words in Australian English. In other parts of the English-speaking world it is marginal (although not totally unknown); OED qualifies it as "Scottish and dialectal" (noun) and "Scottish and northern dialects" (verb), although the Supplement to the OED hedges this qualification by means of the adverb *originally*.

The marginal character of *whinge* and its derivatives such as *whinger* outside Australian English is reflected in the following examples (OEDS 1972):

> Other local terms for crying ... in Dublin the usual word is 'whinging', hence 'whinger', a term also still used in Cumberland, and occasionally heard in Liverpool. (I. and P. Opie 1959)

> Touching the query about 'whinger' ... , 'winjer' was accepted slang for 'grumbler' at Q. Uni. [Queensland University] a few years ago, and probably still is. I have seldom heard it elsewhere, and no one who uses it seems to know the derivation. (Bulletin [Sydney] 1934)

The verb *whinge*, evidently marginal in other varieties of English, in Australia is a household word. It plays a crucial role in the socialization of children ("Stop whingeing"), and in the formation and transmission of the Australian national ethos. As one observer put it, discussing the relative unimportance of the value of "success" and the crucial importance of the values of "toughness," gameness, and resilience in Australian culture:

> There is little public glorification of success in Australia. The few heroes of heroic occasions (other than those of past) are remembered for their style rather than for their achievement. The early explorers, Anzac Day, these commemorate comradeship,

gameness, exertion of the Will, suffering in silence. To be game, not to *whinge*—that's the thing—rather than some dull success coming from organisation and thought. (Horne 1964:31: emphasis added)

The importance of the concept of 'whingeing' in Australian culture is reflected in the very common Australian expression *whingeing Poms* or *whingeing Pommies*— an expression which shows both the Australian perception of English people and their own Australian self-image: English people are, above all, "whingers," whereas Australians are, above all, "non-whingers" (examples from TAND):

The British national pastime of 'grousing' (to use an English phrase) has given rise in Australia to the derisive expression *wingeing* pommy. (Marshall & Drysdale 1962)

It'll pass a law to give every single wingein bloody Pommie his fare home to England. Back to the smoke and the sun shining ten days a year and shit in the streets. Yer can have it. (T. Keneally 1972)

Whingeing Poms make me ill. (W. F. Mandle 1974)

And a recent example:

Brad acted in the gracious manner which epitomizes him as both a rugby league player and a man. Instead of whingeing to the media about being shunted out of the team . . . he knuckled down to business and produced some performances which helped the Dragons make the grand final against Brisbane. (Daley & Clyde 1995:65)

What exactly is 'whingeing'? Clearly, it is a concept closely related to that expressed by the word *complaining*. But, first, *complain* is neutral, and does not imply any evaluation of the activity in question, whereas *whinge* is critical and derogatory. Furthermore, *complain* is purely verbal, whereas *whinge* suggests something that sounds like an inarticulate animal cry. Being purely verbal, *complaining* can be seen as fully intentional, whereas *whingeing* can be seen as only semi-intentional and semi-controlled. Finally, *whingeing*, like *nagging*, and unlike *complaining*, suggests monotonous repetition.

In *English speech act verbs* (Wierzbicka 1987), I posited for *complain* the following semantic structure (reproduced here in a slightly simplified form):

(a) I say: something bad is happening to me
(b) I feel something bad because of this
(c) I want someone to know about this

Whinge appears to attribute to the speaker (the "whinger") an analogous, but more elaborated, attitude:

whinge (e.g. X was whinging)
(a) for some time, X was saying something like this:
     something bad is happening to me
(b) X was saying it as people say things
(c) when they want to say something like this:
(d)   something bad is happening to me
(e)   I feel something bad because of this

(f)   I can't do anything ("about it")
(g)   I want someone to know this
(h)   I want someone to do something because of this
(i)   I think no one wants to do anything
(j)   I want to say this many times because of this
(k) people think: it is bad if someone does this

Component (f) of this formula suggests a feeling of total helplessness, (h) indicates passivity and reliance on others, (i) suggests an element of childish resentment and self-pity, whereas (j) spells out the reliance on the equally childish "strategy" of monotonous repetition (as in an infant's crying). Generally, then, the concept of 'whingeing' likens the attitude of those who indulge in it to that of crying babies, and what Australians think of people who behave like crying babies is best expressed in another important Australianism: the noun *sook* (adj. *sooky*). Some examples from TAND:

(He goes to her and holds her gently. . . . She sobs a little, but then forces a laugh and leaves him.) Ruby: Well! You'll think I'm a sook. (R. J. Merritt 1975)

Annie felt sick with fear. 'Sookie sook, I'm going to tell on you', chanted Rosa. (*Australian Short Stories* 1985)

The girl applied a hefty hip . . . and flattened him. Sprawled on the bitumen, he began to howl. 'Bloody sook!' said the girl, disgustedly. (*Bulletin* 1986)

As noted by Horne, among others, "Australians are cheerful and practical-minded optimists" (1964:44). They admire toughness, resilience, and good humor, in hard times as well as in good times. In the past their folk heroes were Ned Kelly and various other real or legendary "wild colonial boys," for whom the important thing was not so much to live in comfort and security or to succeed as to:

. . . die hard, die game,
die fighting, like that wild colonial boy,
Jack Dowling, says the ballad, was his name.
(a poem by John Manifold, quoted in Ward 1958:217)

According to the same Australian ballad, "'I'll die but not surrender', said the Wild Colonial Boy" (Wannan 1963:16).

The ideal, or myth, of "dying hard" is now a thing of the past, and far more appealing, apparently, is the prospect of "having a good time" (on the growing hedonism of Australians, see Conway 1971 and King 1978); but the contempt for "sooks" and "whingers" has remained part and parcel of the present-day Australian ethos. One could still say, with some justification, that Australians value practicality and self-reliance, and that while they also assume and approve of mutual reliance of "mates" on one another (cf. Renwick 1980:16), any reliance on more powerful "other people" and indulgence in repeated "crying" (instead of a search for practical solutions) is incompatible with the traditional Australian ethos. (As we have seen, even today a footballer can be seen as a sporting hero only if he doesn't "whinge" in the face of a setback but bravely "battles on.") The key verb *whinge* reflects and documents these attitudes.

A full study of Australian colloquial speech act verbs would have to include many more, such as *stir, sledge, skite, rouse on, pimp on, earbash, big-note oneself, knock, (w)rap (up),* and *fang* (see Wilkes 1978, and TAND 1988). I believe, however, that the five which have been discussed here are particularly representative and particularly important.

3. Australian "b-words" (swearwords).

I do not claim that the characteristic Australian "*b*-words" (*bastard, bloody, bugger,* and *bullshit*) are not used at all outside Australia. They are (as is also *mate*). But in Australia, these words play a role that is truly unique. Elsewhere, they are more or less marginal. Here, they are central—in everyday life and even in public discourse (especially on the political scene). Elsewhere, they are regarded as "coarse slang" (as the OEDS [1972] calls *bullshit*), but in Australia, they are part of everyday language; and they are felt to be an important means of self-expression, self-identification, and effective communication with others.

But although the frequency of *b*-words in Australian speech is undoubtedly unique, and although it has often been commented on by visitors from other parts of the English-speaking world, it is, above all, in the meaning of these words, as they are used in Australia, that the Australians have managed to express something of their own cultural identity. As Colin Bowles, the author of the mock textbook *G'day! Teach yourself Australian in 20 easy lessons*! (1986) says with special reference to *bugger*, these words are "the Clayton words of the Australian language," where *Clayton* is itself a peculiarly Australian word, meaning, roughly, that something is not what it appears to be.[1] Strictly speaking, then, it is not the *b*-words themselves but the meanings encapsulated in them that are characteristically Australian.

Baker observed that "In spite of many criticisms Australians do not use more vulgarisms than the English and Americans. They merely use some of those vulgarisms more often" (1970[1945]:200). Among the most common "vulgarisms," Baker includes "the four Indispensable Bs—*bastard, bitch, bloody* and *bugger*." In fact, I believe that *bullshit* is more "indispensable" and more characteristically Australian than *bitch* (which in any case appears to have declined considerably) ever has been. Baker also made the following insightful comments on the "*b*-words":

> The repetitive nature of Australian vulgarism has had the important effect of robbing many allegedly objectionable words—especially the Bs—of their taint of indecency. Offensive they may still be at times, but much depends on the tone of voice in which they are spoken. *Bastard* and *bugger* are frequently used as terms of genial or even affectionate address between men. The fact that Australian women also use the four Bs widely is additional evidence that they are becoming innocuous.
>
> This lack of insult in Australian profanity is a point that should be noted, not as an excuse for the continued use of certain words, but as evidence that even in his employment of vulgar terms imported from the Old World the Australian has managed to express something of his own personality. (201)

I believe that rigorous semantic analysis of the *b*-words allows us to see better in what way they express some aspects of the Australian "personality," and what aspects of this personality they highlight.

3.1   *Bloody*

Bloody has been known as "the great Australian adjective" for more than a century (cf. Baker 1970:196). It is ubiquitous in Australian life, and though not unknown in the other parts of the English-speaking world, "it has always been conspicuous enough to be seen as such [i.e. as "the great Australian adjective"] by overseas visitors" (Wilkes 1978:35). Just one characteristic quote (from William Howitt's *Land, labour, and gold* (1855, quoted in Wilkes 1978:35–36):

> The language of the diggings is something inconceivable in its vileness, and every sentence almost is ornamented with the word *bloody*. That word they seem to think the perfection of phraseology; it is the keystone and topstone of all their eloquence, it occurs generally in every second or third sentence; and, when they get excited, they lard every sentence with it profusely. . . . Two diggers passing our tent one day, saw the thermometer hanging on the post: 'What d—d, blasted, bloody thing is that now?' said one to the other. 'Why I'm blowed if it ain't a d—d, blasted, bloody old weather glass', replied his mate.

But it is not just the frequency of use which makes "the great Australian adjective" so characteristically Australian. Most importantly, this word has developed a new personality in Australian English and, I would claim, a unique meaning.

The syntactic range of *bloody* in Australian English is very wide, as it can modify verbs, nouns, adjectives, adverbs, and even numerals, as in the following example:

> When I asked an old 'cove' when he first arrived in Darwin, he replied, 'Young man, in nineteen bloody eight!' (Hartley 1942, TAND)

It can also be used as an infix:

> Got in a troop train . . . after a fortnight comin' down from Broome across the Transcontibloodynental. (Cusack & James 1951, TAND)

To get some idea of the role this versatile word plays in Australian English, the reader is invited to consider the following characteristic example:

> One of the witnesses, a fettler, came into the inquiry room and tripped on a mat and said, 'What stupid bastard put that bloody mat there?' And he slung it out the door. 'Bull' Mitchell on the inquiry board said to him, 'None of your bloody swearing here, you just remember that you're at a bloody inquiry and bloody well behave yourself.' (Patsy Adam Smith 1968, TAND)

And a further example from a public speech by a public figure (Mr. C. Jones, federal minister for transport):

> There is going to be some bloody mammoth changes—some mammoth changes which the Budget will disclose. Bloody mammoth changes, that is the only way you can describe them. I think Frank [Crean] has done a bloody good job to stand up to

the pace. Bloody oath, he has done a marvellous job in standing up to the bloody pace. (Sydney *Morning Herald* 1973, TAND)

What is particularly interesting about the use of *bloody* in Australia is the range of feelings which it can express: unlike expletives such as *fucking*, more common in American English, *bloody* is by no means restricted to negative feelings; it can also express admiration, enthusiasm, endearment, and so on. Particularly characteristic are the following two phrases: *You bloody beauty*! (for example, watching sport, with admiration), and *You bloody old bastard*! (greeting a friend). One example:

> A short-necked man, with a chest like a barrel, and arms reaching to his knees, forced his way through the crowd, put his hand out and said, 'Frank, you bloody old bastard!' ... They pumped his hand, smacked him on the back, swore at him and each other, then took possession of most of the bar. (H. P. Tritton 1964, recalling the period 1905–1906, in Wilkes 1978)

I would suggest that the meaning of *bloody*, as it is used in Australia, involves five distinct semantic components. First, this crucial word is obviously a tool for expressing emotion ('I feel something'). Second, the speaker is lost for words and unwilling to articulate the emotion ('I don't want to say what I feel'). Third, the feeling is strong and intense, and it is linked with an active impulse (reminiscent of the active impulse of anger): one wants to hit, to kick, to slap someone on the back, or whatever the case may be ('because of this, I want to do something [to X]'). Fourth, to convey the strength of the emotion, the speaker "has to" break a social taboo and show that the feeling cannot be expressed within the conventions of a "polite society" (components [d] and [e] below). Finally, an adequate explication of *bloody* also has to include a reference to some predication, as the "great adjective" can only be used as a modifier, never on its own (unlike, for example, *bugger* or *bullshit*, to be discussed later). Furthermore, as pointed out by Hill (1985:32), *bloody* cannot be used in predicate-less *wh*-exclamations:

(a) What a man!
(b) *What a bloody man!
(c) What a bloody idiot!

In sentence (a), "a man" is not used as a predicate (the speaker doesn't want to express the idea that "he is a man"), but in (c) "an idiot" IS used as a predicate (here, the speaker does want to express the idea that "he is an idiot"). I will represent this aspect of *bloody* as follows: 'when I say something about X I feel something'. This brings us to the following explication:

bloody (e.g. bloody X!)
(a) when I say something about X, I feel something
(b) I don't want to say what I feel
(c) I want to do something else
(d) some people say that some words are bad words
(e) I want to say something of this kind

Montagu described *bloody* as meaning "frightful, beyond description, ghastly" (1967:274). Although the use of the words *frightful* and *ghastly* in this definition is not justified, since, as we have seen, *bloody* can also express very positive feelings (such as enthusiasm), the phrase "beyond description" correctly captures an important dimension of *bloody*—except that it is not the referent which is "beyond description" but the speaker's feeling. For example, when a person who is asked when they first arrived in Darwin replies, "Young man, in nineteen bloody eight!" it is clearly not the date which is "beyond description" but the feeling which goes with it.

The emotional value of *bloody* in Australian English has sometimes been denied, and it has been claimed that *bloody* is often no more than an empty "filler" (cf. e.g. Turner 1966:93). But, as pointed out by Hill (1985:27), *bloody* (unlike *very*) cannot be used in questions:

Is he very tall?
*Is he bloody tall?
He's the very good artist I was telling you about.
*He's the bloody good artist I was telling you about.

This shows that *bloody* does in fact carry the component 'I feel something'.

The "great Australian adjective" epitomizes some of the characteristic features of the traditional Australian ethos, and in particular, unwillingness to describe feelings and the tendency to say "bad things" and to use "bad words"—not only to express negative opinions and negative feelings but also to express "good feelings." It epitomizes the traditional Australian cult of "toughness" and rebelliousness.

3.2   Bastard

Colin Bowles' "textbook" *G'day! Teach yourself Australian in 20 easy lessons* (1986) includes an important section entitled "How and when to use the word *bastard* ":

Correct usage of the word "bastard" is perhaps one of the hardest aspects of the language to learn. A term of endearment (as in "Owyagowin, y'old bastard") or of abuse (as in "You rotten bastard!"), it is most often used simply as a synonym for "person". But as a rule, you don't call someone you don't know a "bastard", as the subtle shades of meaning can be misconstrued.

In describing other people, anyone and everyone is a bastard, unless they're female. If you like someone, they're not a bad bastard, and if you feel sorry for them they're a poor bastard. If you don't like them, they're that bastard and if you don't like them and despise them as well they're that mongrel bastard.

If you don't like them, but you're a bit frightened of them, they're a bad bastard. If they're smart, they're a clever bastard. If they're not, they're a dozey bastard. If they wear their lechery on their sleeves they're a grubby bastard and if they're indolent, they're a lazy bastard. If they have a malevolent streak, they're a nasty bastard. If they have no manners they're a rude bastard. If they're miserly, they're a lousy bastard.

Other popular bastards are unlucky bastards, queer bastards, officious bastards and weak bastards.

The Australian language is built around the bastard. Learn the word, say it correctly, use it wisely. Remember—every Australian is some sort of bastard, but you only say it to his face when you know him well enough to have shouted each other drinks. (12)

The most common use of *bastard* implies that the speaker thinks of another person (a man) as a "bad kind of person" and feels something (clearly, something bad) because of it. Used without modifiers that's what *bastard* normally implies. Typically, it is used with such a negative intent in three syntactic frames: "that bastard" (example 1 below), "to be a bastard" (example 2), and "call someone a bastard" (examples 3 and 1):

1. Digger [paraded before an English officer trying to discover who called the regimental cook a bastard]: 'You keep on asking us who called that cook a bastard; what we want to know is, who called that bastard a cook?' (Piddington 1929, TAND).

2. I want a few quid for th' school tonight, so don't be a bastard. (McLean 1960, TAND).

3. Australian Prime Minister Gough Whitlam addressing the Canberra branch of the Australian Labor Party: "I do not mind the Liberals, still less do I mind the Country Party, calling me a bastard. In some circumstances I am only doing my job if they do. But I hope you will not publicly call me a bastard, as some bastards in the Caucus have." (*Sunday Telegraph* 1974, TAND).

The basic meaning of the Australian *bastard* (in its predicative use) can be portrayed as follows:

a bastard (e.g. he is a bastard)
(a) I think about him like this:
(b)   I know men of this kind
(c)   men of this kind are bad men
(d)   men of this kind can do very bad things
(e) because of this, when I think about him I feel something bad
(f) I want to say something bad about this man
(g) people say that some words are bad words
(h) I want to say something of this kind

Components (a), (b), (c), and (d) indicate that the word *bastard* places a man in a certain recognizable category of men, "bad men who can do very bad things," and (e) reflects the speaker's feelings associated with this categorization. Component (f) indicates that the speaker is not going to describe these feelings but instead will express them by saying "something bad" about the man in question and by using a "bad" word, that is, a word that the society (or some part of it) is known to disapprove of ([g] and [h]).

This is, then, the pejorative meaning of *bastard* (*bastard₁*). But as the passage quoted from *Teach yourself Australian* makes clear, there is also another meaning of the term, *bastard₂*, which does not describe a man as "bad" or as belonging to a "bad kind" of men and which implies "good feelings" rather than "bad feelings." This second meaning can be illustrated with the following examples, which imply something like compassion (1 and 2), friendliness (3) and affection (4):

1. I've knocked around a bit in my time, and I'll tell them that don't know him he's a decent sort of a poor bastard. (Hatfield 1931, TAND)

2. Not such a bad sort of a poor old bastard, but the grog's got him. (Hungerford 1953, TAND)

3. There was a Welsh fellow with us, a lay preacher, and . . . a ganger called him a Welsh bastard. It was friendly you know. But Taffy didn't know and told us that he had evidence of the marriage of his parents. The ganger got heated and said if he himself didn't mind being called a bastard why was this Welsh bastard complaining and with that Taffy up and jobbed him. (Patsy Adam Smith 1969, TAND)

4. 'G'day, ya old bastard,' said Jim, and I was amused again that the Tommies could never get used to our main term of endearment. (Lawson 1944, TAND)

And two more recent examples, from the Macquarie electronic corpus of Australian English:

'Hope the poor bastard has enough money for coffee', Henry said solemnly. (1988)

. . . There's too many rules and regulations nowadays. Surfing used to equate to freedom. It was a way of expressing yourself. Now every bastard looks the same and surfs the same. (1992)

Particularly common and characteristic is the use of the term *bastard* (in this second sense) in friendly greetings (among men), especially in the phrase, "You (ya) old bastard," which can indeed be called, without too much exaggeration, "the main term of endearment." (Recall the quote from Harris 1962 in section 2.)

Clearly, in all its different uses, *bastard* expresses the speaker's feeling ('I feel something'). Since (unlike *bloody*) *bastard* can be used on its own, this word expresses feelings triggered by what one THINKS of a particular person rather than by what one says. Hence in this case the appropriate phrasing appears to be 'when I think about (man) X, I feel something' (rather than 'when I say something about this, I feel something').

Colin Bowles says that *bastard* "is most often used simply as a synonym for *person*," but this statement should be taken with a grain of salt: first, *bastard* is normally used only with reference to men, and not to women,[2] and second, unlike *person*, *bastard* definitely conveys an emotional attitude, and it cannot be used in abstract, impersonal, purely intellectual contexts (although as the quote from Whitlam's speech shows, it can certainly be used in public speeches, in political discourse, and so on).

The fact that *bastard* is so ubiquitous in Australian speech that it can be perceived as "simply a synonym for *person*" highlights the anti-intellectual, down-to-earth, context-dependent flavor of traditional Australian speech. It also highlights the undercurrent of muffled, unarticulated emotion associated with this speech.

Another important aspect of *bastard* is hinted at in Bowles' comment, "You don't call someone you don't know a 'bastard', as the subtle shades of meaning can be misconstrued." The point is that the feeling implied by *bastard* is unspecified, and that when using this word the speaker relies on the addressee's ability to "guess," without words, what is intended in this particular case.

Wishing to hint that the unexpressed emotion is "strong," an Australian speaker can take recourse to one reliable and congenial strategy: saying some words regarded by "polite society" as "bad." Verbal taboos are broken in Australia all the time, but this does not mean that they are not felt to be present. On the contrary, Australian speakers traditionally rely, so to speak, on the existence of such taboos, because they often feel that only by breaking them can they adequately express their emotions.

The emotion hinted at by Australian *b*-words in general and by *bastard* in particular can seldom be articulated because of the traditional Australian mistrust of verbal articulateness and of explicit emotion talk (cf. chapter 2, section 5). But this very fact raises the emotional tension and increases the need for some adequate release. The sense that one is breaking a verbal taboo provides such a release and presumably fulfills an important psychological function. It also appeals to the rebellious and anti-authoritarian side of the historically shaped Australian national character, as well as to many Australian men's culturally shaped need to stress their masculinity and to frequently reaffirm the bonds linking one with like-minded "tough" and "anti-sentimental" "blokes"[3] ("mates" or potential "mates"). I suggest the following explication:

> *bastard*$_2$ (e.g. poor bastard, clever bastard)
> (a) I think about this man like this:
> (b) I know men of this kind
> (c) because of this, when I think about him, I feel something
> (d) I don't want to say what I feel
> (e) I want to say something else
> (f) some people say some words are bad words
> (g) I want to say something of this kind

As this explication suggests, *bastard*$_2$ is close in meaning to *bastard*$_1$—but, unlike *bastard*$_1$, it does not place the person referred to in the category of "bad men who can do very bad things." Rather, it places him in a certain category of men which is familiar to the speaker and which doesn't need to be specified in a given context.

3.3 Bugger

In *Introducing Australia*, C. Hartley Gratton (1944:171–172, quoted in Wilkes 1978:58) writes: "The word bugger is used in numerous forms and contexts. 'Oh, bugger it all.' 'I'll be buggered.' 'Buggered if I will.' 'Bugger him.' 'Oh, go to buggery,' 'The silly bugger.' 'I'm all buggered up.' And triumphantly combining all the favorite words, 'bugger the bloody bastard'. English people profess to find Australian men foul-mouthed."

In a similar vein, Colin Bowles (1986) devotes special attention to the word *bugger*, which he calls "the utility word":

> The Australian language is constructed around utility words like "bugger" and "bastard" that have long lost their offensive nature. They express negatives in a number of different ways and reduce the need for an extensive and complicated vocabulary. Some examples are given below:

go to buggery—a means of letting someone know you no longer care for their future well-being or continuing presence
all to buggery—badly messed up
to play silly buggers—to waste time or badly mismanage a situation
to buggerise around—same as above
I'm buggered if I know—I'm stuck for a solution/I haven't a clue

"Bugger" is the Clayton's word of the Australian language. It's the word you have when you don't have the right word. (18)

Closer examination, however, shows that even when it is used as a noun, *bugger* is not really an equivalent of *bastard*.[4] Evidence for this lack of equivalence is provided by the fact that *bugger* is less likely than *bastard* to co-occur with adjectives such as *clever*, *crafty*, or *nasty*: collocations such as *clever bugger, crafty bugger, nasty bugger*, and *smart-arsed bugger* are not impossible, but they sound less felicitious, or less natural, than *clever bastard, crafty bastard, smart–arsed bastard*, or *nasty bastard*.

Bugger feels most at home with the adjectives *silly*, *poor*, and *old*, and also with their combinations, such as *silly old bugger* and *poor little bugger*. It is worth mentioning in this connection the well-publicized utterance "Silly old bugger!" used in public (in the late 1980s), in front of the television cameras, by the Australian prime minister, Bob Hawke, during a meet-the-public session, when he was goaded by an old-age pensioner about high parliamentary salaries. Another well-publicized utterance, also due to Bob Hawke, was used during the prime minister's visit to Japan, where he announced that "we are not going to play funny buggers" (a phrase that the interpreter found herself unable to translate into Japanese).

Given the Australian value of "irreverence," a prime minister can also be described (in public) as a "poor bugger" himself, as the Australian journalist Philip Adams has done in a recent interview (conducted in Berlin) with a visiting Australian musician (Adams is talking here with the violist Brett Dean):

Adams: Brett, I've been going around the city, explaining Australian irreverence, explaining our quality of cheek, our reluctance to club hierarchies—I've explained how we call the Prime Minister by his first name—and the poor bugger has to sit in the front of the car, he can't get in the back seat. How does an irreverent Australian like you fit into this context? (Adams 1995)

Generally speaking, *bugger* attracts adjectives which evoke an image of resourcelessness, harmlessness, weakness, or silliness. A "silly old bugger" may be a nuisance but cannot be dangerous and, unlike a "bastard," cannot provoke real hostility. Nor can a "bugger" provoke envy or admiration, as a "clever bastard" or a "crafty bastard" might. *Bastard* can be very hostile, but it doesn't express contempt. By contrast, *bugger*—if it is used pejoratively—is contemptuous and dismissive, but it can hardly convey a real hostility. A "bugger" can do something "bad," but he can hardly do something "very bad"; and he can cause bad things to happen, but hardly "very bad things" (if only because "buggers" are ineffectual, weak, silly, senile, or immature). I suggest this is why *bugger* does not attract "active" adjectives such as *clever*, *crafty* and *nasty*, which suggest resourcefulness and an ability to control events.

This "passive," helpless character suggested by *bugger* is highlighted in the use of the verb *bugger-up*, as in the following example:

> But one time I fell off the train and buggered my insides up. (D'Arcy Niland 1957, quoted in Wilkes 1978).

Clearly, a person who "buggered his (her) insides up" is a person to whom something happened (perhaps because of his [her] clumsiness or incompetence), not a person who did something. Admittedly, sometimes "buggers" do things, or rather try to do things, but they are generally ineffectual and don't control events. As the *Macquarie dictionary of Australian colloquial language* (1988) puts it, "to bugger about" or "to bugger around" means something like "to mess about, fiddle around"— that is to say, it implies "causing a mess" rather than achieving something; *buggerise*, and *buggerise about* or *around* are glossed by the same dictionary as "to behave aimlessly or ineffectually"; and the expression *to play silly buggers* is glossed as "to engage in time-wasting activities and frivolous behaviour." (Recall also the variant with "funny buggers," used by Hawke in Japan).

The adjective *buggered*, glossed by Wilkes (1978) as "1. tired out; exhausted, 2. broken; wrecked, 3. damned: I'm buggered if I'll do that," also clearly implies that 'something bad happened or may happen'.

Similarly, the expression *bugger him* (e.g. "Bugger him, I'm going home," MDACL) suggests something like "I'm going home, I don't care if something bad happens because of this." The common expression *Oh, bugger it all,* quoted earlier, has similar implications: 'I don't care if something bad happens, I don't want to think about it'; and so does Wilkes' "triumphant" utterance "bugger the bloody bastard."

The defiant expression *I'll be buggered if . . .* is also very interesting. Its implications are: 'I don't want to do this, I don't care if something bad happens because of this, I don't want to think about it'. The speaker is determined not to do something and feels able to dismiss any possible consequences as something that doesn't count.

The use of *bugger* as a noun referring to inanimate objects or events points in the same direction, as illustrated by the following examples: "that recipe is a real bugger," "it's a bugger of a day" (MDACL). Clearly, a "bugger of a day" is a day when bad things happen (but probably minor "bad things," not intended by anybody); and a recipe which is "a real bugger," too, causes "bad things to happen," but doesn't involve a serious danger, harm, or ill will.

Finally, the interjection *bugger!*, glossed by MDACL as "a strong exclamation of annoyance, disgust, etc." and described by Wilkes as "used most often as an equivalent to 'damn,'" indicates that something has gone wrong and that the speaker is not in control of the situation. For example, if one is attempting to hammer a nail into a wall and instead hits one's own finger, or if one is trying to repair an electric appliance but instead damages it even further, or if one notices that it has started to rain just as one was preparing to hang out the washing, one may well exclaim *bugger!* (and in fact, this is what most Australian men—and quite a few Australian women— can be expected to exclaim in such circumstances).

On the other hand, one can't say *bugger!* if one is suddenly hit by a stone or attacked by a magpie (a common occurrence in Canberra in springtime), because to exclaim *bugger!* the speaker has to be trying to do something and has to be frustrated in his or her efforts. (According to my informants, in a case like this one can be expected to say *shit!* but not *bugger!*)

I suggest that we can capture all this in the following explications:

bugger! (interjection)
(a) I think: something bad happened
(b) I don't want to say "very bad"
(c) because of this, I think:
(d)   I want to do something
(e)   I can't do it
(f) because of this, I feel something bad
(g) because of this, I want to say something
(h) some people say that some words are bad words
(i) I want to say something of this kind

The person exclaiming *bugger!* is not expressing anger or rage; rather, the feeling expressed is closer to annoyance or a combination of annoyance and frustration. Components (d) and (e) account for this. Component (f) shows that, unlike *bloody*, *bugger!* (the interjection) always expresses a 'bad feeling'. Components (h) and (i) are common to *bugger*, *bloody*, and *bastard*.

The noun *bugger* requires, it seems, a very similar explication, except that it refers to another person's actions and another person's incompetence. The interpretation of the "bad feeling," however, is likely to differ, together with the speaker's perspective: if something goes wrong in the course of my own actions, I am likely to feel something like frustration, but if something goes wrong in the course of another person's actions I am more likely to feel pity, condescension, mild contempt, and so on. On the other hand, something like annoyance is quite likely to occur in both cases.

The fact that the phrase *bloody bugger* sounds less felicitious than *bloody bastard* is, I think, due to the clash between the active, vigorous impulse suggested by *bloody* and the weak, passive image suggested by *bugger*. The person who says "bloody X!" has an impulse to do something to X (to hit him, to shake him, or whatever); but the semantics of *bugger*, with its implications of something like condescension, pity, dismissal, or annoyance, suggests a different and rather incompatible attitude.

As a first approximation, then, I would propose the following explication of *bugger* (noun):

bugger (noun)
(a) I know: something bad happened
(b) I don't want to say "very bad"
(c) because of this, I think:
(d)   this man wants to do some things
(e)   this man can't do things (like other people)
(f) because of this, I feel something bad
(g) I want to say something bad about this man
(h) some people say that some words are bad words
(i) I want to say something of this kind

For example, when Bob Hawke, goaded by the old-age pensioner, reacted to the intrusion with the utterance "silly old bugger!" his attitude can be interpreted as follows: (a) something bad happened (a disruption, trouble, etc.); (b) I don't regard this as something serious ('I don't want to say: "very bad"'); (d) this old man wants to do something (confront me, influence the government's policy, and so on); (e) but he is incompetent, silly, ineffectual ('he can't do things like other people'); (f) because of this, I feel something bad (irritation, impatience, a bit of contempt, etc.); (g) I want to say something bad about this man, and I want to do it using a "juicy" expressive word, not of the "polite" kind (h) and (i).

If a mother calls her little boy who has done some mischief or who has been a nuisance "a real bugger of a boy," her attitude is no doubt different in some ways, but in other ways it can be seen as similar. She, too, indicates that 'something bad happened' (the mischief, the nuisance), she, too, downplays the importance of the event or events in question (her little boy didn't commit a real crime), she recognizes that the boy has active impulses (wants to play, wants to do things), but she sees him as in some way different and "worse" (in behavior) than other children. She, too, wants to express a 'bad feeling' (irritation, impatience, exasperation, or the like), and to do so without mincing words.

When the noun *bugger* is used to express something like compassion, a different explication may seem to be called for, but in fact the one proposed here fits such a situation, too. For example, if someone says "poor little bugger" referring to a handicapped child, their attitude can be interpreted as follows: (a) something bad happened (to this child); (b) I don't want to say: a tragedy, I prefer to say something like: a misfortune ('I don't want to say: something very bad'); (c) no doubt this child wants to do things (like other people); (d) unfortunately, this child can't do things like other people; (e) I feel something bad because of this (pity, a bit of sorrow, etc); (f) because of this, I want to say something, but since I don't want to sound sentimental, I'll say a "bad" word rather than some "pretty" word ((n) and (i)).

If *bugger* is used to express something like compassion, it often involves an understatement: what happened to the "poor bugger" may be really something very bad (even death), and the speaker doesn't say that it wasn't something very bad: he only indicates that he doesn't want to say "very bad." For example, the sympathetic comment "poor bugger!" could well refer to a fisherman who drowned when his boat capsized in a gale; on the other hand, a passenger killed in a car accident would normally not be called "a poor bugger"—not because death is too serious an event to cause such a comment but because of the passenger's totally passive role in the event: the fisherman wanted to do something and couldn't do it, so in his case the phrase *poor bugger* is appropriate, but in the case of the car passenger, his totally passive role clashes with the component 'he can't do things like other people'.

What exactly one feels is left unspecified: the collocation *poor bugger* invites the interpretation that the "bad feeling" expressed is akin to pity, whereas the collocation *silly bugger* suggests, rather, something like condescension or mild contempt.

3.4 Bullshit

Bullshit is mentioned in the OED (1972) Supplement with the comment "coarse slang," and with the gloss "rubbish, nonsense." The very fact that it is mentioned in the supplement, not in the OED itself, indicates the compilers' perception that the word is rather marginal in (British) English; and the qualifier "coarse slang" points in the same direction.[5] In America, it must be rather marginal, too, if it is possible for a major dictionary, such as *Chambers English dictionary*, not to include it at all.

But in Australia, *bullshit* is not a marginal word by any means. Nor is it perceived here as "coarse slang." On the contrary, it is a vital ingredient of what Colin Bowles calls "basic Australian." Furthermore, here it doesn't mean "rubbish, nonsense," but something much more complex, and much more culture-specific than that. What exactly, I will try to establish.

First, however, it should be pointed out that in Australian English, *bullshit*, far from being on the outskirts of the lexicon, gave rise to a whole extended family of words and expressions, all expressing a characteristically Australian outlook on life and reflecting characteristic Australian attitudes. This extended family includes *bull*, *bulls*, *bullo*, *bullsh* or *bulsh*, *bullswool* or *bull's wool*, *bull dust*, *bulldust*, *bull crap*, *bullcrag*, *bullock*, *bull artist*, *bullshit artist*, *bulldust artist*, *bulldust* (verb), *bulldusted*, *bullduster*, *bull artist*, *bullshit artist* (and hence a whole chain of other "artists": *booze artist*, *metho artist*, *bash artist*, *gee-up artist* [of a coach], and so on).[6] Most of these, as far as one can tell, are exclusively Australian. As Baker (1970) observed: "We have elaborated few U.S. expressions more than the vulgarism *bullsh*t* for nonsense and humbug. At least, it is to be presumed that this is an Americanism, although the vast number of variants we have evolved shows that we have made it almost native" (134).

It is true that not all of these descendants of *bullshit* flourish in contemporary Australian English: several of them, in particular the euphemistic *bullsh*, *bulldust* (and its derivatives), and *bullswool* are perceived as archaic. No doubt this is related to the general decline of traditional Australian culture and to its growing Americanization. Like other cultures, Australian culture in the twentieth century is undergoing rapid transformation (without, however, losing in the process all its characteristic and unique features). The history of the *bullshit* family in Australia reflects both the continuity and the change.

One thing which is largely gone is the need for euphemism. At a time when words like *fuck* and its derivatives are rapidly spreading, innocent old-time euphemisms like *bullsh*, *bulldust,* and *bullswool* (also *frogsh* and *sheepsh*), sound touchingly prudish, provincial, and somewhat ridiculous.

I have quoted earlier C. Hartley Grattan's comment that "English people profess to find Australian men foul-mouthed." But in the traditional Australian society, men were not always "foul-mouthed": they tended to be "foul-mouthed" among "mates," but not "in front of the ladies" or in "polite society." (In fact, the phrase "excuse the language" is still very common in Australia, witnessing both the generally felt need to use "the language" and the need to restrain oneself in certain circumstances.)

By saying something like *bullsh* or *bulldust,* Australians could, so to speak, have their cake and eat it: they could indulge both their need to express their opinions and their feelings by "saying some bad words" (and thus breaking some social taboos) and their need to show that they can be civil, that they know how to behave (when they are not "with mates"), an attitude which can be illustrated with the following sentence:

Ah bullshit—s'cuse, I mean, I don't believe it. (Macklin 1975, from TAND reject files, quoted in Frigo 1989:4)

This double need, indulged in words like *bulldust*, can be portrayed as follows:

I feel something
because of this, I want to say something
some people say that some words are bad words
I want to say something of this kind
I know some people think it is bad to say something like this
because of this, I will say something else
I think everyone can know what I want to say

In what follows, I will adduce a number of illustrative sentences including *bull*, *bullshit*, *bulldust*, and *bullswool*, assuming that all these words have a common core and differ mainly in the presence or absence of the euphemistic components spelled out above.

In many cases, *bullshit* and its relatives appear to convey something like "non-sense," as OEDS suggests. For example:

He said, with a straight face, that if one wanted to say politely 'nonsense' one used the word 'bulsh' or 'bullshit'. (Barcs 1980, TAND)

In other contexts, *bullshit* and its relatives appear to imply something like "lie," for example:

'I'm seventy-five percent Irish', said Mick.
'You're seventy five percent bulldust, too', said Joe. (J. Cleary 1954, TAND)

'I come here to get the truth out of you, and no bull. See?' (D'Arcy Niland 1959, Wilkes 1978)

In yet another context, *bullshit* and its variants appear to imply above all something like "empty talk," often, sentimental talk, for example:

The old man was always talking about England and calling it the Mother Country and Home, but it sounded all bull to me. (Dal Stivens 1951, Wilkes 1978)

Very often, this "empty talk" is combined, in the speaker's perception, with intellectual pretences, with pomposity, with education, and also with politics, the common implication being that by indulging in that "empty talk" (that is, in that "bull" or "bullshit"), those who do it try to impress other people and obtain in this way some advantages. (As Renwick [1980] points out, "it is very difficult to impress an Australian" [24], and utterances which can be seen as an attempt to do so are likely to be dismissed as "bullshit.") For example:

'The real Aphrodite was supposed to be born in Cyprus.' 'I wouldn't know about all that bullsh.' (R. Beilby 1970, TAND)

Education, if he [the Australian worker] thinks of it at all, seems to him a childish trick whereby the 'bullshit artist' seeks to curry favour with the boss and thus get a better job. (Murray Sayle 1960, Wilkes 1978)

Never mind Billy Hughes. He's a politican, and 'bulsh' is their stock-in-trade. (V.C. Hall 1947, TAND)

The ACT [Australia's capital, and the seat of the Parliament] has long held prior right to the title of Bull-land due to the vast amount of bull's wool issuing from it since the first sod was turned. (Kings Cross Whisper 1968, TAND)

But *bullshit* (and the rest of the family) can also refer to what is perceived as empty talk without any implications of cynical, self-interested deception:

It's an intangible thing, a sort of veneration for an idea for its own sake. It's hard to put into words. You'd probably call it bullshit. (Eric Lambert 1965, Wilkes 1978)

Before I try to posit an explication of *bullshit* that will try to account for all these different aspects, I will first adduce a few more examples of its use collected from recent Australian writings. They refer to art (1), to poetry (2), to bureaucracy (3), to rock music (4), and to sport (5) and (6):

1. 'Life', Billy de Vere raised his glass, 'imitating art. Or should I say', he lowered his voice and winked 'life imitating bullshit'. (Carey 1982:64)

2. 'For Christ's sake', said Timmy, 'not poetry again!' Timmy felt it was sissy. Even that bullshit of Lawson's. (Haylen 1965, TAND reject files)

3. 'Eugene's a good kid, he's very bright around the office on keeping tabs on all the bureaucratic bullshit'. (Rowe 1972, TAND reject files)

4. Australian audiences have a very low bullshit tolerance. There's not much scope for lyrical or musical pretentiousness in Australia. (*The Big Australian Rock Book*, quoted in Fiske & Turner 1987:23)

5. Once you develop a profile as a footballer it is amazing how many bullshit stories start about you. (Daley & Clyde 1995:43).

6. To any player who sobs that he has had to turn to drugs to escape from the pressure and demands of the game, my response is 'What a load of bullshit!' All that shows is a weakness in character. (Daley & Clyde 1995:142).

What does *bullshit* mean, then, in Australia? I propose the following explication:

bullshit
(a) I know: some people say many things
(b)   no one can know anything about anything because of these things
(c)   they want other people to think that they say something good
(d)   some other people think this
(e) I don't want to be like these other people
(f) when I think about it I feel something bad
(g) because of this, I want to say something
(h) some people say that some words are bad words
(i) I want to say something of this kind

Component (a) suggests a distrust of eloquence or verbosity, and of people who say "many things"; (b) indicates that the things people say may be false or represent empty talk; (c) suggests that the things said may sound "good" and that they may be calculated to impress and/or deceive; (d) refers to "other people's" gullibility and naiveté; (e) shows the speaker (the one who says *bullshit*) is not gullible or naive and that he(she) can see through any attempts to deceive or to impress him(her); (f) refers to the speaker's "bad feelings," and (g)–(i) to his or her determination to respond to the provocation with a "bad" word.

As McGregor says, "most Australians dislike what they call bullshit" (1981:46); and "most of what is pumped out of the word factories is 'bullshit'" (Horne 1964:4). The explication given above attempts to articulate what exactly it is that "most Australians" dislike.

Ironically, the kind of language that the "typical Australian" (as described by Russel Ward or Sidney Baker) used to dismiss as "bullshit" is best illustrated by the pronouncements of some contemporary theoreticians who try to define such a "typical Australian" out of existence. One example: "Stereotypes such as the 'bushman' figure described by Russel Ward . . . arise because the discourse of nationalism is operating in the 'distanced zone' of authoritative discourse remote from the exigencies of everyday life" (Ashcroft & Salter 1994:74). (The examples could be multiplied: the "heteroglossia of Australian cultural discourses," "a centripetal force imposing the unity upon the heteroglot," "the exotopic dimension," and so on.)

Although "stereotype" is now used widely as a dirty word, the very existence of words such as *bullshit* (with their distinctive Australian meaning) demonstrates that stereotypes, like clichés, can be true. Such words may seem unworthy of serious attention, but in fact they are more eloquent, in their humble way, than many a heteroglot or exotopic discourse.

4. Conclusion

In the two hundred years of its existence, Australian English has developed many features which reflect Australian national character, values, attitudes, and the Australian collective experience (for further discussion, see Wierzbicka 1986, 1991a, 1992b). This chapter has discussed two categories of words which are particularly revealing of the traditional Australian ethos: uniquely Australian speech act verbs *shout, dob in,* and *whinge,* and some characteristic Australian swearwords (mainly "*b*-words"). Both these categories reflect the traditional Australian cult of "toughness," male solidarity, anti-authoritarianism, antisentimentality, cynicism, anti-intellectualism, dislike of verbosity, pretentiousness, snobbery, articulate speech, social graces, polite conventions, and class distinctions. Last, but not least, they express Australian humor. They are part and parcel of the traditional Australian way of life. This way of life is of course changing, and some of the attitudes and values are changing, too. The fact that the word *mate* is increasingly used by women and with reference to women is significant in this respect, as is also the fact that while the word *bastard* as an expressive epithet is still thriving, the use of its feminine counterpart *bitch* (treated in Baker 1970 [1945] on a par with *bastard*) has apparently declined considerably.

But even the fact that the use of *mate,* instead of dying out, is spreading to women (and, of course, to "New Australians") suggests that there is life in the old dog yet.

It will be fitting, I think, to close this chapter with the words of a respondent quoted in Hugh Mackay's (1994) book *Reinventing Australia: The mind and mood of Australia in the 90s,* a quote which reflects both the changes and the continuity in Australian culture, as reflected in Australian English:

[My mother] was a doormat to my father and I'm buggered if I'm going to end up like that. I'm *buggered* if I am. They can just put up with it. I've got a life too. (3)

Appendix

SUMMARY OF THE FORMULAE

chiack (e.g. X was chiacking Y)
(a) for some time, X was saying some bad things about person Y
(b) X wanted Y to hear it
(c) X was saying these things as people say bad things about someone
(d) when they think something like this at the same time:
(e)   I want to say these things about this person
(f)   because I want people here to feel something good
(g)   not because I want this person to feel something bad
(h)   I can do it because this person is someone like me
(i) people think: men feel something good when they can do this with other men

chat (e.g. X had a chat with Y)
(a) for some time, X was saying some things to Y
(b) as people say things to someone
(c) when they think something like this at the same time:
(d)   I want to say some things to this person
(e)   not because I want this person to know something
(f)   I think this person wants the same
(g)   I think this person will say some things to me during this time
(h)   I think I will feel something good because of this
(i)   I think this person will feel the same

yarn (e.g. X had a yarn with Y)
(a) for some time, X was saying some things to Y about some things
(b) as people say things to someone
(c) when they think something like this at the same time:
(d)   I want to say some things to this person about some things
(e)   I want to do it for some time, not a short time
(f)   I think this person wants the same
(g)   I think this person will say some things to me about these things during this
       time
(h)   I think I will feel something good because of this
(i)   I think this person will feel the same
(j) people think: it is good if men can do this from time to time with other men

shout₁ (e.g. X shouted a round for everyone)
(a) X said something like this:
(b)   I will have a drink now

(c)   I want everyone else to have a drink at the same time
(d)   I will pay for this
(e) X did it as men often do when they are with other men
(f) people think:
> it is good if men do this with other men

(g)   it is good if one person does it after another person
(h)   when men do this, they feel something good because of this

shout₂ (e.g. X shouted Y a trip to Sydney)
(a) X said something like this to someone:
(b)   I want to do something good for you
(c)   I will pay for this
(d) people think:
> it is good if people say this to other people

(e)   when people do this, they feel something good because of this

dob in (e.g. X dobbed Y in)
(a) X said something like this to Z about Y:
(b)   "I want you to know that Y did something bad"
(c) X knew:
(d)   X is someone like Y
(e)   Z is not someone like Y
(f)   Z can do bad things to someone like Y
(g) people think: if someone does something like this, it is very bad
(h) people feel something bad when they think about things like this

whinge (e.g. X was whinging)
(a) for some time, X was saying something like this:
> "something bad is happening to me"

(b) X was saying it as people say things
(c) when they want to say something like this:
(d)   something bad is happening to me
(e)   I feel something bad because of this
(f)   I can't do anything ("about it")
(g)   I want someone to know this
(h)   I want someone to do something because of this
(i)   I think no one wants to do anything
(j)   I want to say this many times because of this
(k) people think: it is bad if someone does this

bloody (e.g. bloody X!)
(a) when I say something about X, I feel something
(b) I don't want to say what I feel
(c) I want to do something else
(d) some people say that some words are bad words
(e) I want to say something of this kind

a bastard (e.g. he is a bastard)
(a) I think about him like this:
(b)   I know men of this kind
(c)   men of this kind are bad men

(d)   men of this kind can do very bad things
(e) because of this, when I think about him I feel something bad
(f) I want to say something bad about this man
(g) people say that some words are bad words
(h) I want to say something of this kind

bastard₂ (e.g. poor bastard, clever bastard)
(a) I think about this man like this:
(b)   I know men of this kind
(c) because of this, when I think about him, I feel something
(d) I don't want to say what I feel
(e) I want to say something else
(f) some people say some words are bad words
(g) I want to say something of this kind

bugger! (interjection)
(a) I think: something bad happened
(b) I don't want to say "very bad"
(c) because of this, I think:
(d)   I want to do something
(e)   I can't do it
(f) because of this, I feel something bad
(g) because of this, I want to say something
(h) some people say that some words are bad words
(i) I want to say something of this kind

bugger (noun)
(a) I know: something bad happened
(b) I don't want to say "very bad"
(c) because of this, I think:
(d)   this man wants to do some things
(e)   this man can't do things (like other people)
(f) because of this, I feel something bad
(g) I want to say something bad about this man
(h) some people say that some words are bad words
(i) I want to say something of this kind

bullshit
(a) I know: some people say many things
(b)   no one can know anything about anything because of these things
(c)   they want other people to think that they say something good
(d)   some other people think this
(e) I don't want to be like these other people
(f) when I think about it I feel something bad
(g) because of this, I want to say something
(h) some people say that some words are bad words
(i) I want to say something of this kind

6

Japanese Key Words and Core Cultural Values

1. How "unique" is Japanese culture?

In his combative book *The myth of Japanese uniqueness*, Dale (1986) argues that there is nothing "particularly unique" about Japanese culture, and he attacks the long tradition of *nihonjiron*, that is, discussions attempting "to define the specificity of Japanese identity." Some of the figures cited by Dale in this connection are indeed striking ("According to the Nomura survey, in the roughly 30 years from 1946 to 1978, approximately 700 titles were published on the theme of Japanese identity, a remarkable 25% of which were issued in the peak three year period from 1976 to 1978" [15]).

I would agree that there is nothing "particularly" unique about Japanese culture, for every culture is unique. For this very reason, however, I cannot agree with the claim that Japanese uniqueness is a myth. It is true, of course, that to study a culture in its uniqueness we need an appropriate methodology. It is also true that "unique systems are intelligible only in reference to wider, general propositions" (33), and that "the unique can only be conceptualized if it has an element of recurrency" (34). But this is not a reason NOT to study Japanese culture in its uniqueness, or to try to "locate Japan uniquely in a universal map" (Lebra 1976:xiv). The fact that "logically, all societies might be placed uniquely on a universal map" (Dale 1986:33) makes the project of studying Japan in this perspective all the more interesting; and the necessary "recurrent elements" are provided by universal human concepts, lexicalized in all the languages of the world.

It is widely agreed (*pace* Dale 1986) that certain crucial features of Japanese culture and society are reflected in Japanese words such as *on*, *giri*, *amae*, and *wa* and that one cannot understand Japan without understanding the concepts encapsulated in these words (cf. e.g. Benedict 1947; Nakane 1973; Doi 1981; Lebra 1976; Moeran 1989). But when commentators try to explain these concepts in terms of English words such as *gratitude*, *justice*, *honor*, *dependence*, and *harmony* the effect is often to obfuscate them rather than clarify.

Of course, English words of this kind are usually offered as approximate glosses, not as exact equivalents; and the use of such glosses is often unavoidable, or at least understandable, as a first approximation. But if one does not move from these approximations and vague analogies to something more precise one remains locked in one's own cultural perspective.

The point is that English words such as those mentioned above are "culture-laden," too—no less than the Japanese words which they are supposed to explain. One cannot clarify culture-laden words of one language in terms of culture-laden words of another. A Japanese scholar, Setsuko Ono (1976) sees many Western misinterpretations of Japan as deriving from an uncritical reliance on "Western words":

> Each Western word is loaded with cultural and historical meanings, associations. A word such as "hierarchy" means automatically an order of power relationships. It has a connotation of oppression, denial of individualism, its rights and freedom which should lead to equality of men. In Japan, hierarchy simply signifies ritual order. It defines neither the location of power nor responsibility. Thus Western words as such are not appropriate for describing non-Western reality. (26)

Clearly, Ono suspects that the word *hierarchy,* frequently used in Western discussions of Japan, not only misrepresents Japanese social reality and cultural assumptions but also implicitly poses a negative judgment (in virtue of its negative connotations). It could be argued, in response, that *hierarchy* doesn't have inherent negative connotations and can also be used in perfectly neutral contexts, but this is not the point. In essence, Ono is quite right in observing that Western literature on Japan abounds in would-be "descriptions" which are in fact misrepresentations and which are often phrased in pejorative terms. Consider, for example, the following passage:

> De Vos and Wagatsuma (1973, p.50) stress that for Japanese adults passive, dependent, yet manipulative roles are acceptable. (. . .) This is possible because, according to Beardsley (1965, p.378), "institutionalized male roles in Japanese society tolerate self-centred, juvenile dependency as one way of performing the role." (Morsbach & Tyler 1986:303)

No doubt, the authors chose the words *manipulative* and *juvenile* with the intention to describe Japanese cultural patterns rather than to condemn or ridicule them, but this doesn't alter the fact that these words are inherently pejorative and that they suggest to the reader a negative evaluation of what they purport to describe.

The problem cannot be solved by the use of overt disclaimers, as in the following passage, where the Japanese value of *amae* ("centering around passive dependency needs in hierarchical relations," Morsbach & Tyler 1986:300) is discussed:

> It is a manifestation of narcissistic selfishness (if that can be said in a non-pejorative way without at the same time getting too clinical) in which the person wishes to merge with others in a loving, heart-warming relationship (Doi, 1972, p.382). It's the expectation that one's dependency is at the same time the other's delight. (301)

Terms like *manipulative, juvenile,* and *narcissistic selfishness* simply *cannot* be used in a non-pejorative way: they are not just "Western" but also heavily prejudicial.

Nor does it help to add a positive-sounding adjective to an inherently pejorative noun, as in the following sentence:

> As a third feature of Japanese socialization, the development of empathetic capacities for vicarious identification is crucial to responsible paternalism. . . . The Western image of "paternalism" connotes an instrumental-exploitative use of a contract-bound labor force towards whom a boss feels little or no sense of personal involvement, let alone belonging. The Japanese, in contrast, tend to believe the political and social myth about their nation, about their company or their occupational groups, or about their family collectivity. (Wagatsuma & De Vos 1984:451)

But in fact, it is not "the Western image of 'paternalism'" which is negative but the English word *paternalism* itself. No matter how much one tries, one cannot present an impartial picture of Japanese cultural patterns if words of this kind are used.

Even when Western students of Japan are aware of the dangers involved in the use of "Western words," they often get tangled in these words and leave their readers bewildered and confused. For example, Zimmerman (1985) writes: "The Westerner is often puzzled by the Japanese use of the word 'sincerity,' because to the Japanese sincerity is not openhearted truthfulness but a complex amalgam of ideas. The basic theme in this is that a 'sincere' person is one who fulfills obligations no matter what and avoids giving offense . . . , or, to put it another way, one who strives for harmony in all relationships" (74).

The Western reader may well wonder what all this has to do with "sincerity" and how Japanese people can use the word *sincerity* in those complex and unfamiliar ways. But of course Japanese people don't use the word *sincerity* at all. What Zimmerman is really trying to say is that Japanese doesn't have a word corresponding in meaning to the English word *sincerity*; and that the Japanese words often glossed as "sincerity" really mean something different and quite culture-specific. But he doesn't say what.

A similar confusion regarding the value of 'sincerity' is evident in Benedict's (1947) discussion of this subject, despite the keen awareness of the problem, evidenced in other chapters of her book: "A basic meaning of 'sincerity', as the Japanese use it, is that it is the zeal to follow the 'road' mapped by the Japanese code and the Japanese spirit" (217). The concept which Benedict really had in mind was not 'sincerity' but *makoto:*

> When modern Japanese have attempted to make some one moral virtue supreme over all the "circles," they have usually selected "sincerity." Count Okuma, in discussing Japanese ethics, said that sincerity (*makoto*) is the precept of all precepts; the foundation of moral teachings can be implied in that one word. Our ancient vocabulary is void of ethical terms except for one solitary word, *makoto*. (212–213).

But if 'makoto' is a uniquely Japanese concept, very different from the English concept of 'sincerity', one cannot explain the former by means of the latter. (The same applies to another Japanese key concept, 'magokoro', also usually glossed as "sincerity.")

How can one, then, explain Japanese key concepts to cultural outsiders? It is all very well for Setsuko Ono to insist that "Western words . . . are not appropriate for describing non-Western reality," but for Westerners, "Western words" are all they have and all they can rely on. If Japanese culture couldn't be explained to Westerners "in Western words," then it couldn't be explained to them at all.

Dale (1986) voices in this context the following complaint: "As Nakane repudiates Western concepts because they make Japan appear feudal, so Ono denies Westerners the right to discuss Japan because their languages impose concepts of political power when only rituals of culture exist" (59).

Clearly, Dale has a point; but so does Ono. The solution to the dilemma is not to dismiss Ono's concerns as unjustified but to try to build on a foundation of shared concepts. Japanese culture—or any other non-Western culture—CAN be explained to Westerners, but not in terms of culture-specific English words such as *sincerity*, *harmony*, and *dependence*. Rather, it can be explained via English words which do have semantic counterparts in Japanese, and in any other language of the world, that is, via lexical universals.

In this chapter, I will explore and analyze seven Japanese words encoding concepts widely regarded as particularly culture-specific and culturally revealing: *amae, enryo, wa, on, giri, seishin,* and *omoiyari.*

The existing literature on these concepts is rich and insightful, but it lacks methodological rigor and doesn't aim at articulating semantic invariants. Nor does it examine minimal pairs, try to determine the role of context, or investigate unacceptable sentences (as a source of insight and evidence, etc.). The relation between the goal of this chapter and those of the existing literature can be compared to that between phonology and phonetics. My goal is not to collect "new data" but to analyze the existing data in a way which would make sense of it all.

Finally, while it is beyond the scope of this chapter to try to show how the key words discussed here explain and epitomize many diverse aspects of the Japanese "ethnography of speaking" (cf. Hymes 1962), it should be noted that (as mentioned earlier) any account of the Japanese "cultural scripts" (see Wierzbicka In press a) must reveal important links between these key words and the Japanese patterns of discourse.

2. Amae

According to Doi, *amae* is "a peculiarly Japanese emotion," although it has "universal relevance" (1981:169). It is "a thread that runs through all the various activities of Japanese society" (26). It represents "the true essence of Japanese psychology" and is "a key concept for understanding Japanese personality structure" (21). It is also a concept which provides "an important key to understanding the psychological differences between Japan and Western countries" (Doi 1986[1974]:310).

The extraordinary success of Doi's book (both critical and popular) is best illustrated by the fact that within little more than a decade it ran to well over one hundred editions (Dale 1986:121). As Dale points out, it was enthusiastically received not only in Japan but also in the West.

But what exactly *is amae*? Doi (1986[1974]) points out that there is no single word in English (or in other European languages) equivalent to it, a fact that "the Japanese find . . . hard to believe" (308). Nonetheless, in his writings, Doi has offered innumerable clues which enable us to construct an English version of the concept of 'amae'—not in a single word, of course, but in an explication. Doi has himself devoted an entire book (Doi 1981) to the elucidation of this concept and its ramifications, and in the decade which followed the publication of this book, numerous other authors have tried to elaborate on Doi's analysis.

Doi explains that "*amae* is the noun form of *amaeru*, an intransitive verb which means 'to depend and presume upon another's benevolence'" (1974:307). It indicates "helplessness and the desire to be loved" (1981:22). The adjective *amai* means 'sweet', both with reference to taste and with reference to human relations: "if A is said to be *amai* to B, it means that he allows B to *amaeru*, i.e. to behave self-indulgently, presuming on some special relationship that exists between the two" (1981:29).

Amaeru can also be defined "by a combination of words such as 'wish to be loved' and 'dependency needs'" (1974:309). The Japanese dictionary *Daigekan* defines *amae* as "to lean on a person's good will" (Doi 1981:72), or "to depend on another's affection" (1981:167). Other dictionary glosses include "to act lovingly towards (as a much fondled child towards its parents)," "to presume upon," "to take advantage of" (Brinkley's); "to behave like a spoilt child," "be coquetish," "trespass-on," "take advantage of," "behave in a caressing manner towards a man"; "to speak in a coquettish tone," "encroach on (one's kindness, good nature, etc.)" (Takenobu); "presume on another's love," "be coquettish," "coax" (Kenkyusha), and so on.

Morsbach and Tyler (1986), who have analyzed fifteen passages from Japanese literature referring to *amae*, used in their translations of these passages the following English glosses, among others: "take advantage of," "play baby," "make up to (someone) and get their sympathy," "coax," and "act spoilt." Morsbach and Tyler comment on the use of *amae* in these passages as follows: "As these fifteen examples illustrate, *amae* has a variety of meanings centering around passive dependency needs in hierarchical relationships" (300). But the term *hierarchical relationship* is misleading. For example, it doesn't seem to fit the popular song (quoted by the authors) in which a female singer is asking her lover to permit her to *amaeru* to him:

On the day
we are finally one
hug me,
hug me,
and you'll let me play baby, won't you?

Morsbach and Tyler point out "that at the time this song was popular there were no less than three pop tunes in which the word *amaeru* was used" (296).

Many scholars link the importance of *amae* in Japanese culture with specific features of Japanese social structures. For example, De Vos (1985) writes:

In the traditional Japanese system there were no "rights" on the part of the subordinate. The only recourse for subordinates in the past, since they had no contractual relationships, was to hope to induce kindness and benevolence in their superiors. These feelings were induced by invoking potential feelings of nurturance and appreciation from them. This capacity to induce kindness and benevolence in superiors in a manipulative manner is called *amaeru* in Japanese. (160)

This is helpful but not entirely satisfactory either. In particular, the term *superior* has all the disadvantages of the term *hierarchical,* and the term *manipulative* carries with it a negative value judgment and reflects a Western perspective.

The most useful clue to the concept of 'amae' is provided by the reference to the prototype on which this concept is based—a prototype which is not difficult to guess. "It is obvious that the psychological prototype of *amae* lies in the psychology of the infant in its relationship to its mother"; not a newborn infant but an infant who has already realized "that its mother exists independently of itself. As its mind develops it gradually realises that itself and its mother are independent existences, and comes to feel the mother as something indispensable to itself, it is the craving for close contact thus developed that constitutes, one might say, *amae*" (Doi 1981:74).

This is the prototype. But—according to Doi—in Japan, the kind of relationship based on this prototype provides a model of human relationships in general.

> The Japanese term AMAE refers, initially, to the feelings that all normal infants at the breast harbour towards the mother—dependence, the desire to be passively loved, the unwillingness to be separated from the warm mother-child circle and cast into a world of objective "reality". It is Dr Doi's basic premise that in a Japanese these feelings are somehow prolonged into and diffused throughout his adult life, so that they come to shape, to a greater extent than in adults in the West, his whole attitude to other people and to "reality." (Bester 1981:8)

Gibney (1975) elaborates this theme as follows:

> The Japanese have their own word for extreme dependency, which has a simple equivalent in no other language. The word *amaeru* is related to the word *amai* ("sweet"). It means literally, "to presume on the affections of someone close to you." When the Japanese say someone is *amaete iru*, or in extreme cases, an *amaembo*, they mean that the person in question has an excessive need to be catered to, protected, or indulged, but not by just anybody. The person you depend on, the object of your passive *amae* is invariably your senior. He may be your father or your older brother or sister (the case of the dependent member of the family, who sponges on his relatives from cradle to grave, is familiar enough in any society). But he may just as well be your section head at the office, the leader of your local political faction, or simply a fellow struggler down life's byways who happened to be one or two years ahead of you at school or the university. . . . The *amae* syndrome is pervasive in Japan. (119)

But although *amae* is by no means restricted to family relationships, it is generally agreed that extrafamilial *amae* relationships are perceived in terms of a metaphor based on the relationship between parent and child.

> The leader's responsibility for attending to the needs and wants of those under him is indeed great. In return for the *amae* he satisfies and indulges, he exacts strong loyalty. He gets a big press, in a society which prefers people to principles more than most. He is constantly deferred to. One goes back again to the prototype of the *oyabun* ("the boss," "the parent") and the *kobun* ("the child," "the follower"). (Gibney 1975:164)

The *kobun* depends on and counts on the *oyabun's* good will—a good will which is expected to be unconditional, like a mother's love.

De Vos (1985), who compares the role of the *amae*-senior to that of a rabbi in Jewish society, emphasizes in particular the unconditional character of *amae*.

Basically, a Japanese expects his rabbi (who can be an older relative, someone who graduated from his college a year or two earlier, a corporate superior or the leader of a political clique) to help him cope with all of life's challenges—emotional, social and economic. The rabbi may well arrange his protegé's marriage; he will certainly give counsel on all sorts of personal problems and, above all, intercede with the powers-that-be to get the younger man promotions and to advance his career ambitions generally. But in sharp departure from the usual situation in the United States, a protegé in Japan does not necessarily feel obliged to justify such intercessions in his behalf by performing his job with uncommon competence or even by effective office politicking in support of his rabbi. All he feels his rabbi can legitimately expect of him is that he be loyal, sincere and dutiful. Mama, after all, did what she did out of love and not—ostensibly at least—because she expected any payback. (169)

Given all the complexity and versatility of the 'amae' concept, some have doubted that a unitary definition of it can be given at all. For example, Morsbach and Tyler (1986) observed: "As it is apparent even from Doi's definitions, *amae* has several levels of meaning and will not readily yield to a comprehensive definition" (290). I would argue, however, that while *amae* has indeed several semantic components and while it does not yield to a comprehensive definition easily, nonetheless such a definition is possible. In the light of the foregoing discussion, I propose the following:

amae
(a) X thinks something like this about someone (Y):
   I know:
   (b) when Y thinks about me, Y feels something good
   (c) Y wants to do good things for me
   (d) Y can do good things for me
   (e) when I am with Y nothing bad can happen to me
   (f) I don't have to do anything because of this
   (g) I want to be with Y
(h) X feels something good because of this

Doi stresses that *amae* presupposes conscious awareness. The component 'X thinks something like this . . .' reflects this. The presumption of a "special relationship" is reflected in the component 'when Y thinks about me, Y feels something good'. The implication of self-indulgence is rooted in the emotional security of someone who knows that he (she) is loved: "it is an emotion that takes the other person's love for granted" (Doi 1981:168). This is accounted for by the combination of components: 'Y wants to do good things for me', 'X can do good things for me', and 'when I am with Y nothing bad can happen to me'. The component 'I don't have to do anything because of this' reflects the "passive" attitude of an *amae* junior, who doesn't have to earn the mother-figure's good will and protection by any special actions.

A great deal has been written on the reasons for "the prominence of *amae* in Japanese society" (Doi 1981:173). According to Doi himself (1981:16), and to a number of other observers of Japanese society, this is linked with an "affirmative attitude toward the spirit of dependence on the part of the Japanese." Murase (1984) points out that "Unlike Westerners, Japanese children are not encouraged from an early age to emphasise individual independence or autonomy. They are brought up in a more or less 'interdependent' or *amae* culture" (319). He contrasts the Western culture, which he calls "ego culture," with the Japanese culture, which he calls "*sunao* culture," where *sunao*—like *amae*—symbolizes "trustful relationships" fostering "openness and dependence" (325). He also cites some other key words (besides *amae*) which "have been proposed as representing the essential nature of Japanese culture" and notes that they all point in the same direction: "empathy culture" (Minamoto 1969), "maternal principle" (Kawai 1976), "egg without eggshell" (Mori 1977), and so on.

Some aspects of Doi's discussion of *amae* have been challenged, perhaps not entirely without justification, by Dale (1986). But one doesn't have to accept all of Doi's ideas uncritically to agree with him that, first, the verb *amaeru* doesn't have an exact semantic equivalent in English (or, apparently, in any other European language), and also that the concept embodied in this word seems to be indeed extremely salient in Japanese culture (as documented, for example, by Morsbach & Tyler 1986). The frequent use of this word in Japanese pop tunes (as well as in other literary genres) shows that its status in Japanese culture is quite different from that of words like *coax* (repeatedly used by Dale as the supposed English equivalent of *amaeru*) in Anglo culture.

According to Murase (1984), the Western "ego culture" is individual-centered; and the personality type which it promotes is "autonomous," "self-expanding," "harsh and solid," "strong," "competitive," "active, assertive, and aggressive"; by contrast, the Japanese "*sunao* culture" is "relationship-oriented," and the personality type which it promotes is "dependent," "humble," "self-limiting," "mild and tender," "flexible and adaptable," "harmonious," "passive, obedient, and non-aggressive" (327). The relationships fostered by the "ego culture" are "contractual," whereas the relationships fostered by the "*sunao* culture" are "unconditional." Murase links this with the prevalence of the "maternal principle" in Japan as against the prevalence of the "paternal principle" in the West. He also stresses such specifically Japanese values as "adaptation through accommodation," "conformity, or the merging of self and other," "a naive, trusting and empathic relationship with others," "obedience and docility" ("without the negative connotation in English"), and, again and again, "dependence."

Clearly, perceptions of this kind are indeed highly consistent with the prominence of the feelings of trustful dependence elucidated in Doi's (1974 and 1981) discussions of *amae*. I hope that the explication of this crucial concept proposed here can help to make it a little more intelligible to the cultural outsider.

Challenging what he calls "the myth of *amae*" (1986:141), Dale observes that "until Doi's intervention," the word *amae* "was innocently translated into English by such words as 'coaxing', 'fawning', 'wheedling', etc. In short *amaeru* is the word habitually used to describe the behaviour of spoilt children when they play up to their parents to gain their indulgent attention" (122). But the fact that an attitude which in English could only be described with pejorative words in Japanese represents a cultural ideal sung about in popular songs (like "love" in English) confirms the basic validity of Doi's insight.

3. Enryo

Enryo expresses one of the greatest Japanese cultural values. It is frequently translated into English as "reserve" or "restraint," but Japanese-English dictionaries assign to it a bewildering variety of other English glosses. These include, in addition to "reserve" and "restraint," also "constraint," "diffidence," "coyness," "discretion," and "hesitation" (*Takenobu*), "reservation," "deference," "regard" (Kenkyusha), "ceremony," "modesty," and "shyness" (Takehara), and "backwardness" (Brinkley's). On the other hand, the English words offered in such lists as suitable glosses for *enryo* themselves are hardly ever matched with *enryo* in the opposite direction, that is in English-Japanese dictionaries. (As a rare exception to this, Hyojun Romaji Kai (1973) glosses the English phrase "stand on ceremony" as *enryo suru*, that is, "do *enryo*.")

It seems clear, therefore, that trying to understand the concept of *enryo* we cannot rely on any global English equivalents, because there simply aren't any. On the other hand, the literature on Japanese culture and society abounds in analytical comments on this concept, and these can be very helpful. For example, Lebra (1976) offers the following comment: "Pressure for conformity often results in a type of self-restraint called *enryo*, refraining from expressing disagreement with whatever appears to be the majority's opinion" (29).

In a similar vein, Smith (1983) remarks:

> Japanese children generally employ no self-referents at all in ordinary speech. It is also the case that a person is generally expected to call as little attention to himself as possible. The word most commonly used in this connection is *enryo*, 'restraint' or 'reserve'. One way to express *enryo* is to avoid giving opinions. (83)

Many students of Japan have pointed out that this avoidance of giving opinions is often a major obstacle in business negotiations between the Japanese and Westerners. For example, Reischauer (1988) observes:

> To Americans the Japanese style of negotiation can be confusing and even maddening, just as our style can seem blunt and threatening to them. An American businessman may state his case clearly from the start and in maximal terms for bargaining purposes. The Japanese may be appalled at this as an opening gambit, wondering what more the American may really have in mind. And the American in turn may feel that the cautious indirection of the Japanese is not only unrevealing but also smacks of deceit. (137)

Reischauer (1988:138) also notes that the Japanese often find Westerners "immature" because of the "frankness" with which they express their opinions.

But while the Japanese tend to refrain from expressing their opinions in general, there is an even stronger tendency to refrain from expressing dissenting opinions—and not only when one disagrees with what appears to be the majority's opinion but also when one disagrees with one's addressees in general, whoever they might be. For example, Smith comments: "The Japanese are at pains to avoid contention and confrontation . . . much of the definition of a 'good person' involves restraint in the expression of personal desires and opinions" (1983:44). This culturally endorsed restraint in the expression of opinions can be represented as follows:

I can't always say to other people: "I think this, I don't think this"

The avoidance of dissent includes, crucially, a reference to "the same":

> when someone says something
> I can't say to this person: "I don't think the same"

But this is only one aspect of *enryo*. As the quote from Smith's discussion of this concept adduced above suggests, *enryo* concerns not only people's personal opinions but also their desires, their preferences, their wishes. It calls for a self-effacement or an apparent self-effacement, which would stop people from saying clearly not only what they think but also what they want. As Smith points out, to show *enryo* one is expected not only to refrain from expressing one's opinions but also to "sidestep choices when they are offered. As a matter of fact, choices are less often offered in Japan than in the United States" (1983:87). Smith quotes in this context Japanese psychiatrist Takeo Doi's account of the strain he experienced on a visit to the United States, where he was constantly offered choices:

> Another thing that made me nervous was the custom whereby an American host will ask a guest, before a meal, whether he would prefer a strong or a soft drink. Then, if the guest asks for liquor, he will ask him whether, for example, he prefers scotch or bourbon. When the guest has made this decision, he next has to give instructions as to how much he wishes to drink, and how he wants it served. With the main meal, fortunately, one has only to eat what one is served, but once it is over one has to choose whether to take coffee or tea, and—in greater detail—whether one wants it with sugar, milk, and so on . . . I couldn't care less. (Doi 1981:12)

Smith comments:

> The strain must have been considerable, for in Japan, by contrast, the host, having carefully considered what is most likely to please this particular guest, will simply place before him a succession of an overwhelming number of items of food and drink, all of which he is urged to consume, in the standard phrase, 'without *enryo*'. It is incumbent on the guest to eat and drink at least part of everything offered him, whether or not he likes the particular item, in order not to give offence by appearing to rebuke his host for miscalculating what would please him. (1983:87).

A similar point was made by Morsbach and Tyler (1986:304), who link the Anglo-American cultural emphasis on personal choice with the Protestant tradition and who contrast the Anglo-American attitude to personal choice with the Japanese one:

> It is this particular insistence on individual choice (perhaps largely due to the basically Protestant heritage) that de-emphasizes emotional dependence in the Anglo-American culture which most readers basically accept as the norm. Whereas it is regarded as polite in Western society to present a visitor with as large a choice as possible when offering, say, food or drink, it is thought far more polite for the Japanese host to pre-select what his/her guest is likely to want. A dialogue such as the one described in Kingsley Amis's *The Anti-Death League* (set in England) would tend to embarrass the guest if he were a Japanese, whereas in its Western setting it is a ritual absolved with ease by most hosts and guests:

'Now,' said Dr Best, 'what's it to be? Sherry or Martini?'
'Sherry, please', said Leonard.
'Manzilla, fino or amontillado?'
'Amontillado, please'
'Pedro Domeq or Harvey's?'
'Harvey's, please'
'A lot or a little?'
'A little please'

Dialogues of this kind go against the grain of Japanese cultural norms because they are inconsistent with *enryo*. Since Japanese culture places a taboo on direct expression of one's wishes, it is culturally inappropriate to ask other people directly what they want. "Brutal," direct questions such as "Do you want X or Y?" force the addressee to violate *enryo*. In Anglo-American culture, they are "polite" and solicitous, but they are out of place in Japanese culture, with its emphasis on *enryo*. Thus, Mizutani and Mizutani (1987) state:

> Asking someone's wishes directly is also impolite in Japanese. Saying things like
>
> *Nani-o tabetai-desu-ka. (What do you want to eat?)
> *Nani-ga hoshii desu-ka. (What do you want to have?)
>
> should be limited to one's family or close friends. . . . To be polite, one should ask for instructions rather than directly inquire into someone's wishes.

The same cultural constraint prevents people in Japan from clearly stating their preferences, even in response to direct questions. As Mizutani and Mizutani (1987:117-118) point out, many Japanese, when asked about their convenience, decline to state it, saying instead, for example: "any time will do," "any time will be all right with me": "In actuality, one cannot always agree to what another person wishes, and one will then have to state one's own convenience anyway, but it is regarded as childish to immediately start stating one's own convenience when asked" (117–118).

To account for this aspect of *enryo,* I will add to its explication the following component:

> X thinks: I can't say: "I want this, I don't want this"

The Japanese tendency to shrink from saying what one wants or doesn't want is sometimes attributed to excessive shyness and uneasiness in relations with non-intimates. For example, Reischauer (1988) writes: "Each Japanese seems to be constantly worrying about what the other person thinks of him. He tends to be painfully shy in many of his personal relations and bound down by *enryo*, 'reserve' or 'constraint.' One of the commonest polite phrases is 'please do not have *enryo*,' but it seems to have little effect" (147).

Other writers interpret *enryo* as, above all, a form of social ritual. For example, Honna and Hoffer (1989) define this concept as follows:

> *Enryo*, or holding back, is a form of politeness, a device for maintaining a certain distance from those one does not know well or one considers as one's superiors. . . .

Since aggressiveness and frankness are considered rather negatively in Japanese social etiquette, it is graceful to behave in a 'holding back' way. For example, when they are offered a drink or food, it is courteous to refuse what is offered at least once in order to show that they are 'holding back,' that is, they are polite.[1]

But whether in any particular case *enryo* is due primarily to culturally induced "shyness" or to "courtesy" or "politeness," it appears that the primary motivation implied by the word itself can be identified as a desire not to hurt, offend, inconvenience, or embarrass anybody. This can be generalized in the form of the following semantic component:

(if I said/did this), someone could feel something bad because of this

Lebra (1976) comments on this aspect of *enryo*:

the virtue of *enryo*, 'self-restraint', is exercised not only to respond to group pressure for conformity but to avoid causing displeasure for others, regardless of their group membership. . . . The imposition of self-restraint to avoid hurting Alter's feelings . . . can reach an extreme that reveals immaturity even to most Japanese. The individual may acquiesce in the face of an intrusion on his rights or autonomy only because he is reluctant to offend another person by claiming his right. (71–72)

It seems to me, however, that the term *Alter* used here by Lebra is perhaps too restrictive: the "self-restraint" implied by *enryo* can be motivated not only by a concern for other people but also by a concern for oneself. By refraining from saying what one wants, one can protect oneself from embarrassment, or from a loss of face (cf. Zimmerman 1988:65–66). In fact, Lebra herself has suggested in a different context that *enryo* can be aimed at preventing Ego's own "bad feelings," and not only those of Alter's:

Enryo, social self-restraint, is a product of the suppression of individuality under the pressure of group solidarity and conformity, empathetic considerations for Alter's convenience or comfort, concern to prevent Ego's own embarrassment, and the wish to maintain Ego's freedom by avoiding social involvement without hurting Alter. Both achievement and *enryo* contain two mutually opposed motivations, altruistic and egoistic; the same style of behavior, in other words, can satisfy two or more, often contradictory, desires. (1976:252)

The formula 'if I said/did this, someone could feel something bad because of this' can account for both the "altruistic" and the "egotistic" dimensions of *enryo*. It invites the inference that the speaker is concerned about someone else's feelings, but it does not exclude the possibility that he is also trying to avoid any "bad feelings" for himself.

This vague, open-ended phrasing ('if I said/did this someone could feel something bad because of this') also accords well with the very wide range of situations to which *enryo* can apply, and with the wide range of its possible functions—features which are explicitly emphasized in Lebra's discussion. For example:

The more obtrusive Ego's behavior is, the more liable Ego is to lose face or to injure Alter's face. Cultural wisdom encourages Ego to be unobtrusive. Modesty and subtle refinement can thus be considered necessary qualities to display to defend face. Even shyness, bashfulness, or anticipatory embarrassment may be viewed as defensive in this light. Humility, besides being a virtue, is a social weapon to defend one's own and another's face. *Enryo* refers to the restraint Ego imposes upon himself in interaction with Alter when he is offered help, a treat, a gift, and the like. The same term describes both polite hesitation to accept a desired offer and polite refusal of an undesired offer. Thus, Alter does not always know how to take Ego's expression of *enryo*. Since *enryo* refers to polite hesitation in most instances, Alter is generally supposed to keep insisting that his offer be accepted. (1976:125)

At times, in discussing *enryo* Lebra adopts a somewhat skeptical or even critical tone, highlighted by her use of the word *immaturity*. This is in contrast to her other comments on *enryo*, such as the following: "Lack of aggression . . . can be taken as the very sign of maturity and humanness if considered in the light of empathetic consideration and self-restraint practiced so as not to offend others" (1976:41).

A number of other Japanese scholars have displayed a similarly ambivalent attitude to *enryo* as a cultural value and pointed to the difficulties which it creates for the Japanese in contact with Westerners. For example, Suzuki (1986) states:

We, used to assimilation and dependency, expect to project ourselves onto the other, and expect him to empathise with us. We have great difficulty with the idea that so long as our addressee is not Japanese we can't expect to have our position understood without strong self-assertion. But establishing our own viewpoint or position before our addressee has understood is not our forte . . . So when Japanese, who aren't good at foreign languages, don't show their true ability in international conferences and scholarly meetings, it is less because of their language skills than because of the weak development of the will to express themselves linguistically to sufficient degree. It lies furthermore in the underdeveloped ability to stand apart from the position taken by another and at least assert oneself to the extent of saying, "This is where I stand at this moment."(157)

It seems, however, that the concept of 'enryo' as such is neither negative nor positive, and that it lends itself to both negative and positive uses.

Dictionary glosses such as "discretion" and "modesty" suggest a positive evaluation, and so does the fact that the phrase *enryo naku* (literally "without enryo") is often glossed negatively: "boldly," "bluntly," "ruthlessly" (Kenkyusha); "boldly," "bluntly," "pitilessly," "indelicately" (Takenobu). On the other hand, the fact that people can be encouraged, cordially, to behave "without *enryo*" (for example, to eat and drink "without *enryo*") suggests that a positive evaluation is not part of the semantic invariant. To account for all these different features of *enryo*, I propose the following explication:

enryo
(a) when X is with person Y, X thinks something like this:
(b)   I can't say to this person:
(c)   "I want this, I don't want this"
(d)   "I think this, I don't think this"
(e)   if I did this, someone could feel something bad because of this
(f)   someone could think something bad about me because of this
(g) because of this X doesn't say things like this

(h) because of this X doesn't do some things
(i) people think: this is good

Component (a) shows that *enryo* is a conscious, or semi-conscious, attitude, based on certain thoughts; (b) shows the perceived need for self-restraint in a particular relationship; (c) shows that this self-restraint can apply to one's wants, and (d) that it can apply to the expression of opinions; (e) accounts for the fear of hurting or embarrassing someone; (f) accounts for the link between *enryo* and "face"; and (g) and (h) show that *enryo* manifests itself in people's behavior, both verbal (g) and non-verbal (h).

Going back now to the list of dictionary glosses (while keeping this explication in mind), it is easy to understand their heterogeneity. They are different from one another because they don't capture the concept as such but, for the most part, the different likely motivations of the behavior in question. For example, "deference" and "regard" are not part of the meaning of *enryo* as such, but given Japanese cultural attitudes, it is also easy to see why concepts of this kind can easily come to mind as a likely motivation of an *enryo* type of behavior. The same kind of behavior, however, can be motivated by "shyness" or "diffidence"—again, traits which are extrinsic to *enryo* as such but which can be naturally associated with it. The same applies to "discretion," "ceremony," "modesty," and the other glosses usually offered by dictionaries. I believe that the explication proposed here makes sense of all such associations; at the same time, it presents *enryo* as a unified Japanese concept, and it shows explictly how it is related to some basic features of Japanese culture and society.

4. Wa

> When we trace . . . the progress of our history, what we always find there is the spirit of harmony. Harmony is a product of the great achievements of the founding of the nation, and is the power behind our historical growth; while it is also a humanitarian Way inseparable from our daily lives . . . our country makes harmony its fundamental Way. Herein indeed lies the reason why the ideologies of our nation are different from those of the nations of the West. (*Kokutai no Hongi* 1949:93)

According to all students of Japan (writing in English), "the key Japanese value is harmony" (Reischauer 1988:136); and when they say "harmony" they really mean not "harmony" but *wa*. (Significantly, English-Japanese dictionaries never gloss *harmony* as "wa," although Japanese-English dictionaries do gloss *wa* as "harmony.")

Rohlen (1974), the author of an ethnography of a Japanese bank, used the company motto, *wa to chikara* (translated as "For harmony and strength"), as the title of his book, thus drawing special attention to the importance of *wa* in the Japanese business world. Rohlen comments on the meaning of *wa* as follows: "This important concept has received little attention from Western scholars, and no succinct expression of its meaning exists in English. . . . The precise sense of this notion is not . . . easily defined. The usual translations of 'harmony' or 'concord' are inadequate to convey the full sense of the word" (46–47).

Whatever *wa* means, all students of Japan agree on its vital importance in Japanese culture. Nakamura (1962:633) quotes in this connection the classical statement from the first article of Prince Shotoku's seventh-century constitution, widely regarded as a keystone of Japanese political tradition: "Above all else esteem concord" (that is, *wa*).

The prewar nationalist publication, *Principles of the national polity* (*Kokutai no Hongi*), which I quoted earlier, contrasts Western individualism with the Japanese emphasis on *wa* as a central value:

> In individualism there can exist co-operation, compromise, self-sacrifice, and so on, in order to adjust and reduce contradictions and oppositions, but in the final analysis there exists no real harmony (*wa*) . . . the *wa* of our country is not mechanical co-operation, starting from reason, of equal individuals independent of each other, but the grand harmony (*taiwa*) which maintains its integrity by proper statuses of individuals within the collectivity and by acts in accordance with these statuses. . . . After all, oppositions of opinions, as well as differences of interests deriving from [various] standpoints, are integrated into a unity of grand harmony proper to Japan and originating from a common source. Not conflicts, but harmony is final. (Kawashima 1967:264)

Rohlen stresses the "pre-eminent position of *wa* in the hierarchy of Japanese values" (1974:47). He draws attention to the fact that *wa* "is undoubtedly the single most popular component in mottos and names of companies across Japan," and he generalizes: "To achieve *wa* is certainly a major goal for any Japanese group, and it also is an essential ingredient in the attainment of other goals. In this regard, it is something like 'love' in American popular culture, for it is both a major means to social improvement and an end in itself."

Rohlen illustrates this claim as follows: "The term is also to be found in descriptions of the pleasures of company recreational outings, and the New Year's greetings from some offices (which the company magazine publishes) show individual pictures of the staff grouped around the character *wa* written large in the center of the design."

So what is *wa?*

Honna and Hoffer write: "There is no doubt that harmony within the group is a key value in Japanese society" (1989:122). This may seem virtually identical to Reischauer's statement quoted earlier, but in fact there is a difference: Honna and Hoffer do not speak about "harmony" in general but about "harmony within the group." This points to one of the differences between the English concept of 'harmony' and the Japanese concept of 'wa'. The way Honna and Hoffer continue the passage in question highlights this difference: "There is no doubt that harmony within the group is a key value in Japanese society, so that Japanese people tend to think and behave as a group. . . . the emphasis on the group often causes a Japanese to refrain from standing up for himself and follow the group instead."

Thus, *wa*—unlike *harmony*—has clear implications of "groupism" and "anti-individualism." (As has often been pointed out, the only Japanese word for something like "individualism"—*kojinshugi*—is pejorative; cf. Moeran 1986:85.) Honna and Hoffer (1989) explain:

> Conformism fosters a great sense of oneness shared by all the members in the same group. . . . A member who deviates from the group norms or disturbs the group consensus may have to take the risk of being excluded from the group. In fact, there is a Japanese saying which goes, "The nail that stands up will be pounded down." (122)

Trying to account for the group orientation of *wa*, we could start our explication of this concept as follows:

> all these people are like one thing
> all these people want the same

This formula corresponds very closely to the assessment of the social psychologist De Vos (1985):

> Japanese organisations are based on the implicit idea that group members are somewhat merged in their collectivity. They share the same goals and have similar implicit interpersonal affective patterns which allow them to work together in harmony without any form of individualistic or "alien" notions which would break up the basic melded harmony of the group. (170)

De Vos' idea of a "merger" of group members is reflected in the component 'all these people are like one thing', and his idea that group members share the same goals is reflected in the component 'all these people want the same'.

There are reasons to think, however, that (as suggested to me by Enoch Iwamoto), *wa* implies not so much a unity which is already there as a unity which is desired and aimed for. This would explain why *wa* is so often used in slogans and mottos and why it is used by companies rather than by naturally cohesive groups such as families. By appealing to *wa*, company management, coaches of sports teams and other people responsible for the success of group effort are trying to forge *wa* rather than to acknowledge what is already there. This suggests that it may be more justified to phrase the explication as follows:

> all these people think: we want to be like one thing
> all these people want the same

It might be added that De Vos' idea of group members being able to work together in harmony suggests one further component: 'they can do some things (together) because of this'. I will argue later that some such component is indeed justified. But first let us return to the Honna and Hoffer passage quoted above, and to its key terms *conformism* and *consensus*.

I believe that *conformism* is not a very helpful word in the present context because it is a culture-laden concept itself, which imposes on a Japanese concept a thoroughly non-Japanese perspective. But the word *consensus* is more helpful, because it is more readily replaceable with a culture-independent formula along the lines of what we have already proposed for *enryo*:

> they don't want this:
>   one of them says: "I want this"
>   another one says: "I don't want this"

According to all students of Japan, the role of consensus in Japanese culture can hardly be overestimated, and it is clearly an idea highly relevant to *wa*. The Japanese concept of 'nemawashii' (glossed sometimes as "Japanese-style spadework") is often invoked in this connection, with good reason.[2] Naotsuka et al. (1981) explain this concept as follows:

> Since group decisions are made on the basis of unanimous group consensus, and since direct and open confrontation is avoided whenever possible in Japan in the interest of harmony and smooth functioning, any plan up for decision needs a great deal of preliminary *nemawashii* [Japanese style spadework or the advance notice of plans pending]. . . . The plan is adapted and re-adapted to the feelings and attitudes of all concerned, these attitudes being painstakingly elicited during many individual informal conversations, so that a group consensus has gradually emerged before the formal decision meeting actually takes place. (quoted in Arima 1991:46)

Reischauer (1988) makes the following interesting comment on the links between *wa, consensus,* and *nemawashii* (cf. also Kume 1985):

> . . . they seek to achieve [harmony] by a subtle process of mutual understanding, almost by intuition, rather than by a sharp analysis of conflicting views or by clear-cut decisions, whether made by one-man dictates or majority votes. Decisions, they feel, should not be left up to any one person but should be arrived at by consultations and committee work. Consensus is the goal—a general agreement as to the sense of the meeting, to which no one continues to hold strong objections. One-man decrees, regardless of that man's authority, are resented, and even close majority decisions by vote leave the Japanese unsatisfied. (136)

It is worth noting in this connection that dictionaries often gloss *wa* not only as "harmony" but also as "peace" and "unity." "Peace" implies an absence of overt conflict and confrontation (that is, an absence of a situation where one person says, "I want this," and another, "I don't want this"); and "unity" implies that 'all these people are like one thing' and 'all these people want the same'. To quote Reischauer once more:

> Through consensus decisions achieved by negotiation and compromise, they tend to avoid the losses of open conflict and much of the wasteful friction produced by litigation, to which Americans are so prone. They also build up a solidarity that is invaluable both to small groups and to the nation as a whole. Japanese business prowess depends heavily upon this solidarity, and group identification lies at the heart of their national strength. (139)

The point about the relative absence of litigation in Japan is worth noting, as this aspect of Japanese society has always intrigued and fascinated Western observers. It seems clear that this absence of litigation is linked to the core value of *wa,* as has indeed been argued by Kawashima:

> . . . it is the concern for harmony that lies at the heart of the avoidance of litigation, which is unacceptable in that it "presupposes and admits the existence of a dispute and leads to a decision which makes it clear who is right or wrong in accordance with

standards that are independent of the wills of the disputants." (quoted in Smith 1983:41)

Smith also quotes in this connection another Japanese scholar, Ono Seichiro's, definition of *wa*: "Harmony [that is, *wa*] consists in *not making* distinctions; if a distinction between good and bad can be made, then there *wa* does not exist" (41).

This brings us to another aspect of *wa*, which was best elucidated by Smith himself. In particular, Smith cites a most illuminating article from the American magazine *Sports illustrated*, entitled "You've got to have *wa*," which discusses some characteristic features of Japanese baseball:

> . . . the piece deals with the impact of the concept of *wa* on American players who have been hired by Japanese teams. From this admirable essay, consider the following passage: "If you ask a Japanese manager what he considers the most important ingredient of a winning team, he would most likely answer, *wa*. If you ask him how to knock a team's *wa* awry, he'd probably say, 'Hire an American'." (50)

Smith implies that the most important ingredients of a Japanese winning team include not only a sense of group unity, a shared goal, and an absence of internal conflict, but also no visible desire for individual success as opposed to group success—no desire for individual "stardom," no desire for open distinctions between "good" and "not so good" members of the team. One must recall in this connection the Japanese saying reported earlier (following Honna and Hoffer): "The nail that stands up will be pounded down." It is not only a dissenting member of a group which is seen in Japan as such an obnoxious nail, but also a would-be star.

Obviously, it is not just team sports groups in Japan which cultivate *wa* (recall Rohlen's statement: "to achieve *wa* is certainly a major goal for any Japanese group"). In fact, De Vos (1985) argues that Japanese social groups in general can be compared to harmonious team sports groups. He points out that in contrast to America, where the emphasis is on personal autonomy and individual achievement, in Japan,

> the within-group emphasis is on cooperative behavior and the necessary social subordination of oneself, on the surface at least, into a harmonious mode of instrumental realization with others of one's own group. . . . Such cooperative behavior in turn can be put in a highly competitive frame of reference with respect to others outside the group. The ritually reinforced sense of social belonging within an organization takes precedence over any forms of individual realization of goals. Competitive inclinations cannot be released toward others close by, but are expressed through regulated competition as part of a group. The Japanese sense of accomplishment can be realized in group success. The analogy that comes immediately to mind is that Japanese groups are like football teams or other forms of team sports in which one can successfully compete only if one subordinates oneself to the group. Single stars who overemphasize their individual prowess may be disruptive to group spirit and, at least overtly, they must contain themselves within the group purpose in order to continue to function as part of the group. (178–179).

Any visible bid for individual stardom would of course be incompatible with the high value of "modesty," "self-effacement," and "humility" in Japan (cf. e.g. Honna and Hoffer 1989:20). Smith (1983) makes the following pertinent comment in this connection: "This outward humility is the *tatemae* (superficial appearance) used to maintain harmony, or *wa,* in human relations" (21).

Once again, then, what exactly does the word *wa* mean?

Rohlen (1974) offers the following explication of this crucial concept:

> *Wa* is not a metaphor. Nor is it some abstract or logical part of a system of distinctions. Rather, it is a quality of relationship, particularly within working groups, and it refers to the cooperation, trust, sharing, warmth, morale, and hard work of efficient, pleasant, and purposeful fellowship. Teamwork comes to mind as a suitable approximation. It is the complex of qualities that makes working relationships successful and enjoyable. Thus, *wa* is far from a concept of static harmony. It is a directly tangible thing that easily accommodates human frailties and differences as long as participants share a devotion to the success of the common effort and a respect for one another as partners in the enterprise. (47)

This is very helpful indeed, and yet—like all such definitions—it is also vague and elusive, and it suffers from the inevitable ethnocentric bias inherent in culture-specific English terms such as *cooperation*, *warmth*, and *morale*. Trying to free ourselves from such a bias, and to formulate our tentative analysis of *wa* in precise and culture-independent terms, we can propose the following:

wa
(a) these people want to be like one thing
(b) they all want the same
(c) they don't want this:
(d)   one of them says: "I want this"
(e)   another one says: "I don't want this"
(f) they don't want to say about some of them:
(g)   "these people did something good,
(h)   these people did something bad"
(i) they don't want to say about one of them:
       "this person did something very good"
(j) they want to do some things because of this
(k) they all feel something good because of this
(l) they can do many good things because of this
(m)they couldn't do these things if they didn't all want the same
(n) people think this is very good

Component (a) reflects the desire for unity and closeness; (b) spells out the unity of purpose; (c), (d), and (e) explain why *wa* is also glossed as "concord" and "peace"; (f), (g), (h), and (i) reflect "the absence of distinctions," the refusal to credit or blame individuals within the group or to treat one member of the group as a star; (j) shows the common effort; (k) shows the resulting "good feelings"; (l) and (m), the group's capacity for success, and finally, component (n) reflects the fact that *wa* is seen as a great social value.

I agree with Dale (1986:220) that the importance of interpersonal "unity" or "the unity of self and other" in Japanese culture can be exaggerated and misconstrued, and, like he, I do not believe that in this culture the concept of 'we' (*wareware*) can be more basic than the concept of 'I', or that the distinction between

'I' and 'thou' is blurred. Dale (1986:222) criticizes in this connection attempts at "constructing a mythology of culture which denies the existential distinction between 'I' and 'thou'".

But the concept of 'wa' as analyzed here does not blur the distinction between 'I' and 'thou' or 'I' and 'other people', and it is presented as based, ultimately, on the concept of 'I', not of 'we'. It is one thing to defend the universality of basic concepts such as 'I', and basic distinctions such as that between 'me' and 'other people', and another to deny well-documented salience and importance of concepts such as 'wa' in Japanese culture. Here as elsewhere, language itself provides clear evidence for the objective validity of the "myth."

5. On

5.1. A preliminary analysis of the concept 'on'

It has been said that societies can be divided into two types, those which are preoccupied with rights, and those which are preoccupied with obligations, and that while the West is very much "right-oriented," Japan is clearly an "obligation-oriented" society (cf. Kawashima 1967, quoted in Lebra 1986:107).

Nothing reflects this centrality of obligations in Japanese culture better than its two key words, *on* and *giri*, to be discussed in this and in the following section, respectively.

There is a wide consensus among students of Japan that, to quote Lebra, "the concept of 'on' . . . has played an essential role in Japanese culture" (1986:194). Some have even claimed that it "constitutes a basis for Japanese morality" (Lebra 1976:92). What exactly, then, does the word *on* mean? Dictionaries usually include long lists of alternative glosses which to an outsider may appear to be quite disparate. These include, among others, "favor," "kindness," "grace," "goodness," "benefit," "bene-factions," "obligation," and "a debt of gratitude."

More helpful, but still insufficient and puzzling, I think, is, a single gloss offered by Bellah (1985:225): "blessings." But of course more illuminating than any glosses are analytical definitions, such as the following one, offered by Mitsubishi (1987:151): "*On* is the act of bestowing on another person something (usually goods) which makes the receiver feel grateful and arouses in him a sense of obligation" (151).

The origin of the 'on' concept lies clearly in the samurai ethics: "In the old days, when a feudal samurai received an *on* from a lord, he repaid the favor by offering his service (military service). In this case, the *on* was the bestowal of a fief" (Mitsubishi 1987:151). In contemporary usage, the term is said to refer "at once to a favor granted by A to B and to a resultant debt B owes to A" (Lebra 1986:194).

As a first approximation, then, we could portray the meaning of *on* as follows:

X thinks about someone:
    this person did something good for me
    I didn't do something like this for this person
    I have to do something good for this person because of this

5.2. *On* and "good feelings"

A more detailed examination of the writings on *on* suggests that this concept is really much richer and much more complex than this simpler definition would imply. In particular, this definition ignores the question of the benefactee's feelings. Lebra (1986) writes: "An *on* must be accepted with gratitude since it is an evidence of the giver's benevolence or generosity; at the same time it must be carried as a burden, because the *on*, once granted, makes the receiver a debtor and compels him to repay" (194).

The word *gratitude* used by Lebra and by many other writers on the subject suggests that the *on* benefactee is expected to feel "something good" toward the *on*-benefactor (or *onjin*, as such a person is called in Japanese). At the same time, the word *burden*, also commonly used in connection with *on*, suggests that the benefactee feels "something bad."

The famous discussion of the concept 'on' in Ruth Benedict's book *The chrysanthemum and the sword* (1947) suggests a similar ambivalence. Benedict, too, used the word *burden*, which suggests "something bad." At the same time, however, she repeatedly mentioned the benefactee's expected "love" or "devotion" for the benefactor. For example, she writes: "'Remembering one's *on*' may be a pure outpouring of reciprocal devotion. A little story in a Japanese second-grade school reader entitled 'Don't forget the *on*' uses the word in this sense. It is a story for little children in their ethics classes" (100).

The story is about a cute little dog, Hachi, who was loved by his master "like a child of the house," and who after the master's death remains faithful to his memory and for years keeps looking for him every day. Benedict comments: "The moral of this little tale is loyalty, which is only another name for love." This, of course, implies, that the benefactee is expected to feel "something good" toward the *onjin*. If we tried to reflect this ambivalence in the definition of *on,* we would have to expand it along the following lines:

X thinks something like this about someone:
  this person did something good for me
because of this, when X thinks about this person X feels something good
at the same time, X thinks something like this:
  I didn't do something like this for this person
  I have to do something good for this person
X feels something bad because of this

But are both these feelings—the bad one and the good one—really parts of the semantic invariant of *on*? Benedict (1947) comments:

> A son who cares deeply for his mother can speak of not forgetting the *on* he has received from his mother and mean that he has for her Hachi's single-minded devotion to his master. The term, however, refers specifically not to his love, but to all that his mother did for him as a baby, her sacrifices when he was a boy, all that she has done to further his interests as a man, all that he owes her from the mere fact that he exists. It implies a return upon this indebtedness and therefore it means love. But the primary meaning is the debt, whereas we think of love as something freely given unfettered by obligation. (100).

Thus, according to Benedict, the emphasis is not on "love" but on "debt." But is the idea of "love" or (something like love) included in that concept at all? (In our terms, is it justified to include in the definition of *on* the component 'when X thinks about this person, X feels something good'?) Benedict herself seemed rather ambivalent on this point, but on the whole her comments do not seem to support this. For example, in her general discussion of *on* she writes:

> Both the Chinese and the Japanese have many words meaning 'obligations'. The words are not synonyms and their specific meanings have no literal translation into English because the ideas they express are alien to us. The word for 'obligations' which covers a person's indebtedness from greatest to least is *on*. In Japanese usage it is translated into English by a whole series of words from 'obligations' and 'loyalty' to 'kindness' and 'love', but these words distort its meaning. If it really meant love or even obligation the Japanese would certainly be able to speak of *on* to their children, but that is an impossible usage of the word. Nor does it mean loyalty, which is expressed by other Japanese words, which are in no way synonymous with *on*. *On* is in all its uses a load, an indebtedness, a burden, which one carries as best one may. A man receives *on* from a superior and the act of accepting an *on* from any man not definitely one's superior or at least one's equal gives one an uncomfortable sense of inferiority. When they say, 'I wear an *on* to him' they are saying, 'I carry a load of obligations to him', and they call this creditor, this benefactor, their '*on* man'. (99)

Comments of this kind seem to suggest that "good feelings" for the benefactor (gratitude, love, devotion, or whatever) are not really included in the concept of 'on'. At the most, this concept might include an EXPECTATION of such feelings, which is a different thing altogether ('people can think: I will feel something good because of this', or even, 'I have to feel something good because of this', rather than 'X feels something good because of this'). An expectation of this kind may in fact contribute to the "burden" of the benefactee, a burden which can at times be quite crushing. One more quote from *The chrysanthemum and the sword*:

> Love, kindness, generosity, which we value just in proportion as they are given without strings attached, necessarily must have their strings in Japan. And every such act received makes one a debtor. As their common saying has it: 'It requires (an impossible degree of) inborn generosity to receive *on*.' (113)

On the other hand, Lebra (1976) has claimed explicitly that an *on* debtor is not only expected to feel grateful but really "does" feel that gratitude (or at least that that is what the word *on* implies). "First of all, the *on* receiver is expected to feel, and does feel, grateful to the *on* giver" (92).

But the idea that *on* might imply "good feelings" on the part of the benefactee seems incompatible with the common view that *on* can be more or less cynically imposed on people, as evidenced by the common expressions *on o uru*, or *on ni kiseru*. For example, Mitsubishi (1987) states: "Any act of bestowal which is obviously motivated by the expectation of a repayment becomes a not too laudable act of *on wo uru* (to sell *on*). When one forces another to feel obligated and seeks repayment it becomes an act of *on ni kiseru* (to fasten *on*)" (151).

Incidentally, expressions of this kind demonstrate that the concept 'on' does not imply any kindness or benevolence on the part of the benefactor, even though both these words are commonly mentioned in the discussion of *on*. For example, Mitshubishi (1987:151) states: "When one returns kindness with ingratitude or bites the hand that feeds him, it is a depraved act described as '*on wo ada de kaesu*'" (151). But in fact, *on* implies that it is not just kindness which has to be "repaid" with something good, but any "debt"—or at least any major debt, whatever the creditor's motivations might be. The words *obligation* or *favor* are therefore more helpful in the description of *on* than words such as *kindness*.

But returning to the question of the debtor's expected "gratitude," I am inclined to think that the word *gratitude* is simply badly chosen. What Lebra really means, I think, is not "gratitude" but something else—and if I understand her intended point correctly, I think it is quite valid. This real point has to do not with the debtor's feelings but with his or her memory or thoughts. Lebra herself (1976) explains this point as follows:

> The moral significance of gratitude, however, lies not so much in an external demonstration as in Ego's awareness of being in debt, Ego's internalization of Alter as a benefactor, and Ego's retention of the memory of having received the *on*. Not to forget a received *on* is as important, if not more so, as to repay it; to be forgetful of a received *on* or to refuse to repay it would equally incur the accusation of being *on-shirazu* ('unaware of *on*', implying 'ungrateful'). (92)

This suggests that what is really at issue is not a matter of feelings ('X feels something good toward this person because of this') but a matter of a permanent awareness of the incurred debt:

> X thinks something like this: I have to always think about this

5.3 What kinds of debts come under *on*?

The question of whether *on* concerns any debts whatsoever or only major debts deserves to be considered a little more closely, since different views have been expressed on this point in the literature. For example, Zimmerman (1985) writes: "The Japanese word for the obligation incurred by the giving and granting of major favors (such as giving birth to someone or assuming responsibility for his or her education) is *on*" (67).

On the other hand, Ruth Benedict (as we have seen) links *on* with both major and minor "debts" ("The word for *obligations* which covers a person's indebtedness from greatest to least is *on*"), and she illustrates the concept of 'on' with some examples of very trivial services.

It seems to me, however, that in fact not all "debts" would be covered by *on*, but only those which are perceived as "unpayable"; and if some debts are seen as unpayable then they can indeed come under *on* even if they are small and trivial. The following passage in *The chrysanthemum and the sword* is particularly illuminating in this respect (cf. also the discussion in Coulmas 1981):

Especially in unformalized situations the Japanese are extremely wary of getting entangled in *on*. Even the offer of a cigarette from a person with whom a man has previously had no ties makes him uncomfortable and the polite way for him to express thanks is to say: 'Oh, this poisonous feeling (*kino doku*). 'It's easier to bear', a Japanese said to me, 'if you come right out and acknowledge how bad it makes you feel. You had never thought of doing anything for him and so you are shamed by receiving the *on*. '*Kino doku*' therefore is translated sometimes as 'Thank you', i.e., for the cigarettes, sometimes as 'I'm sorry', i.e., for the indebtedness, sometimes as 'I feel like a heel', i.e., because you beat me to this act of generosity. It means all of these and none. . . . In English, *sumimasen* is translated 'Thank you', 'I'm grateful' or 'I'm sorry', 'I apologize'. You use the word, for instance, in preference to all other thank-you's if anyone chases the hat you lost on a windy street. When he returns it to you politeness requires that you acknowledge your own internal discomfort in receiving. 'He is offering me an *on* and I never saw him before. I never had a chance to offer him the first *on*. I feel guilty about it but I feel better if I apologize to him. *Sumimasen* is probably the commonest word for thank-you in Japan. I tell him that I recognize that I have received *on* from him and it doesn't end with the act of taking back my hat. But what can I do about it? We are strangers'. (105)

This "unpayability" implied by *on* is not reflected, so far, in our attempted explication of this word. We can account for it, however, by replacing the component 'I didn't do something like this for this person' with the following: 'I could never do anything like this for this person'. This phrasing, which seems to be fully consistent with the foregoing comments and examples offered by Ruth Benedict, would also account for the much commented on asymmetric nature of *on*. To quote Lebra (1986):

It is asymmetric in that the *on* is considered limitless and unpayable and that the receiver feels urged to return at least 'one-ten-thousandth' of the received sum through total, sometimes life-long, devotion to the donor. Bellah (1957:73) paid special attention to this relentless demand of *on* which puts one in the status of a permanent debtor, and equated it to the idea of original sin with all its dynamic potentialities. (195)

Bellah's reference to original sin is extremely interesting, and it is tempting to expand the definition of *on* sketched here in such a way as to reflect this analogy with original sin more closely. This could be done by including components such as 'this is bad' and 'I have to think about it always' in the proposed definition . But perhaps the component 'this is bad' is unnecessary, and the combination of components:

X thinks:
  I can never do something like this for this person
  I have to think about it always
X feels something bad because of this

accounts sufficiently for Bellah's intended point. On the other hand, it might be justified to posit a general cultural norm for Japan, along the following lines:

if someone does something good for me
I have to do something like this for this person

if I can't do it this is bad
I have to do something because of this

A norm of this kind would explain not just one concept ('on') but a whole range of phenomena, both linguistic and nonlinguistic.

5.4   *On* and status hierarchy

One of the most interesting and most controversial questions which arise in connection with the concept of 'on' is the nature of the relationship implied by it. According to many writers on the subject, this relationship has to be hierarchical. According to others, however, it can be a relationship among equals. The prototypical *on* situation is no doubt hierarchical. It involves, as mentioned earlier, the relationship between a samurai and a lord; the lord bestowed on a samurai a fief, and the samurai repaid him by lifelong loyal service.

But *on* has other prototypes as well—in the realm of politics (political authorities), religion (benevolent supernatural beings) and family (parents). For example, with respect to the political sphere, Bellah (1985) writes:

> First of all the compelling and overriding loyalty toward the political authority must be seen in the context of the idea of *on*. The political authority has the obligation of bestowing blessings (*on*) on the people subject to it. In the case of the samurai this takes the direct form of receiving a stipend, but the concept is much more general. For instance one of the great blessings which the shogunate bestowed on all the people was peace. (20)

With respect to religion (primarily Buddhism), the same author writes:

> Action with respect to deity as a benevolent superordinate gets us at once into the theory of *on*. Deity in some form dispenses blessings (*on*) and it is the obligation of the recipient to make return for these blessings (*hoon*). Religious action, then, is the various forms this *hoon* may take. . . .
>   Religious action conceived as a return for blessings from a benevolent superordinate, then, is based on a view of man as weak and helpless by himself. Only with the help of benevolent beings can he live, and the blessings he receives are so much greater than his ability to return them that actually he can only return an infinitesimal amount. (70–73)

At the same time, Bellah's sources (e.g. the early Buddhist work *Anguttara Nikaya*) link *on* also with filial piety and with the unpayable debt toward one's parents:

> We may carry our mothers on one shoulder, and our fathers on the other, and attend on them even for a hundred years, doing them bodily services in every possible way, and establishing them in the position of universal sovereignty: still the favour we have received from our parents will be far from requited.

But to what extent are all these different prototypical relations valid to the modern concept of 'on'?

Evidence suggests that, in fact, none of them should be reflected explicitly in the semantic formula of *on*, and that at the same time the general type of relationship should be somehow hinted at—as essentially and inherently asymmetrical and, so to speak, "vertical." The exact nature of the "asymmetry" and the "verticality" implied by this word, however, remains to be clarified.

Sakurai (1961), quoted in Lebra (1974:194), "characterized *on* as a contractual relationship between a master and his subordinate bound by a double contingency of expectations: the master bestows an *on* provided the subordinate performs loyal service, whereas the subordinate fulfils the obligation of loyalty on the condition that the master rewards him with an *on*" (194). Lebra herself has opposed this view, arguing:

> . . . the asymmetric norm of *on* has been socially determined by the cultural emphasis upon status hierarchy. Ordinarily an *on* is granted by a superior-status holder and the burden of repayment falls on the inferior person's shoulders; hence, the *on* reinforces the inferior's loyalty and obedience to the superior. The hierarchical relationship underlying the *on* is reminiscent of the historically specific meaning of *on*, that is, the territorial grant or stipend bestowed by the feudal lord upon his vassal. In modern Japan every Japanese was supposed to owe the heaviest *on* to the emperor as the sovereign. This does not, however, preclude the possibility that *on*-reciprocity takes place between equals. In this case, status hierarchy is generated after an *on* is granted rather than the other way around as is a more common case. The point is that *on*-reciprocity is inseparably entangled with status difference and status orientation in general, whether status hierarchy precedes or is preceded by *on*-granting. (195)

Thus, according to Lebra, *on* always implies "status difference," "status orientation," and "status hierarchy," yet an *on*-relationship can also take place between equals (and not necessarily between a master and a subordinate, or between a "superior" and an "inferior" status holder). This may sound somewhat confusing, and in any case, terms such as *superior* and *inferior status holders* are inherently obscure and culture-specific and couldn't, needless to say, be used in a universally interpretable semantic metalanguage. Furthermore, to the extent to which such terms are clear at all they do not mean the same as Sakurai's terms *master* and *subordinate* (rendered as such by Lebra).

Despite these difficulties, Lebra's comments are very helpful and insightful, and her intentions can, I hope, be fully clarified by means of the following semantic formula:

On
(a) X thinks something like this about someone:
(b)   this person did something very good for me
(c)   I couldn't do something like this for this person
(d)   I have to think about this always
(e)   I have to do good things for this person because of this
(f)   if this person wants me to do something I have to do it
(g) X feels something bad because of this

This formula seems to account for all the different aspects of *on* discussed in the literature. It presents this relationship as asymmetrical, and it invites the inference that the *onjin* is X's superior without, however, precluding the possibility that the "status difference" and the "hierarchical relationship" is created by, rather than prior to or independent of, the "unpayable debt" itself.

5.5 Is *on* still on in Japan?

In modern Japan, the principle of *on* has often been attacked as feudal and un-democratic (cf. Lebra 1974:203), and it would seem that its importance in Japanese culture has diminished. Nonetheless, Lebra (1974) argues convincingly (drawing on contemporary studies devoted to this problem) that "it would be far from the truth to say that the norm of *on* has completely broken down." In particular, she reports a study in which the subjects were asked to imagine that they were the president of a company recruiting new employees on the basis of a competitive examination:

> The president is free to choose between two candidates; the candidate who ranks highest in the examination and the candidate who is second highest but the president's relative. Seventy-five percent of the respondents chose the first candidate, and only 19 percent favored the relative. In response to the next question, which replaced the relative by a child of the president's *onjin* (benefactor), the proportion changes to 48 percent (in favour of the highest candidate) vs. 44 percent. (205)

These results support the view that, despite all the changes which have taken place in postwar Japan, *on* is still a powerful cultural norm.

5.6 *On*—a final illustration

As a final illustration of the concept of 'on', I will quote here a dialogue from Kazuo Ishiguro's remarkable novel *An artist of the floating world* (1986)—written in English but set in Japan and reflecting a Japanese point of view. The hero, Masuyi Ono, an artist, has written a letter of recommendation (to an acquaintance in the State Depart-ment) for the younger brother of one of his pupils, and now the two brothers have come to thank him. They refuse to come inside, but stand in the doorway, bowing and giggling (in embarrassment). Finally, Shintaro, the older brother, turns to his younger brother and whispers his name:

> For the first time, the young man stopped bowing and looked up at me nervously. Then he said: "I will be grateful to you for the remainder of my life. I will exert every particle of my being to be worthy of your recommendation. I assure you, I will not let you down. I will work hard, and strive to satisfy my superiors. And however much I may be promoted in the future, I will never forget the man who enabled me to start on my career.'
> "Really, it was nothing. It's no more than you deserve."
> This brought frantic protests from both of them, then Shintaro said to his brother: "Yoshio, we have imposed enough on Sensei as it is. But before we leave, take a good look again at the man who has helped you. We are greatly privileged to have a benefactor of such influence and generosity."
> "Indeed," the youth muttered, and gazed up at me.
> "Please, Shintaro, this is embarrassing. Please come in and we'll celebrate with some sake."

"No, Sensei, we must leave you now. It was the greatest impertinence to come here like this and disturb your afternoon. But we could not delay thanking you for one moment longer."

6. Giri

6.1 What is *giri*? A preliminary discussion

According to Mitsubishi, "*giri* is the linchpin of human relations among Japanese" (1987:40). The importance of this concept in Japanese culture is acknowledged by all students of Japan. Some, for example, Roberts (1974), have claimed that it was *giri* which "enabled the shattered Japanese economy to recover so rapidly after the war" (399). According to the same author, *giri* is a power "that gives Japanese society its stability." Zimmerman (1988), an outstanding businessman and for many years the president of the American Chamber of Commerce in Tokyo, emphasizes in particular the importance of *giri* in the world of business. He calls it "a powerful force" (73) and says, for example: "The implications of *giri* . . . pervade Japanese society, and the business world is no exception" (69).

But students of Japan agree not only that *giri* is a powerful force but also that it is a "culture-laden," uniquely Japanese concept, without an equivalent in English or in other Western languages. Japanese-English dictionaries offer a bewildering variety of alternative glosses: "justice," "honour," "duty," "obligation," "a debt of gratitude," "respectability," "decency," "courtesy" (Kenkyusha); "propriety," "rectitude," "moral cause" (Brinkley's); and others.

As Ruth Benedict (1947) pointed out half a century ago, monolingual all-Japanese dictionaries are not very helpful on this point either. One of them, quoted by Benedict (in translation) offers: "*giri*—righteous way; the road human beings should follow; something one does unwillingly to forestall apology to the world" (137).

The most commonly given English gloss is "duty" or "obligation" (although, significantly, English-Japanese dictionaries never gloss either of these words as *giri*). Benedict commented:

> There is no possible English equivalent [for *giri*], and of all the strange categories of moral obligations which anthropologists find in the cultures of the world, it is one of the most curious. It is specifically Japanese. . . . it is not possible to understand their courses of action without taking it into account. No Japanese can talk about motivations or good repute or the dilemmas which confront men and women in his home country without constantly speaking of giri. (133)
>   To an Occidental, giri includes a most heterogenous lot of obligations . . . ranging from gratitude for an old kindness to the duty of revenge. It is no wonder that the Japanese have not tried to expound giri to Westerners. (139).

Since Ruth Benedict wrote these words, several Japanese scholars *have* tried to expound *giri* to Westerners. Unfortunately, the explanations are often as bewildering as the explicandum itself. Lebra (1976) regards as the best explanation of *giri* the one offered by Kawashima (1951), which she summarizes as follows:

Giri refers to a social order consisting of a set of social norms that assign every status holder a certain role to be carried out. More specifically, *giri* is generated by and in turn maintains gemeinschaft relationships between particular individuals. The gemeinschaft relationships involving *giri* can be characterized by: (1) duration . . . , (2) total involvement . . . , an imposition on the individual by virtue of his status . . . , (4) a personal, particularistic relationship involving face-to-face interaction in a physical sense, (5) emotional ties, and (6) a hierarchical relationship involving an unequal distribution of obligations. (93)

This is all very helpful, but it would be hard to maintain that it fully clarifies the concept of 'giri' for Westerners (especially since the concepts 'gemeinschaft' and 'gesellschaft', on which Kawashima's discussion relies, also call for an explanation). Perhaps a greater clarity can be achieved by trying to decompose this concept into simple components. Since *giri* implies, above all, a sense of obligation, one component seems rather obvious:

X thinks: I have to do something

Clearly, though, there is much more to *giri* than that.

6.2   Does *giri* have to involve human relations?

The bulk of the literature on *giri* implies that *giri* refers not simply to an "obligation"—a kind of Kantian abstract moral imperative—but to an obligation toward somebody, and, more specifically, toward a particular person. Furthermore, it appears that the obligation in question has to be seen as the obligation 'to do something good', despite Benedict's claim, quoted earlier, that *giri* ranges "from gratitude for an old kindness to the duty of revenge." According to my informants, in contemporary Japanese revenge cannot come under *giri*.

This would suggest that our initial semantic component should be expanded as follows:

X thinks: I have to do something good for person Y

I have quoted earlier the opening statement of the Mitsubishi (1987:40) entry devoted to *giri* ("*Giri* is the linchpin of human relations among Japanese"), and this statement is fully consistent with other writings on the subject, which also stress the relational aspect of this concept. Many sources also stress that *giri* is concerned specifically with relations between individual human beings. For example, Zimmerman states: "*Giri* can also be expressed as overriding loyalty to an individual that transcends loyalty or obligation to the firm" (1988:70).

This idea that *giri* is concerned with individual, private relations is also supported by Kawashima's remark quoted earlier that *giri* refers to "a personal, particularistic relationship involving face-to-face interaction in a physical sense." This appears to be one of the crucial differences between *giri* and *on*: *on* refers to a kind of obligation which can have as its target one's ancestors, a faraway inaccessible emperor, one's country, and so on, but *giri* has to have as its target another person, with whom one can interact face to face.

The idea that *giri* is necessarily concerned with private, personal relations is also fully consistent with Benedict's discussion of possible conflict between *giri* and *chu* (emperor worship) and the "atomism of Japanese morals." According to Benedict, in modern times, great effort has been invested into developing a more general, national code of morals, which would be centered on emperor worship rather than on personal obligations to individuals:

> The best and most authoritative statement of this program is the Imperial Rescript to Soldiers and Sailors given by the Emperor Meiji in 1882. . . . The Rescript warns its hearers not to be like heroes of old who died in dishonor because, "losing sight of the true path of public duty, *they kept faith in private relations*" [Benedict's emphasis] . . . . The whole Rescript shows an official attempt to minimize giri and to elevate chu. Not once in the whole text does the word giri appear in the sense in which it is a household word in Japan. Instead of naming giri, it emphasizes that there is a Higher Law, which is chu, and a Lower Law, which is "keeping faith in private relations." (209)

Finally, the idea that *giri* has to involve "direct," face-to-face interaction between individuals is also supported by Dore's (1958) observation: "The immediate sanction which would attend non-fulfilment of the obligation is the displeasure or the distress of this specific person or group of persons" (254) (an observation which echoes Kawashima's point about "emotional ties" involved in a *giri*-relationship). This suggests that the semantic formula for *giri* should indeed relate individual human beings (person X and person Y) and in fact should also refer to the target person's possible feelings:

X thinks something like this:
  I have to do something good for person Y
  if I don't do it, Y can feel something bad

Nonetheless, there is also some evidence against such an analysis of *giri*. In particular, this analysis seems hard to reconcile with Benedict's statement that "the stoicism, the self-control that is required of a self-respecting Japanese is part of his *giri* to his name" and that "a woman may not cry out in childbirth because of *giri*" (148). Examples of this kind appear to indicate that *giri* does not have to involve the relation between two people, X and Y, but can be a matter of something like self-respect. (Benedict compared this aspect of *giri* with the European concept of 'honor' and, more particularly, with the German concept of 'Ehre'.)

The problem requires further investigation, but my own tentative conclusion is this: the meaning of *giri* has changed in the relevant respect over the last fifty years or so. In Benedict's time, *giri* apparently could refer to a person's obligation toward himself or herself, but this is no longer the case. Thus, my informants reject examples such as that of self-control or stoicism as examples of *giri*. According to them, if one behaves in some way because one thinks one "owes it to oneself," this would not come under *giri*. Accordingly, for the present-day concept of 'giri,' it does appear justified to phrase the component in question in terms of one's obligation to another person:

X thinks: I have to do something good for person Y

6.3 Is *giri* a permanent relationship?

Assuming that 'giri' IS a relational concept, should we specify that the relationship in question has to be permanent or semi-permanent? As it stands, our explication so far allows also for purely transient relationships—but is this right?

Many writers on the subject would presumably say that this is wrong. For example, both Kawashima and Lebra quoted earlier insist that *giri* "is not a temporary relationship but a permanent one" and, moreover, that it occupies "not just a small part of life . . . but the whole sphere of life" (Lebra 1976:93). Kawashima'a idea that *giri* "maintains gemeinschaft relationships between particular individuals" is consistent with this view.

Other writers are not equally explicit on this point, but what they say is usually consistent with the idea. For example, Roberts (1974), quoted in Zimmerman (1988), speaks of *giri* as "the peculiar sense of obligation that makes Japanese society so cohesive" (72). It seems reasonable to assume that the cohesiveness of Japanese society is attributed here to a network of more or less permanent sets of loyalties and obligations. It cannot be an accident that so many commentors speak not simply of a "*giri* obligation" but of a "special bond of *giri*" (Roberts 1974:398). The word *bond* suggests, I think, something strong and enduring. There may even be a link in this respect between *giri* and *enryo*, because, as Reischauer (1988) observes, it may be due to *enryo* that "Japanese do not develop new associations lightly" and "are less inclined than Westerners to enter into casual contacts" (147). Thus, *enryo* may stop people from developing new relationships with other people, whereas *giri* may strengthen the existing ones. As Reischauer (1988) put it, in Japan, "Friends are less easily made, but once made may be held onto with a strength that the more socially casual Westerner finds puzzling" (147).

Christopher (1983) comments in this connection on the difficulties in relations between the Japanese and the Americans: once a relationship is established,

> a Japanese comes to expect more of an American acquaintance than the American is prepared to give—with the result that the Japanese is confused and sometimes embittered by the American's sudden and, to the Japanese way of thinking, inexplicable evasion of the unspoken obligations of their relationship. On more than one occasion in my own experience Japanese friends have wanted me to do things that were either legally impossible or incompatible with American journalistic ethics, and I know that my failure to oblige them has put serious though unacknowledged strains on our friendship. (172)

Trying to account for this binding and permanent character of a *giri* relationship we could expand the explication as follows:

X thinks something like this:
  I have to do good things for person Y
  if I don't do it Y can feel something bad
  I have to think about this

This does not imply that to comply with *giri* one would have to always think about the person to whom *giri* is due, yet it does imply that the relationship is seen as more or less permanent.

6.4   Is *giri* a repayment?

According to many writers on the subject, a *giri* relationship involves crucially the idea of repayment, along the lines of:

> you did something good for me
> because of this I have to do the same for you

For example, Smith (1983) defines *giri* as follows: "*Giri* is a duty or obligation of a person to behave in certain loosely prescribed ways towards another to whom the person is indebted" (45) Similarly, Mitsubishi states: "When a person says, 'I owe that man *giri*', he means that he had received some favor from him at one time and that he must eventually return the obligation" (1987:40). This tallies well with the folk definition of *giri* reported by Lebra (1976): "The villagers whom Kawashima studied defined *giri* as *okaeshi* ('return', that is, repayment for *on*)" (93).

But even if the word *giri* does evoke, primarily, a return of favors, this does not mean that a return of favors necessarily belongs to the semantic invariant of this word. The association between *giri* and a balance of favors may be a matter of cultural knowledge rather than of the semantics of *giri*.

Of course, meaning is not independent of, or unrelated to, cultural knowledge; and *giri* itself is a clear example of a word whose meaning is shaped by culture and embodies cultural knowledge. But cultural knowledge also goes beyond the meaning of individual words. The fact that in Japan repayment of debts is seen as a prime example of "*giri* obligation" may be cultural knowledge which—at this stage at least—is not a part of the meaning of this word as such. The crucial question is this: Can the word *giri* also be applied to situations which do not involve any repayment of debts or can't it?

The answer to this question appears to be: Yes, it can. For example, as one informant explained, if a friend is giving a party, one may feel that one has to go to that party "because of *giri*" (*giri de*), and this does not seem to refer to any favors received previously from the friend, but simply to the bond of a permanent relationship.

Similarly, it is reported in the literature that in business relationships a person may feel bound in *giri* to do business with another person (or firm) simply because they have done business with them before—as if such a relationship created obligations, regardless of any exchange of favors. For example, Honna and Hoffer (1989) state (in connection with *giri*): "The feelings of obligation also extend to relations between businesses, for example, between a firm and a supplier. If the two have done business together for some time, the firm is most likely to retain the supplier even if another supplier proposes a somewhat better offer" (116–117). (I don't think, incidentally, that this statement contradicts our conclusion that *giri* involves relations between individuals, because relations between businesses would normally involve relations between individuals.)[3]

Consider also the following Western analogue of a "*giri* obligation" offered by Dore (1958): "'We really ought to go and see Auntie Mabel when we are in London. She's a bit of a bore, but she will be upset if we don't' is a perfect example of a *giri*-act and a *giri*-relation" (254).

Clearly, this example of a *giri*-act does not involve "repayment," although Dore also points out that "Aunt Mabel may be 75 and tolerably well off, so the action does not have to be disinterested" (257), and that "'support and be supported', 'live together, prosper together' were traditional phrases quoted as justifications for maintaining such relationships" (257). Dore offers also the following comment, which clarifies Kawashima's point about "an imposition on the individual by virtue of his status":

> *Giri*-relationships may be 'ascribed' in the sense that they are implied in the very nature of the positions occupied by two parties in any kinship, community or economic organization. Such are relations between relatives not of the same house-hold group, relations between employer and employee, between landlord and tenant, between neighbours or between fellow-employees. They may also arise as the result of a particular favour conferred, for example, relations between marriage go-between and married pair, or between an employee and the man who found him his job. (254)

Thus, according to Dore, *giri* MAY arise as the result of a particular favor, but this doesn't have to be so.

It would seem, then, that although in rural Japan *giri* appears to consist largely in "compulsory" reciprocal gift-giving, this is probably a cultural rather than semantic fact, even if for many rural Japanese there is a very strong association between the two, as described by Befu (1986):

> *Giri* is a moral imperative to perform one's duties toward other members of one's group. Gift-giving falls squarely in the sphere of *giri*; one is morally obligated to give a gift when custom demands it. *Giri* is bound up with the institution of gift-giving in another way, namely, reciprocation. . . . The concept of *giri* evokes in the tradition-minded rural Japanese the obligation to reciprocate. Since gift-giving is an act of *giri*, and since *giri* requires reciprocation, a gift naturally calls for a return gift. . . . So important is the concept of *giri* in gift-giving that many rural Japanese interpret *giri* to mean strict observance of the etiquette of gift-giving. (162)

This suggests that in Befu's view, *giri* is something like "a social obligation," and that since in rural Japan reciprocal gift-giving constitutes a major social obligation, in many people's perception *giri* and reciprocal gift-giving are much the same thing.

I conclude, tentatively, that while "repayment" is strongly associated in Japanese culture with the idea of *giri,* nonetheless the semantic invariant of *giri* does not include any reference to it.[4] This takes us back to the formula:

> X thinks something like this:
> I have to do good things for person Y
> if I don't do this Y can feel something bad
> I have to think about this

It is possible, of course, that on further investigation the word *giri* will prove to be polysemous, or subject to regional variation (cf. Dore 1958:253) and that one will have to recognize that in one of its meanings *giri* does mean something like "repayment of favor." But neither polysemy nor variation in meaning should be postulated without proven necessity. At this stage, nothing forces us to conclude that *giri* has more than one meaning; and if so, "repayment of favors" is not part of this word's semantic invariant.

6.5 The moral and social character of *giri*

The components sketched above cannot be regarded as an exhaustive explication of *giri* because they do not account for the semi-moral and semi-social character of this concept, reflected in dictionary glosses such as "decency," "respectability," "propriety," and even "honor." To account for these larger implications of *giri,* I propose to add two further components [(c) and (e)] to the explication:

(a) X thinks something like this:
(b)   I have to do good things for person Y
(c)   if I don't do this it will be bad
(d)   if I don't do this Y can feel something bad
(e)   people will say bad things about me because of this
(f)   I have to think about this

Taken by itself, component (c) could be seen as implying a purely moral dimension, but the combination of (c), (d), and (e) suggests that *giri* is concerned not so much with some moral absolute as with social consequences of one's behavior.

It is interesting to note how discussions of *giri* in the literature almost invariably include references to other people's opinion, such as the following ones:

> To the Japanese it is sufficient reward to be respected in his world and 'a man who does not know giri' is still a 'miserable wretch'. He is scorned and ostracized by his fellows. (Benedict 1947:176).

> Giri remains today a virtue with great authority and to say of a man that 'he does not know giri' is one of the most drastic condemnations in Japan. (Benedict 1947:212).

The fear of such a condemnation is apparently extremely effective, despite the absence of any formal sanctions. Smith (1983) emphasizes this point with respect to reciprocal *giri* relationships: "no one ever thought to take another to court to secure repayment of a debt of *giri*—but the person who violates the reciprocal relationship will be branded as without integrity or honor, and subjected to substantial informal sanctions" (46). Benedict (1947) stressed the same point speaking of people's duties to their in-laws, called in Japan "relatives in giri": "A person fulfills his duties to his in-laws punctiliously . . . because at all costs he must avoid the dreaded condemnation: 'a man who does not know giri'" (135)

Interestingly, although *giri* is often glossed as "rectitude," "righteousness," or "what is right," in fact, *giri* can also be contrasted with such notions. For example, Bellah (1985) always translates *giri* as "right" and glosses it as such in his list of key Japanese words. Yet, as Benedict (1947) pointed out, "every Japanese knows the phrase, 'I could not do righteousness (gi) because of giri'" (213). Similarly, Zimmerman (1988) states: "The Japanese businessman may find himself torn between *giri* to a friend or a benefactor and his sense of right or wrong" (68). A good example of such a conflict between *giri* and impersonal moral laws is provided by Dore (1958):

> A nephew employed in his uncle's firm as under-manager is convinced of the justice of the workers' case in a strike conflict. Should he suppress his 'sympathies' and

loyally support his uncle as the ethics of *giri* prescribe? Or should he work for what he believes to be just even though it does bring on him the accusation that he does not know *giri*? (380)

Having examined several examples of this kind, Dore comments:

> . . . the sort of situations outlined above present dilemmas of a different kind, conflicts between, on the one hand, particularistic loyalties, and on the other either individual aspirations which it is held to be the right of everyone to hold, or generalized principles of conduct which are held to be applicable to all situations. (381)

But the contrast between "what is right" and "what is *giri*" can be interpreted in two different ways, and perhaps it should be interpreted in both these ways at once. First, *giri* has to do with private relations, and private obligations could be seen as coming into conflict with "what is right" in some more abstract sense. Second, "what is right" can be interpreted in an absolute sense, as something independent of "what people might say," whereas *giri* is never independent of "what people might say."

It has often been pointed out that the Japanese ethical system is "oriented more to specific relationships than to abstract principles" (Reischauer 1988:147), that "the Japanese on the whole think less in terms of abstract ethical principles than do Westerners and more in terms of concrete situations and complex human relationships" (Reischauer 1988:172), and also that the Japanese are more concerned with other people's opinion than with abstract moral principles—or rather, that they tend to be guided in their behavior by other people's opinions about them, or their anticipated opinions. As Benedict put it, "The Japanese . . . need terribly to be respected in the world" (1947:173). Furthermore, several students of Japan have noted that the fear of losing face before other people plays a crucial role in the socialization of Japanese children. For example, "The mother tells the child that he will be laughed at or ridiculed by neighbours, his playmates, his relatives, or anyone whose opinion the child values most" (Lebra 1976:152).

The concept of 'giri', as explicated here, reflects these features of Japanese culture.[5]

6.6   *Giri* as a burden

According to Benedict, there is a common Japanese saying: "*giri* is hardest to bear. . . . As one Japanese said, 'If a grown son does things for his own mother, it is because he loves her and therefore it couldn't be giri. You don't work for giri when you act from the heart'" (1947:133, 135).

Comments of this kind suggest that *giri* necessarily implies unwillingness. Of course, one could say that the notion of obligation or duty as such implies a degree of unwillingness. But obligations don't have to be "burdensome," "hard to bear," or incompatible with an impulse from the heart. *Giri*, on the other hand, appears to suggest that natural inclination and obligation go in opposite directions. The traditional pair of opposites—*giri* and *ninjo*, 'obligation' and 'human feeling'—reflects this "unwanted" character of whatever *giri* requires.

Benedict stressed this in particular with respect to the modern use of *giri*, and she documented this aspect of the modern concept of 'giri' with linguistic evidence such as the following:

> Today's constantly used phrases are full of resentment and of emphasis on the pressure of public opinion which compels a person to do giri against his wishes. They say, 'I am arranging this marriage merely for giri'; 'merely because of giri I was forced to give him the job'; 'I must see him merely for giri.' They constantly talk of being 'tangled with giri', a phrase the dictionary translates as 'I am obliged to it.' They say, 'He forced me with giri', 'he cornered me with giri', and these, like the other usages, mean that someone has argued the speaker into an act he did not want or intend by raising some issue of payment due upon an *on*. . . . All these usages carry the implication of unwillingness and of compliance for 'mere decency's sake', as the Japanese dictionary phrases it. (140)

Observations of this kind suggest that the explication of *giri* developed thus far should be expanded by a further component, along the following lines:

> (if I don't do this), people will say bad things about me because of this
> I don't want this
> because of this, I want to do good things for Y

This stops short of saying bluntly "I don't want to do it," because a person "forced by *giri*," may, in a sense, want to do what *giri* requires, not because they want to do that particular thing but because they want to comply with *giri*.

This brings us to the following explication of *giri*:

giri
(a) X thinks something like this about someone (Y):
(b)   I have to do good things for person Y
(c)   if I don't do this it will be bad
(d)   if I don't do this, Y can feel something bad
(e)   people will say bad things about me because of this
(f)   I don't want this
(g)   because of this, I have to do good things for Y
(h)   I have to think about this

This explication reflects the importance of personal obligations in Japanese culture, the link between obligations and permanent bonds, the crucial role of consideration for others and anticipation of other people's feelings (see Section 8), and the relativistic and opinion-oriented character of moral norms.

7. *Seishin*

The English language literature about Japan is often a meeting place of words which in other contexts would hardly ever come together. One particularly interesting example of this phenomenon involves the words *spirit*, *spiritual*, and *spiritualism*, which in books and articles on Japan (written in English or translated into English) often keep company with such unlikely (from a Western point of view) words as *military, police, business,* and *sport*.

For example, Minami speaks of "military education based on spiritualism" and asserts that in Japan, "military education was itself spiritualistic" (1971:136). He also links "spiritualism" with the use of formal clothing, and comments: "Men's summer short-sleeved shirts and shorts also seem to be evidence of the influence of physicality in terms of dispensing with the formalities of spiritualism and adopting physically comfortable conditions in daily living" (146).

Similarly, Frager and Rohlen (1976) discuss "the place of spiritual education in . . . the military and the police. They both share a tradition of 'spiritualism' that requires very little explicit educational enhancement" (266). And further: "One effect of more leisure time and more personal income has been a rapid growth of people taking up some form of traditional art on what we would term a hobby basis. The pursuit of any of these, from flower arrangement to judo, involves the student in a serious program of spiritual education" (273).

Finally, Moeran (1986) remarks that, according to Japanese radio and television commentators reporting on high school baseball tournaments, "It is the player's 'spiritual' attitude and strength which makes or breaks him when it 'comes to the crunch'" (68).

When one comes across the words *spiritual* or *spiritualism* used in such unusual contexts, one is bound to wonder whether they are not clumsy translation equivalents of Japanese words whose meanings are perhaps rather different; and one discovers that the Japanese concept behind such "odd" combinations of ideas is *seishin:* "a key element in [Japanese] national mores" (Austin 1976:255). As Frager and Rohlen (1976) point out:

> At various times in recent history this term has been a prominent rallying cry for those wishing to preserve or reassert Japanese traditional ways, and during the 1930s and 40s it was extensively utilized by military and right-wing leaders in their efforts to inspire the nation. It is very important to note that, despite its history as a panacea of nationalist and militaristic movements, the Japanese orientation to *seishin* has a much broader and deeper basis in the ongoing life of most Japanese . . . in fact, virtually all aspects of life and behaviour are grist for the *seishin* perspective. (256)

Austin concurs: "The vitality of *seishin* is not least among the paradoxes of progress" (1976:255).

What does the word *seishin* mean?

In Japanese-English dictionaries, *seishin* is glossed as, for example, "mind, spirit, soul" (Kenkyusha); "mind, spirit, mental power, intellect, will, motive" (Brinkley's); "mind, spirit, soul, will, mentality, intuition" (Takehara). In the literature on Japan, *seishin* is usually rendered as "spirit." It is clear, however, that although it IS sometimes used for translating English words such as *spirit*, *mind*, and *psyche*, *seishin* stands for a uniquely Japanese concept which cannot be satisfactorily explained by matching it with any supposed English equivalents.

Rohlen (1986) observes in this connection:

> The term *seishin* has many applications, including *seishin no ai* (platonic love), *seishin bunseki* (psychoanalysis), *seishin kagaku* (mental science), and *dokuritsu seishin* (the spirit of independence). Many of these are Japanese translations of foreign concepts

and perhaps it is not correct to argue for a single meaning for the word, yet, once the broad, inclusive perspective of human psychology at the foundation of the *seishin* concept is grasped the differences among the various applications recede in significance. (335)

Although the different senses of the word *seishin* are undoubtedly related, it would be wise, no doubt, to follow Rohlen's initial point and assume that the sense or senses implied by the use of this word in translations of foreign concepts may be somewhat different from the "native" Japanese concept—and clearly, it is this "native" Japanese concept which we should, above all, try to elucidate.

As our starting point, we will take, once again, some descriptive explanations suggested by various students of Japanese culture and society. To begin with, Austin (1976) characterizes the meaning of *seishin* as follows:

Seishin is antithetical to modernization as generally conceived. It is not democratic, not universalistic, not individualistic, not materialistic. It is rather the complex of loyalty, discipline, esprit de corps, and indomitable perseverance that is central to so many of the historical accomplishments of Japanese civilization, from art to economic growth. (255)

Other comments on *seishin*, however (made, for example, by Morsbach 1980 and Moeran 1986), suggest that of the four elements mentioned by Austin—loyalty, discipline, esprit de corps, and perseverance—only two are really pertinent: discipline and perseverance. "Loyalty" and "esprit de corps" may be among the fruits of a well-developed *seishin,* but they do not seem to be implied by the term as such. In particular, Morsbach (1980) argues: "While much has been written on the group orientation found in Japanese social interaction, it should not be overlooked that there is a strong tradition of *seishin*, which is basically an individualistic trait" (331).

While in its essence *seishin* "primarily operates on the individual level" (332), it can, nonetheless, be used "for promoting positive group interaction." Furthermore, "through the *seishin* concept one can also understand the functioning of groups better: situations where the words *gaman* and *gambatte!* ('endurance' and 'hold out!') are frequently heard" (332). Morsbach's point is that while *seishin* "has nothing to do with groups" (332) or with social values such as "loyalty" and "esprit de corps," it does have a great deal to do with individual traits such as "perseverance" and "endurance," and that these are socially useful.

Morsbach himself defines *seishin*, succinctly, as "a personality syndrome centred on inner mental strength which can be developed through long years of training" (331). He elaborates:

Seishin is seen by Japanese as being the opposite of materialism and easy-going self-gratification. It involves a singlemindedness of purpose and often has practical aims: a strong-willed person can conquer physical illness, selfish desires and can accept whatever comes, including unreasonable demands by superiors and the pressures of group life. (331)

This tallies well with Smith's (1983) remarks made in the context of his discussion of *seishin*: "Through discipline and adversity a person achieves self-development and, crucially, self-mastery" (99). And also: "Unlike the heroes of Horatio Alger's stories, who seem to be born honest and true and strong, those of the typical Japanese success story become all these things through suffering, perserverance, and obedience" (101).

This suggests that, in addition to something like "perseverance" or "endurance," *seishin* also crucially involves something like "strong will" and "singlemindedness of purpose." This is consistent with Rohlen's analysis of "the meaning of *seishin*", which stresses, in particular, "fortitude," "single-mindedness," "strength" or "will power," "discipline," and "perseverance and hard work in training" (1986:257–262).

It has often been pointed out that in World War II, Japanese soldiers were urged to demonstrate their *seishin* by matching "our training against their (i.e. Americans') numbers and our flesh against their steel" (Benedict 1947:24), and that this attitude culminated in the "Special Attack Corps" (that is, kamikaze units). For example, Minami (1971) writes:

> . . . man can do the unexpected and superhuman when his "spiritual force" works upon a condition that seems to be beyond human wisdom and strength. . . . Spiritualism, the belief that that spirit displays superhuman power under conditions actually beyond human wisdom or judged to be beyond human wisdom, was quite dominant among Japanese military men. (134)

He also quotes the authors of *The kamikaze suicide units* (Inokuchi and Nakajima 1951), who wrote (with reference to the deployment of kamikaze in World War II): "The situation was already beyond the control of human wisdom. This being so, there could be no other means to achieve a miracle except the pure and innocent spirit of these youth and their fresh vigor to retain their spiritual purity."

It is true that at the end of World War II the Japanese faith in *seishin* appears to have diminished, and the concept itself appears to have lost some of its appeal in Japanese society. Moeran (1986) quotes in this connection Dore's (1958:67) comment:

> The old Japanese belief that *seishin*—spirit, will-power—could conquer matter, that the human body would endure loss of sleep, starvation, and physical pain to an almost unlimited degree provided the will was strong enough, has demanded some modification ever since the central war time inference from the premises—that Japanese spirit would be superior to American guns and bombs—has been falsified. (69)

Yet, as pointed out by Frager and Rohlen (1976:255), "The future of a tradition: Japanese spirit in the 1980s," the concept of 'seishin' has survived the wartime defeat and continues to act "as a kind of interpretative lens through which the Japanese like to view their own culture and society" (Moeran 1986:69–70). It is particularly interesting to note that an increasingly large proportion of Japanese companies conduct regular programs of "*seishin* training" for all their employees. Rohlen (1986) provides a fascinating account of such a program (in which he himself participated) in "'Spiritual education' in a Japanese bank." He reports that the program included, among other things, an arduous "endurance walk," Spartan sessions of Zen meditation, visits to military bases (involving military exercises, fitness tests, and listening to lectures on military history), and exercises in cramped "group living."

Recalling the pain and the exhaustion associated with one of these exercises, Rohlen (1986) comments revealingly: "I vowed over and over never to get involved in such a situation again, and yet, within days, when the memory of the physical pain had dimmed, I was taking great pride in my accomplishment and viewing my completion of the twenty-five mile course as proof that I could do anything I set my mind to" (325).

Trying to articulate his understanding of *seishin*, based both on research and on personal experience, Rohlen writes:

> How may we define the term *seishin*? If the frame of reference is a very general one contrasting physical and mental, the concept *seishin* would most likely be placed in the mental column. Attitudes, will power, concentration, and many other "mental" qualities are important aspects of spiritual power. Yet this kind of distinction obscures more than it clarifies, for the physical/mental distinction is not central to the concept. . . . The standard by which spiritual strength (*seishinryoku*) is measured is performance. The outward manifestations of strength are such things as the ability to endure trouble and pain, a coolness in the face of threat, patience, dependability, persistence, self-reliance, and intense personal motivation; qualities we would associate with "strong personal character." (328)

Let us reiterate Rohlen's question: How may we define the term *seishin*? My own answer is as follows:

seishin
(a) X thinks something like this:
(b)   I want to do something very good (Y)
(c)   I know: I can't do it now
(d)   I can do it after now if I do other things now
(e)   I know: I will have to do these other things for a long time
(f)   I know: I will feel something bad because of this
(g)   I don't want not to do these other things because of this
(h)   I want to do these other things
(i)   X does these other things because of this
(j)   X can do something very good (Y) because of this
(k) X can do many other good things because of this

Component (a) reflects the "mental" basis of *seishin*, whereas component (b) accounts for its volitional character, reflected in dictionary glosses such as "will," "motive," and "intention." Components (c) and (d) account for the fact that *seishin* cannot refer to a "natural" quality but only to something due to personal development. They also account for the emphasis on training as a basis of *seishin*. Component (e) accounts for the necessity of perseverance and endurance, (f) for the "endurance" and "hardships," and (g) and (h) for determination and "will power." Component (i) refers to the actual "training," and component (j) to the resulting mastery and attainment of self-imposed goals. Component (k) accounts for the fact that, despite the singlemindedness reflected in component (b), if one has *seishin* one could do not just one thing but many different things (even if not exactly as Rohlen put it, anything one sets one's mind to).

8. *Omoiyari*

Omoiyari is generally regarded as one of the most important ideals in Japanese society. Variously translated into English with nouns such as "empathy," "sympathy," "compassion," and "consideration," and with adjectives such as "thoughtful," "sensitive," and "considerate," *omoiyari* cannot, of course, correspond in meaning to all of them, and, as demonstrated in detail by Travis (1992), it doesn't correspond exactly to any of them. Nor does it correspond to any "mixtures" of English words, such as those offered by Rohlen: "concerned sensitivity," "empathetic sensing," "concerned empathy," or "concerned empathic kindness" (quoted in Travis 1992:23). Lebra (1976) comments on the first of these aspects of *omoiyari*:

> Inward communication of unity and solidarity stems from the notion that in perfect intimacy Ego does not have to express himself verbally or in conspicuous action because what is going on inside him should be immediately detected by Alter. The Japanese glorify silent communication, *ishin denshin* ('heart to heart communication'), and mutual 'vibrations', implying the possibility of semi-telepathic communication. Words are paltry against the significance of reading subtle signs and signals and the intuitive grasp of each other's feelings. The ultimate form of such communication is *ittaikan* ('feeling of oneness'), a sense of fusion between Ego and Alter. (115)

In addition, Lebra speaks of "anticipating and taking care of Alter's wants," of "understanding of Alter's feelings without verbal communication," and of "providing what Alter needs or likes and . . . avoiding whatever might cause discomfort for him" (40–41).

As Lebra and others point out, the ideal of *omoiyari* is closely linked with the communicative style prevailing in Japanese society, and in particular with what she calls "anticipatory communication":

> Ego does not express his wish but expects Alter or a third person to anticipate his wish. The burden of communication falls not on the message sender but on the message receiver. Instead of Ego's having to tell or ask for what he wants, others around him guess and accommodate his needs, sparing him embarrassment. This sort of anticipatory communication was referred to in the context of empathy. . . .
>
> For anticipatory communication to be possible, Ego must be trained to be both receptive to the offer of such service by Alter and sensitive to Alter's unexpressed needs. The extreme of such sensitivity merges with silent communication in intimate behavior. *Omoiyari* ("empathy") cuts across the two situations, ritual and intimate, obviating verbal communication in both. (123).

Clearly, there is no word in English combining the same configuration of ideas.

On the basis of careful analysis of numerous sentences including the word *omoiyari*, Travis (1992) proposed a rigorous explication of this concept phrased in lexical universals. I will reproduce, and comment on, this explication later on. For the time being we can characterize *omoiyari*, loosely, as an ability to "read other people's minds" and a willingness to respond to other people's unspoken feelings, wants, and needs.

What needs to be stressed is not only the semantic uniqueness of *omoiyari* but also its cultural salience: not only is *omoiyari* a common everyday word, but it is also one of the highest-ranking words among those cited by Japanese informants as referring to particularly desirable human characteristics.

Thus, in a survey conducted among Australian and Japanese speakers in Australia, Travis (1992) asked what kind of personal characteristics the respondents valued most, and she found that while the Australians mentioned most commonly the words *honest, intelligent,* and *kind,* the Japanese top-ranking words were *yasahii* (roughly, 'gentle'), *akarui* (roughly 'bright, cheerful'), and *omoiyari.* The figures cited by Travis are as follows:

honest	70%	yasashii	77%
intelligent	50%	akarui	68%
kind	20%	omoiyari	58%

The special importance of *omoiyari* in the Japanese hierarchy of values is reflected in Lebra's suggestion that Japanese could be called an "omoiyari culture" (1976:38; cf. also Minamoto 1969). Lebra comments:

> For the Japanese, *empathy* (*omoiyari*) ranks high among the virtues considered indispensable for one to be really human, morally mature, and deserving of respect. I am even tempted to call Japanese culture an "omoiyari culture." *Omoiyari* refers to the ability and willingness to feel what others are feeling, to vicariously experience the pleasure or pain that they are undergoing and to help them satisfy their wishes . . . kindness or benevolence becomes *omoiyari* only if it is derived from such sensitivity to the recipient's feelings. The ideal in *omoiyari* is for Ego to enter into Alter's kokoro, "heart," and to absorb all information about Alter's feelings without being told verbally. (38)

The importance of the ideal of *omoiyari* in Japanese culture is also highlighted by Nakatsugawa's (1992) observation that in a reader's column in the Japanese newspaper *Shikoku Shimbun,* where parents can publish a photo of a baby together with their hopes and expectations about the qualities he or she will develop, often the parents' first comment is "omoiyari-no aru ko-ni natte-ne," that is, 'Please become a person with *omoiyari*'. Furthermore, Nakatsugawa points out that *omoiyari* has an important place in educational guidelines for teachers, the first of which is "omoiyari-no kokoro-o taisetsu-ni shimashoo," that is, 'Let's treasure the mind (spirit) of *omoiyari*'.

Trying to capture the elusive "spirit of *omoiyari*" in a semantic formula, Travis (1992) proposed an explication phrased in lexical universals, justifying every component on the basis of a meticulous analysis of numerous examples. I will reproduce this explication here in a slightly modified form:

> *omoiyari* (e.g. X has *omoiyari*, X is a person with *omoiyari*)
> (a) X often thinks something like this about other people:
> (b)   I think I can know what this person feels
> (c)   I think I can know what this person wants
> (d)   I can do something good for this person because of this
> (e)   I want to do this
> (f)   this person doesn't have to say anything

(g) because of this, X does something
(h) people think: this is good

As Clancy (1986) and others (cf. e.g. Conroy et al. 1980) have pointed out, "*omoiyari* training" occupies a prominent place in the socialization of children of Japan (Clancy calls it "empathy training," but it is clear that what she really means is "*omoiyari* training").[6] She comments: "In giving directives, Japanese mothers strongly emphasized sensitivity to the needs, wishes, and feelings of others. In fact, such appeals for empathy, both implicit and explicit, constituted 45 percent of all the rationales given by mothers for their directives" (232). Often, the mothers in Clancy's data simply informed their children of the needs of other people, for example, by saying, "If you don't speak more clearly, older sister won't understand" or "Older sister is hungry." But clearly, the mothers were trying not only to make the children responsive to the needs of others but also to anticipate and "guess" these needs:

> One might well wonder how Japanese children learn to "read the minds" of other people in this way. . . . A common behavior for all three mothers in the sample was to attribute speech to people who had not actually spoken, thereby indicating to the child what might be on their minds. . . . Attributing speech to others is one way Japanese mothers teach their children to be sensitive to others. (233)

Clancy's examples include the following (all addressed to two-year-olds):

> Older sister says, "Show me your toys."
> The girls also say, "We want to eat" [said to a child eating a tangerine].

> Older sister says, "ouch ouch."

Clearly, pedagogical practices of this kind are fully consistent with the ideal of *omoiyari,* as explicated in the proposed semantic formula.

Lebra's comments on the importance of *omoiyari* in Japanese culture have been questioned (as have those of Doi's on *amae*) by Dale (1986):

> To substantiate this myth, reference is frequently made to the clipped laconic exchanges between boss and employee, husband and wife, or intimates. But such abbreviated discourse is nothing other than what in Western linguistics is described as 'exophoric or context-dependent speech', and is hardly unique. Indeed, many celebrations of the *sui generis* silence of the Japanese versus the verbose rhetoric of Westerners tend to remind one of Basil Bernstein's classification of working-class speech style and middle-class language in the United Kingdom. (103)

What Dale doesn't take into account is the evidence provided by the word *omoiyari* itself. While the attitude reflected in this word is of course not unknown in Anglo culture, the fact that English has no word for it suggests that it is not as salient as it is in Japanese culture—a fact dramatically confirmed in Travis's survey cited at the outset (and supported by Nakatsugawa's observations).

9. Conclusion

Like many others before her, the Japanese American anthropologist Harumi Befu wonders whether one can meaningfully compare differing concepts between two cultures given that "no matter how one might rephrase the statement, one cannot eliminate the uniqueness of the meaning inherent in each language" (1989:331). Like many others, too, Befu sees comparing cultures on the one hand, and recognizing the uniqueness of each culture on the other, in terms of an insoluble dilemma. As an example she offers one of the words discussed in this chapter, namely, *on*:

> To give a simple example, the Japanese concept of 'on' may be translated as "debt" or "indebtedness" in English. But *on* singularly lacks the monetary connotation which the English terms include. 'On' implies certain social relationships such as the parent-child, teacher-student, or employer-employee relationship, and it evokes a feeling that one is associating with Japan's feudal or traditional values. When Japanese are asked to think of *on*, they think of all these and more. When Americans think of *debt*, none of these connotations are central, though Americans may have some sense of social indebtedness. Thus, the use of *on* in Japanese and *debt* as its English equivalent would likely lead to erroneous conclusions. Much the same can be said of questionnaires asking about the existence of *kami* in Japanese and about the existence of *God* in English. (331)

Befu doesn't fully spell out her pessimistic conclusion, but the editors of the volume, Sugimoto and Mouer (1989), do it for her:

> The paper by Befu on *emic* (cultural-specific) and *etic* (universalistic cross-cultural) modes of analysis demonstrates clearly that the language barrier is more than a problem of translation. Befu argues that the use of language as a tool for analysis, for transcription and for communicating the results of one's research on one culture to persons in another often involves the imposition of categories from the one culture onto those of another. (15)

> As Befu hints in Chapter 10, there may be no truly *etic* concepts; the best we have are the *emic* concepts of the most influential society which may be superimposed on world society as a kind of lingua franca. (23)

I hope I have shown in this chapter and in this book as a whole, that pessimistic conclusions of this kind are unwarranted, and that the culture-specific ("emic") concepts of Japanese culture, like those of any other culture, can be described and explained to outsiders in terms of universal ("etic") concepts. There is no need to deny the uniqueness of Japanese key words such as those discussed in this chapter in order to portray them in terms comprehensible to outsiders and free of ethnocentric bias.

Appendix

SUMMARY OF THE FORMULAE

amae
(a) X thinks something like this about someone (Y):
(b)   when Y thinks about me, Y feels something good

(c)   Y wants to do good things for me
(d)   Y can do good things for me
(e)   when I am with Y nothing bad can happen to me
(f)   I don't have to do anything because of this
(g)   I want to be with Y
(h) X feels something good because of this

enryo
(a) when X is with person Y, X thinks something like this:
(b)   I can't say to this person:
(c)   "I want this, I don't want this"
(d)   "I think this, I don't think this"
(e)   if I did this, someone could feel something bad because of this
(f)   someone could think something bad about me because of this
(g) because of this X doesn't say things like this
(h) because of this X doesn't do some things
(i) people think: this is good

wa
(a) these people want to be like one thing
(b) they all want the same
(c) they want to do some things because of this
(d) they don't want this:
(e)   one of them says: "I want this"
(f)   another one says: "I don't want this"
(g) they don't want to say about some of them:
(h)   "these people did something good,
(i)   these people did something bad"
(j) they don't want to say about one of them
     "this person did something very good"
(k) they all feel something good because of this
(l) they can do some good things because of this
(m) they couldn't do these things if they didn't all want the same
(n) people think this is very good

on
(a) X thinks something like this about someone:
(b)   this person did something very good for me
(c)   I couldn't do something like this for this person
(d)   I have to think about this always
(e)   I have to do good things for this person because of this
(f)   if this person wants me to do something I have to do it
(g) X feels something bad because of this

giri
(a) X thinks something like this about someone:
(b)   I have to do good things for person Y
(c)   if I don't do this it will be bad
(d)   if I don't do this, Y can feel something bad
(e)   people will say bad things about me because of this
(f)   I don't want this

(g) because of this, I have to do good things for Y
(h) I have to think about this

seishin
(a) X thinks something like this:
(b) I want to do something very good (Y)
(c) I know: I can't do it now
(d) I can do it after now if I do other things now
(e) I know: I will have to do these other things for a long time
(f) I know: I will feel something bad because of this
(g) I don't want not to do these other things because of this
(h) I want to do these other things
(i) X does these other things because of this
(j) X can do something very good (Y) because of this
(k) X can do other good things because of this

omoiyari
(a) X often thinks something like this about other people:
(b) I think I can know what this person feels
(c) I think I can know what this person wants
(d) I can do something good for this person because of this
(e) I want to do this
(f) this person doesn't have to say anything
(g) because of this, X does something
(h) people think: this is good

Notes

Chapter 1

1. As a matter of fact, the concept of 'pošlost' did survive into the Soviet era and was even made use of by the official ideology. For example, Dovlatov (1986:125) reports (tongue in cheek?) that the song "Ja pit' želaju gub tvoix nektar" ("I desire to drink the nectar of your lips") was forbidden by the censorship as anti-Soviet, with the justification: "pošlost'."

2. I hasten to add that the expression "Anglo culture" (which some find objectionable) is meant to refer to the common core of the different "Anglo cultures," and does not imply homogeneity.

3. On the notion of "core cultural values," see Smolicz 1979.

4. A colleague who teaches Asian studies comments: "If I tell my Australian students that cultural norms prevailing in a particular Asian society are different from the Australian ones I am attacked by the politically correct for 'essentializing cultures', but if I don't tell them about such differences the results will be disastrous for them when they go to that country." My colleague's solution is to present his students with a series of case studies, without, however, making any generalizations, and to let the students make such generalizations (which cannot be stated overtly) in their heads. Of course, a lot of time is wasted in this way, and often students do get things wrong, but at least this colleague is now seldom accused of "stereotyping" and "cultural racism" (in contrast to some others who still dare to make generalizations).

5. Tyler (1987) speaks of the "impossibility of translation" as if it didn't matter whether we were never able to understand people from other cultures. He considers it "a silly idea to suppose that one might render the meanings of another folk in terms already known to us just as if the others had never been there at all. It is not for us to know the meaning for them unless it is already known to us both, and thus needs no translation, but only a kind of reminding" (214). Fortunately, the important truth that languages embody different systems of meaning does not have to lead us to such a nihilistic conclusion: we can understand the meanings of another folk via linguistic universals.

Chapter 2

1. Unless otherwise specified, the examples quoted in this section come from Stevenson (1949).

2. Undoubtedly, patterns of interpersonal relations among women tend to differ from those among men, in America as elsewhere. With respect to America, Packard notes that "keeping friendships bland and readily disconnectable seems harder on women than on men"(1974:189). No doubt, these differences are reflected in various ways in the ways of speaking. The fact that heterosexual women can have "girlfriends" whereas heterosexual men don't have "boyfriends" is a good case in point. But the changes in the use of the word *friend*, discussed in this chapter, apply across the board.

3. While I am not in a position to offer any statistical evidence to support the notion, it is my impression that as the use of the "a friend of mine" construction grew, the use of another construction involving the word *friend*, namely, the symmetrical use of "friends" in the sense of "mutual friends" (not "someone's friends" but "each other's friends"), declined. The word *friend* seems to be still commonly used as a symmetrical predicate, as in the following example:

We are still friends (lovers, neighbors).

In referential use, however, phrases such as "the friends" or "the two friends" (without a possessive modifier) sound now old-fashioned, as the following examples from the beginning of the century illustrate:

Fastening their boat to a willow, the friends landed in this silent, silver kingdom, and patiently explored the hedges, the hollow trees, the tunnels and their little culverts, the ditches and dry waterways (Grahame 1980[1908]:135).

The affair was soon over. Up and down, the whole length of the hall, strode the four Friends, whacking with their sticks at every head that showed itself; and in five minutes the room was cleared (Grahame 1980[1908]:247).

Similarly, the phrase "the Society of Friends" sounds today quaint and archaic and to many present-day speakers it suggests the question "Whose friends?" Today, one could form, for example, "the society of friends of the whale," but hardly "the society of friends" *tout court*.

The apparent decline of the symmetrical referential use of "friends" is consistent with the shift in perspective discussed throughout this chapter. The symmetrical construction (as in "the two friends," or even "the four friends") suggests a small group of people, seen as mutually closely related. With the increase in the expected number of "friends" and with their increased mobility and transience, the image of one stable point of reference with various (not necessarily stable) adjuncts is more relevant than that of a "twosome," or a trio, seen as some kind of collective unit.

4. The Russian word *znakomyj* can refer to a fairly wide range of relationships, from a *blizkij* ('close') or *xorošij* ('good') to *dal'nij* ('distant') and even *šapočnyj znakomyj* (literally 'a hat znakomyj', analogous to 'a nodding acquaintance'). The point is that this range (and the underlying conceptualization) is different from that of the English word *acquaintance*; and the fact that in English one can't say *close acquaintance* or *good acquaintance* at all highlights the nature of this difference. To illustrate:

Esenin ne čuvstvoval raznicy meždu dnem i noč'ju. . . . Nočami zvonil po telefonu, podnimalsja noč'ju s posteli i otpravljalsja k znakomym, ne gladja na časy. (Vinogradskaja 1991:7)

'Esenin never distinguished between night and day. At night he would be on the phone or get out of bed and visit "acquaintances" [*znakomye*] regardless of the hour.'

Odnaždy . . . on prišel k znakomoj, byl nevesel, poprosil xorošij karandaš i bumagu i skoro ušel, skazav, čto idet pisat'. (Vinogradskaja 1991:23)

'Once he arrived at a "woman acquaintance's" (*znakomaja*) house in a gloomy mood, and having asked for paper and a decent pencil, he left, saying he was going away to write something.'

Esenin's behavior can be said to be unusual by any standards, but if the word *znakomye* in these sentences were to be translated as "acquaintances" rather than "friends," it would make no sense at all.

5. It is probable that the prodigious figure of 817 covers not only the use of the word *drug* in the sense of "close friend" but also its use in the phrase *drug druga* "each other". The contrast between the frequency of *družba* (155) and that of *friendship* (27 and 8) suggests that even if the uses of *drug* in *drug druga* were to be subtracted from the overall frequency of *drug*, the remaining figure would still be extremely high.

6. Even Pushkin's mock definition of *drug* (applied to Bordeaux wine) focuses on a *drug*'s reliable help in need, as well as his or her readiness to be with us and to share our moods:

No ty, Bordo, podoben drugu,
Kotoryj, v gore i v bede
Tovarišč zavsegda, vezde,
Gotov nam okazat' uslugu
Il' tixij razdelit' dosug.
Da zdravstvuet Bordo, naš drug!

'But you, Bordeaux, are like a friend [*drug*]
who is, in grief and in calamity,
at all times, everywhere, a comrade,
ready to render us a service
or share our quiet leisure.
Long live Bordeaux, our friend!'
(Nabokov's translation, in Pushkin 1975:196)

7. I am not saying that it is absolutely impossible for the word *podruga* to refer to a small boy's female friend. SSRLJ cites one example from the nineteenth century writer's, Aksakov's, childhood memoirs in which *podruga* is in fact used like that:

Ja stroil iz nix [kusočkov dereva] kakie-to kletki, i moja podruga ljubila razrušat' ix, maxnuv svoej ručonkoj. (S. Aksakov)

'I used to build cages from them [little pieces of wood], which my *podruga* liked to knock over, with a quick movement of her hand [literally "little hand," a diminutive].'

But normally, a boy's *podruga* implies something like "girlfriend" rather than "cherished female companion" or "female friend."

8. As noted by Windle (in press), in prisons and camps, a prisoner who used the word *tovarišč* to address his guards could expect to hear "ty mne ne tovarišč" ('you're not a *tovarišč* to me'), often followed by "brianskij volk tebe tovarišč" ('the Briansk wolf is your *tovarišč*'). This contrast between *tovarišč* and the "Briansk wolf" is immortalized in the popular underground Russian song "Tovarišč Stalin" (Comrade Stalin), whose many different variants are analyzed in Windle's article.

9. For example, Hollander (1973) writes:

The survivals of a traditional peasant society are still perceptible in Soviet family life. For example, it is common for three generations to live together—a practice that cannot be attributed *solely* to the housing shortage or the desirability of free domestic help even in a society where most mothers work and there is a shortage of kindergartens and day care centers. The traditional aspects of the family also survive in collective farms, where the family retains many of its economic functions and where the household is the membership unit. The survival of traditional attitudes is apparent in the findings of the Soviet sociologist Kharchev, who reported that 80 per cent of the respondents (in a sample of young couples drawn from Leningrad) sought parental consent before marrying and almost 78 per cent obtained it. It will also strike many American readers as anachronistic that among Soviet parents obedience from their children is still a fairly widespread expectation, as is respect for adults, including the aged (256).

Although these observations are more than twenty years old, one can presume that they have retained some degree of validity (cf. e.g. Shlapentokh 1989).

10. To quote one social commentator (Inkeles 1968):

It appears that despite the massive destruction of the main formal elements of the old social structure and the extensive elaboration of new social forms, a large number of basic attitudes, values, and sentiments, as well as traditional modes of orientation, expression, and reaction were markedly persistent . . . we come in contact here with national character, or better, the modal personality patterns of the population, which show a marked propensity to be relatively enduring despite sweeping changes in the formal structure of society. Certain core or primary institutional forms, notably the kinship structure and the pattern of interpersonal relations within the family, show a comparable resistance and delayed reaction to change despite the revolutionary process (14–15).

11. In German, too, one waiter can refer to another as *mein Kollege* 'my fellow-waiter ("colleague")'. But in German, soldiers were normally referred to as *Kameraden* (Pl.), not as *Kollegen* (Pl.). While the German taxonomy of human relations has points in common with the Polish one (with the word *Freund* and *Bekannte* being quite close to the Polish *przyjaciel* and *znajomy*), the overall system is different, and the crucial Polish category of *koledzy* can be equated with neither *Kollegen* nor *Kameraden*.

12. It is interesting to note that Polish has also preserved, as an archaism, the older word *druh*, cognate with the Russian *drug*, and that the collocation *wierny druh* ('a faithful *druh*') appears to have implications similar to those of the Russian phrase (as does also *niezawodny druh*, comparable to *nadežnyj drug* 'reliable friend'). *Druh*, marginal as it is in modern Polish, implies loyalty and support, and the use of this word as a title among scouts builds on those implications. There is also a conceptual link between *druh* and *drużyna* 'team'. But the key word *przyjaciel* does not have such an association.

13. Of course, restrictions of this kind can always be violated for an expressive purpose, as when Czesław Miłosz (1972:83) speaks of a *daleki przyjaciel* by analogy with a *daleki kuzyn* 'distant cousin':

Mycielski, mój przyjaciel też, ale daleki, tak jak mówi się "daleki kuzyn". Choć więcej niż tylko kolega.

'Mycielski, my *przyjaciel*, too, but a distant one, as one says "a distant cousin." Although more than just a *kolega*.'

14. Although the Polish word *znajomi* is, as mentioned earlier, similar in meaning to the Russian word *znakomye*, the two meanings are not identical. For example, one would be unlikely to use the Polish word *znajomy* in a context discussing casual "prison acquaintances," as in the following two Russian sentences:

V kamere, kuda menja vveli vmeste s tatarinom i šulerom, okazalos' neskol'ko staryx znakomyx, v tom čisle Genka i narkoman, kotoryx ran'še dernuli iz Sverdlovska. (Amal'rik 1970:132):

'In the cell, where I was introduced together with the Tatar and the cardsharper, I saw some old acquaintances (*znakomye*), among them Genka and the drug addict, who had both been yanked out of the Sverdlovsk prison.'

The exact meaning of the Russian word *znakomye* and the relationship between *znakomye* and *znajomi* requires further investigation.

15. Forms of names such as "Lozza" (from Laurie), "Bazza" (from Barry), and "Tezza" (from Terry) are typical of Australian English. They embody culture-specific pragmatic meanings and reflect cultural values closely related to the value of "mateship," especially equality and congenial fellowship. For detailed discussion, see Wierzbicka 1986 and 1991a.

16. Of course not everyone that can be casually addressed as "mate" is regarded as one of the speaker's mates. In fact, in Australia a perfect stranger is still often addressed as "mate"—sometimes threateningly or mockingly—as was also the case a century and a half ago: " 'Your licence, mate', was a peremptory question from a six-foot fellow in blue shirt, thick boots, the face of a ruffie, armed with a carbine and fixed bayonet" (1855, R. Carboni; TAND).

17. As Ian Green pointed out to me (personal communication), the role of "not talking" in "mateship" is sometimes exaggerated, or misinterpreted, as for example in the following quotes: "The best of bloody mates don't say anything" (Hawkes 1990:32). "Silence was the essence of traditional mateship. The gaunt man stands at his wife's funeral; his mate comes up, says nothing but rests a gentle hand briefly on his shoulder" (1986, *Bulletin* [Sydney], quoted in TAND). "Mateship" does not require silence on all topics, and under some circumstances (while drinking) it is even compatible with garrulousness (e.g. on sport, politics, sex). On the other hand, "mates" normally do not discuss their innermost feelings, or ideas in general.

18. An Australian friend has told me that once when she was in hospital, awaiting an operation, her thirteen-year-old son, who came to visit and who was worried about her, asked the other women in the room anxiously, "You're all mates here?" whereupon he was reassured by those other patients that they would look after his mother and that she would be all right. This example illustrates nicely how the use of the word *mate* can be extended to include women, and how this extension happens most naturally when the focus is on the attitude of the person involved: "mates" will not let anything bad happen, or anyone do anything bad, to one of their own.

19. Writing about the common distinction between "close" and other friends "in western societies," Garrett (1989) refers to a study by Morse and Marks (1985), which "found that Australian males routinely distinguished between 'mates' and 'friends'—a 'mate' being a non-intimate friend. . . " Morse and Marks back up the idea that "mateship" is more casual with their findings that work problems would often be discussed with mates (but not personal problems) and that friends, but never mates, might be asked for a financial loan or advice (139).

Statements of this kind misrepresent the nature of Australian "mateship." The fact that Australian "mates" might be reluctant to discuss personal problems with one another does not show that the relation between "mates" is more "casual" than that between "friends." The fact that the bond between "mates" is not based on "intimacy" and personal confidences does not mean that this bond is "casual" or that it is more similar to that between "just friends" than to that between "close friends." Any attempts to interpret the sociocultural category of "mates" through the prism of the concept 'friend' can only lead to distortion and misinterpretation. Both concepts can, however, be described without distortion through lexical universals.

Chapter 3

1. My interest in the concepts discussed in this chapter was stimulated by several conversations with Professor Andrzej Walicki, to whom I would like to express my sincere gratitude.

2. For example, Oppenheim argues that "freedom" should be defined in "non-valuational terms," because since "political science includes value judgements . . . its key concepts must be defined by purely empirical, i.e., non-normative terms" (1962:274). This means that he doesn't see the concept of 'freedom' as an objective datum, which one should seek to elucidate, but as a tool which one can model at will. Since in his view it would be good for the key concepts of political science to be "non-valuational," he thinks he can take for this purpose the concept of 'freedom' and use it as if it were purely descriptive. Such an attitude could be said to be quite legitimate, of course, if the author acknowledged that he was construing his own concept of 'freedom', not necessarily coinciding with that encoded in the English word *freedom*; but this awareness seems to be lacking.

3. Among scores of examples of different uses of *liberty* cited by OED (1933), there is one including *liberty from*: "Political or civil liberty is the liberty from legal obligation which is left or granted by a sovereign government to any of its subjects" (Austin, "Jurisprudence," 1832). It should be noted, however, that this sentence comes from a treatise on legal philosophy, not from ordinary language, and that philosophers writing about ideas often feel free to depart from ordinary usage. Thus, if Isaiah Berlin can say, for example, "liberty in this sense means *liberty from*" (1969:127), this does not mean that *liberty* can take *from* in present-day ordinary English either. Significantly, only one example of *liberty from* is cited in the entire (20 million words) corpus of COBUILD, and this example comes from a technical exegesis of St. Paul's Epistle to the Hebrews.

4. An expression such as *free from help* (an analogy with *free from interference*) would be judged as either ungrammatical or ironic. Expressions such as *free of admirers, free of relatives,* and *free of fans* would imply that admirers, relatives and fans are seen as a nuisance. Collocations such as *tax free* and *pollution free* imply that taxes and pollution are seen as something bad for the persons affected by them, and that their absence is good for them. On the other hand, an expression such as *X is free to do Z* implies that being able to do Z is seen as something of value for X (even if the speaker regards doing Z as something bad).

Admittedly, an expression such as *pupil-free day*, used in the education system in Australia, could be seen as a counter-example to the claim made here. But first, many parents in Australia find this expression offensive and see it as implying that the educators regard pupils as a nuisance, and that a day without students is felt as something good for the teachers, and second, this expression belongs to a bureaucratic jargon, and like many phrases which have been coined artificially, it may run counter to common intuitions of ordinary language users.

I must conclude that claims such as those made by Sommerville (1962) that "there is no necessary relation between freedom and value, that it is impossible to define freedom consistently as a value term" (780) are not justified. It is true that "concepts like honesty or justice are of a different nature" (781), but they are not different because "concepts like justice or honesty are, by their very nature, value concepts" whereas 'freedom' is not. 'Freedom', too, is a value concept, but in a different way. Not all value judgments are moral judgments. There is a difference between an assumption that something is "good," and an assumption that something is "good for someone."

5. Cf. in this connection Walicki's (1984) analysis of what he calls the "classical liberal conception of freedom":

> A man is free when *nobody forbids* him to act in accordance with his own will, and it is inessential whether those actions *can* bring about the results expected by him. . . . Freedom thus conceived is therefore not *positive liberty*, or the ability to attain desired ends: it is *negative liberty*—freedom from commands and prohibitions imposed on an individual by other men. One may add that legal norms do not contradict freedom, since their character is universal and impersonal. Rule of law excludes arbitrariness and therefore secures freedom; admittedly it sets definite limits to freedom, but within those limits it guarantees the individual a sphere of privacy free from the interference of any other persons and any authority. It is just that sphere of independence, in which the individual is free from all interference and at the same time left at his own risk, which is the proper sphere of freedom (226).

In another highly relevant work, Philip Pettit (1997:21) contrasts the modern idea of "freedom as non-interference" with the "republican" idea of "freedom as non-domination," and he argues that "the originators of the negative, purportedly modern idea of freedom as non-interference were not those who welcomed the American revolution," and that "it was precisely the conception of freedom as non-domination, not the negative conception of freedom as non-interference, that was embraced among writers in the republication tradition." I think the lexical and semantic shift from *liberty* to *freedom* (in the modern sense of the word) supports Petti's argument. But the picture suggested by linguistic evidence is perhaps more complex than that presented by Pettit. In particular, his notion of "non-domination" is too broad to tally well with the linguistic facts. The English *liberty*, conceived in opposition to, roughly speaking, oppression in a hierarchical feudal society, did not (and does not) mean the same as the Latin *libertas*, conceived in ancient Rome in opposition to slavery.

6. For Shakespeare, the exact figure is 83 occurrences of *liberty* per 880,000 words, whereas for COBUILD, it is 222 occurrences per 20 million, if we include *Liberty*, and 100 if we exclude it.

7. Other uses of *liberty* are not impossible, but they sound archaic, stylized, or elevated, as in the following examples (from the COBUILD data on *liberty*):

> Killer on run fears liberty.

> . . . to preserve and extend the sacred fire of human liberty.

8. In a pre-summit interview with the BBC (October 1985), President Reagan made a much-commented-on remark that there is no Russian word for freedom. *Time* magazine (November 1985) retorted, "There is: svoboda," and added that "it has long been Reagan's style to avoid cluttering his mind with the complexities of a subject." *Time* magazine didn't offer any explanation as to the source of Reagan's error, but it may well be that he was reproducing an element from a Sovietological briefing referring to Amal'rik's comments on the concept of 'svoboda'. Reagan's remarks could better be countered with the observation that there is no English word for *svoboda* than with a flat assertion that there IS a Russian word for 'freedom'.

9. The fact that twentieth century Russian developed a separate concept of 'volja' as life outside the prison system seems to reflect a conscious or subconscious perception on the part of the Russian people of living in the shadow of a gigantic Gulag archipelago.

10. The fact that Russian has two words, *svoboda* and *volja*, corresponding to the English *freedom* (but very different from one another and from *freedom*), reminds one of another pair of Russian key words, *istina* and *pravda*, both translated into English as *truth*, but very different from one another and from their supposed English equivalent (for two insightful analyses, see Mondry & Taylor 1992 and Šmelev 1996).

11. It is also interesting to note that one of the secondary senses of the English adjective *free* ('without paying') is based on a negative component which is absent from the meaning of *libre*. For example, *free copies* are copies which one can obtain without having to do something that one wouldn't want to do (i.e. without paying). The corresponding adjectives in Latin, German, and French don't have such a meaning, and *free* in this sense has to be translated as *gratis*, *kostenlos*, and *gratuit*. For this reason, the French feminist slogan: "l'avortement libre gratuit" "free free abortion" (i.e. "abortion at will, without pay") cannot be easily rendered in English.

12. Cf. the following couplet from a popular operetta by Wojciech Bogusławski, reflecting the emerging Polish self-image after the partitions of Poland (by Russia, Austria, and Prussia) at the end of the eighteenth century:

> Polak nie sługa, nie zna co to pany
> nie da się okuć przemocą w kajdany.
> Wolnością żyje, do wolności wzdycha,
> Bez niej jak kwiatek bez rosy usycha.

> 'A Pole is not a slave, he doesn't know the meaning of the word master,
> he will not let himself be put by force in chains.
> He lives by freedom, dreams of freedom,
> And without freedom dies like a flower without water.'

The operetta was first staged in Warsaw in 1794, just after the outbreak of the Kościuszko insurrection (against the foreign powers dominating Poland). For the benefit of the Russian censor, the intended and understood word *Polak* 'a Pole' had to be replaced in this couplet with the word *serce* 'the heart'; but, as a German writer present at the spectacle reported it, "A few chief actors, probably by arrangement, were singing textual variations to the melody, and these parodies soon overshadowed the original text. They were repeated by everybody with joy. They spread quickly from the theater to the street, and after the events of Krakow, the battle of Racławice, they changed all the Warsavians into opera singers" (Miłosz 1983:175). After three evenings, the play was forbidden by the Russians, but the defiant patriotic couplet became entrenched in the Polish national lore.

Chapter 4

1. The phrasing of component (k), 'I was like a part of these places when I was a child', may be objected to, as somewhat bizarre. Why not say simply that I "belonged" to that place? But "belong," though more idiomatic in English, is not a lexical universal, so it cannot be used for interpreting the notion of 'Heimat' for cultural outsiders.

2. As an illustration, consider the following quote:

> Gestern abend traf ich Herrn R. . . . . . Und ich fragte Herrn R., der aus Wien war, und
> seit bald dreißig Jahren in New York lebte, und jetzt auf dem Wege in die DDR für

einen Abend in Frankfurt Station machte, wie das denn bei ihm sei—mit dem Vaterland? Sei er nun Amerikaner? Sei er Österreicher? Oder fühle er sich vielleicht gar also Israeli? Man könne doch schließlich das Vaterland nicht einfach so wechseln—sagt man bei uns. Das feine, ironische Lächeln erstarb um seinen Mund, als ich das mit dem Vaterland fragte. Er richtete sich streng auf, legte die Hände flach auf den Tisch und sagte: "Was heißt denn Vaterland, lieber Freund? Bei mir war das so: Die sagten in Österreich eines Tages zu mir, daß ich kein Mensch sei, sondern irgend etwas darunter: ein Untermensch oder ein Blutsauger oder auch eine Wanze— das war 1938. Da bin ich aus diesem Lande gegangen. "Na und?" frage ich, "reicht das denn, um Amerikaner zu werden?"—"Ja", sagte er, "das reicht, es reicht vollkommen, das ist überhaupt das einzig Entscheidende. In New York nahmen sie mich auf, und die New Yorker sagten zu mir, das mit der Wanze sei falsch, ich sei ein Mensch. Sie ließen mich Mensch sein. Sehen Sie, dort ist mein Vaterland." (Krüger 1969:100)

'Last night I met, accidentally, Mr. R. . . . . And I asked Mr. R., who was from Vienna, and had been living for nearly thirty years in New York, and now stopped in Frankfurt for the evening on his way to the GDR; what was, for him, his fatherland? Was he an American? Was he an Austrian? Or perhaps he even felt himself to be an Israeli? After all, one couldn't simply change one's fatherland—as we say. . . . The fine, ironic smile faded when I asked about the fatherland. He sat bolt upright, placed his hands flatly on the table, and said: "What does fatherland mean, my friend? For me, it was like this: One day they told me in Austria that I was no longer a human being, but something lower than that: a subhuman creature or a blood-sucker or even a bed-bug—that was around 1938. So I left this country."—"So?" I asked, "is that enough to become American?"—"Yes," he said, "that is enough, it is completely sufficient, it is in fact the only deciding factor. They accepted me in New York, and the New Yorkers told me, the stuff about the bed-bug was wrong, I was really a human being. They let me be a human being. So you see, that is where my fatherland is."'

3. The special role of the word *Vaterland* in German historical debates is well illustrated by the following fragment from Peter Lotar's (1962) radio play, *Das Bild des Menschen*, first produced in 1952 and set in a wartime German prison:

> GRAF: Sie müssen den Mut haben, konsequent zu Ende zu denken: Was ist das für ein Vaterland, das für Sie zur toten, unbarmherzigen Maschinerie werden konnte?
>
> STUDENT: Es ist immer noch mein Vaterland.
>
> GRAF: Ja, es ist unser aller Vaterland. Aber es ist entehrt und geschändet.
>
> STUDENT: Deshalb müssen wir es nur noch mehr lieben.
>
> GRAF: Ja. Und diese Liebe gebietet uns, das Erniedrigte wieder aufzurichten und das Entehrte zu reinigen.
>
> STUDENT: Wie kann ein einzelner das tun?
>
> GRAF: Nur der einzelne kann es. Was ist das Vaterland? Ist es durch Grenzen bestimmt? Die ändern sich. Durch Sprache oder Rasse? Viele Sprachen und Rassen bilden oft ein Vaterland, und zuweilen teilt sich die gleiche Sprache in zwei Völker. Es ist der große Gleichklang von Millionen einzelner Seelen, verbunden durch ein gemeinsames Ideal. Stirbt dieses, dann stirbt früher oder später auch das Vaterland.

> GRAF: You have to have the courage to think it all through logically: What kind of *Vaterland* is it that turns itself into an inhuman, merciless machine?
>
> STUDENT: It is still my *Vaterland*.

GRAF: Yes, it's our *Vaterland,* for all of us. But it's dishonored and covered in
shame.

STUDENT: Therefore we must love it even more.

GRAF: Yes. And this love requires that we lift it out of this shame and purify
it.

STUDENT: How can an individual do that?

GRAF: Only an individual can do that. What is the *Vaterland?* Is it determined
by borders? Borders change. By language or race? But a *Vaterland* may
have many languages and races, and sometimes the same language is
shared by two peoples. The *Vaterland* is a unison of millions of
individual souls, bound together by one common ideal. If this dies, then
sooner or later the *Vaterland* also dies.

4. Some of the references to quotes adduced in Bartmiński 1993b are given here without
page numbers because the quotes in question were deleted by the author from the published
version of his article.

5. From personal experience, I would add that one may never use a word actively (and
find it hard to imagine doing so) and yet feel that the concept encoded in this word is an important
part of one's personal and cultural identity. This is, for example, how I feel about the word
ojczyzna.

6. Konrad is a romantic hero, a symbol of national martyrology and the struggle for
national freedom.

7. In the Soviet era, the word *rodina* (referring to the country as a whole) was frequently
a subject of political manipulation, as was *ojczyzna* in "People's Poland," and as *Vaterland* was
in the "German Democratic Republic," and earlier, in Nazi Germany. For this reason, today
many Russians avoid using the word *rodina,* just as many Poles avoid the word *ojczyzna* and
many Germans the word *Vaterland.*

Chapter 5

1. The word *Clayton* or *Clayton's* is a recent neologism in Australian English. *The
Australian national dictionary* defines the word *Clayton's* as follows: "Clayton's. [The propri-
etary name of a soft drink]. Something which is largely illusory or exists in name only." This
is illustrated, among others, with the following examples: "1985 *Canberra Times* 13 July B1/1
Australian English is not a Clayton's sort of English, a sort of colonial doggerel you speak when
you cannot manage Standard Southern. 1986. *Ibid.* 16 Feb. 6/5 I'm not sure if the advertisements
boosted sales of Claytons Tonic, but they certainly made 'Claytons' a household word and one
that will make 'The Macquarie Dictionary' before too long."

2. It should be added that *bastard* can also be used in Australia with respect to things, or
situations, as in the following examples from Wilkes (1978):

Of all the bastards of places this is the greatest bastard in the world.
(Idriess 1915)

It's like one of your mates going out on patrol and not coming back.
It's a bastard, but you can't do anything about it. (Glassop 1944)

Sometimes a man began with a question seeking an explanation of my crutches:
'What's wrong with you?' 'Paralysis.' 'Bastard, isn't it. . .?' (Marshall 1962)

The air-conditioner's . . . on the blink. Bastard's not worth two bob.
(Power 1974)

This use, however, would require a separate explication, since a broad formula covering both uses would also include women and thus would be too broad.

3. The word *bloke*, described by the SOED (1964) as "slang" and by *The American Heritage dictionary of the English language* (1973) as "British slang" (and glossed as "man, fellow"), is an extremely common word in Australian English, rich in culture-specific connotations. Far from being perceived as "slang," it is seen in Australia as one of the basic everyday words. The use of this word in Australian speech, which deserves a separate study, can be illustrated with the following passage:

> Canterbury's Terry Lamb is . . . a fierce competitor who loves winning, while a bloke like the Sydney Tigers' Paul Sironen would be a great asset because 'Sirro' is just about the funniest bloke I know and great for morale in touring teams. But if the Raiders gave me complete control of recruiting one bloke for the team I would head for Newcastle to talk to the 'Chief', Paul Harragon. (Daley & Clyde 1995:63)

4. Unlike *bastard* (or *bloody*), *bugger* appears to be losing ground in the speech of the younger generation of Australians. To my daughters' generation, this word, though very frequently heard, already sounds slightly archaic.

5. Eric Partridge's *A dictionary of slang and unconventional English* (1967:105) describes *bullshit* as "mostly Australian" and *bullsh* or *bulsh* (to be discussed later) as "mostly Australian and New Zealand."

6. Baker (1970[1945]:134) lists also the following examples, now obsolete: *bull fodder, bullock waggon, buffalo chips, cowsh, cowflop, cowyard confetti, Flemington confetti, heifer dust, meadow mayonnaise, bumfluff, bovril,* and *alligator bull.*

Chapter 6

1. It is worth noting the use of the word *aggressiveness* in this passage; it is clearly intended here as a descriptive term for something like "assertiveness," but from the point of view of Japanese cultural norms it is difficult to distinguish "assertiveness" from "aggressiveness" since they both violate *enryo*.

2. Hendry (1993) points out that the role of consensus in Japanese culture is sometimes misunderstood:

> This is also a case where misunderstanding is very likely at an intercultural level. The idea, prevalent in the West for some time, that groups of Japanese people make decisions "by consensus" is patently open to suspicion, and I would suggest that this is simply a misreading of a layer or two of wrapping. It is quite possible that meetings may appear to achieve unanimous decisions—indeed, they very often do—but this must simply mean that these decisions have been reached somehow before the meeting ever started. Even a cursory investigation will uncover the practice known as *nemawashii*, the literal "tending of the roots," or groundwork, which precedes most meetings in Japan, as indeed elsewhere. (144)

But while something like *nemawashii* may indeed occur elsewhere, the very word *nemawashii*—which has no equivalent in English or in other European languages—provides evidence for the special importance of this practice (and of something like "consensus") in Japanese culture.

3. It is interesting to note Kiefer's (1976) remark: "When I questioned a group of white-collar salaried men about their loyalty to their company, they considered the idea of loyalty *to company* ludicrous. They would not change jobs, if the opportunity arose, because

they felt intense loyalty to the 'office gang' with whom they worked and relaxed during the largest percentage of their waking lives" (299).

4. No "repayment" appears to be involved in some of the situations which Benedict (1947) linked with one's "giri to one's name" (see also Minami 1971:165). But since present-day informants reject such cases anyway (as instances of *giri*), I have not included them in the present discussion. For the same reason, I have not included in the present discussion duties to uncles and aunts, or nephews or nieces, which according to Benedict (1947:136) also come under *giri*.

5. Both the "private" character of *giri*-relationships and their link with reputation are sometimes interpreted as responsible for the differences between private and "anonymous" behavior in Japan. For example, Dore (1958) writes:

> The man who is punctilious in performing all his obligations towards people with whom he has a *giri*-relationship will, it is said, nevertheless fight tooth and nail to be the first on the train, scatter litter in public parks, sell adulterated food and fail to put himself out to help strangers in distress. "Other people" outside of his *giri* world, people whose displeasure is of no importance to him do not count. The only way, says one newspaper writer, to prevent Japanese from using train lavatories while trains are standing in a station is to provide automatic locking devices on the doors. (386)

Cf. also the Japanese proverb quoted by Lebra: "A traveller can do anything without shame (1976:80)."

6. For a detailed argument showing why *empathy* (which is not an everyday English word anyway) cannot be regarded as a semantic equivalent of *omoiyari*, see Travis (1992). It should be immediately clear, however, that while *empathy* does imply something like "intuitive" understanding of other people, it does not imply a wish to do good things for them.

References

Adamova-Sliozberg, Ol'ga. 1993. *Put'*. Moscow: Vozvraščenie.

Adams, Philip. 1995. Transcript of ABC Radio's "Late Night Live," July 11, 1995.

Adler, Lenore L., ed. 1977. *Issues in cross-cultural research*. New York: New York Academy of Sciences. (Annals, 285)

Allan, Graham A. 1979. *A sociology of friendship and kinship*. London: Allen and Unwin.

Amal'rik, Andrej. 1970. *Will the Soviet Union survive until 1984?* London: Penguin.

———. 1978. *SSSR i zapad v odnoj lodke*. London: Overseas Publications Interchange.

———. 1982. *Zapiski dissidenta*. Ann Arbor, Mich.: Ardis.

Ameka, Felix. 1986. The use and meaning of selected particles in Ewe. M.A. thesis. Australian National University.

———. 1987. A comparative analysis of linguistic routines in two languages: English and Ewe. *Journal of Pragmatics* 11:299–326.

———. 1990. The grammatical packaging of experiencers in Ewe. *Australian Journal of Linguistics*. Special issue on emotions. 10.2:139–182.

———. 1991. Ewe: Its grammatical constructions and illocutionary devices. Ph.D. thesis. Australian National University.

———. 1994. Ewe. In Goddard and Wierzbicka 1994:57–86.

The American Heritage dictionary of the English language. 1973. Boston: Houghton Mifflin.

Amis, Kingsley. 1966. *The anti-death league*. Harmondsworth: Penguin.

Antipenko, L.A., and G.N. Karnaušenko. 1993. Rodina glazami xar'kovskogo studenčestva. In Bartmiński, ed. 1993:105–126.

Appignanesi, Richard, and Chris Garratt. 1995. *Postmodernism for beginners*. Cambridge: Icon Books.

Applegate, Celia. 1990. *A nation of provincials: The German idea of Heimat*. Berkeley: University of California Press.

Arima, Michiko. 1991. Creative interpretation of the text and the Japanese mentality. In Ikegami 1991:33–55.

Aschroft, Bill, and John Salter, 1994. 'Australia': A rhizomic text. In Dobrez, ed. 1994:15–24.

Atsumi, Reiko. 1980. Patterns of personal relationships in Japan. *Social Analysis* 5/6.43,4:483–492.

———. 1989. Friendship in cross-cultural perspective. In Sugimoto and Mouer 1989:130–156.

Austin, Lewis. 1976. The political culture of two generations: Evolution and divergence in Japanese and American values. In Austin, ed. 1976:231–254.

———. 1976. *Japan: The paradox of progress.* New Haven: Yale University Press.

Australian Newspaper (Sydney). July 11, 1995.

Baker, Sidney J. 1959. *The drum: Australian character and slang.* Sydney: Currawong.

———. 1970 [1945]. *The Australian language.* 2d ed. Melbourne: Sun Books.

Barańczak, Stanisław. 1990. *Breathing under water and other East European essays.* Cambridge: Harvard University Press.

Barnlund, Dean. (1975). *Public and private self in Japan and in the United States.* Tokyo: Simul Press.

Bartmiński, Jerzy. 1989. Jak biegną drogi ojczyzny? *Ethos* (Lublin) 2,5 1:165–171.

———. 1993a. Polskie rozumienie ojczyzny i jego warianty. In Bartmiński, ed. 1993:23–48.

———. 1993b. Ojczyzny europejskie—duże i małe. In Bartmiński, ed. 1993:5–11.

———, ed. 1993. Pojęcie ojczyzny we współczesnych językach europejskich. Lublin: Instytut Europy Środkowo-Wschodniej.

Bauer, Raymond, Alex Inkeles, and Clyde Kluckhohn. 1956 *How the Soviet system works.* Cambridge: Harvard University Press.

Befu, Harumi. 1986. Gift-giving in a modernizing Japan. In Lebra and Lebra 1986:158–170.

———. 1989. The emic-etic distinction and its significance for Japanese studies. In Sugimoto and Mouer 1989:323–343.

Bell, Robert. 1973. *Mateship in Australia and its implications for gender relations.* La Trobe Occasional Papers in Sociology, 1. Melbourne: La Trobe University.

Bellah, Robert. 1957. *Tokugawa religion: The values of pre-industrial Japan.* New York: Free Press.

———. 1985. *Tokugawa religion: The cultural roots of modern Japan.* New York: Free Press.

Bellah, Robert N., Richard Madsen, William M. Sullivan, Ann Swidler, and Steven M. Tipton. 1985. *Habits of the heart: Individualism and commitment in American life.* Berkeley: University of California Press.

Benedict, Ruth. 1947. *The chrysanthemum and the sword.* London: Secker and Warburg.

Benet, Sula. 1953. Courage: Cumulative effects of sacrifice. In Mead and Métraux 1953:415–421.

Berlin, Brent, and Paul Kay. 1969. *Basic colour terms: Their universality and evolution.* Berkeley: University of California Press.

Berlin, Isaiah. 1969. *Four essays on liberty.* Oxford: Clarendon Press.

Berry, John Widdup, S.H. Irivine, and Earl Hunt, eds. 1988. *Indigenous cognition: Functioning in cultural context.* Dordrecht-Boston: Martinus Nijhoff.

Bester, John. 1981. Forward. In Doi 1981:7–10.

Bevan, E. Dean. 1971. *A concordance to the plays and prefaces of Bernard Shaw.* Detroit: Gale Research.

Blieszner, Rosemary, and Rebecca G. Adams. 1992. *Adult friendship.* Newbury Park, Calif.: Sage.

Bloomsbury. 1991. *Bloomsbury dictionary of quotations.* London: Bloomsbury.

Bogusławski, Andrzej. 1966. *Semantyczne pojęcie liczebnika.* Wrocław: Ossolineum.

———. 1970. On semantic primitives and meaningfulness. In Greimas, Jakobson, and Mayenowa 1970:143–152.

———. 1975. On "the world." *Linguistica Silesiana* 1:63–70.

———. 1981. Wissen, Warheit, Glauben: zur semantischen Beschaffenheit des kognitiven Vokabulars. In Bungarten 1981:54–84.

———. 1985. Sur les expressions d'addresse avec reference particulière au polonais. *Revue des études slaves* 57. 3:469–481.

————. 1989. Knowledge is the lack of lack of knowledge, but what is that lack lack of? *Quaderni di semantica* 10.1:15–31.

————. 1990. Semantic primes for agentive relations. *Lingua Posnaniensis* 32/33:39–64.

Böll, Heinrich. 1980. *Ansichten eines Clowns*. Köln: Kiepenheurer and Witch.

Bolle, Kees. 1979. *The Bhagavadgita: A new translation*. Berkeley: University of California Press.

Bowles, Colin. 1986. *G'day! Teach yourself Australian in 20 easy lessons*. Sydney: Angus and Robertson.

Brinkley's Japanese English dictionary. 1963. Cambridge: Heffer.

Brockhaus Wahrig. 1981. *Deutsches Wörterbuch*. Ed. Gerhard Wahrig, Hildegard Krämer, and Harald Zimmerman. 6 vols. Wiesbaden: F.A. Brockhaus.

Brookner, Anita. 1993. *Fraud*. London: Penguin.

————. 1994. *A family romance*. London: Penguin.

Bruner, Jerome. 1990. *Acts of meaning*. Cambridge: Harvard University Press.

Bugenhagen, Robert. 1990. Experiential constructions in Mangap-Mbula. *Australian Journal of Linguistics*. Special issue on emotions. 10.2:183–215.

Bungarten, T., ed. 1981. *Wissenschaftssprache: Beiträge zur Methodologie, theoretischen Fundierung und Deskription*. Munich: Fink.

Canberra Times. July 13, 1985.

Carey, Peter. 1982. *Bliss*. Australia: Picador.

Carnegie, Dale. 1982 [1936]. *How to win friends and influence people*. New York: Pocket Books.

Carroll, John B., Peter Davies, and Barry Richman. 1971. *The American Heritage word frequency book*. Boston: Houghton Mifflin.

Carter, David. 1994. Future pasts. In Headon, Hooton, and Horne 1994:3–15.

Chambers English dictionary. 1975. Cambridge: Chambers.

Chappell, Hilary, 1983. A semantic analysis of passive, causative and dative constructions in standard Chinese. Ph.D. thesis. Australian National University.

————. 1986a. Formal and colloquial adversity passives in standard Chinese. *Linguistics* 24.6:1025–1052.

————. 1986b. The passive of bodily effect in Chinese. *Studies in Language* 10.2:271–283.

Chappell, Hilary M. 1994. Mandarin semantic primitives. In Goddard and Wierzbicka 1994:109–147.

————. Forthcoming. *Analytic syntax in standard Chinese*. Lanham, Md.: United Press of America.

Chotomska, Wanda. 1967 *Przygody jeża spod miasta Zgierza*. Warsaw: Nasza Księgarnia.

Christopher, Robert C. 1983. *The Japanese mind: The goliath explained*. New York: Linden Press/Simon and Schuster.

Chryssides, Helen. 1995. *In a different light: Ways of being Australian*. Victoria, Australia: HarperCollins.

Clancy, Patricia. 1986. The acquisition of communicative style in Japanese. In: Schieffelin and Ochs 1986:213–250.

Clyne, Michael, ed. 1976. *Australia talks: Essays on the sociology of Australian immigrant and Aboriginal languages*. Canberra: Australian National University. (Pacific Linguistics, D23)

COBUILD. 1987. *Collins Cobuild English language dictionary*. Eds. John Sinclair and Patrick Hanks. London: Collins.

Coleman, Peter, ed. 1968. *Australian civilization: A symposium*. Melbourne: Cheshire.

Collins-Robert. 1983. *French-English English-French dictionary*. London: Collins.

Conklin, Harold. 1957. *Hanunóo agriculture*. Rome: Food and Agriculture Organization of the United Nations.

Conquest, Robert. 1973. *The great terror: Stalin's purges of the thirties*. London: Macmillan.

Conroy, Mary, Robert Hess, Hiroshi Azuma, and Keiko Kashigawa. 1980. Maternal strategies for regulating children's behaviour. *Journal of Cross-cultural Psychology* 11:153–172.

Conway, Ronald. 1971. *The great Australian stupor: An interpretation of the Australian way of life*. Melbourne: Sun Books.

Coulmas, Florian. 1981. Poison to your soul: Thanks and apologies contrastively viewed. In Coulmas, ed. 1981:69–91.

——, ed. 1981. *Conversational routine*. The Hague: Mouton.

Crawford, Raymond M. 1960. *An Australian perspective*. Madison: University of Wisconsin Press.

——. 1970. *Australia*. London: Hutchinson.

Dal', Vladimir. 1955 [1882]. *Tolkovyj slovar' živago velikorusskago jazyka*. 4 vols. Moscow: Gosudarstvennoe Izdatel'stvo Inostrannyx i Nacional'nyx Slovarej.

——. 1977 [1862]. *Poslovitsy russkago naroda; sbornik*. Leipzig: Zentralantiquaria der DDR.

Dale, Peter. 1986. *The myth of Japanese uniqueness*. New York: St. Martin's Press.

Damborsky, Jiři. 1993. Discussion. In Bartmiński, ed. 1993:62–63.

Darder, Antonia. 1995. Introduction. The politics of biculturalism. In: Antonia Darder, ed., *Culture and difference: critical perspective on the bicultural experience in the United States*. Westport, Connecticut: Bergin & Garvey. 1–20.

Darnell, Regna. 1994. Comments on Wolf's "Perilous ideas: Race, culture and people." *Current Anthropology*. 35.1:7–8.

Davies, Norman. 1981. *God's playground: A history of Poland*. Oxford: Clarendon.

——. 1984. *Heart of Europe: A short history of Poland*. Oxford: Clarendon.

Davis, Keith E., and Michael J. Todd. 1985. Assessing friendship: Prototypes, paradigm cases and relationship description. In Duck and Perlman 1985:17–38.

Dean, Jenny. 1985. Poms, wogs, dagos and others: Ethnic labelling in Australia. B.A. honors thesis. Australian National University.

Denisov, Petr Nikitič, and Valerij Veniaminovič Morkovkin. 1978. *Učebnyj slovar' sočetaemosti slov russkogo jazyka*. Moscow: Russkij Jazyk.

Derrida, Jacques. 1982. *L'oreille de l'autre*. Montréal: VLB.

——. 1991. From 'Des tours de Babel'. In Kamuf 1991:243–253.

Der Spiegel Dokument. March 2, 1994.

Descartes, René. 1931 [1701]. The search after truth by the light of nature. In *The philosophical works of Decartes*. Trans. Elizabeth S. Haldane and G.R.T. Ross. 2 vols. Cambridge: Cambridge University Press, 1:305–327.

De Vos, George (with Hiroshi Wagatsuma). 1973. *Socialization for achievement: Essays on the cultural psychology of the Japanese*. Berkeley: University of California Press.

De Vos, George A. 1985. Dimensions of the self in Japanese culture. In Marsella, De Vos, and Hsu 1985:141–184.

Diller, Anthony. 1994. Thai. In Goddard and Wierzbicka 1994: 149–170.

Dirven, René, ed. Forthcoming. *The language of emotions*. Amsterdam: John Benjamins.

Dixon, R.M.W. 1980. *The languages of Australia*. Cambridge: Cambridge University Press.

Dobrez, Livio. 1994. Introduction. In Dobrez, ed. 1994:i–xvii.

——, ed. 1994. *Identifying Australia in postmodern times*. Canberra: Bibliotech, Australian National University.

Doi, Takeo. 1981. *The anatomy of dependence*. Tokyo: Kodansha.

————. 1986. Amae: A key concept for understanding Japanese personality structure. In Lebra & Lebra 1986:145–54.

————. 1988. *The anatomy of self.* Tokyo: Kodansha.

Dore, Ronald P. 1958. *City life in Japan: A study of a Tokyo ward.* Berkeley: University of California Press.

Dovlatov, Sergej. 1983. *Naši.* Ann Arbor: Ardis.

————. 1986. *A foreign woman.* New York: Grove Weidenfeld.

Duck, Steven. 1977. *The study of acquaintance.* Farnborough, Hants: Saxon House.

Duck, Steven, and Daniel Perlman, eds. 1985. *Understanding personal relationships: An interdisciplinary approach.* London: Sage.

Duden. 1980. *Das grosse Wörterbuch der deutschen Sprache.* Ed. Günther Drosdowski. 6 vols. Mannheim: Dudenverlag.

Durie, Mark, Daud Bukhari, and Mawardi Hasan. 1994. Acehnese. In Goddard and Wierzbicka 1994:171–201.

During, Simon. 1995. Fighting words. *The Age,* April 13, 1995, Extra 9. Review of John Willinsky's *Empire of words: The reign of the OED.* Princeton: Princeton University Press.

Erikson, Erik H. 1963. *Childhood and society.* 2d ed. New York: Norton.

Ernst, Thomas M. 1990. Mates, wives and children: An exploration of concepts of relatedness in Australian culture. In Marcus 1990:110–118.

Evans-Pritchard, Edward Evan. 1968 [1940]. *The Nuer: A description of the modes of livelihood and political institutions of a Nilotic people.* Oxford: Clarendon.

Fedotov, Georgij. 1981. *Rossija i svoboda: Sbornik statej.* New York: Chalidze.

Fetscher, Iring. 1992. Heimatliebe—Brauch und Mißbrauch eines Begriffs. In Görner 1992:15–35.

Fishman, Joshua, ed. 1968. *Readings in the sociology of language.* The Hague: Mouton.

Fiske, John, Robert Hodge, and Graeme Turner. 1987. *Myths of Oz: Reading popular Australian culture.* Sydney: Allen and Unwin.

Frager, Robert, and Rohlen, Thomas P. (1976). The future of a tradition: Japanese spirit in the 1980s. In Austin, ed. 1976:225–278.

Friedrich, Carl, ed. 1962. *Liberty. Nomos IV.* New York: Atherton Press.

Frigo, Lisette. 1989. Australian English and Australian culture. Unpublished paper. Australian National University, Canberra.

Füllerborn, Ulrich. 1992. ". . . die sich gebar im Verlust": Heimat in Rilkes Dichtung. In Görner 1992:90–105.

Garrett, Stephanie. 1989. Friendship and the social order. In Porter and Tomaselli 1989:130–142.

Garton Ash, Timothy. 1983. *The Polish revolution: Solidarity 1980–82.* London: Jonathan Cape.

Garvin, Mal. 1988. *Us Aussies: The fascinating history they didn't tell us at school.* Sole, Australia: Hayzan.

Geertz, Clifford. 1979. *Meaning and order in Moroccan society: Three essays in cultural analysis.* Cambridge: Cambridge University Press.

Gibney, Frank. 1975. *Japan: The fragile superpower.* New York: Norton.

Gladwin, Thomas, and William Sturtevant, eds. 1962. *Anthropology and human behavior.* Washington, D.C.: Anthropological Society of Washington.

Goddard, Cliff. 1990. The lexical semantics of "good feelings" in Yankunytjatjara. *Australian Journal of Linguistics.* Special issue on the semantics of emotions. 10.2:257–292.

————. 1991. Anger in the Western Desert. A case study in the cross-cultural semantics of emotion. *Man* 26:602–619.

————. 1992a. *Pitjantjatjara/Yankunytjatjara to English dictionary.* 2d ed. Alice Springs, Australia: Institute for Aboriginal Development.

————. 1992b. Traditional Yankunytjatjara ways of speaking: A semantic perspective. *Australian Journal of Linguistics* 12.1:93–122.

————. 1994b. The meaning of *lah*: Understanding 'emphasis' in Malay (Bahasa Melayu). *Oceanic Linguistics* 33.1:245–265.

————. 1994a. Lexical primitives in Yankunytjatjara. In Goddard and Wierzbicka 1994:229–262.

————. In press. The 'social emotions' of Malay (Bahasa Melayu). *Ethos.*

Goddard, Cliff, and Anna Wierzbicka, eds. 1994. *Semantic and lexical universals: Theory and empirical findings.* Amsterdam: John Benjamins.

Görlach, Manfred, ed. 1991. *Englishes: Varieties of Englishes around the world.* Amsterdam: John Benjamins.

Görner, Rüdiger, ed. 1992. *Heimat im Wort: die Problematik eines Begriffs im 19. und 20. Jahrhundert.* Munich: Iudicium Verlag GmbH.

Grahame, Kenneth. 1980 [1908]. *The wind in the willows.* London: Methuen Children's Books.

Gratton, C. Hartley. 1944. *Introducing Australia.* New York: J. Day.

Greiffenhagen, Martin, and Sylvia Grieffenhagen. 1979. *Ein schwieriges Vaterland.* Munich: List.

Greimas, Algirdas J., Roman Jakobson, and Maria Renata Mayenowa, eds. 1970. *Sign, language, culture.* The Hague: Mouton.

Greverus, Ina-Maria. 1972. *Der Territoriale Mensch. Ein literaturanthropologischer Versuch zum Heimatphänomen.* Frankfurt am Main. Athenaüm.

Grimm, Jacob. 1956 [1886]. *Deutsches Wörterbuch.* Vol. 12. Leipzig: S. Hirzel.

Gudykunst, William B., et al. 1985. *Communication, culture and organizational processes.* Beverly Hills, Calif.: Sage.

Hale, Ken. 1994. Preliminary observations on lexical and semantic primitives in the Misumalpan languages of Nicaragua. In Goddard and Wierzbicka 1994:263–283.

Hanrahan, Jo. 1989. *Verbs of love and dependence in the Japanese language.* M.A. thesis, Australian National University.

Harkins, Jean. 1986. Semantics and the language learner. *Australian Journal of Pragmatics.* 10:559–573.

————. 1990. Shame and shyness in the Aboriginal classroom: A case for 'practical semantics'. *Australian Journal of Linguistics.* Special issue on emotions. 10.2:293–306.

————. 1992. Throat and desire in Arrernte: Metaphor or polysemy? Unpublished manuscript. Australian National University.

————. 1994. *Bridging two worlds: Aboriginal English and cross-cultural understanding.* Brisbane: University of Queensland Press.

Harkins, Jean, and David P. Wilkins. 1994. Mparntwe Arrernte and the search for lexical universals. In Goddard and Wierzbicka 1994:285–310.

Harré, Rom, ed. 1986. *The social construction of emotions.* Oxford: Blackwell.

Harris, Max. 1962. Morals and manners. In Coleman 47–67.

Harzmann, Friedrich. 1930. *Burschenschaftliche Dichtung von der Frühzeit bis auf unsere Tage.* Eine Auslese. Heidelberg: Carl Winters Universitätsbuchhandlung.

Hasada, Rie. 1994. The semantic aspects of onomotopoeia in Japanese. M.A. thesis. Australian National University.

Hawkes, Ponch. 1990. *Best mates.* Melbourne: McPhee Gribble.

Headon, David, Joy Hooten, and Donald Horne, eds. 1995. *The abundant culture: Meaning and significance in everyday Australia.* Sydney: Allen and Unwin.

Hendry, Joy. 1993. *Wrapping culture: Politeness, presentation, and power in Japan and other societies.* Oxford: Clarendon.

Herder, Johann Gottfried. 1966 [1772]. *On the origin of language.* Trans. John H. Moran and Alexander Gode. New York: Frederick Ungar.

Hill, Deborah. 1985. *The semantics of some interjectional constructions in Australian English.* B.A. honors thesis. Australian National University, Canberra.

————. 1994. Longgu. In Goddard and Wierzbicka 1994:311–329.

Hirschfeld, Lawrence A., and Susan A. Gelman, eds. 1994. *Mapping the mind: Domain specificity in cognition and culture.* Cambridge: Cambridge University Press.

Hoffman, Eva. 1989. *Lost in translation: A new life in a new language.* New York: Dutton.

Hollander, Paul. 1973. *Soviet and American society: A comparison.* New York: Oxford University Press.

Honna, Nobuyuki, and Bates Hoffer. 1989. *An English dictionary of Japanese ways of thinking.* N.p.: Yuhikaku.

Hornadge, Bill. 1980. *The Australian slanguage: A look at what we say and how we say it.* Sydney: Cassell Australia.

Horne, Donald. 1964. *The lucky country.* Sydney: Angus and Robertson.

————. 1989. *Ideas for a nation.* Sydney: Pan Books.

Hudson, Joyce. 1985. Selected speech act verbs in Walmatjari. In Hutter and Gregerson 1985:63–83.

Hunt, Earl, and Mahzarin R. Benaji. 1988. The Whorfian hypothesis revisited: A cognitive science view of linguistic and cultural effects on thought. In Berry et al. 1988: 57–84.

Huston, Nancy, and Leila Sebbar. 1986. *Lettres parisiennes.* Paris: Bernard Barrault.

Huttar, G., and K. Kenneth Gregerson, eds. (1985). *Pragmatics in non-Western perspective.* Dallas: Summer Institute of Linguistics.

Hymes, Dell. 1962. The enthnography of speaking. In Gladwin and Sturtevant 1962:15–53. Reprinted in Fishman 1968:99–138.

————. 1964. *Language in culture and society: A reader in linguistics and anthropology.* New York: Harper and Row.

Hyojun Romaji Kai. 1973. *All-Romanized English-Japanese dictionary.* Rutland, Vt. and Tokyo: Tuttle.

Ihlenfeld, Kurt. 1966. 'Verbotene Frucht'/Gedanken zum Vaterlandsproblem. In *Eckart Jahrbuch* 1966/67. Eckart Verlag. Berlin/Witten Verlag. 47–60.

Ikegami, Yoshihiko, ed. 1991. *The empire of signs: Semiotic essays on Japanese culture.* Amsterdam: John Benjamins.

Inkeles, Alex. 1968. *Social change in Soviet Russia.* Cambridge: Harvard University Press.

Inkeles, Alex, and Kent Geiger, eds. 1961. *Soviet society: A book of readings.* Boston: Houghton Mifflin.

Inokuchi and Nakajima. 1951. *The Kamakaze suicide units.* Quoted in Minami 1971.

Ishiguro, Kazuo. 1986. *An artist of the floating world.* New York: Putnam.

Jamrozik, Wanda. 1995. Fatty can't win this game on heart alone. *The Weekend Australian,* April 22–23:36.

Janion, Maria. 1979. *Reduta: romantyczna poezja niepodległościowa.* Krakow: Wydawnictwo Literackie.

Jespersen, Otto. 1965. *A modern English grammar on historical principles,* part 3, *Syntax.* Vol. 2. London: Allen and Unwin.

Johnson, Curtis. 1980. 'Libertas' and 'res publica' in Cicero and Tacitus. Ph.D. thesis, Columbia University. (University microfilms)

Johnson, Samuel. 1968 [1755]. *A dictionary of the English language.* Hilersheim: F. Olms.

Kamuf, Peggy, ed. 1991. *A Derrida reader.* New York: Columbia University Press.

Kapferer, Bruce. 1988. *Legends of people, myths of state: violence, intolerance, and political culture in Sri Lanka and Australia.* Washington, D.C.: Smithsonian Institution Press.

Kataoka, Hiroko C., with Tetsuya Kusumoto. 1991. *Japanese cultural encounters and how to handle them.* Chicago: Passport Books.

Kawai, Hayao. 1976. *Bosei shakai: Nihon no byori.* Tokyo.

Kawashima, Takeyoshi. 1951. Giri. *Shiso* (September):759–766.

———. 1967. *Nipponjin no ho-ishiki.* Tokyo: Iwanami.

Kefer, Michael, and Johann van der Auwera, eds. 1991. *Meaning and grammar.* Berlin: Mouton de Gruyter.

Kenkyusha's new Japanese-English dictionary. (1954). Tokyo: Kenkyusha.

Kerblay, Basile. 1983. *Modern Soviet society.* Trans. Rupert Sawyer. London: Methuen.

Kiefer, Christie W. 1976. The *Danchi Zoku* and the evolution of metropolitan mind. In Austin, ed. 1976:279–300.

King, Jonathan A. 1978. *Waltzing materialism.* Sydney: Harper and Row.

King, Petrea. 1992. *Quest for life.* Milson's Point, Australia: Random House.

Kleine-Brockhoff, Thomas, Kuno Kruse, and Michael Sontheimer. 1989. *Die Mauer. Die Zeit* 47(November 24):9.

Klemperer, Victor. 1946. *Die unbewältigte Sprache.* Darmstadt: Joseph Melzer.

Kloskowska, Agnieszka. 1993. "Kraj, do którego się wraca". Czym jest ojczyzna dla lubelskich studentów. In Bartmiński, ed. 1993:49–56.

Kloskowska, Antonina. 1991. Kultura narodowa. In *Encyklopedia kultury polskiej XX wieku.* Wrocław: Ossolineum, pp. 51–56.

Kokutai no Hongi: Cardinal principles of the national entity of Japan. 1949. Trans. John Own Gauntlett. Cambridge, Mass.: Harvard University Press.

Kon, Igor. 1987. *Družba.* Moscow: Politizdat.

Kornacki, Pawel. 1995. Aspects of Chinese cultural psychology as reflected in the Chinese lexicon. Ph.D. thesis. Australian National University.

Kościuszko Foundation dictionary: English–Polish, Polish–English. 1959–1961. By K. Bulas and F.J. Whitifield. The Hague: Mouton.

Krüger, Horst. 1969. *Deutsche Augenblicke.* Munich: R. Piper & Co.

Kučera, Henry, and Nelson Francis. 1967. *Computational analysis of present-day American English.* Providence: Brown University Press.

Kume, Teruyuki. 1985. Management attitudes towards decision making: North America and Japan. In Gudykunst et al. 1985:231–251.

Kurcz, Ida, Andrzej Lewicki, Jadwiga Sambor, Krzysztof Szafran, and Jerzy Worończak. 1990. *Słownik frekwencyjny polszczyzny współczesnej.* Krakow: Polska Akademia Nauk.

Kurokawa, Shozo. 1972. Japanese terms of address: Some usages of the first and second person pronouns. *Papers in Japanese Linguistics* 1.2:228–238.

Langacker, Ronald W. 1987. *Foundations of cognitive grammar,* vol. 1: *Theoretical prerequisites.* Stanford: Stanford University Press.

———. 1990. *Concept, image and symbol: The cognitive basis of grammar.* Berlin: Mouton de Gruyter.

Lazarus, Richard. 1995. Vexing research problems inherent in cognitive-mediational theories of emotion—and some solutions. *Psychological Inquiry* 6. 3:183–196.

Lebra, Takie S. 1974. Reciprocity and the asymmetric principle: An analytical reappraisal of the Japanese concept of *on.* In Lebra and Lebra 1986:192–207.

———. 1976. *Japanese patterns of behavior.* Honolulu: University Press of Hawaii.

———. 1987–88. The cultural significance of silence in Japanese communication. *Multilingua* 6-7:347–357.

Lebra, Takie S., and W.P. Lebra, eds. 1986 [1974]. *Japanese culture and behavior.* Rev. ed. Honolulu: The University Press of Hawaii.

Leibniz, Gottfried Wilhelm. 1961 [1903]. *Opuscules et fragments inédits de Leibniz.* Ed. Louis Couturat. Hildesheim: Georg Olms Buchhandlung.

————. 1981 [1709]. *New essays on human understanding.* Trans. Peter Remnant and Jonathan Bennett. Cambridge: Cambridge University Press.

Lewis, Charlton, and Charles Short. 1962. *A Latin dictionary.* Oxford: Clarendon.

Lewis, Clive S. 1990. *Studies in words.* Cambridge: Cambridge University Press, Canto.

Libelt, Karol. 1967 [1844]. *O miłości ojczyzny.* Warsaw: PWN.

Litvinova, Flora. 1994a. Zapisi ob Anatolli Marčenko. *Russkaja mysl'* 4055.

————. 1994b. Zpisi ob Anatolli Marčenko. *Russkaja mysl'* 4056.

————. 1994c. Zpisi ob Anatolli Marčenko. *Russkaja mysl'* 4057.

————. 1994d. Zpisi ob Anatolli Marčenko. *Russkaja mysl'* 4058.

Locke, John. 1959 [1690]. An essay concerning human understanding. Ed. A.C. Fraser. Oxford: Clarendon.

Lotar, Peter. 1962. Das Bild des Menschen. In Schmitthenner 1962:73–100.

Lutz, Catherine. 1990. *Unnatural emotions.* Chicago: University of Chicago Press.

Mackay, Hugh. 1993. *Reinventing Australia: The mind and mood of Australia in the 90s.* Sydney: Angus and Robertson.

Macquarie electronic corpus of Australian English. Sydney: Macquarie University.

Macquarie dictionary of Australian colloquial language (MDACL). 1988. McMahons Point N.S.W.: Macquarie Library/Pty Ltd.

Malotki, Ekkehart. 1983. *Hopi time: A linguistic analysis of the temporal concepts in the Hopi language.* Berlin: Mouton.

Marcus, Julie, ed. 1990. *Writing Australian culture: text, society and national identity.* Social Analysis Special Issue Series, no. 27. Adelaide: Department of Anthropology, University of Adelaide.

Marsella, Anthony, George De Vos, and Francis Hsu, eds. 1985. *Culture and self: Asian and Western perspectives.* New York: Tavistock.

Marsella, Anthony, and Geoffrey White, eds. 1984. *Cultural conceptions of mental health and therapy.* Dordrecht: Reidel.

Mayenowa, Maria Renata, and Zenon Klemensiewicz, eds. 1962. *Odrodzenie w Polsce: Historia języka.* Vol. 2. Warsaw: Państwowy Instytut Wydawniczy.

Mazour, Anatole. 1962. *Russia: Tsarist and communist.* Toronto: D. van Nostrand.

McCall, George. 1970. *Social relationships.* Chicago: Aldine.

McGregor, Craig. 1981. *The Australian people.* Sydney: Hodder and Stoughton.

Mead, Margaret, and Rhoda Métraux. 1953. Formulation of a working hypothesis: The swaddling hypothesis. In Mead and Métreaux, eds. 1953:107–115.

————, eds. 1953. *The study of culture at a distance.* Chicago: Chicago University Press.

Medding, Peter Y., ed, 1973. *Jews in Australian Society.* Clayton, Monash University: Macmillan.

Mel'čuk, Igor, and Alexandr Žholkovskij. 1984. *Tolkovo-kombinatornyj slovar' sovremennogo russkogo jazyka.* Vienna: Wiener Slawistischer Almanach. (Sonderband 14)

Merriam-Webster. 1972. *The Merriam-Webster pocket dictionary of synonyms.* New York: Pocket Books.

Mickiewicz, Adam. 1955. *Dzieła.* Warsaw: Czytelnik.

Miłosz, Czesław. 1972 *Prywatne obowiązki.* Paris: Instytut Literacki.

————. 1983. *This history of Polish literature.* 2d ed. Berkeley: University of California Press.

Minami, Hiroshi. 1971. *Psychology of the Japanese people.* Toronto: University of Toronto Press.

Minamoto, Ryoen. 1969. *Giri to ninjo.* Tokyo: Japan Times.

Mitsubishi Corporation. 1987. Japanese business language. London: KPI.

Mizutani, Osamu, and Nobuko Mizutani. 1987. *How to be polite in Japanese.* Toyko: Japan Times.

Moeran, Brian. 1986. *Individual, group and seishin: Japan's internal cultural debate.* In Lebra and Lebra 1986:62–79.

————. 1989. *Language and popular culture in Japan.* Manchester and New York: Manchester University Press.

Mondry, Henrietta, and John R. Taylor. 1992. On lying in Russian. *Language and communication* 12.2:133–143.

Monk, Ray. 1991. *Ludwig Wittgenstein: The duty of genius.* London: Jonathan Cape.

Montagu, Ashley. 1967. *The anatomy of swearing.* New York: Macmillan.

Moore, Charles A., ed. 1962. *Philosophy and culture: East and West.* Honolulu: University Press of Hawaii.

Mori, J. 1977. *Nihonjin: 'kara-nashi-tamago' no jigazoo.* Tokyo: Kodansha.

Morsbach, Helmut. 1980. Major psychological factors influencing Japanese interpersonal relations. In Warren 1980:317–344.

Morsbach, Helmut, and W.J. Tyler. 1986. A Japanese emotion: Amae. In Harré 1986:289–307.

Morse, S.J., and A. Marks. 1985. "'Cause Duncan's me mate": A comparison of reported relations with mates and with friends in Australia. *British Journal of Social Psychology* 24:283–292.

Mosel, Ulrike. 1994. *Samoan.* In Goddard and Wierzbicka 1994:331–360.

Mróz-Ostrowska, Ewa. 1962. Rzeczowniki z przyrostkiem -ość w języku XVI w. In Mayenowa and Klemensiewicz 1962:303–503.

Murase, Takao. 1984. Sunao: A central value in Japanese psychotherapy. In Marsella and White 1984:317–329.

Myers, Fred R. 1986. *Pintupi country, Pintupi self: Sentiment, place and politics among Western Desert Aborigines.* Washington, D.C.: Smithsonian.

Nabokov, Vladimir. 1961. *Nikolai Gogol'.* New York: New Direction.

Nakamura, Hajime. 1962. Basic features of the legal, political, and economic thought of Japan. In Moore 1962:631–647.

Nakane, Chie. 1973. *Japanese society.* Harmondsworth: Penguin.

Nakatsugawa, Kyoko. 1992. Japanese cultural values reflected in educational guidelines. Unpublished paper. Department of Linguistics, Australian National University.

Naotsuka, Nancy, et al. 1981. *Mutual understanding of different cultures.* Tokyo: Taishukan.

Needham, Rodney. 1972. *Belief, language and experience.* Oxford: Blackwell.

New Shorter Oxford English dictionary (NSOED). 1993. Oxford: Clarendon.

O'Grady, John. 1965. *Aussie English: An explanation of the Australian idiom.* Sydney: Ure Smith.

Onishi, Masayuki. 1994. Semantic primitives in Japanese. In Goddard and Wierzbicka 1994:361–385.

Ono, Setsuko. 1976. Fragile blossom, fragile superpower: A new interpretation? *Japanese Quarterly* 23:12–27.

Oppenheim, Felix. 1962. Freedom: An empirical interpretation. In Friedrich 1962:274–288.

Oxford English dictionary (OED). 1993 [1933]. 2d ed. Vols. 1–2. Oxford: Clarendon.

Oxford English dictionary. Supplement (OEDS). 1972. Oxford: Clarendon.

Oxford Latin dictionary. 1968–82. Oxford: Clarendon.

Oxford Russian-English dictionary. 1980. London: Clarendon.

Oxley, Harry G. *Mateship in local organization: A study of egalitarianism, stratification, leadership, and amenities projects in a semi-industrial community of inland New South Wales.* St. Lucia: University of Queensland Press.

Ožegov, S.I. 1978. *Slovar'* russkogo jazyka. 12th ed. Ed. N.J. Švedova. Moscow: Russkij Jazyk.

Packard, Vance. 1974. *A nation of strangers.* New York: Pocket Books.

Pares, Bernard. 1955. *A history of Russia.* London: Jonathan Cape.

Parkin, David. 1978. The cultural definition of political response: Lineal destiny among the Luo. London: Academic Press.

————, ed. 1982. Semantic anthropology. London: Academic Press.

Partridge, Eric. 1967. *A dictionary of slang and unconventional English.* London: Routledge and Kegan Paul.

Pascal. 1954 [1667]. De l'esprit géométrique et de l'art de persuader. In *Oeuvres complètes.* Ed. J. Chevalier. Paris: Gallimard, pp. 570–604.

Pawley, Andrew. 1994. Kalam exponents of lexical and semantic primitives. In Goddard and Wierzbicka. 1994:387–421.

Pawley, Andrew, and Frances H. Syder. 1983. Two puzzles for linguistic theory: Native-like selection and native-like fluency. In Richards and Schmidt 1983:191–227.

Peeters, Bert. 1994. Semantic and lexical universals in French. In Goddard and Wierzbicka 1994:423–442.

Pełczyński, Zbigniew, and John Gray, eds. 1984. *Conceptions of liberty in political philosophy.* London: Athlone Press.

Pettit, Philip. In press. *Republicanism.* Oxford: Clarendon Press.

Pinker, Steven. 1991. Rules of language. *Science* 253:530–535.

————. 1994. *The language instinct.* New York: William Morrow.

Piper, Henry Dan. 1970. *Fitzgerald's The Great Gatsby: The novel, the critics, the background.* New York: Scribner.

Popiełuszko, Jerzy. 1992. *Kazania 1982–1984.* Warsaw: Wydawnictwo Archidiecezji Warszawskiej.

Porter, Roy, and Sylvana Tomaselli, eds. 1989. *The dialectics of friendship.* London: Routledge.

Potapov, Viktor. 1993. Put' k duxovnomu vozroždeniju Rossii. [The road to the spiritual regeneration of Russia]. *Russkaja Mysl'* 3986.

Pullum, Geoffrey K. 1991. *The great Eskimo vocabulary hoax and other irreverent essays on the study of language.* Chicago: University of Chicago Press.

Pushkin, Alexandr. 1981. *Evgenij Onegin: Roman v stixax.* Moscow: Gosudarstvennoe Izdatel'stvo Xudožestvennoj Literatury.

Pushkin, Alexandr. 1975. *Eugene Onegin: A novel in verse.* Trans. Vladimir Nabokov 4 vols. Princeton: Princeton University Press.

Rees, Nigel. 1990. *Dictionary of popular phrases.* London: Bloomsbury.

Reischauer, Edwin O. 1988. *The Japanese today.* Cambridge, Mass.: Belknap.

Renwick, George W. 1980. *Interact: Guidelines for Australians and North Americans.* Yarmouth, Me.: Intercultural Press.

Richards, Jack, and Richard Schmidt, eds. 1983. *Language and communication.* London: Longman.

Roberts, John G. 1974. *Mitsui: Three centuries of Japanese business.* New York: Weatherhill.

Rohlen, Thomas P. 1974. *For harmony and strength: Japanese white-collar organization in anthropological perspective.* Berkeley: University of California Press.

————. 1986. Spiritual education in a Japanese bank. In Lebra and Lebra 1986:307–338.

Rosaldo, Michelle Z. 1980. *Knowledge and passion: Ilongot notions of self and social life.* Cambridge: Cambridge University Press.

Rozanova, V.V. 1978. *Kratkij tolkovyj slovar' russkogo jazyka dlja inostrancev.* Moscow: Russkij Jazyk.

Russell, James, José-Miguel Fernández-Dols, Anthony Manstead, and Jane Wellenkamp, eds. 1995. *Everyday conceptions of emotion: An introduction to the psychology, anthropology and linguistics of emotion.* Dordrecht: Kluwer.

Sakurai, Shotaro. 1961. *On to giri.* Tokyo: Asahisha.

Sanseido's new concise Japanese-English dictionary. 1967. Tokyo: Sanseido.

Sapir, Edward. 1949. *Selected writings of Edward Sapir in language, culture and personality.* Ed. David Mandelbaum. Berkeley: University of California Press.

Schiefflin, Bambi, and Elinor Ochs, eds. 1986. *Language socialization across cultures.* Cambridge and New York: Cambridge University Press.

Schmitthenner, Hansjörg. 1962. *Sechzehn Deutsche Hörspiele.* Munich: R. Piper.

Serpell, James. 1989. Humans, animals, and the limits of friendship. In Porter and Tomaselli 1989:111–129.

Seymour, Alan. 1962. *The one day of the year.* Sydney: Angus and Robertson.

Shlapentokh, Vladimir. 1984. *Love, marriage and friendship in the Soviet Union.* New York: Praeger.

———. 1989. *Public and private life of the Soviet people: Changing values in post Stalin Russia.* New York: Oxford University Press.

Shorter Oxford English dictionary (SOED). 1964. Oxford: Clarendon.

SJP. 1958–69, *Słownik języka polskiego.* Ed. W. Doroszewski. 11 vols. Warsaw: PWN.

Skorupka, Stanisław. 1974. *Słownik frazeologiczny języka polskiego.* Warsaw: Wiedza Powszechna.

Słonimski, Antoni. 1964. *Poezje zebrane.* Warsaw: Państwowy Instytut Wydawniczy.

Šmelev, Aleksej. 1996. Leksičeskij sostov russkogo jazyka kak otraženie "russkoj duši." *Russkij Jazyk v Škole* 4:83–90.

Smirnickij, A.I. 1961. *Russko-anglijskij slovar'.* Moscow: Gosudarstvennoe Izdatel'stvo Inostrannyx i Nacional'nyx Slovarej.

Smith, Hedrick. 1976. *The Russians.* London: Sphere Books.

Smith, Robert J. 1983. *Japanese society: Tradition, self and the social order.* Cambridge: Cambridge University Press.

Smolicz, Jerzy. 1979. *Culture and education in a plural society.* Canberra: Curriculum Development Centre.

Sokolov, Vladimir. 1981. *Nravstvennyj mir sovetskogo Čeloveka.* Moscow: Politizdat.

Solov'ev, Vladimir. 1966–70. *Sobranie sočinenij.* 14 vols. St. Petersburg: Prosveščenie; and Brussels: Foyer Oriental Chrétien.

Solzhenitsyn, Aleksandr. 1973–75. *Arxipelag gulag.* 5 vols. Paris: YMCA Press.

———. 1993. [An interview]. *Russkaja Mysl'* 3986.

Sommerville, John. 1962. Towards a consistent definition of freedom. In Friedrich 1962:289–300.

Spevack, Marvin. 1968. A complete and systematic concordance to the works of Shakespeare. Hildesheim: Goerg Olms.

SRJ. 1957–62. *Slovar' russkogo jazyka.* Ed. Akademija Nauk SSSR. Moscow: Gosudarstvennoe Izdatel'stvo Inostrannyx i Nacional'nyx Slovarej.

SSRJ. 1971. *Slovar' sinonimov russkogo jazyka.* Ed. Akademija Nauk SSSR. 2 vols. Leningrad: Nauka.

SSRLJ. 1950–65.1. *Slovar' sovremennogo russkogo literaturnogo jazyka.* 17 vols. Moscow: Izdatel'stvo Academii Nauk SSSR.

Stevenson, Burton. 1949. *Stevenson's book of proverbs, maxims and familiar phrases.* London: Routledge and Kegan Paul.

————. 1958. *Book of quotations: Classical and modern.* London: Cassell.

Stewart, Edward C. 1972. *American cultural patterns: A cross-cultural perspective.* Yarmouth, Me.: Intercultural Press.

Storck, Joachim W. 1992. "Meine Herkunft ist mein Schicksal." Heimat als Problem beim "zweisprachigen Grenzvogel" René Schickele. In Görner 1992:106–116.

Sugimoto, Yoshio, and Ross E. Mouer, eds. 1989. *Constructs for understanding Japan.* London: Kegan Paul.

Suttles, Gerald. 1970. Friendship as a social institution. In McCall 1970:95–135.

Suzuki, Takao. 1986. Language behavior in Japan: The conceptualization of personal relations. In Lebra and Lebra 1986:142–157.

Svartvik, Y., and R. Quirk, eds. 1980. *A corpus of English conversation.* Lund: CWK Gleerup.

Taborska, Hanna. 1993. Discussion. In Bartmiński, ed. 1992:57–58.

Takehara, Tsuneta. 1924. *A standard Japanese-English dictionary.* N.p.

Takenobu Japanese-English dictionary. 1918. Tokyo: Kenkyusha.

TAND. 1988. *The Australian national dictionary: A dictionary of Australianisms on historical principles.* Ed. W.S. Ramson. Melbourne: Oxford University Press.

Taube, A.M. 1978. *Russian English dictionary.* Moscow: Russian Language.

Taylor, Brian A. 1976. Towards a sociolinguistic analysis of 'swearing' and the language of abuse in Australian English. In Clyne 1976:43–62.

Taylor, Charles. 1982. *Philosophical papers,* vol 2: *Philosophy and the human sciences.* New York: Cambridge University Press.

Taylor, Ken. 1994. Things we want to keep: Discovering Australia's cultural heritage. In Headon, Hooton, and Horne 1994:26–33.

Thomas, L. 1987. Friendship. *Synthese* 72:217–236.

Thompson, Elaine. 1994. *Fair enough: Egalitarianism in Australia.* Sydney: University of New South Wales Press.

Tocqueville, Alexis de. 1953 [1835–40]. *Democracy in America.* Trans. Henry Reeve. Ed. Phillips Bradley. New York: Knopf.

Todorov, Tzvetan. 1986. Le croisement des cultures. In Todorov, 1986:5–26.

————, ed. 1986. *Le croisement des cultures.* Paris: Hérissey à Évreux.

Tolstoy, L.N. 1930–1931. *War and peace.* Trans. Louis Maude and Aylmer Maude. 2 vols. London: Humphrey Milford.

Toystoy, Lev. 1964. *Vojna i mir.* Moscow: Detskaja Literatura.

Travis, Catherine. 1992. How to be kind, compassionate and considerate in Japanese. Honors thesis. Department of Linguistics, Australian National University.

TSRJ. 1935–1940. *Tolkovyj slovar' russkogo jazyka.* 4 vols. Ed. D.N. Ušakov. Moscow: Gosudarstvennoe Izdatel'stvo Inostrannyx i Nacional'nyx Slovarej.

Turner, George William. 1966. *The English language of Australia and New Zealand.* London: Longman.

Turner, Ian. 1968. *The Australian dream: A collection of anticipations about Australia from Captain Cook to the present.* Melbourne: Sun Books.

Tyler, Stephen A. 1987. *The unspeakable: Discourse, dialogue, and rhetoric in the postmodern world.* Madison: University of Wisconsin Press.

USSSRJ. 1978. *Učebnyj slovar' sočetaemosti slov russkogo jazyka.* Moscow: Russkij Jazyk.

Vinogradskaja, Sof'ja. 1991. Kak žil Esenin? In Vinogradskaja et al. 1991:5–28.

Vinogradskaja, Sof'ja, Anatolij Mariengof, Vol'f Erlix, Vadim Šeršenevič, Nadežda Vol'pin. 1991. *Kak žil Esenin.* Čeljabinsk: Južno-Uralskoe Knižnoe Izdatel'stvo.

Volkov, Viktor. 1993. Interview. *Russkaja Mysl'* 3986.

Wagatsuma, Hiroshi. 1977. Problems in language in cross-cultural research. In Adler 1977:141–150. (Annals, 285)

Wagatsuma, Hiroshi, and George De Vos. 1984. Heritage of endurance: Family patterns and delinquency formation in urban Japan. Berkeley: University of California Press.

Walicki, Andrzej. 1980. *A history of Russian thought: From the enlightenment to Marxism.* Oxford: Clarendon.

————. 1984. The Marxian conception of freedom. In Pełczyński and Gray 1984:217–241.

————. 1987. *Legal philosophies of Russian liberalism.* Oxford: Clarendon.

Wallerstein, Immanel. 1994. Comments of Wolf's 'Perilous ideas: race, culture and people'. *Current anthropology.* 35.1:9–10.

Wannan, Bill. 1963. *Tell 'em I died game.* Melbourne: Landsdowne Press.

Ward, Russel. 1966 [1958]. *The Australian legend.* 2d ed. Melbourne: Oxford University Press.

Warren, Neil, ed. 1980. *Studies in cross-cultural psychology.* Vol. 2. London: Academic.

Wassman, Jürg. 1995. The final requiem for the omniscient informant? An interdisciplinary approach to everyday cognition. *Culture and Psychology* 1.2:167–202.

Webster's third new international dictionary of the English language. 1976. Springfield, Mass.: Merriam.

Wedel, Janine. 1986. *The private Poland.* New York: Facts on File.

Weidle, Wladimir. 1952. *Russia: Absent and present.* Trans. A. Gordon Smith. New York: John Day.

Weil, Simone. 1972. *Gravity and grace.* London: Routledge.

Weisgerber, Leo. 1959. *Die geschichtliche Kraft der deutschen Sprache.* Düsseldorf: Pädagogischer Verlag Schwann.

Wheeler, Marcus. 1972. *The Oxford Russian English dictionary.* Oxford: Clarendon.

White, Merry. 1987. *The Japanese educational challenge: A commitment to children.* New York: Free Press.

Whiting, Robert. 1979. You've got to have *wa. Sports Illustrated* (September 24):60–71.

Whorf, Benjamin Lee. 1956. *Language, thought and reality: Selected writings of Benjamin Lee Whorf.* Ed. John B. Carroll. New York: Wiley.

Wierzbicka, Anna. 1972. *Semantic primitives.* Frankfurt: Athenäum.

————. 1980. *Lingua mentalis: The semantics of natural language.* Sydney: Academic.

————. 1985. *Lexicography and conceptual analysis.* Ann Arbor, Mich.: Karoma.

————. 1986. Does language reflect culture? Evidence from Australian English. *Language in Society* 15:349–374.

————. 1987. *English speech act verbs: A semantic dictionary.* New York: Academic.

————. 1988a). L'amour, la colère, la joie, l'ennui: la sémantique des émotions dans une perspective transculturelle. *Langages* 89:97–107.

————. 1988b. *The semantics of grammar.* Amsterdam: John Benjamins.

————. 1989a. Semantic primitives and lexical universals. *Quaderni di semantica* 10.1:103–321.

————. 1989b. Semantic primitives—the expanding set. *Quaderni di semantica* 10.2:309–332.

————. 1990a. Duša (soul), toska (yearning) and sud'ba (fate): Three key concepts in Russian language and Russian culture. In Zygmunt Saloni, ed., *Metody formalne w opisie języków słowiańskich.* Białystok: Białystok University Press, 13–36.

————. 1990b. The semantics of emotion: *Fear* and its relatives in English. *Australian Journal of Linguistics.* Special issue on the semantics of emotions. 10.2:359–375.

————. 1991a. *Cross-cultural pragmatics: The semantics of social interaction.* Berlin: Mouton de Gruyter.

————. 1991b. Japanese key words and core cultural values. *Language in Society* 20:333–385.

————. 1991c. Lexical universals and the universals of grammar. In Kefer and van der Auwera 1991:385–415.

————. 1992a. Defining emotion concepts. *Cognitive Science* 16:539–581.

————. 1992b. *Semantics, culture, and cognition: Universal human concepts in culture-specific configurations.* New York: Oxford University Press.

————. 1992c. Talking about emotions: Semantics, culture and cognition. *Cognition and Emotion.* 6.3/4:289–319.

————. 1992d. Australian b-words (*bloody, bastard, bugger, bullshit*): An expression of Australian culture and national character. In André Clas ed. *Le mot, les mots, les bons mots/Word, words, witty words: Festschrift for Igor Mel'čuk.* Montréal: Les Presses de L'Université de Montréal, 21–38.

————. 1994. Cognitive domains and the structure of the lexicon: The case of emotions. In Hirschfeld and Gelman 1994:771–797.

————. 1995. Everyday conceptions of emotion: A semantic perspective. In Russell et al. 1995:17–47.

————. 1996. *Semantics: Primes and universals.* Oxford: Oxford University Press.

————. In press a. Japanese cultural scripts: Cultural psychology and "cultural grammar." *Ethos.*

————. In press b. "Sadness" and "anger" in Russian: The non-universality of the so-called "basic human emotions." In Dirven (forthcoming).

Wilkes, Gerald Alfred. 1985 [1978]. *A dictionary of Australian colloquialisms.* 2d ed. Maryborough: Fontana/Collins.

Wilkins, David. 1986. Particles/clitics for criticism and complaint in Mparntwe Arrente (Aranda). *Journal of Pragmatics* 10:575–596.

Williams, Raymond. 1976. *Keywords: A vocabulary of culture and society.* London: Flamingo, Fontana.

Wimbush, S. Enders, and Alex Alekseev. 1982. *The ethnic factor in the Soviet Armed Forces.* Santa Monica, Calif.: Rand.

Windle, Kevin. In press. Yuz Aleshkovskii, "Pesnja o Staline" and "Sovetskaia paskhal'naia": A study of competing versions. *Slavonic and East European Review.*

Winstead, Barbara A., and Valerian J. Derlega, eds. 1986. *Friendship and social interaction.* New York: Springer.

Wirszubski, Chaim. 1950. *Libertas as a political idea at Rome during the late republic and early principate.* Cambridge: Cambridge University Press.

Wittfogel, Karl. 1963. *Oriental despotism: A comparative study of total power.* New Haven: Yale University Press.

Wolf, Eric R. 1994. Perilous ideas: race, culture and people. *Current Anthropology* 35.1:1–7.

Wuthnow, Robert. 1987. *Meaning and moral order: Explorations in cultural analysis.* Berkeley: University of California Press.

————, ed. 1992. *Vocabularies of public life: Empirical essays in symbolic structure.* London: Routledge.

Wuthnow, Robert, James Davison Hunter, Albert Bergesen, and Edith Kurzweil. 1984. *Cultural analysis: the work of Peter L. Berger, Mary Douglas, Michel Foucault and Jürgen Habermas.* Boston and London: Routledge and Kegan Paul.

Zasorina, L.N., ed. 1977. *Častotnyj slovar' russkogo jazyka.* Moscow: Russkij Jazyk.

Zimmerman, Mark A. 1985. *How to do business with the Japanese.* New York: Random House.

————. 1988. *Dealing with the Japanese.* London: Unwin.

Znaniecki, Florian. 1965. *Social relations and social roles: The unfinished systematic sociology.* San Francisco: Chandler.

Index

Acehnese (Austronesian), 26
acquaintance (English), 85, 86, 95, 97, 282
Adams, Henry, 36
Adams, Philip, 224
akarui, 276 (Japanese)
allolex, allolexy, 27, 28–29
alphabet of human thoughts, 22, 27
amae (noun) (Japanese), 152, 153, 198, 235, 238–242
   amaeru (verb), 239
   amai (adjective), 239
   explication, 241, 278
Amal'rik, Andrej, 143, 144, 287
American English, 71
ami, amie (French), 33, 66
amicitia (Latin), 52
amico (Italian), 33
amicus (Latin), 33, 52
anger, 9
Anglo-American culture, 244, 245
Anglo-Australian culture 35, 199, 200
Anglo cultural norms, 15
Anglo culture 21, 39, 55, 120, 130, 242, 281
Anglo society, 74
   individual rights, 133, 142
Applegate, Celia, 157, 160, 161
Armia Krajowa (Polish). *See* kraj
Arnauld, Antoine, 25
Arndt, Ernest Moritz, 162
Arrernte (Aranda) (Australian), 26, 30
asobinakoma (Japanese), 35
Austin, Lewis, 271, 272, 286
Australian Aboriginal culture(s), 199

Australian (Aboriginal) languages, 11, 26, 152
Australian "bush ethos," 102, 207
Australian (colloquial) speech act verbs, 217
Australian culture, 21, 103, 114, 117, 198
   anti-sentimentality of, 202
Australian English 21, 35, 198–234, 285, 286, 290, 291
   abbreviations, 201
   interjections, 201, 202, 208, 276: *g'day*, 202; *good on ya*, 201, 202; *goodo* (*good-oh*), 201, 202; *how ya going*, 202; *no worries*, 201, 202, 208; *righto* (*right-oh, rightio*), 201, 202; *she'll be right*, 208
Australian ethos, 91, 101, 102, 109, 205, 212, 214, 216
Australian humor, 231
Australian school ethos, 213
Australian slang, 211

"b-words" (Australian English), 217
Baker, Sidney, 109, 212, 217, 218, 228, 231, 291
Barańczak, Stanisław, 97
barszcz (Polish), 2
Bartmiński, Jerzy, 176, 177, 181, 182, 185–188, 290
bastard (Australian English), 198, 202, 212, 217, 220–223, 226, 231, 233, 234, 290, 291
   explication, 221, 223, 233, 234
   grammatical frames, 221